*An Introduction to the
Law and Institutions of the European
Communities*

An Introduction to the Law and Institutions of the European Communities

SECOND EDITION

D. LASOK,
L.en Dr., LL.M., Ph.D., Dr. Juris,

of the Middle Temple, Barrister;
Professor of European Law and Director
of the Centre of European Legal Studies
in the University of Exeter

and

J. W. BRIDGE, LL.B., LL.M., Ph.D.,

Professor of Public Law in the University of Exeter

Scire leges non hoc est verba earum tenere, sed vim ac potestatem.
Celsus, 1.3.17

BUTTERWORTHS
1976

ENGLAND: BUTTERWORTH & CO. (PUBLISHERS) LTD.
LONDON: 88 Kingsway, WC2B 6AB

AUSTRALIA: BUTTERWORTHS PTY. LTD.
SYDNEY: 586 Pacific Highway, Chatswood, NSW 2067
Also at Melbourne, Brisbane, Adelaide and Perth

CANADA: BUTTERWORTH & CO. (CANADA) LTD.
TORONTO: 2265 Midland Avenue, Scar-borough M1P 4S1

NEW ZEALAND: BUTTERWORTHS OF NEW ZEALAND LTD.
WELLINGTON: 26–28 Waring Taylor Street, 1

SOUTH AFRICA: BUTTERWORTH & CO. (SOUTH AFRICA) (PTY.) LTD.
DURBAN: 152–154 Gale Street

USA: BUTTERWORTH & CO. (PUBLISHERS) INC.
BOSTON: 19 Cummings Park, Woburn, Mass. 01801

ISBN Casebound: 0 406 26892 4
Limp: 0 406 26893 2

Preface

In preparing this revised edition the authors have not attempted to depart from their original concept of this book as an introductory text which is intended primarily for those embarking on the study of the novel and complex system of Community Law. As explained in the Preface to the First Edition, the intention is to deal in some detail with the genesis, nature and general principles of Community Law and with Community institutions and to provide no more than an outline of the substantive economic law of the Communities. More detailed treatment of the latter and of other topics may be found in the works listed in the Appendix.

This edition largely follows the pattern of the first edition. The dynamic nature of the Community legal system, the enlargement and the impact of three years of British membership on the law of the United Kingdom are responsible for the slight increase in the length of the text. There has also been some rearrangement of material as between Chapters 10 and 11 in order to produce what is hoped to be a more logical treatment.

Exeter,   D.L.
June, 1976   J.W.B.

Preface to the First Edition

Ubi Societas Ibi Jus

To understand the nature of the law one must understand the nature of the society from which it emanates and which it purports to govern. We are used to the concepts of national and international law. The former is the law of a sovereign state and as such it governs the society comprised in a state that is a group of people living within a defined area under a government which has executive, legislative, judicial and administrative powers. International law, on the other hand, is the body of rules which governs relations between states and such international organisations as are set up and recognised by states as bearers of rights and duties. In exceptional situations individuals may be regarded as subjects of international law. As a body of rules international law is derived partly from custom and state practice, partly from the will of states expressed in treaties and partly generated by institutions (e.g. the United Nations Organisation) set up by states and based on a treaty.

The object of this book is to define and analyse a nascent body of law which can be described as the law of the European Community. It is neither a national nor an international system of law in the accepted sense of these terms but a *sui generis* system emanating from the will to create a European Community. It reflects, of course, the nature of this design. At this stage we can speak of the European Community only in general political terms as an organisation with limited, mainly economic objectives and a potential for development towards a federal organisation. In strictly juristic, institutional terms we have to speak of the European Communities, that is the European Coal and Steel Community, the European Atomic Energy Community and the European Economic Community and, therefore, a distinction between "Community" and "Communities" has to be borne in mind. The law of the European Community, as we understand it, comprises consequently elements of international and national law as well as the rules generated by the Communities, of which the European Economic Community may be regarded as a cornerstone of future developments. This we shall endeavour to emphasise.

The genesis of this book lies in the authors' experience of teaching European Community Law in the University of Exeter. They wish to express their thanks to their students, both undergraduate and post-graduate, for the patience and forbearance with which they endured the authors' experimental first steps in this field. The authors claim to have written no more than an introduction to the complex system of Community Law. In order to explain its working to the reader it was thought necessary to stress the institutional aspects of the Community and matters of principle at the expense of the details of the law of the economy which is still at a formative stage. It is hoped, however, that it is informative and provocative in that by setting out the rudiments it will make the reader aware of the unprecedented challenge facing Europe, the United Kingdom and the citizen, be he lawyer or layman. The aim throughout has been to approach the subject from the standpoint of the United Kingdom joining a continental Community which is already a going concern and this explains the emphasis placed on the political background of the Community and the civil law framework within which it functions. The authors owe a considerable debt to the numerous pioneer writers on the Communities and their law and pay them generous tribute.

This is a joint work. Chapters 1, 3, 4, 10, 11, 13 and 14 were drafted by D. Lasok; Chapters 5, 6, 7, 8, 9 and 12 were drafted by J. W. Bridge; Chapter 2 was drafted jointly. The work of each author has been subject to the comments and criticisms of the other and both authors are in agreement on and each accepts responsibility for the form and content of the whole book.

The authors' gratitude is due to all the members of the secretarial staff of the Faculty of Law of the University of Exeter who, with their accustomed cheerfulness and efficiency, undertook the typing of the manuscript; to the Publishers; and to their wives and families to whom this book is dedicated.

Exeter,   D.L.
Michaelmas, 1972   J.W.B.

Table of Contents

PART IV THE LAW OF THE ECONOMY

Table of Treaties

List of Cases

List of Principal Abbreviations

A.J.C.L.—American Journal of Comparative Law
A.J.I.L.—American Journal of International Law
Art.—Article
Benelux—Belgium, The Netherlands and Luxembourg
B.G.B.—Bürgerliches Gesetzbuch (Germany)
B.Y.B.I.L.—British Year Book of International Law
C.E.C.A.—Communauté Européenne du Charbon et de l'Acier (see
    E.C.S.C.)
C.E.E.—Communauté Economique Européenne (see E.E.C.)
C.E.E.A.—Communauté Européenne de l'Energie Atomique (see
    E.A.E.C./Euratom)
C.M.L.R.—Common Market Law Reports
C.M.L.Rev.—Common Market Law Review
Comecon—Council for Mutual Economic Co-operation
E.A.E.C./Euratom—European Atomic Energy Community
E.C.S.C.—European Coal and Steel Community
E.E.C.—European Economic Community
E.F.T.A.—European Free Trade Association
E.R.T.A.—European Road Transport Agreement
G.A.T.T.—General Agreement on Tariffs and Trade
Gaz.Uff.—Gazetta Ufficiale (Italy)
I.C.J. Reports—International Court of Justice Reports
I.C.L.Q.—International and Comparative Law Quarterly
I.L.O.—International Labour Organisation
I.M.F.—International Monetary Fund
J.O.—Journal Officiel des Communautés Européennes
J.O.R.F.—Journal Officiel de la République Française
L.Q.R.—Law Quarterly Review
M.B.—Moniteur Belge
M.L.R.—Modern Law Review
N.A.T.O.—North Atlantic Treaty Organisation
O.E.C.D.—Organisation for Economic Co-operation and Development
O.E.E.C.—Organisation for European Economic Co-operation
P.C.I.J. Rep.—Permanent Court of International Justice Reports
Recueil—Recueil de la Jurisprudence de la Cour de Justice des Com-
    munautés Européennes
Reg.—Regulation
R.P.—Rule of Procedure of the Community Court
U.N.T.S.—United Nations Treaty Series

PART I

The Nature of the European Communities and of Community Law

CHAPTER ONE

The European Community and its Law

THE FORMATION OF THE EUROPEAN COMMUNITY

The recurrent dream of a unified Europe is part of our cultural heritage. Students of history are familiar with the attempts to create a united Europe mainly by force, for conquest and universalism go often hand in hand. Only within living memory have two powerful ideologies, Communism and Nazism, endeavoured to unify Europe in their own fashion. In August 1920 the advance of the Red Army "through the heart of Poland to the conquest of Europe and world conflagration"[1] was brought to a halt at the gates of Warsaw in what was described[2] as the eighteenth decisive battle of world history. In 1945 ended the Second World War, unleashed by one Adolf Hitler who dreamed of a millennium of German domination over Europe. After six years of struggle most of Europe was reduced to smouldering heaps of rubble, physically and politically. The old Europe became just a phase in the Continent's saga and history began to work towards a different concept of unification.

Students of political thought are familiar with the rivalries for excellence between the concept of the sovereign state and federal ideas. From the middle ages right up to our time the state was regarded as the ideal self-sufficient unit, capable of securing protection and self-fulfilment of individuals. The 19th and the first half of the 20th centuries witnessed the apotheosis of the sovereign state as the supreme and sublime goal of human organisation. Everything was to be subordinated to the state. This Hegelian ideal, no doubt rooted in Plato's philosophy, being an element of the explanation of the universe and of historical determinism, was eagerly adopted by modern dictatorships both of the fascist and communist type and soon brought into disrepute. The

---

[1] General Tukhachevski in an order to his armies quoted by Umiastowski, R., *Russia and the Polish Republic* 1918–1941 (1944), p. 84.
[2] By Lord D'Abernon; Fuller, J.F. C., *The Decisive Battles of the Western World*, 1792–1944, Vol. 2 (1970), p. 411.

3

Second World War did not solve Europe's problems but resulted in a new division based on the conquest of its eastern half and a status of satellite states. In a sense it contributed to the creation of two European Communities; of the West (which is the subject of the present study) and of the East (which marks a political and ideological dependency on the Soviet Union). The Second World War, however, demonstrated the futility of conquests and the vulnerability of the sovereign state concept. The sovereign state could no longer guarantee the protection of the citizen and so the traditional concept of allegiance based on a *sui generis* contract broke down. Interdependence of states rather than independence became the key to post-war international relations, and was reflected in current trends of international law, especially in the ideology and structure of the United Nations. The slogan *si vis pacem para bellum* had to give way to the quest for justice among men and nations and *si vis pacem para pacem* had to become the order of the day. An admirable example of co-operation and a practical application of the call for peace is the European Coal and Steel Community built on the premise that, if the basic raw materials for war (coal and steel) are removed from national control, wars between the traditional enemies, France and Germany, will become virtually impossible as long as both are prevented from developing a substantial war industry. A corollary benefit of the international control of these resources, accruing not only to France and Germany but also to the other members of the Community, was brought about by the rationalisation of the coal and steel industries and the economic stimulus created by an enlarged market.

With the demise of the state ideology, federalism found a new lease of life. Federal doctrines have, in the past, set their face against the idolatry of the state, but physical, territorial federalism in Western Europe proved politically impossible. Federalism had to search for other, more realistic forms. Harold Laski, in an introduction to his book, *Liberty in the Modern State*,[3] argued that the Second World War and its antecedents had shown that "the principle of national sovereignty has exhausted its usefulness". He wrote further: "it is through supra-national planning in fields like electric power, or transport, an integrated economy of coal and steel, that we can best hope to attain this end [i.e. to make liberty possible]. It is, of course, impossible to leave such planning in private hands". Laski dubbed his idea "functional federalism" because he was opposed to the concept of territorial federation, that is to say a United States of Europe or a Federal Western Europe, an enlarged version of Switzerland, which he regarded as both obsolete and impractical.

---

[3] Re-published in 1948.

Whilst "functional federalism" has been accepted by the architects of the West European Community, Laski's pessimism about territorial federalism may yet prove unfounded. It is clear that economic co-operation and integration will tighten the political and organisational bonds between states and from this reality new political forms will emerge. Territorial federalism is not just round the corner but is not as remote as it may seem. It may well be that it will not be heralded by political theory but will grow up as a child of evolution. In the Community institutions, which we shall examine in detail, the stage seems to have been set for such a development.

The post-war practical exercise in international co-operation in Western Europe has proved that nations can live together and work together, that they can solve their differences amicably and, where need be, through appropriate legal and judicial process. It has demonstrated that the concept of a Community is not only viable but also capable of growth and development. The Community institutions have already been working for a generation and their very existence and practical usefulness will inevitably lead to their refinement. In due course the child will become man.

If we cast our minds back to the early post-war days we will realise that a Community approach was the practical answer to many problems Europe was in ruins politically and economically; the European colonial empires faced liquidation; the importance of the single European states which dominated the League of Nations was diminished; the "dollar-gap" resulted in great influence of the United States of America not only as a benevolent saviour but also as a potential master; an "iron curtain" was drawn across Europe and the world cowered in the shadows of great powers: the United States of America and Soviet Russia facing each other menacingly across Europe. Only rapid recovery in concert could restore Europe's self respect. What is more it became only too obvious that economic reconstruction had to match political aspirations. Thus the idea of a European Community was forced upon Europeans as an economic and political necessity. As for grand designs, the architects of the Community soon realised that great ideologies and elaborate blueprints were of little practical use and that nothing could be achieved at one stroke. Robert Schuman,[4] the great French European, said: "L'Europe ne se fera pas d'un coup dans une construction d'ensemble, elle se fera par des réalisations concrètes créant d'abord une solidarité de fait . . ."

This factual solidarity can be traced to events of great importance to Europe and the world at large, as the work of world recovery and

---

[4] Quoted by Lorette, L. de Sainte, *Le Marché Commun* (1961), p. 17.

reconstruction began to create a fabric of international economic co-operation. We should mention, if only briefly, these events and forms of co-operation because they too contributed to European solidarity and in a sense paved the way for the institutional framework of the European Community.

THE INTERNATIONAL MONETARY FUND AND THE WORLD BANK

The I.M.F. was created at a conference at Bretton Woods in 1946, with the object of maintaining the stability of national currencies, reducing restrictions on the currency exchange and helping countries to maintain a balance of payments. The subscribing countries participate on a share basis: U.S.A. 28%, U.S.S.R. 12·5% and Europe only 16%. The size of the share determines the voting power of the subscribers. Countries (including the United Kingdom) often borrow money to maintain their solvency. The World Bank was also created at Bretton Woods. Here again states participate on a share basis. The U.S.A. alone provides 38% of the capital. The Bank offers not only financial assistance but also provides experts in various fields. It has been useful to finance projects incapable of being financed otherwise, especially in the developing countries.

THE HAVANA CHARTER AND G.A.T.T.

Fifty-five countries, assembled at Havana on the initiative of the U.S.A. in 1947–48, drafted a Charter of International Commerce which envisaged a gradual reduction of customs tariffs; proposed suppression of import quotas (except in the case of agricultural produce) and imbalance of payments; prohibited discrimination in commerce (except in the case of former colonies, customs unions and free exchange areas); encouraged investments in the developing countries and suggested an International Trade Organisation. Liberia was the only country which ratified the Charter.

The idea of this Charter was nevertheless accepted by 38 countries which in October 1947 signed the General Agreement on Tariffs and Trade (G.A.T.T.). It is concerned with customs and commercial policy. The Agreement has been in operation without being ratified and the number of participants increased with the admission of some 12 countries (including countries defeated at war). Under the auspices of G.A.T.T. frequent meetings of experts are held and many customs laws have been modified.

The members of G.A.T.T. have set up a permanent commission

with a secretariat in Geneva. Moreover, member countries adhere, as a rule, to the principles propounded by G.A.T.T. in the matter of customs, import quotas and preferences and enter into bi-lateral agreements in these fields. It is significant that the so called Schuman Plan and the European Economic Community Treaty were submitted to G.A.T.T. to ensure conformity with its principles.

Although G.A.T.T. has not been ratified by any country it nevertheless plays an important part in international trade.

THE U.N. ECONOMIC COMMISSION FOR EUROPE

This Commission was established in 1947 in Geneva for the purpose of exchanging information and statistical data on coal, electricity and transport in Western and Eastern Europe. Twenty-eight countries, including the U.S.A., are involved. The Commission has published analytical studies of the economic situations of several European countries, but as the division between the Western and Eastern blocs deepened, it failed as an instrument of co-operation.

THE MARSHALL PLAN AND THE ORGANISATION FOR EUROPEAN ECONOMIC CO-OPERATION

In a speech at Harvard on 5 July 1947 General George Marshall, the U.S. Foreign Secretary, announced a plan for European relief. Instead of loans to individual countries the U.S. offered economic aid on the sole condition that the Europeans work out a common programme for the relief of poverty and economic reconstruction. His appeal was addressed to Europe as a whole stating that ". . . our policy is not directed against any country or against any doctrine but against hunger, poverty, despair and chaos; its aim is the renewal of active economy throughout the world".[5] The plan was welcomed in Western Europe and the Foreign Secretaries of France and the United Kingdom invited Soviet Russia to join them. Ten days later Molotov scorned the invitation and enjoined Czechoslovakia, Poland and Finland, who expressed interest, to have nothing to do with the Plan.

Sixteen West European countries participated in the conference and the ensuing Committee of Economic Co-operation which led to the creation of the Organisation for the European Economic Co-operation in April 1948. More than 13 milliard dollars were poured into Europe out of the American bounty. This was undoubtedly the first substantial

---

[5] Lorette, *op. cit.*, p. 22.

move towards economic co-operation in Europe and the Americans quite rightly take pride in their contribution.

At first the O.E.E.C. examined the various national plans of economic reconstruction and then worked out a programme of distribution of the American aid. From a legal point of view the important feature of the O.E.E.C. was its inter-governmental structure. The sovereignty of each country was safeguarded and no political strings were attached, so much so that even Switzerland, sworn to perpetual neutrality, could participate. The Organisation, which consisted of a Council of Ministers, an Executive Committee and a Secretariat, survived the completion of the Marshall Plan. It embraced 18 countries, including West Germany since 1949 and Spain since 1959 and Yugoslavia represented by an observer. The O.E.E.C. could take decisions which were binding on members. It endeavoured to co-ordinate national economic policies and provide experts who serve in an advisory capacity in special fields, i.e. transport, electricity, textiles, etc. It even tried to bring together rival groups like the E.E.C. and the E.F.T.A.

From its inception the O.E.E.C. endeavoured to liberalise European trade. It brought about a reduction of import quotas without tampering with the customs laws, which resulted in a short-lived trade boom. In 1952 the United Kingdom and France, contrary to the O.E.E.C.'s advice, lapsed into import quotas and so exposed the weakness of the Organisation. As new forms of economic co-operation began to take shape, the O.E.E.C. exhausted its usefulness. In 1961 it was transformed into an Organisation for Economic Co-operation and Development (O.E.C.D.) for the purpose of assisting the developing countries. The European countries were joined by the U.S.A. and Canada as well as the E.E.C. in its corporate capacity, i.e. independently of its members.

THE COUNCIL OF EUROPE

Parallel to this economic co-operation there was a movement towards political and military integration. The various European movements joined forces in a Congress of Europe held in May 1948 in the Hague under the presidency of Winston Churchill. This resulted in the Council of Europe inaugurated in 1949 at Strasbourg. It started with the five countries of the Brussels Military Alliance (now the Western European Union), viz. the U.K., France, Belgium, Holland and Luxembourg, and now embraces 18 countries of Western Europe. Spain and Portugal are excluded and Greece was suspended from membership in 1967 and re-admitted in 1974.

The Council of Europe consists of a Consultative Assembly composed of parliamentary delegates of the member states, a Committee of

Ministers and a Secretariat. It has a permanent seat at Strasbourg. As a political design it has proved a failure since it has not developed beyond the nuclear stage of a federal organisation. Its main achievements lie in the field of Human Rights, having established a Commission and a Court of Human Rights. But, above all, it has kept the idea of a United Europe alive.

In the economic field the Consultative Assembly in 1951 formulated proposals to turn Europe into a "low tariff club" through the lowering of customs barriers. It also put forward, under the name of the "Strasbourg Plan", ideas for the economic development of the former colonies of the European powers and for the adoption of preferential tariffs between these territories; the British Commonwealth on the one hand and the European countries on the other. Further initiatives aimed at the organisation of European agriculture (the so called green pool) and transport.

Whilst the economic initiatives of the Council of Europe have been superseded by the E.E.C. and the political initiatives remain in an embryonic stage, the Council provides a forum for cultural and political contacts extending beyond the E.E.C. and so preserves the concept of European unity.

THE NORTH ATLANTIC TREATY ORGANISATION AND TRANSPORT

N.A.T.O. developed from the North Atlantic Treaty of 1949 which was an extension of the Brussels Treaty of 1948. It now embraces all the West European countries (except Eire, Sweden and Switzerland) as well as the U.S.A., Canada, Greece, Turkey and West Germany. France has withdrawn from N.A.T.O. but remains party to the North Atlantic Treaty. It is important to note that, without a surrender of sovereignty, decisions within N.A.T.O. are taken collectively and that this co-operation, though confined to military matters, contributes to the cohesion of Western Europe.

In another technical field, that of transport, the Conference of European Ministers of Transport has for some years now achieved rationalisation of railway transport and, incidentally, enabled the 17 countries involved to make substantial economies. This means that railway carriages marked E.U.R.O.P. can be used and repaired anywhere within the organisation and need not be returned empty to their countries of origin. Complementing E.U.R.O.P. is E.U.R.O.F.I.M.A. (*Société de financement de matériel ferroviaire*) which by international agreement is entitled to exemption from customs and taxes in respect of railway equipment no matter where it is ultimately used within the organisation. The more complex problem of the rationalisation of transport by road is currently under consideration within the E.E.C. Transport Policy.

THE BENELUX COUNTRIES

For the purpose of customs, the three countries (Belgium, Netherlands, Luxembourg) have become one. This has been achieved by stages in spite of the disparity of their economic systems and policies. As from 1 January 1948 they removed customs barriers between themselves and agreed upon common customs tariffs *vis-à-vis* the outside world. In 1951 they adopted a common scheme of customs and excise duties, with the exception of excise on alcohol, sugar and petrol. In 1954 they authorised a free flow of capital which meant a freedom of investment and unrestricted transfer of currency within the three countries. Since 1956 they have entered into common commercial treaties with other countries and accepted a free movement of labour. In 1958 they signed a treaty of economic union which came into force on 17 November 1960. As from that date the economy of the Benelux countries was geared to the basic assumptions of an internal market, that is the removal of customs barriers, resulting in a free movement of goods and the free movement of capital and manpower. These three elements were adopted later on for the formation of the E.E.C. by the Treaty of Rome.

The Benelux union did not destroy the national sovereignty of the three countries or affect their identity as subjects of International Law. Though economic integration led inevitably to a greater cohesion in a political and military sense, each country has preserved its political and legal system. The economic integration of the Benelux countries was not a painless operation for there were rival interests of industries across the border. However, as a result, the internal trade of these countries increased by 50% whereas their external trade jumped to fifth place after the U.S.A., the U.K., West Germany and Canada, thus surpassing France even though the population of France was twice that of the Benelux countries.

From 1948 to 1956 the national revenue of Belgium and the Netherlands increased considerably and so did their trade with the outside world. This minute Common Market proved to be profitable, not only to the three countries but also to others. Its unqualified success whetted the appetites of neighbouring states and the question arose whether the Benelux experiment could be projected on a larger scale.

THE SCHUMAN PLAN

Robert Schuman and Count Sforza thought that a customs union between France and Italy would be beneficial to both countries. A customs treaty was signed in 1949 but France and Italy lacked the will to see it through. This failure indicated that a less ambitious approach, limited perhaps to one basic industry, should be attempted. Thus coal and steel was selected as the industry basic to many other industries and one especially relevant to the business of war. If war were to be eliminated coal and steel must be put under international control and if economic progress were to breach the national frontiers this basic industry must be made to serve a community of nations.

This was not a novel philosophy, for back in 1948 the European Movement proclaimed at the Hague the need for an industrial programme especially for the production and distribution of coal. A year later, at Westminster, the European Movement proposed a scheme for several basic industries, i.e. coal, steel, electricity and transport, envisaging a European Institution responsible for a general policy in respect of each of these four industries especially in the field of investments, the volume of production and prices and a consultative body consisting of employers and employees as well as representatives of the public interest.

This, in turn, led to the so called Schuman Plan. In May 1950 France, through her Minister of Foreign Affairs, Robert Schuman, proposed to place all the Franco–German production of coal and steel under a common authority and invited other countries to do the same. Schuman declared: "... Par la mise en commun de productions de base et par l'institution d'une Haute Autorité nouvelle, dont les décisions lieront la France, l'Allemagne et les pays qui adhéreront, cette proposition réalisera les premières assises concrètes d'une Fédération Européenne indispensable à la préservation de la paix . . ."[6]

THE EUROPEAN COAL AND STEEL COMMUNITY

On 18 April 1951 the Ministers representing France, Germany, Italy, Belgium, Holland and Luxemburg signed in Paris a treaty which established the European Coal and Steel Community (*Communauté Européenne du Charbon et de l'Acier*). The Treaty was ratified, not without national opposition, e.g. it was ratified by the French Chamber of Deputies by 377 votes against 235 and by the Senate by 182 votes against 32. The industries concerned were unhappy as the Treaty was imposed upon them without prior consultation but it was, no doubt, a wise scheme.

The Treaty of Paris, this first instrument of European integration, consists of 100 articles, three annexes, three protocols and a convention of transitory provisions. The most important feature of the Coal and Steel Community is its supra-national character. It is no longer an

---

[6] Lorette, *op. cit.*, p. 38.

inter-governmental but a truly supra-national organisation. It was aptly described[7] as "a quasi federation in an important economic sector, the member-states retaining their sovereignty in all other sectors".

Apart from supra-national organs the Community enjoys a faculty of self-administration manifested in the choice and recruitment of officials, a financial autonomy marked by the power of levying taxes and a measure of self-control vested in a parliamentary assembly.

The Community was endowed with five organs:
- (1) an executive, called the High Authority,
- (2) a Consultative Committee attached to the High Authority,
- (3) a Special Council of Ministers,
- (4) an Assembly, and
- (5) a Court of Justice.

The High Authority was the permanent executive of the Community. It consisted of nine members, eight chosen unanimously by the six governments and the ninth co-opted by the eight members to emphasise the supra-national character of the Community. A third of the High Authority retired every second year and was replaced by new members irrespective of nationality. The functions of the High Authority included the launching and management of a common market in coal and steel, development and control of investments and scientific research, action to curb unemployment, discrimination and restrictive practices, the imposition of common taxes upon the production of coal and steel; all this without reference to the governments of the member states, subject only to responsibility to the Court and the Assembly. It is true that the field of independent action of the High Authority was restricted, but where it could act it took decisions which were binding upon the member states.

The High Authority was assisted by a Consultative Committee consisting of representatives of employers, trade unions and consumers designated by the Special Council of Ministers on the advice of the trade unions and the producer and consumer organisation.

The Special Council of Ministers represented the sovereign power. Its function was to harmonise the national economies on the recommendation of the High Authority in the fields of coal and steel. Political control was in the hands of the Assembly of the Coal and Steel Community, which consisted of 68 members, of which France, Germany and Italy provided 18 each and the remaining 24 represented the Benelux countries. Members were elected by their national Parliaments though they could have been elected directly. By a two-thirds majority the Assembly could dismiss the High Authority and together with the member states propose amendments to the Treaty.

---

[7] By Guy de Carmay, *Fortune d'Europe* (1953).

The Court consisted of seven members. Its function was to act as a watch-dog over the application of the Treaty, examine the decisions of the High Authority in the light of the Treaty provisions and adjudicate upon the alleged breaches of the Treaty. During the seven years of its existence the Court gave 137 decisions which were of a considerable importance to the Community. These decisions had a binding force in the member states. They are still relevant to Community Law.

Several lessons could be drawn from this experiment. It proved that supra-national institutions could function in spite of diverse national interests; that far from being an economic disaster this first European common market greatly contributed to the economic progress of the member states. The enlarged market activated industries far beyond those directly connected with coal and steel. The greatest benefit accrued to Italy, the economically weakest member. However, all was not well all the time. In 1959 there was a crisis in the coal industry caused mainly by over-production and an increase in the use of oil which rendered coal mines, especially in Belgium and Germany, redundant. The High Authority endeavoured to finance stock-piling, to reduce production and even to lower wages, but the Council of Ministers refused to sanction these measures clearly because national interests were at stake. The High Authority was, therefore, forced to provide a special aid to Belgium, which was hit very badly, for the rehabilitation and re-training of miners and to restrict imports from outside the Community. The very existence of the Community enabled it to relieve at least one country but it also became clear that there must be a common European policy in the field of energy. Whilst the Community was successful in its field it was not able to cope with other economic problems and its success certainly did not satisfy those who worked for a United Europe in their lifetime.

TOWARDS THE TREATIES OF ROME

The greater integration of Europe owes a great deal to military considerations for it is evident that military alliances have political and economic consequences.

The problem of the defence of Western Europe, especially the American insistence on the participation of Germany in the defence of the Continent, raised delicate political and economic questions. The Germans were doing well without having to spend vast sums on defence, yet there was an aversion to their having a finger on the common trigger and some fear of the revival of German military might. These fears were assuaged partly by the international control of coal and steel, partly by the pacific stance of the German people. Moreover, in view of the cost of defence, it was quite inequitable that Germany should be shielded by her neighbours at their expense. A German contribution had to be sought within an international framework. France, especially, insisted on a supra-national control of the armed forces and so in 1952 the European Defence Treaty was signed.

The Treaty envisaged a European Defence Community as a kind of federation without a central federal government. The organisation was to consist of a Commissariat, an Assembly, a Council of Ministers and a Court of Justice, all modelled upon the Coal and Steel Community. It is interesting to note that whilst internationalist France actively promoted the idea it was nationalist France which wrecked the edifice, as on 30 August 1954 the French National Assembly refused to ratify the treaty already ratified by other countries.

The failure to create a European Army led to the London Conference in September 1954 which resulted in turn in the admission of Italy and West Germany to the alliance by virtue of the Protocols to the Brussels Treaty signed in Paris in October 1954. The Final Act of the London Conference gave birth to yet another organisation, i.e. the Council of Western European Union embracing the United Kingdom, Belgium, Holland, Luxembourg, France, Germany and Italy. It has subsequently passed through certain mutations but achieved no prominence apart from defence in the N.A.T.O. setting though logically it set the United Kingdom into the picture of West European integration.

For a while the unionist movement lay dormant, though on the Continent there were encouraging stirrings among the various industries, especially agriculture and the trade unions. The idea was resurrected at the meeting of the Foreign Ministers of the six members of the Coal and Steel Community in June 1955 at Messina. They were unanimous in their resolve to pursue the concept of an economic union and they were encouraged to do so by the governments of the Benelux countries.

At the beginning of the Conference the Ministers proclaimed their intention to "pursue the establishment of a United Europe through the development of common institutions, a progressive fusion of national economies, the creation of a Common Market and harmonisation of social policies".[8] During the Conference the Ministers became more precise as they considered that a "constitution of a European Common Market must be their objective" though they realised that this could only be achieved by stages. To do this, again on the advice of the Benelux countries, the Ministers set up an Inter-Governmental Committee to study the various problems. The United Kingdom was invited to attend and indeed a minor official from the Board of Trade took part in the preliminary discussions.

---

[8] Quoted by Lorette, *op. cit.*, p. 60.

In July 1955 the Committee met in Brussels with the object of co-ordinating the work of the various sub-committees set up to study the problems of investment, social policy, fuel and power, atomic energy and transport. The work continued during the summer and autumn of 1955 and among the sixty or so experts there were representatives of the Coal and Steel Community, the Organisation for European Co-operation, the Council of Europe and, for a while, of the United Kingdom. Then followed a period of considerable activity and several meetings of the Foreign Ministers of the six countries. Reports of experts were considered, until finally a treaty was drafted and signed in Rome on 25 March 1957. This was the first Treaty of Rome which established the European Economic Community (the E.E.C.) commonly known as the Common Market. The Treaty consists of 248 articles, 4 appendices, 9 protocols and a convention relating to the association with the Community of the Overseas Countries and Territories which have special relations with Belgium, France, Italy and the Netherlands.

The second Treaty of Rome, setting up the European Community of Atomic Energy (Euratom) was signed on the same day. It consists of 225 articles, 5 appendices and 1 protocol.

Both treaties had to be ratified by the parliaments of the signatory states. The reaction of these parliaments is worthy of a comparison. In Germany both Houses of Parliament ratified the Treaties unanimously. In Belgium in the Chamber of Deputies 174 voted for and 4 against ratification; in the Senate 134 and 2 against. In France in the Chamber of Deputies 342 voted for and 239 against the ratification; in the Senate 222 for and 70 against. In Italy in the Chamber of Deputies 311 voted for and 144 against the ratification; the Senate voted unanimously for ratification. In Luxembourg 46 votes were cast for and 3 against ratification. In the Netherlands in the Chamber of Deputies 114 votes were cast for and 12 against ratification; in the Senate 44 for and 5 against. The numerical opposition in France and Italy is significant but can easily be explained by the existence of large Communist parties in those countries and the attitude of the mother-country of communism to European Unity.[9]

The Treaties became operative on 1 January 1958.

THE THREE COMMUNITIES

The two Treaties of Rome added two new Communities to the Coal and Steel Community.

The European Atomic Energy Community (Euratom) was created as a specialist market for atomic energy. Atomic energy is a relatively new

---

[9] "Soviet unease over U.K. entry", *European Community* (February 1972), p. 16.

source of power with a virtually unlimited potential. It is hoped, therefore, that it will satisfy the demands of our technological era. In the sixties the Six imported about a quarter of their energy from countries outside the Community. By 1975, it was considered, they will have to import 40% of their needs unless atomic energy takes over from the traditional sources of power. However this target was not realised as in 1973 the Community was importing some 63% of its energy and the oil crisis aggravated the situation. A common energy policy embracing the Euratom for which the Community has been striving, albeit without success, has become not only a matter of economic urgency but also a factor in European integration.

The object of Euratom is to develop nuclear energy, distribute it within the Community and sell the surplus to the outside world. In view of the development costs involved the Community must collectively engage in the necessary research and disseminate the accumulated knowledge. It must develop industry in a rational way ensuring a fair distribution within the Community and, finally, it must, as a body, consider the international implications of the pacific use of nuclear energy. In many respects Euratom corresponds to the Coal and Steel Community.

The objectives of the European Economic Community (E.E.C.) are wider than the objectives of the remaining two Communities, for the E.E.C. is not a mere specialist organisation but an instrument of economic integration with a considerable political potential. Therefore whilst bearing in mind the three separate juristic entities the E.E.C. is by far the most important and may be regarded as a prototype of an integrated European Community.

THE MERGER OF THE COMMUNITIES

The main institutions of the E.C.S.C. as we have seen were five in number: an executive body known as the High Authority; a Consultative Committee; a Special Council made up of the representatives of the governments of the member states; a Parliamentary Assembly made up of representative parliamentarians of the national parliaments of the member states; and a Court of Justice. When the E.E.C. and Euratom were established, their institutions were modelled upon those of the E.C.S.C. and this naturally suggested the merger of the separate institutions so as to avoid a multiplicity of institutions responsible for the achievement of similar tasks. This merger has taken place in two stages.

A Convention relating to certain Institutions common to the European Communities was concluded simultaneously with the Rome Treaties and provided for the establishment of a single Court of Justice and a single Parliamentary Assembly to serve all three Communities. The completion of this process of institutional merger was not immediately realised with the result that for some years each of the Communities retained its own executive body (High Authority in the case of the E.C.S.C. and Commissions in the case of the E.E.C. and Euratom) and Council. This institutional separatism resulted from the adoption of a functional approach to European integration; three Communities were established by separate treaties and charged with the achievement of specific objectives. Further, the role of the Commissions and Councils in relation to the E.E.C. and Euratom differed significantly from that of the High Authority and Special Council in relation to the E.C.S.C., and so in 1957 separate institutions seemed appropriate. In practice this separation was found to be unsatisfactory. Whilst the objectives of each Community are distinct they also overlap and form part of a larger economic whole. In several fields, such as coal and steel and atomic energy, it was desirable for the Communities to co-ordinate their policy; the existence of separate institutions each with its own personnel with different views and ideas militated against this. Eventually a treaty was signed in May 1965 and took effect on 1 July 1967, providing for further fusion of the Communities.[10] This treaty instituted a single Commission to replace the High Authority of the E.C.S.C. and the Commissions of the E.E.C. and Euratom, and a single Council to replace the separate Councils of the three Communities.

This "Merger Treaty", which completed the institutional merger of the Communities, represents a further step towards the eventual merger of the three Communities to form a single European Community; but this will require the negotiation of a new treaty to replace the Treaty of Paris and the Treaties of Rome. For the time being "the three Communities can be regarded as facets of one basic experiment, stages in an unfinished process, the future development of which cannot yet be foreseen".[11]

THE UNITED KINGDOM AND EUROPEAN SOLIDARITY

The United Kingdom has contributed to European solidarity (particularly in the field of military co-operation) but has tended to remain aloof. It is true that in 1946 in his famous Zurich speech

---

[10] The entry into force of this treaty was delayed by the crisis resulting from a clash between France and her five partners over the agricultural policy of the E.E.C.

[11] Palmer, M., Lambert, J. *et al.*, *European Unity* (1968), p. 169. On the background to and effects of the Merger Treaty, see Houben, P. H. J. M., "The Merger of the Executives of the European Communities" (1965–66), 3 C.M.L. Rev. 37 and Weil, G. L., "The Merger of the Institutions of the European Communities" (1967), 61 A.J.I.L. 57.

Winston Churchill urged the establishment of a United States of Europe based on a partnership between France and Germany. But the role which he assigned to the United Kingdom was that of a friend and sponsor of the new Europe, clearly a role which fell far short of full participation.[12]

Successive British post-war governments adopted a lukewarm and sceptical attitude towards developments on the Continent. There were, perhaps, two main reasons for this. In the first place, unlike her continental allies, Britain had not endured defeat and enemy occupation. Although she had suffered economically as a result of the war, British institutions and the British way of life were not only preserved intact but could in a sense be said to be triumphant. From such a standpoint the prospect of compromising British independence in favour of union with continental Europe was not very attractive. In addition, at that time Britain was still in possession of a considerable colonial empire to which, as well as to the independent members of the Commonwealth, she looked rather than to the Continent. There was also the special relationship which had been forged between Britain and the United States. The British attitude to European integration in the years immediately following the Second World War is, perhaps, summed up by the reaction of Ernest Bevin, when Foreign Secretary, to the proposal that Britain should participate in a European Assembly as part of the Council of Europe: "I don't like it. I don't like it. If you open that Pandora's Box you will find it full of Trojan horses."[13]

By the late 1950s British exclusion from the advantages which became apparent within the Community and the fear that she might lose political influence made her realise that the idea of the European Community, far from being a failure, was a force to be reckoned with. The United Kingdom never joined the Coal and Steel Community (although she did establish a form of association with it) and cold-shouldered the Common Market negotiations. In 1957 Britain proposed a "free trade area" (the so called Maudling Plan) and, when this failed, created a rival organisation, the European Free Trade Association (E.F.T.A.) in 1959. However, in some respects E.F.T.A., which embraced Austria, Denmark, Norway, Portugal, Sweden, Switzerland and the United Kingdom, proved less successful than the European Economic Community and a positive policy towards the European Community emerged.

In 1961 the Macmillan Government applied for membership of the E.E.C. The negotiations (the British team was headed by the Lord

---

[12] Kitzinger, U., *The European Common Market and Community* (1967), p. 37.

[13] Robertson, A. H., *The Council of Europe* (2nd Edn., 1961), p. 6, note 23.

Privy Seal, Mr. Edward Heath) dragged on, but when the British side, leaving some problems to further negotiations, was ready to sign in 1963 the French President, General de Gaulle, vetoed the British entry. In 1967 the Wilson Government renewed the application but it was vetoed again by France before negotiations could take place. The third attempt was made by the Heath Government in 1970 and the negotiations for entry were successfully concluded in January 1972.

Grand debates were held in Parliament and elsewhere during the summer and autumn of 1971 and the Government mounted a massive information service. Opinion polls revealed a considerable opposition to British entry into Europe and party politics obscured the discussion on the merits of the entry. It transpired that the Labour Party, who would have been happy to accept the terms of the British accession when in power, was opposed to the terms when in opposition. The declared reasons that the situation had changed and that the country's economy did not warrant accession at this time, though hardly convincing, were vigorously advanced by the Labour Party opposition. Opponents in principle argued that there was anything but advantage in accession to the Community, whilst the surrender of sovereignty was an unforgiveable folly. On 28 October 1971 the Government secured a reasonable majority[14] with the support of the Liberals and Labour dissenters from the official party policy who voted for the entry in principle but pledged themselves to oppose the consequential legislation. The historic decision, which merited a national unity, was soured by the antics of party politics. On 20 January 1972 the eleventh hour attempt to prevent the signing of the Treaty of Accession until the full text "has been published and its contents laid before the House" failed, but the vote on the motion produced a majority of only 21 for the Government,[15] the Conservative opponents abstaining and the Labour members voting under a three line whip.

THE TREATY OF ACCESSION AND BEYOND

In simple legal terms the Treaty of Accession, signed on 22 January 1972 on behalf of the six member states, the Communities (represented by Mr. Gaston Thorn, Foreign Minister of Luxembourg and Chairman of the Council of Ministers) and the four prospective members Denmark, Eire, Norway and the United Kingdom, is a Treaty signifying admission of new members to the three Communities. The Treaty consists of three articles stating that the new members accede to the

---

[14] *Hansard, House of Commons* 1970–71, Vol. 823, col. 2212.
[15] *Ibid.*, 1971–72, Vol. 829, col. 800.

existing Communities and accept all their rules. A lengthy Act, signed at the same time, confirms the results of the negotiations and gives details of what membership entails. Full membership as from 1 January 1973 is conditional upon the incorporation of the Community Law into the municipal laws of the new members. It also imports the methods of phasing into the Community over the five years from 1973 to 1978.

We shall discuss elsewhere the effects of the Treaty for the United Kingdom and the Community. It will suffice to say, at this stage, that neither the texts of the foundation Treaties nor the institutions established under these Treaties were radically changed, though they were adjusted to give effect to the enlarged membership.

Long term adjustments postulate a new treaty. Such a treaty would provide an opportunity for a revision of the three foundation treaties, elimination of what has become obsolete and incorporation of the multifarious experience of the Communities as well as new ideas. The merger of the Communities could be brought to its logical conclusion, that is a complete fusion of the three Communities into a single legal entity. The present vague political idea of a Community of West European nations could be transformed into a more meaningful juristic concept.

An evolutionary approach to the problem of integration was advocated in the Tindemans Report published in January 1976. In his cautious Report the Belgian Prime Minister postulated a gradual development towards European Union building on the existing institutions and the practices which have evolved outside the Treaty framework. The Report envisaged a closer co-operation between the member states, notably a co-ordination of their foreign policy and regular meetings of heads of government acting as the "European Council".[16] It proposed "to put an end to the distinction which still exists to-day between ministerial meetings which deal with political co-operation and those which deal with the subjects covered by the Treaty". It proposed to strengthen the role of the European Council by making the Council of Ministers of Foreign Affairs responsible for the preparation of its meetings and by the European Council indicating the institution or organisation responsible for the execution of its decisions.

The Report emphasised further the need to develop a common foreign policy along with extended external economic relations and a common defence policy, converting policy commitments into "legal obligations". It advocated recourse to majority voting in the Council

---

[16] Based on the recommendations of the Heads of Government meeting in Paris in December 1974.

as a "normal practice of the Community". Avoiding any rigid time-table or development by stages the Report suggested a "two-speed plan of economic integration" in which the weaker members, i.e. Eire, Italy and the United Kingdom, shall proceed at a slower pace than the others. Above all the Report urged European Unity as a self-evident good.

It is evident that if, and when, such Unity comes about, the form of the new Community will have to be considered. The Community may continue as an association of sovereign states (*l'Europe d'Etats*) or develop into a federal structure heralded by the E.E.C. Political developments will, no doubt, influence the institutions and the law of the Community. At present we have the world's largest trading unit with a total population of over 250 million consisting of states of different size, cultural heritage, wealth and aspirations.

CHAPTER TWO

The Concept and Status of the European Communities

I THE LEGAL STATUS OF THE EUROPEAN COMMUNITY

The European Community is a result of international solidarity which we have considered in the light of post-war developments in international relations, and of the conscious effort to create a kind of unity in Western Europe. When political unification proved premature the architects of the Community seized upon the economic elements of inter-state relations and built these into the three "Communities" (Coal and Steel, Euratom and E.E.C.), so much so that today within the vague notion of a political Community we have three legally definable treaty-based "Communities". It follows that in spite of the machinery for defence (N.A.T.O.) and economic co-ordination (the three Communities), and a friendly understanding in matters of foreign policy (which should not be overrated) the political structure remains still in the sphere of speculation. Political scientists offer a variety of ideas but a blueprint which can become the basis of discussion at a Government level is yet to emerge. No doubt statesmen have their ideas too but at an official level less adventurous schemes can be expected. General de Gaulle spoke of a Europe of States and M. Pompidou,[1] speaking on the challenge of the enlarged E.E.C. spoke guardedly about a confederation. Occasionally the E.E.C. is described as a federation but, as we shall see later, neither the federal nor the confederal label fits the organisation.

In the long history of mankind only a few confederations can be recorded: Switzerland 1291–1848; The Netherlands 1581–1795; the U.S.A. 1776–1788; Germany 1815–1866. Since these confederations developed either into unitary states or federations it is worthwhile contrasting the confederal with the federal type of constitution. In a federal state the sovereign power is apportioned between a central

---

[1] *The Times*, 12 May 1972.

government and a number of member states. There are two versions of federal states which can be best illustrated by a comparison between the U.S.A. and Canada. The U.S. constitution is so arranged that power flows from the state to the federal government which has no powers, apart from those delegated to it by the states. The exact opposite obtains in Canada where the power flows from the Dominion Government to the Provinces, which have no powers apart from those delegated to them by the Dominion Government. For the purpose of international relations a federal state is represented by a central government. Internally, the legislature, the judiciary, the administration and indeed the law can be divided into federal and state.

In a confederation the sovereignty enjoyed by the individual member states is said to be complete. It can be defined as a relationship of sovereign states, each member state retaining its status as a subject of international law. In a federation, on the other hand, the sovereignty of the individual member states merges into the one sovereignty of the federation. In a confederation the central government acts directly on the member states but only through the member states upon individuals. It follows that outwardly each member of a confederation can enter into separate relations with foreign states and, of course, may of its own right be a member of U.N.O., whereas members of a federation, as a rule,[2] cannot enter into separate relations with foreign states. Inwardly members of a confederation maintain their independent and separate form of government, legislature, judiciary, administration and system of law, their relation to the central government being contractual rather than organic. A confederation has no distinct legal order for it is a political association of states rather than a composite state.

On balance the emerging European Community fits, in the light of the E.E.C. Treaty, better into a federal than confederal form.

Since, of the three Communities, the E.E.C. is the prototype of the legal structure of the European Community it is essential to examine its legal status, for it is a *pointer* to the relationship between the member states *inter se*, the member states to the Community and the Community to the outside world. The status of the E.E.C. rests upon its constitution, i.e. the Treaty of Rome, and the appropriate rules of International Law, as well as the constitutional laws of the member states.

It is clear that the E.E.C. is not a state[3] for it has no territory of its

---

[2] Cf. the anomalous position of two member republics of the U.S.S.R.: Ukraine and Byelo-Russia; Dolan, E., "The Member-Republics of the U.S.S.R. as Subjects of the Law of Nations," [1955] I.C.L.Q. 629–36.

[3] According to art. 1 of the Montevideo Convention of 1933 on the Rights and Duties of States, "the state as a person of international law should possess the following qualifications: (a) a permanent population, (b) a defined territory, (c) a government and (d) a capacity to enter into relations with other states".

own, no population which is not a citizenry of the member states, whilst its "government" has no powers except those defined by Treaty. However, it would be quite inadequate to define the E.E.C. as the association of states which subscribe to the Treaty of Rome, since the Treaty lays down a foundation for something more than a loose partnership of states involved in a joint economic enterprise. The Treaty is not a mere contractual compact, it is an institutional stage of European unity.

The E.E.C. though consisting of sovereign states, is a separate, albeit supra-national, entity, and in this respect it is governed by the law of international institutions in general and its own constitution in particular. In this context the law of international institutions, an offshoot of public international law, applies to the E.E.C. as a regional arrangement.

It is perfectly legitimate for sovereign states in their capacity as the makers of international law to act in concert in setting up institutions and organisations furthering the interests of mankind. Of these the most impelling precedent is the U.N. which, though universal in character and purpose, does not exclude regional organisations. Indeed it has been pointed out[4] that the difficulty of developing global institutions raised the hope of a greater success in the field of regional organisations. Unlike its predecessor, the League of Nations, which was conceived merely to be an association,[5] the United Nations Organisation[6] has the status of a legal person, i.e. it is a bearer of rights and duties pertinent to legal personality because it was so willed by the founder states. The same is the position of the E.E.C. In their terse statement that "the Community shall have legal personality" (E.E.C., art. 210) the founder states unequivocally created a new international entity independent of its component parts and endowed it with the status and attributes of a legal person.

By virtue of customary international law two attributes, viz. the treaty-making power and the capacity of sending and receiving envoys, mark out an entity as a sovereign body and a subject of international law. The Holy See[7] was a classic example of this doctrine from 1870

---

[4] Jenks, C. W., "World Organisation and European Integration", *European Yearbook*, Vol. I, p. 173; see also Scheuner, U., "Europe and the United Nations", *European Yearbook*, Vol. VIII, pp. 67–90.

[5] Although the Covenant did not confer juristic personality upon the League of Nations it was often argued that such personality was necessary for the League to fulfil its functions; cf. Jenks, C. W., [1945] B.Y.I.L. 267.

[6] United Nations Charter, art. 104; Advisory Opinion on Reparation for Injuries suffered in the Service of the United Nations, *I.C.J. Reports* (1949), p. 174.

[7] Kunz, J. L., "The Status of the Holy See in International Law" (1952), 46 A.J.I.L. 308 *et seq.*

when it lost territorial sovereignty until 1929 when it re-gained a symbolic territory by the Lateran Treaty. The E.E.C. need not resort to custom to support its claim for the Treaty provides for both the legal personality (art. 210) and the treaty-making power (arts. 113, 114, 228 and 238)[8]. The capacity to enter into diplomatic[9] relations derives generally from the legal personality of the E.E.C. and specifically from art. 17 of the Protocol on the Privileges and Immunities of the European Communities. By the end of 1975 the E.E.C. as a legal person distinct from its members has established diplomatic relations with more than 80 countries including the Holy See and China and maintains a delegation at the U.N.O. However, whilst there is no doubt about the international status and personality of the E.E.C. *vis-à-vis* the member states and countries which treat with it as a corporate body, the question of a universally recognised personality must still remain open.

The E.E.C. was set up by a treaty of unlimited duration (art. 240), and so was the E.A.E.C. (art. 208), but the E.C.S.C. only for fifty years (art. 97). By its design the Community is committed to a continuous progress, by its nature it appears irreversible. Theoretically it is possible for a member state to withdraw as long as it remains sovereign, that is as long as the political integration or transformation of the economic community into a more homogenous body politic has not materialised. However, in reality the economic structure of the member states and their national interests may become so intertwined in the course of time that a break-away may prove well-nigh impracticable. On the other hand it is always possible to maintain the status quo and so reduce the Community to political stagnation. The Community itself has a built-in system which may either advance it towards political and institutional integration or preserve the self-contained units of sovereign states whilst developing the economy and creating wealth within the existing institutions. This depends on whether the Community institutions are strengthened at the expense of sovereignty or whether the sovereign element keeps the Community institutions in the servile role of functional bureaucracy.

Article 236 provides for revision of the E.E.C. Treaty. The initiative rests with the government of any member state or the Commission who may submit to the Council of Ministers proposals for the amendments of the Treaty. The scope seems unlimited including, presumably, the winding-up of the Community. However, amendments must be passed by a unanimous conference of representatives of the govern-

---

[8] Cf. U.N. Charter, art. 75. E.A.E.C., arts. 101 and 206; The treaty making power of the E.C.S.C. was implicitly recognised by the U.K. in the agreement of 1954 between the U.K. and the E.C.S.C., 258 U.N.T.S. 322.
[9] Cf. U.N. Charter, art. 105.

ments of the member states, convened by the President of the Council on the recommendation of the Council, having previously obtained an approval of such conference by the Assembly and, in unspecified appropriate cases, by the Commission. However, any amendment must be ratified by all the member states in accordance with their respective constitutions (art. 236 (3)). In this way sovereignty of the member states has been safeguarded but also changes in the structure of the Community have been made dependent upon the common will of the member states. It follows that the position of the member states *inter se* and *vis-à-vis* the Community, as stated in the Treaty, will remain static unless there is a unanimous desire for change.

Enlargement of the Community is also subject to a unanimous decision of the member states followed by amendment of the Treaty duly ratified by all contracting states in accordance with their respective constitutions (art. 237). This means that the composition of the Community and the conditions of admission of new members are subject to negotiations between the member states and may be vetoed by a single vote of a mighty or not so mighty state.

It follows that the organisation as well as the relations between the Community and its members, on the one hand, and the member states, *inter se*, are fixed by the Treaty in so far as the scope of the Treaty is concerned. In a sense this resembles the constitutional position within a composite state.

The constitution of the E.E.C. has clearly been devised upon a federal pattern. As in a state, the direction of the Community is in the hands of political organs which comprise the Assembly, the Council of Ministers and the Commission.

The Assembly consists of "representatives of the peoples of the States brought together in the Community" (art. 137) but the strength of this representation is weighted in accordance with the size of the population of the member states. The Assembly exercises a political control and acts as a deliberative and consultative body. In a sense it is the Parliament, albeit a weak one, of the Community.

The Council of Ministers is the supreme organ of the Community for it represents the sovereignty of the member states. It consists of the representatives of the governments, each government sending one delegate to their meetings (art. 148). The responsibility for the execution of the objectives laid down by the treaty falls upon this body. It is the Council which takes the most important decisions and co-ordinates the economic policies of the member states (art. 145). However, these powers are exercised in conjunction with the Commission.

The Commission is a truly Community institution. Until the enlargement of the Community it consisted of nine members chosen on account of their general competence and independence (art. 157) by member states unanimously (art. 158). Only the citizens of the member states are eligible but there may be no more than two from one particular state. With the admission of Denmark, Ireland and the United Kingdom the size of the Commission was increased to 13 but the same criterion of membership applies. The powers of the Commission can be described as the powers of initiative, preparation and decision. The Commission formulates recommendations and opinions on matters with which the Treaty is concerned and participates in the work of the Council and the Assembly. It also has executive powers to carry out the tasks entrusted to it by the Council and impose fines upon undertakings which break the rules on competition (art. 87 (2) (*a*)).

The judicial power of the Community is in the hands of the Court of Justice, whose main function is to "ensure that in the interpretation and application of this Treaty the law is observed" (art. 164). Composed of nine Judges and assisted by four Advocates-General chosen from persons of proven independence and qualified to hold the highest judicial offices in their countries (art. 167 (1)) the Court is really not an international court. If anything it resembles more a federal court than the International Court of Justice at The Hague. It is in fact an internal court of the Community. Its jurisdiction, as defined by the Treaty, is not a substitute for the jurisdictions of the national courts of the member states since it is confined to the administration of Community Law. It is, however, a fully-fledged judicial body with the power of arbitration, adjudication, repression and advice. The power of interpretation of the Treaty, of the acts of the Community institutions and of the bodies established by the Council, which is sometimes exclusive, enables the Court to exercise a quasi-legislative function and thus build up a body of case law which, like the continental administrative tribunals, especially the French Conseil d'Etat, contribute to the development of the law. The power of annulment, which is an instrument of the control of the acts of the Council and the Commission, puts the Court into the unique position of authority. The Court is the custodian of the Treaty, the watchdog of legality within the Community and the executor of the supremacy of the Community Law over the national laws of the member states in case of conflict between the two systems. Indeed the principle of supremacy of Community Law is perhaps the most important aspect of the status of the Community *vis-à-vis* the member states.

The powers of the Community organs, which we have briefly outlined above, would be quite meaningless if it were not for the corresponding surrender of sovereignty by the member states. The surrender of sovereignty is only partial and circumscribed by the Treaty obligations, but it is sufficient to mark a relationship between the member states and the Community. The relationship is based not only on treaty obligations of a contractual type but also on obligations which result in supra-national institutions and a separate body of law. The relationship resembles more a federation than a confederation and the Treaty is the Constitution, as it were, of the Community.[10] The Law of the Community, on the other hand, is a distinct order from the municipal laws of the member states but it is of a limited scope. The relationship of Community Law to the laws of the member states resembles that of a federal structure where federal law is directly binding within the member states and directly enforced by the federal judiciary. The acceptance of the Treaty, the law enacted by the Community organs, and the obligation to enact municipal legislation in accordance with the Treaty and the directives of the Community organs emphasise still further the federal concept of the Community. All power of the Community flows from the member states but it would be premature to ascribe to the Community the status of a federation.

In spite of its status at International Law (art. 210) the Community has in the territory of the member states no more than the "most extensive legal capacity accorded to legal persons under their Laws" (art. 211). The latter is insufficient as a criterion of a federal state, for federal states are based on constitutions which define the apportionment of power in terms of sovereignty. In the terms of the E.E.C. Treaty the states endeavour to build Community institutions and to create a body of law to regulate the economic activities of the members. Although surrender of a certain portion of sovereignty is necessary in order to achieve these objectives the pooling of sovereignty is not explicit enough to create a federal state or a federal government of the Community. Therefore, at this stage of its development, the Community is an association of sovereign states with a federal potential.

II THE STATUS OF THE COMMUNITIES IN THE LAW OF THE MEMBER STATES

The three Treaties constituting the Communities are identical and quite explicit on the legal status of the Communities in the member states. Thus art. 211 of the E.E.C. Treaty provides that "in each of the Member States, the Community shall enjoy the most extensive legal capacity accorded to legal persons under their laws; it may, in particular,

---

[10] Wagner, H., *Grundbegriffe des Beschlussrechts der Europäischen Gemeinschaften* (1965).

acquire or dispose of movable and immovable property and may be party to legal proceedings".

It is clear from the Treaties that it is only the Communities themselves and not their separate institutions which have legal personality. In a case arising under the E.C.S.C. Treaty, *Algera* v. *Common Assembly*,[11] the Court of Justice laid it down in as many words: "only the Community and not its institutions possess legal capacity". Although the Court in that case was referring to the institutions of the E.C.S.C., it is equally applicable to the merged institutions which serve the three Communities. It is clear that the legal personality and capacity of the Communities, following the classic theory of the personality of corporations, is quite distinct from those of the member states. In a case before an Italian court in 1963 it was argued that the acts of the E.C.S.C. should be regarded by Italian law as the acts of the Italian state so that the E.C.S.C. could enjoy the preferential status in the Italian law of bankruptcy which is enjoyed by the Italian state. But the Court rejected that argument and held "that the Community, while it is composed of the member states is . . . a distinct and autonomous corporation which cannot be identified with them . . . [It is] a free and autonomous private corporation, under no control from the State institutions".[12]

Whilst the Communities are "private" corporations in the sense that they are autonomous and quite distinct from the member states because they regard themselves to be in a similar position towards the Communities as the promoters of a joint stock company towards the company itself, the Court of Justice of the Communities has held that the legal personality of the Communities is governed by public law. Thus in *Von Lachmüller* v. *E.E.C. Commission*[13] the Court stated that the legal personality of the Community is a personality which "exists in public law by virtue of the powers and functions which belong to the Community". This statement was made in accordance with the continental practice of classifying corporate bodies. Thus in French law, for example, the category *personnes morales de droit public* includes the state itself, administrative sub-divisions of the state and state enterprises such as universities, hospitals and nationalised industries. The competence of such corporate bodies is governed by public law and not by the civil law which would govern the competence of *per-*

---

[11] Cases 7/56 and 3–7/57; 3 Rec. 81; Valentine, *op. cit.*, Vol. 2, p. 748; cf. Case 63–69/72: *Wilhelm Werhahn Hansamühle* v. *E.C. Council*, [1973] E.C.R. 1229 at p. 1246.
[12] *High Authority* v. *C. O. Elettromeccaniche Merlini*, [1964] C.M.L.R. 184 at p. 194.
[13] Cases 43, 45 and 48/59; 6 (II) Rec. 933; Valentine, *op. cit.*, Vol. 2, p. 777.

sonnes morales de droit privé, such as commercial companies.[14] In the *Von Lachmüller* case the Court held that contracts of employment between the E.E.C. and its employees were governed by public law and as such were subject to the procedures of administrative law. This is a distinction quite unknown to English law which has a single concept of contract. Thus in English law whether a contract is between John Brown and Bill Smith or between John Brown and the Department of the Environment or between John Brown and the National Coal Board all will be subject to the jurisdiction of the High Court. But in French law, which makes a distinction between the public sphere and the private, contracts to which at least one of the parties is a *personne morale de droit public* tend to be subject to the jurisdiction of the administrative courts, whereas contracts between private individuals or *personnes morales de droit privé* are subject to the jurisdiction of the ordinary civil courts. This jurisdictional distinction is thus reflected in Community law.

Since 1 January 1973, and by virtue of s. 2 (1) of the European Communities Act 1972, the Communities have enjoyed corporate status under the laws of the United Kingdom. But this was no innovation, for such a status is already enjoyed by other international organisations of which the United Kingdom is a member under the terms of the International Organisations Act 1968. That Act makes it possible for a special statutory status of a body corporate to be conferred upon such organisations.[15]

Given that it is the Communities themselves which possess legal personality and not the individual institutions, this raises the practical question of how the Communities are represented in law. The Treaties answer this question. In the case of the E.C.S.C., art. 6 of the Treaty provides that "the Community shall be represented by its institutions, each within the limits of its powers". This has been interpreted in the sense that the E.C.S.C. may be represented by its institutions each within the limits of the field of competence given it by the Treaty. The Court of Justice has also held that the term "institutions" means the institutions named in the Treaty and does not include the departments into which those institutions may be divided for administrative purposes.[16] In the cases of the E.E.C. and Euratom the position is much simpler since, at art. 211 and art. 185 of their Treaties respectively, it is stated that "the Community shall be represented by the Commission".

---

[14] See Amos and Walton, *Introduction to French Law* (3rd Edn. 1967), pp. 47 *et seq.*

[15] Cf. Bridge, J. W., "The United Nations and English Law" (1969), 18 I. & C.L.Q. at pp. 694 and 702.

[16] Case 66/63: *Netherlands Government* v. *High Authority*, [1964] C.M.L.R. 522; 10 Rec. 1047.

This is a role which the Commission, with its expert Legal Service, is particularly well equipped to fill.

While the Communities enjoy an extensive legal capacity in the territories of the member states, they also enjoy privileges and immunities of the type usually accorded to the premises and officers of the international organisations. Article 28 of the Merger Treaty provides that the European Communities shall enjoy in the territories of the member states "such privileges and immunities as are necessary for the performance of their tasks". The terms and conditions of those privileges and immunities are set out in a Protocol annexed to the Merger Treaty. The protocol provides that the premises, buildings and archives of the Communities shall be inviolable.[17]. The assets and revenues of the Communities shall be exempt from taxation.[18] Customs duties and restrictions shall not apply to either goods intended for official use or to Community publications.[19]. The official communications of the Communities shall enjoy the treatment accorded to diplomatic missions and shall not be subject to censorship.[20]. The members and servants of Community institutions shall be issued with *laissex-passer* for the purposes of travel.[1] The members of the Assembly shall enjoy freedom of movement to and from the meetings of the Assembly and their opinions expressed or votes cast in the course of Assembly proceedings shall not be the subject of inquiry or legal proceedings.[2] Both representatives of the member states taking part in the work of Community institutions and the officials and servants of such institutions shall enjoy the customary privileges and immunities. The Community Court, distinguishing between private and official business, held in *Sayag* v. *Leduc*[3] that a Euratom official, not being employed as chauffeur by the Commission, was not entitled to immunity in respect of liability arising from a road traffic accident caused whilst carrying guests of the Commission in his own car.

The diplomatic missions of non-member states to the Communities shall equally enjoy such privileges and immunities.[4] Finally, the Protocol stresses that all these privileges, immunities and facilities are accorded solely in the interests of the Communities and that immunity should be waived whenever waiver is not contrary to Community interests.[5]

---

[17] Protocol on Privileges and Immunities, arts. 1 and 2.
[18] *Ibid.*, art. 3.
[19] *Ibid.*, art. 4.
[20] *Ibid.*, art. 6.
[1] *Ibid.*, art. 7.
[2] *Ibid.*, arts. 8–10.
[3] *Ibid.*, arts. 11–16; see Case 5/68: *Sayag* v. *Leduc*, [1969] C.M.L.R. 12.
[4] *Ibid.*, art. 17.
[5] *Ibid.*, art. 18. Cf. Bridge, *op. cit.*, at pp. 694 *et seq.*

The laws of the member states also impinge on the life of the Communities in connection with contractual and non-contractual liability both of which are covered by art. 215 of the E.E.C. Treaty.[6] As far as the contractual liability of the Communities is concerned it is governed by the law applicable to the contract in question. Thus contracts of employment with the Community are subject to the Staff Regulations[7] (formerly Statute of Service) whilst other contracts to which one of the Communities is a party are subject to the rules of private international law. In practice arbitration clauses are inserted in the latter type of contract with the object of conferring upon the Community Court jurisdiction to hear disputes arising from such cases.

In the case of non-contractual liability art. 215 provides that "the Community shall, in accordance with the general principles common to the laws of the Member States, make good any damage[8] caused by its institutions or by its servants in the performance of their duties". Thus the Court of Justice is required to apply these general principles as an additional source of law in much the same way that the International Court of Justice can resort to "the general principles of law recognised by civilised nations" as a source of international law.[9]

A fundamental question which arises here is whether in order to be recognised and applied by the Court of Justice such general principles must be known to the municipal laws of all the member states. Certainly in connection with the International Court of Justice such an exacting condition has not been applied. Sir Hersch Lauterpracht has defined general principles of law as "those principles of law, private and public, which in contemplation of the legal experience of civilised nations lead one to regard as obvious maxims of jurisprudence of a general and fundamental character".[10] Thus the International Court of Justice must enquire of "the way in which the law of States representing the main systems of jurisprudence regulates the problem in the situations in question".[11] The Court of Justice of the Communities has adopted a

---

[6] See art. 188 of the E.A.E.C. Treaty, and cf. art. 40 of the E.C.S.C. Treaty.
[7] Council Regulation 259/68 (J.O. L. 56 of 4 March 1968, as subsequently amended; consolidated text J.O. C. 12 of 24 March 1973; cf. Case 31/72; *Angelini* v. *European Parliament*, [1973] E.C.R. 403; Case 18/74; *Syndicat Général du Personnel des Organismes Européens* v. *E.C. Commission*, [1975] 1 C.M.L.R. 144.
[8] Cf. Cases 5, 7 and 13–24/66; *Kampffmeyer* v. *E.C. Commission* (1967–68), 5 C.M.L. Rev. 208; 13 Rec. 339; Case 153/73; *Holtz and Willemsen* v. *E.C. Council and Commission,* [1974] E.C.R. 692; Case 169/73: *Compagnie Continentale France* v. *E.C. Council,* [1975] I.C.M.L.R. 578; Case 74/74: *Comptoir National Technique Agricole (CNTA) S.A.* v. *E.C. Commission,* [1975] E.C.R. 533.
[9] See art. 38 (1) (c) of the Statute of the International Court of Justice.
[10] *International Law, being the Collected Papers of Hersch Lauterpacht* (1970), Vol. 1, p. 69.
[11] *Ibid.*, p. 71. For an account of the practice of the International Court also, see *ibid.*, pp. 68–77.

similar approach. As one commentator has put it, "whilst it is not necessary . . . that *all* states concerned agree on a certain principle of law, it is equally true that such a principle must not merely exist in the law of one country or only in a minority of legal systems . . . [It] is not desirable to have a *brouillard* consisting of diverse national legal systems, but rather an adequate solution which is germane to the legal order of the Communities. This result will be reached only after thorough comparative analysis of the legal systems. To the extent that such research reveals a common core, it is not unlikely that the solutions adopted will readily be approved by the member states in their national laws as well".[12] Thus in the words of Advocate-General Lagrange the spirit which has guided the Court has been "not simply [to] take a more or less arithmetical average of the different municipal solutions, but [to] choose those solutions from among the various legal systems prevailing in the different member states as, having regard to the objectives of the Treaty, appeared to it the best or, if one may use the word, the most progressive".[13]

In recent years the Court of Justice of the Communities has made a similar use of general principles of law recognised by the member states in the context of protecting human rights.[14] The Court has interpreted its duty to ensure that the law is observed as permitting it to apply as part of Community law a body of unwritten, fundamental legal principles which are common to the national legal and political systems of the member states. The function of these fundamental principles in the Community legal order is, in the words of Advocate-General Dutheillet de Lamothe, "to contribute to forming that philo-sophical, political and legal substratum common to the member states from which emerges through the case law an unwritten Community law, one of the essential aims of which is precisely to ensure respect for the fundamental rights of the individual."[15] The Court has demon-strated its willingness to test the validity of Community acts against such criteria.[16]

---

[12] Lorenz, K., "General Principles of Law: Their Elaboration in the Court of Justice of the European Communities" (1964), 13 A.J.C.L. at pp. 9, 10, 11.
[13] Case 14/61: *Hoogovens* v. *High Authority*, [1963] C.M.L.R. 73 at pp. 85, 86; 8 Rec. 485 at p. 539. On the practice of the Community Court see Lorenz, *op. cit.* at pp. 12 *et seq.*
[14] See generally Pescatore, P., "Fundamental Rights and Freedoms in the System of the European Communities" (1970), 18 A.J.C.L. 343; Zuleeg, M., "Fundamental Rights and the Law of the European Communities," (1971) 8 C.M.L. Rev. 446; Bridge, J. W., *et al., Fundamental Rights* (1973), Chapter 20.
[15] Case 11/70: *Internationale Handelsgesellschaft mbH* v. *Einfuhr-und Vorrats-stelle für Getreide und Futtermittel*, [1972] C.M.L.R. 255, at p. 271.
[16] E.g. Case 29/69: *Stauder* v. *City of Ulm*, [1970] C.M.L.R. 112. Also see Case 4/73: *Nold* v. *E.C. Commission*, [1974] 2 C.M.L.R. 338.

In the course of time it is probable that this process of drawing upon the common legal experience of the member states will, in a general way, advance the legal integration of the member states.

III THE EXTERNAL RELATIONS OF THE COMMUNITIES

(A) THE INTERNATIONAL PERSONALITY AND CAPACITY OF THE COMMUNITIES

It has already been pointed out that the Communities have personality and capacity under international law. Their personality and capacity may be classified as of the functional sort referred to by the International Court of Justice in its advisory opinion in the *Reparation for Injuries* case.[17] That is to say that the Communities at international law have the degree of personality and capacity which is necessary to enable them to carry out their functions on the international plane. This general view is substantiated by the terms of the Treaties themselves. Article 6 of the E.C.S.C. Treaty states clearly that "in international relations the Community shall enjoy the legal capacity it requires to perform its functions and attain its objectives". The E.E.C. and Euratom Treaties, on the other hand, merely state that the Communities have legal personality but do not refer to any specific attribution of capacity in international law.[18] Nevertheless such latter capacity may not only be inferred from the nature of the Communities as the creatures of treaties but it has also been expressly confirmed by the Court of Justice in its judgment in the *Re ERTA, E.C. Commission* v. *E.C. Council.*[19] There the Court observed that art. 210 of the E.E.C. Treaty, by stating that the Community has legal personality, "means that in its external relations the Community enjoys the capacity to establish contractual links with non-member States over the whole field of the objectives defined in Part One of the Treaty".[20]

An examination of the E.E.C. Treaty reveals numerous provisions concerned in one way or another with external relations. Article 3 (*k*) provides that the purposes of the Community are to be achieved in part through "the association of the overseas countries and territories in order to increase trade and to promote jointly economic and social

---

[17] I.C.J. Reports 1949, p. 174. See generally Campbell, *op. cit.*, Vol. 1, Chap. 8; Henig, S., *External Relations of the European Community* (1971) and Costonis, J. J., "Treaty Making Powers of the E.E.C." (1967) European Yearbook 31.
[18] E.E.C. Treaty, art. 210 and Euratom Treaty, art. 184.
[19] Case 22/70, [1971] C.M.L.R. 335; 17 Rec. 263.
[20] [1971] C.M.L.R. 335, at p. 354.

development". This theme is taken up by art. 131, whereby the member states agree to associate with the Community their former colonial possession with whom they have maintained a special relationship subsequent to independence. A similar agreement has been reached on the association of the non-European territories maintaining special relations with the United Kingdom and the Anglo–French Condominium of the New Hebrides.[1] Articles 111–116 contain provisions concerned with trading relations between member and non-member states. Articles 228–231 and 238 provide for the conclusion of agreements and maintenance of relations between the Community and both non-member states and international organisations. It is clear from art. 238 that any such agreements must be compatible with the Treaty, and if not the Treaty must first be amended in accordance with the terms of art. 236 in order to accommodate such an agreement. This has also been confirmed by the Court which has held that in order "to determine in a particular case the Community's authority to enter into international agreements, one must have regard to the whole scheme of the Treaty no less than to its specific provisions".[2] Article 228 (1) is equally clear on this point and enables the Council, the Commission or a member state to obtain a prior opinion from the Court of Justice on the compatibility of a proposed agreement with the terms of the Treaty. Where the opinion of the Court is adverse the Treaty must be amended before the agreement in question may enter into force.[3]

(B) THE CONDUCT OF THE EXTERNAL RELATIONS OF THE COMMUNITIES

The authority to conclude agreements between the Communities and non-member states or international organisations is, in all cases, vested in the Council, although the other institutions do have a role to play. Under the terms of art. 238 of the E.E.C. Treaty agreements establishing an association, involving reciprocal rights and obligations, between the Community and a third state, a union of states or an international organisation shall be concluded by the Council, acting unanimously after consulting the Assembly. Somewhat similarly applications by European states for full membership of the Community under the terms of art. 237 shall be addressed to the Council which shall act unanimously after obtaining the opinion of the Commission. In

---

[1] See Act annexed to Treaty of Accession, art. 117.
[2] [1971] C.M.L.R. 335, at p. 354.
[3] For the first instance of the use of this jurisdiction see Opinion 1/75, *Re the O.E.C.D. Understanding on a Local Cost Standard* [1976] 1 C.M.L.R. 85.

connection with the negotiations for the admission of the United Kingdom, Ireland, Denmark and Norway the Commission suggested in its Opinion of 1 October 1969 that the negotiations should be divided into two phases: the first to be conducted by the Commission on behalf of the Community and subject to the directives of the Council; the second to be conducted by the Council in the light of the results of the first phase. Such a procedure had been successfully used in connection with the Kennedy Round tariff negotiations.[4] The Council rejected the Commission's suggestion and decided that the conduct of the negotiations with the candidate states should be in the hands of the Council, after the Council, acting upon a proposal from the Commission, had settled the joint position of the Communities on the problems raised by the negotiations. The business of the Council in connection with the negotiations was prepared by the Committee of Permanent Representatives.[5] In these negotiations the role of the Commission upon the instructions of the Council was (i) to submit possible compromise solutions to particular problems; (ii) to explain ths scope of Community law to the delegations of the candidate countries; (iii) to act as a go-between between the Council and candidate countries in the resolution of key political issues; and (iv) to study and report on the technical and linguistic problems facing Community law as a consequence of the enlargement of the Communities.[6]

Although the role of the Commission in the procedure for the admission of new member states is only a subsidiary one it is given a leading role in those cases where the E.E.C. Treaty provides for the conclusion of agreements between the Community and one or more states or an international organisation. Article 228 (1) provides that while such agreements shall be concluded by the Council, after consulting the Assembly where the Treaty so requires, the negotiations shall be conducted by the Commission. The respective roles of the Commission and Council under the terms of art. 228 (1) were recently considered by the Court of Justice.[7]

In January 1962, under the auspices of the U.N. Economic Commission for Europe, a European Road Transport Agreement (E.R.T.A.) was signed by a number of European States including five of the members of the Community. That Agreement has not yet come into force because of an insufficient number of ratifications. In 1967 negotiations were resumed to revise the E.R.T.A. In 1969 the Council of the Communities made a regulation dealing with the harmonisation

---

[4] See *Bulletin of the European Communities* (1969), Supplement to Part 9/10 at pp. 39–41.
[5] See *Bulletin of European Communities* (1970), Part 8 at pp. 115–16.
[6] See the Commission's Report, *The Enlarged Community* (1972) at pp. 22–24.
[7] Case 22/70: *Re ERTA E.C. Commission v. E.C. Council,* [1971] C.M.L.R. 335; 17 Rec. 263.

of certain social provisions in the field of road transport. In March 1970 at a meeting of the Council the attitude to be taken by the member states of the Communities in the final stage of the E.R.T.A. negotiations to be held in April 1970 was discussed. Those negotiations were then undertaken and concluded by the member states in the light of that discussion and the Economic Commission for Europe declared that the E.R.T.A. would be open for signature from July 1970. In May 1970 the Commission of the Communities instituted proceedings seeking an annulment of the Council's discussion of March 1970 on the grounds that the Council had acted in breach of art. 228 of the E.E.C. Treaty. This challenge raised the whole issue of the relative roles of Council and Commission in the conduct of the Community's external relations.

The Court stated that under art. 228 the right to conclude an agreement with non-member states lay with the Council, with the Commission cast in the role of negotiator. But those institutions could only play those roles under the authority of either an express Treaty provision or a decision taken under the Treaty.[8] The bulk of the negotiations for the E.R.T.A. had been concluded before the Community had a developed transport policy, therefore the Community as such had no authority to negotiate and ratify the E.R.T.A. At the time of the Council discussions which were in issue, the E.R.T.A. negotiations had already reached such an advanced stage that it would have jeopardised the whole Agreement to have attempted to re-open them. Thus the Court held that the procedures specified in art. 228 were clearly inapplicable. The only obligation on the member states was to ensure that nothing was done to prejudice the interests of the Community and so that the Council in co-ordinating the attitudes of member states to the E.R.T.A. in the light of Community interests had acted quite properly.[9] Thus even where the provisions of the Treaties are not directly applicable to the external relations of the member states they are nevertheless under a continuing obligation, under the terms of art. 5 of the E.E.C. Treaty, to "abstain from any measure which could jeopardise the attainment of the objectives of the Treaty".

(C) THE ESTABLISHED EXTERNAL RELATIONS OF THE COMMUNITIES

This capacity to enter into external relations which has been described above has been frequently exercised by the Communities, particularly

---

[8] The Court also pointed out that where the Council and Commission are acting by virtue of such authority the member states have no right to act individually in such a matter: [1971] C.M.L.R. 335 at p. 355.

[9] It was also pointed out that the Commission had not exercised its right under arts. 75 and 116 to make proposals concerning the E.R.T.A. negotiations: [1971] C.M.L.R. 335, at pp. 361, 362.

in the case of the E.E.C. Firstly, in connection with individual states, the Communities have entered both association and external trade agreements. The purpose of an association agreement is to create a customs union as between Community members and the associated state with, in some cases, the provision of financial loans to the associated state and in others the extension of other Community benefits such as rights of establishment. Such association agreements have been entered into with Greece, Turkey, Malta, Cyprus, Morocco and Tunisia, which, in the former two cases, by progressive stages are intended to lead to full membership of the Communities.[10]

External trade agreements have been concluded with a number of states. These usually provide for preferential reductions in Community tariffs in relation to such states. Some of these agreements, such as those with India, Pakistan and Switzerland are limited to certain sorts of goods; other, such as those with Israel, Spain and Yugoslavia, are more general in scope.

By virtue of the terms of Article 108 of the Act of Accession, from the date of accession the new member states must apply the terms of the agreements with Greece, Turkey, Tunisia, Morocco, Israel, Spain and Malta. This obligation is subject to the transitional measures and any specially negotiated adjustments which may prove to be necessary.

In addition to these bilateral agreements, multilateral association agreements have been entered with those non-European states which have a special relationship with the member states. These agreements have been designed to promote the economic and social development of those countries and to establish economic links between them and the Community as a whole, such as giving their exports preferential treatment by bringing them within the European customs union. On a provisional basis a form of association was set up by a convention annexed to the E.E.C. Treaty. That was replaced in 1964 by a new Association Convention signed by 18 independent Associated African States and Madagascar. The Convention was signed at Yaoundé, the capital of Cameroon. The original Yaoundé Convention lasted five years and was replaced in 1969 by the Second Yaoundé Convention which remained in force until January 1975. The precedent of the Yaoundé Convention was applied to three Anglophonic countries of East Africa, Kenya, Uganda and Tanzania, in what was known as the Arusha Convention which was signed at Arusha in Tanzania in 1968 and renewed in 1969. The terms of the Arusha Convention were broadly similar to the Yaoundé Convention subject to the important difference that there was no provision for financial aid.

---

[10] Between the coup d'état in 1967 and the restoration of democratic government in 1974 no progress was made with the Association with Greece.

In February 1975 a new agreement was concluded at Lomé, the capital of Togo.[11] This agreement, known as the Lomé Convention replaces both the Second Yaoundé and Arusha Conventions and establishes an association between the Community and 46 African, Caribbean and Pacific States including 21 members of the British Commonwealth. The Convention will remain in force until March 1980 and is subject to renegotiation. It establishes three institutions, a Council of Ministers, a Committee of Ambassadors and a Consultative Assembly to direct the relations between the Community and the Associated States. Any disputes arising under the Convention are initially referred to the Council of Ministers and, as a last resort, to a specified arbitration procedure. The terms of the Convention give free entry to the Community, without reciprocity, to goods from the Associated States; financial aid principally in the form of grants to develop small and medium sized industries; and stabilise the export earnings of the Associated States by protecting them against fluctuations in commodity prices.

As far as non-member states in Europe are concerned, apart from the possibility of a form of association with the Communities, there is also the possibility of applying for full membership.

In addition to having relations with non-member states the Communities have established relations with a number of international organisations. Relations are maintained with the United Nations and particularly those of its specialised agencies concerned with economic affairs. An agreement for the exchange of information and for technical assistance has been made with the I.L.O. Through the Commission the Communities engage in tariff negotiations with G.A.T.T. The Commission is represented at inter-governmental meetings of the Council of Europe and there is an annual joint session of the Assembly of the Communities and the Consultative Assembly of the Council of Europe. The Commission also participates in the work of the O.E.C.D. The Community has also negotiated free trade area agreements with the remaining E.F.T.A. countries (Austria, Switzerland, Finland, Sweden, Portugal, Norway and Iceland).[12] For some time contract has also been maintained with the East European Council for Mutual Economic Co-operation (Comecon) with a view to finding a common platform for trade between the two European economic organisations. Thus in these various ways mutually advantageous links are established with other international and European organisations.

---

[11] For the text of the Convention see *Encyclopedia of European Community Law*, Vol. BII, p. B 12475.
[12] See *E.F.T.A. Bulletin*, No. 8 (1972) and Nos. 5 and 8 (1973).

CHAPTER THREE

Nature and Challenge of Community Law

THE MEANING OF COMMUNITY LAW

It is axiomatic that a body which itself is a distinct legal entity will have its own law either infused into its forms by a superior legislator or generated by its organs or both. In the Community legal order both elements are present: the law of the Treaty and the law generated by the Community organs. Moreover, a certain area of the law will be enacted by the member states themselves in accordance with the Treaty and, although this law is, strictly speaking, a product of the sovereign legislatures of the member states it should be included in the wider concept of Community Law.[1] These are the dimensions of Community Law in the light of its sources. However, before analysing the sources of Community Law it seems necessary to consider its nature and scope. This is particularly important from a British point of view, bearing in mind that after all, we had no hand in the drafting of Community Law.

Community Law defies the accepted classifications of law; it is both international and municipal, public and private, enacted and formulated in precedents. It is a *sui generis* law and must be treated as such. Therefore it has to be studied in its international setting with due attention to its impact upon the laws of the member states and the quasi-autonomous law-making capacity of the Community organs.

The three Communities, being a result of Treaties, are subject to public international law as far as the relations between the member states are concerned. The treaty obligations are defined in terms of duties of states *vis-à-vis* the contracting parties and the Community

---

[1] The Second European Conference of Law Faculties held in April 1971 in Strasbourg under the aegis of the Council of Europe recommended that the authorities in member states be urged to introduce or reinforce the teaching of (1) the law of European Organisations, (2) the substantive law created by or within European Organisations, and (3) the law of European States.

institutions. The execution of the Treaties is in the hands of the Community organs and the Community Court has the exclusive power of authoritative interpretation of the Treaties (art. 177 (1)).[2] Disputes between states (art. 182) and complaints against states (arts. 169 and 170) are resolved judicially in a manner appropriate to inter-state relations rather than relations between private parties where the court exercises a sovereign authority. In other words, unlike individuals who have no choice, states submit to the jurisdiction of the Court either by agreement (art. 182) or by virtue of treaty obligations. In adjudicating upon disputes in which states are involved the Court, like the International Court of Justice, determines the legal position of the parties and recommends, rather than orders, the state in default to take the necessary measures to comply with the judgment (art. 171). The sanctions are also limited (arts. 169 and 171) and appropriate to the status of states at international law. The cardinal rule of public international law that states, large and small, are equal applies in principle within the Community though in the government of the Community and in the financial contribution to the budget of the Community consideration is given to the size of the member states.

However, the Community, as stated by the Community Court,[3] "constitutes a new legal order in International Law for whose benefit the states have limited their sovereign rights, albeit within limited fields, and the subjects of which comprise not only the member states but also their nationals".

By incorporation of the Treaties into the municipal law of the member states Community Law becomes part of the internal legal structure of the member states. Moreover, under the doctrine of the approximation of laws a wide area of commercial law will, in due course, become uniform throughout the Community. This in a sense will become both Community and municipal law of the member states. It is apposite to mention in this context the conflict of laws or private international law. It is a system of rules designed to facilitate enforcement of foreign judgment and to solve problems which involve a foreign element and, therefore, in justice and convenience cannot be left to the exclusive power of domestic law. Each country has its own conflict rules. However, the primary object of the Community is cohesion. This is achieved partly by incorporation of Community Law into the municipal systems and partly by approximation of laws in the areas of a

---

[2] Unless otherwise stated references are to articles of the E.E.C. Treaty.
[3] In Case 26/62: *Van Gend en Loos* v. *Nederlandse Administratie der Belastingen*, [1963] C.M.L.R. 105 at p. 129; 9 Rec. 1.

specific Community interest. In this way it is expected conflicts will be eliminated. Outside the scope of Community Law the member states are left to their own devices as to how to solve the problems arising from the co-existence of several systems of law, though the Community promotes a rational approach to the enforcement of foreign judgments in the territory of the member states (art. 220).[4] A process of approximation of substantive rules of the Conflict of Laws has begun with a Draft Convention on the Law applicable to Contractual and Non-Contractual Obligations.[5]

The once (so it seemed)[6] clear-cut distinction between public and private law has been blurred in the course of time. If we consider that public law is concerned with the organisation of the state and the relations between the citizen and the state whilst private law governs relations between individuals and/or corporations we shall observe that Community Law contains both elements. It has an impact upon the constitutions and public powers of the member states, it is concerned with the creation of a supra-national organisation out of the pooled sovereignty of the member states and brings the citizen politically and in his economic activities face to face with a supra-national authority and a new "European" allegiance. Private law relations (and here we can safely discard the controversy whether "commercial law" is "private law" or a separate branch of the law) are affected too but only to a degree, that is to say in so far as the economic policies enforced by Community Law impinge upon such relations. As legal machinery is used for the execution of the economic policies enshrined in the Treaty some aspects of Community Law can be described for the want of a better term as "economic law" or the law of the economy. This phenomenon, characteristic of the Community, will be considered in detail.[7] The bulk of private law relations comprised in the law of contract, tort, property, family relations and succession remains outside the scope of Community Law. So does Criminal Law, though criminal sanctions will have to be developed in order to check abuses of the Community system.[8]

True to the civil law tradition the corpus of Community Law has been laid down in treaties and derivative legislation but it would be a

---

[4] Cf. Convention on Jurisdiction and the Enforcement of Judgments in Civil and Commercial Matters 1968.

[5] Lando, O., *et al. European Private International Law of Obligations* (1975).

[6] Publicum jus est, quod ad statum rei Romanae spectat, privatum quod ad singulorum utilitatem: sunt enim quaedam publice utilia, quoadem privatim, *Digesta* 1, 1, 1, 2; cf. Llewellyn, K., *The Bramble Bush* (1960), p. 18.

[7] See Part IV, below.

[8] See Bridge, J. W., "The European Communities and the Criminal Law", *Criminal Law Review*, February 1976, p. 88.

mistake to assume that precedent plays no active role in the Community law-making process. We shall discuss the sources of Community Law in detail and it may suffice to say that the Community Court, like the French Counseil d'Etat upon which it has been modelled, often has an opportunity of explaining the law and laying down rules in precedents and it has not refrained from using this power. As practice develops the Community Court tends to follow its own decisions in the spirit of *jurisprudence consistente*[9] but will not hesitate to deviate for good reason.[10] And so the Court considers itself free to decide in a different way the same legal point if it arises between different parties and in a different context.[11]

Without attempting a definition of Community Law (which, incidentally, cannot be found in the Treaties) we should re-iterate that Community Law consists of that portion of public international law which governs treaties and international institutions, of the Treaties and their Annexes, of the rules generated by the Community organs and those portions of the municipal laws of the member states which they are bound to enact in the execution of their obligations. These are not distinct branches but merely the dimensions of Community Law.

LEGAL STYLES

Community Law is a new legal order but to a British lawyer it is also an alien order because it has emanated from the civil law systems. This does not necessarily mean that it is inferior or oppressive, as has been suggested from time to time in the passion of debate, but that it is simply different from ours. It should be borne in mind that in its background lies the philosophy of sophisticated, long-established legal systems and the will to create a better Europe. Being intertwined with the legal systems of the founder states Community Law cannot be isolated from these but historically and philosophically has to be seen as a child of civil law.

In order to make a valid comparison between civil law and common law and thus elicit some general features of the Community legal system it will first be necessary to debunk some popular myths. There is in England some, albeit unfounded, aversion to codes of law and even

---

[9] Case 32/58: *Aciéries du Temple* v. *Haute Autorité*, 5 Rec. 300.
[10] Case 48/72: *Brasserie de Haecht* v. *Wilkin* (*No.* 2), [1973] E.C.R. 77; [1973] C.M.L.R. 287; see p. 87.
[11] Cases 28–30/62: *Da Costa en Schaak N.V.* v. *Nederlandse Administratie der Belastingen*, [1963] C.M.L.R. 244; 9 Rec. 59.

the Code Napoléon, of which the French are justly proud, does not escape criticism as if no branch of English Law had been codified or codification had not been the long-term aim of the Law Commission. Critics believe that codes of law stultify the growth of the law and turn it into a pool of stagnant water whilst common law for ever remains a stream of fresh water. Forgetting that codes are essentially a work of compromise they assume that they are the tools of autocracy. Moreover, it is readily assumed that, whilst in this country we are governed by the wisdom of judges contained in precedents, the continentals are denied this privilege and, because of their rejection of *stare decisis*, suffer from the uncertainty of the law. It would be futile to recite the various misconceptions and try to rebut them. What has to be recognised is the fact that the origins and the evolution of the civil law and common law systems happen to differ and that as a result two different legal styles have developed. Comparative studies help one to understand these differences but not being engaged in a comparative study we have to content ourselves with few generalities. Because we join the Community as a going concern, with a legal system well on its way, the British lawyer has to face the unprecedented challenge of the continental legal style.[12]

Codes of law are not mere comprehensive, systematically arranged statutes. In a sense they are also codes of morals for in their legal institutions, especially general principles of the law, they offer guidelines to a way of life. The law tends to proceed from general principles to particular rules of conduct and so the administration of justice tends to be deductive rather than inductive. Contrast the British fragmentary legislation and tightly drafted statutes which, according to Lord Justice Scarman,[13] "are elaborate to the point of complexity; detailed to the point of unintelligibility; yet strangely uninformative on matters of principle". The English administration of justice tends, therefore, to be inductive, so much so that one can say that we have a system of remedies established by precedent and statute rather than a plain statement of rights and duties from which remedies can be deduced. Community Law follows this latter style as it tends to prescribe the right conduct for government and individuals and grants remedies in the event of derogation.

The codes of law, being systems of generalities provide but a façade for case law, because decided cases are the real witness of the living law.

---

[12] See Lord Denning, M.R. in *H. P. Bulmer, Ltd.* v. *J. Bollinger S.A.* [1974] 2 All E.R. 1226 at pp. 1231–1232; [1974] 2 C.M.L.R. 91; Scarman, Sir Leslie, *English Law: The New Dimension*, Hamlyn Lectures, Twenty-sixth Series, 1974, p. 21 *et seq.*

[13] B.B.C. Third Prgramme, *The Listener*, 9 January 1969, pp. 44–46.

However, in view of the supremacy of legislation and the constitutionally limited power of judges to adjudicate not *legislate*, precedents have only a persuasive authority and cannot be cited as the source of law or superior authority. The theory that codes have no gaps enables the courts to legislate by way of extensive interpretation from analogy or simply through *equitas*. The European Court of Justice is in a similar position though its scope for legislative activities is wider than that of the civil courts of the member states.

In England the judge comes, as a rule, from the Bar and remains a member of his Inn of Court even when elevated to the Bench. On the Continent the judge is a product of special training and a judicial career, he stands aloof from the Bar and resembles more an academic lawyer than an advocate. The English administration of justice has a strong personal flavour because as a rule the judge sits alone and delivers a personal judgment of "his court". In the Court of Appeal or the House of Lords, though no longer alone, he still delivers his personal, concurring or dissenting, judgment which often conceals an advocate in judicial robes. The continental judge as a rule, sits as a member of a team, does not deliver his individual judgment whether or not he agrees with the judgment of his brethren and so preserves a kind of judicial anonymity. The European Court of Justice is a "continental" court in all respects, sits as a team and delivers a single judgment. It is assisted by advocates-general (an office unknown in this country), whose functions shall be considered elsewhere.[14]

The style of the administration of justice is greatly influenced by the scope and rules of judicial interpretation. As compared with their continental brethren and the European Court, English judges seem to have a narrower scope in the field of interpretation. The *Bosch*[15] case is a good illustration. Whilst our judges are not allowed to study the *"travaux préparatoires"*, that is the materials and debates in Parliament leading to the passing of legislation, in order to find out the mind of the legislature, the continental judges are allowed to do so and base their judgment on their study. The *Bosch* case involved cartel agreements under art. 85 of the E.E.C. Treaty and Regulation 17 which implemented arts. 85 and 86 of the Treaty. More precisely the question was whether or not art. 85 came into effect before Regulation 17. The Dutch court of the first instance ruled that art. 85 was not operative before Regula-

---

[14] See Chap. 9.
[15] Case 13/61: *Robert Bosch, GmbH* v. *Kledingverhoopbedrijf de Geus en Uitdenbogerd*, [1962] C.M.L.R. 1; 8 Rec. 89; D. Thompson, "The Bosch Case" (1962), 11 I.C.L.Q. 721; Case 14/70: *Deutsche Bakels GmbH* v. *Oberfinauzdirektion München*, [1971] C.M.L.R. 188; Case 42/72: *Alfons Lütticke GmbH* v. *Hauptzollant Passau*, [1973] E.C.R. 57 at pp. 74–75; [1973] C.M.L.R. 309, at pp. 316–317.

tion 17 was made; the Court of Appeal referred the case to the Community Court under E.E.C. art. 177 and the plaintiff appealed to the Dutch Supreme Court. The final ruling was that it was the intention of the E.E.C. that art. 85 shall not be operative until the appropriate machinery has been created and so Bosch, though involved in a restrictive practice, had not at that time contravened Community Law. An English Court would have accepted art. 85 without considering the purpose of the delegated legislation embodied in Regulation 17 and probably decided against Bosch.

Another attribute of the continental courts is the power to resort to teleological interpretation of codes and statutes which enables them to apply old law in the context of social change or give the rules of law a dynamic and functional effect.[16] In this country (perhaps with the exception of the House of Lords) courts have no such power and, indeed, should an iconoclast judge venture into such practices he would soon find his judgments overruled by higher courts. The Community Court, it seems, enjoys this attribute of judicial power in the best traditions of continental courts and, having established its authority, does occasionally resort to this kind of interpretation. Unlike literal interpretations the Court puts into the mouth of the legislator the meaning of words he should have used rather than words he has actually used to express his intention.[17]

The Courts' role is much coloured by the rules of procedure. The predominant feature of continental procedural law is the inquisitorial system. This system places a heavy duty on the court to enquire into the facts of the case in order to ascertain the objective truth. Unlike the English judge the continental judge is not an impartial umpire watching the contest of the parties and seeing that the rules of the game are observed. The inquisitorial system requires a greater involvement of the court which, among others, manifests itself in the examination of witnesses and parties by the judge. Although the inquisitorial powers have not been expressly spelt out in the foundation Treaties they can be found in the Protocol on the Statute of the Court of Justice[18] and the

---

[16] Cf. Pescatore, P., Interpretation of Community Law and the Doctrine of Acte Clair, in Bathurst, M., *et al.* (editors) *Legal Problems of an Enlarged European Community,* 1972, 27 at pp. 32–34.

[17] E.g. Case 14/63:*Forges de Clabecq High Authority* (1963) 9 Rec. 718, [1964] C.M.L.R. 176; Case 9/73: *Schlüter* v. *Hauptzollamt Lorrach,* [1973] E.C.R. 1135, at p. 1153; Case 6/72: *Europemballage Corporation and Continental Can Inc.* v. *E.C. Commission* [1973] E.C.R. 215; [1973] C.M.L.R. 199; Case 8/73: *Hauptzollamt-Bremerhaven* v. *Massey-Ferguson,* [1973] E.C.R. 897; 37–38/73: *Sociaal Fonds voor de Diamant Arbeiders* v. *N.V. Indiamex,* [1973] E.C.R. 1609; Case 151/73: *Government of Ireland* v. *E.C. Council,* [1974] E.C.R. 285; [1974] 1, C.M.L.R. 429 at pp. 446–447.

[18] E.E.C. Statute, arts. 21, 22, 26, 28; E.C.S.C. Statute, arts. 24, 25, 28 (3), E.A.E.C. Statute, arts. 22, 23, 27, 29; Rules of Procedure, arts. 47 (1), 77, 94.

Rules of Procedure. It is clear that the European Community Court functions like any continental court and this involves a tight control of the proceedings, powers to require parties to produce documents and supply the information the court deems necessary as well as the examination of witnesses and parties by the court.

Other salient features of continental procedure are the predominance of written pleadings which contain mainly legal arguments, hence the art of written advocacy somewhat similar to our Chancery proceedings; the absence of drama in court engineered in this country by the public examination and cross-examination of witnesses; oral procedure involving a report of a judge acting as Rapporteur and finally a collective judgment of the court, after due deliberations in private, usually read in open court on the appointed day together with other judgments. The report of the court is brief and concise drafted by the Registrar. All these features are attributable to the European Community Court and will, no doubt become a challenge our lawyers will have to meet in Community practice.

THE CHALLENGE OF COMMUNITY LAW

Because of its wide dimensions, Community Law offers a challenge to three types of lawyers. Lawyers in government service, lawyers in commerce and industry, and lawyers in private practice.

The three Communities fashioned and worked their institutions through civil servants drawn from the member countries. Since policies enshrined in the foundation treaties had to be carried out through the instrumentality of legal machinery and since legal studies are regarded, on the Continent, as the most appropriate background for the civil service, it is not surprising that lawyers form a considerable proportion of the European bureaucrats. These lawyers have managed to overcome the language barriers and have acquired a community spirit. Through working together with those who initiate and carry into effect the various policies they have developed their own style. They have also perfected the skill of working with non-lawyers and as a supranational bureaucracy they have become a force to be reckoned with. After all, they draft the various rules and regulations which by virtue of the Treaty obligations become the municipal law of the member states. The enlarged Community will provide an opportunity for the newcomers to contribute to the growing body of Community Law. The national impact will always depend on the quality of the civil servants detailed to the Community service.

The task of the lawyer in commerce and industry is different from that of the Community lawyer and those who are engaged as managers, administrators and legal advisors need little adaptation. Large corporations, already straddling several countries, have perforce become international and Community-minded. They are most likely to draw on local talent and gear their activities to their respective fields of operation. Their lawyers would by now have acquired the essential skills and will keep abreast of the developments of Community Law and the relevant areas of the domestic law of the member states. Their main interest lies in the economic directions of the Community and the impact of these directions in the member states in addition to the fiscal and business laws of the member states. More particularly they are likely to encounter problems arising from the law of corporations, restrictive practices, establishment, social security and labour relations, taxation, trade marks and patents, bankruptcy, sale of goods and agency in addition to the mass of the Community rules and regulations which affect investments and commercial operations in their various ramifications. Whilst the importance of Community Law for commercial operations must not be underrated, it has to be borne in mind that the role of the corporation lawyer is somewhat limited. In more complex cases, especially litigation, his employers will rely on the services of lawyers in private practice with whom, no doubt, he will co-operate in the initial stages.

The most formidable is the challenge of Community Law in the field of practice of the law in a strictly professional sense. Broadly speaking the lawyer's work consists of consultancy, litigation and all sorts of paper work where drafting skills take precedence over counselling and advocacy. Two aspects can be distinguished here: the conduct of legal business from a home base or agency abroad, and practice before the Community Court and the national courts of the member states.

The greater proportion of legal business will be conducted on home ground and in this respect no difficulty should arise given a knowledge of Community Law and its effect in this country. In the context of Community Law the solicitor may have to advise his British clients on matters affecting their position here or abroad or foreigners on matters of English Law and Community Law applicable to foreigners in this country. In most cases he will be on familiar ground at home, but far more challenging is the prospect of advising clients on Community matters abroad because these matters have to be considered in the light of the Community and the municipal law of the country concerned. Specialisation will be needed and firms of solicitors practising in this field will establish close relations with foreign practitioners or open branches abroad. Undoubtedly skilled people will be needed to man the branch or do the liaison work. An agency system, on the basis of reciprocity, will probably develop as the cheaper and more effective method. In the initial stage the most essential will be the classification of the business into domestic and Community matters and, where necessary, the engagement of a specialist.

Turning now to a more daunting, though not impossible proposition: art. 52 of the Treaty of Rome gives the "right of establishment" on the basis of free movement within the Community. So far this right has not resulted in a migration of lawyers within the Community simply because the practice of law is essentially national. However, difficulties have come to light because admission to practise is, in most countries, governed by law and restrictive practices of the profession. In accordance with art. 52 (2) the Community Court held, in *Reyners* v. *The Belgian State*,[19] that a Dutch national living in Belgium and having appropriate Belgian professional qualifications was unlawfully excluded from the exercise of the profession of *avocat* on the ground that according to Belgian law only Belgian nationals were admitted to practice. The principle was applied to remove a disqualification on the ground of the lack of habitual residence of a Dutch lawyer who lived in Belgium but wished to practise in the Netherlands.[20]

Assuming that we continue with the divided profession, there is at present no rule to prevent an alien, as an alien, becoming a member of the Bar. Solicitors, allegedly on the basis of s. 3 of the Act of Settlement 1701 (which declared aliens incapable of enjoying certain offices or places of trust) and a counsel's opinion of some vintage, had to be British subjects but this discrimination has now been removed.[1] As far as practice is concerned solicitors must observe the general code of their profession whether they handle "domestic" or "foreign" business. A foreign lawyer wishing to practice in England and Wales must, subject to professional qualifications, elect to practise either as a barrister or a solicitor. He cannot do both. A British solicitor cannot enter into a partnership with a foreign lawyer in England and Wales but may do so abroad subject to local rules. He may however allow his foreign associate to have a seat in his office.[2]

Under the freedom of establishment British lawyers will be entitled to set up in practice abroad on an equal footing, their success depending, of course, on their proficiency in foreign and Community law. Presumably they can offer their services as consultants but whether they can act in a professional capacity is another matter now under consideration in the Community.[3] There is a theoretical and practical

---

[19] Case 2/74, [1974] E.C.R. 631; [1974] 2 C.M.L.R. 305.
[20] Case 33/74: *J. H. M. Van Binsbergen* v. *Bestuur van de Bedrijfsvereniging voor de Metaalnijverheid*, [1974] E.C.R. 1299; [1975] 1 C.M.L.R. 298.
[1] Solicitors' Amendment Act 1974, s. 1; Solicitors' Act 1974, s. 29.
[2] Further details, *Law Society's Gazette*, Vol. 70 (1973), p. 1568.
[3] Schneider, H. H., "Towards a European Lawyer" (1971), 8 C.M.L. Rev. 44.

side to it. In theory the right of establishment and the principle of non-discrimination apply. By art. 52 of the E.E.C. Treaty the freedom of establishment includes the right to engage in and carry on self-employed occupation under the conditions laid down by the law of the country of establishment for its own nationals. The treaty is clear—free movement of persons—but how does it affect lawyers? Article 60 (1) (*d*), defining the term "service", refers to "liberal professions" and this, traditionally, includes the legal profession. But lawyers are, in some respect, involved in the administration of justice which is a public process and an exercise of the authority of the state, not just commercial enterprise or service with which the Common Market is concerned. English solicitors are designated as "Officers of the Supreme Court" and barristers are supposed to be helping the court in its work. German *Rechtsanwälte*, who combine the work of the English barrister and solicitor and are engaged more in litigation than conveyancing, are too "officers of the court". The French have a diversified profession but those who are involved in court work are regarded auxiliaries "of justice" or of "tribunals". The *avocats*, who are the aristocracy of the French legal profession may be called to the Bench or replace public prosecutors, so there is too a considerable involvement in the administration of justice.

For practical purposes one could divide the various functions of lawyers and single out those which can be exercised freely under the right of establishment. This may be a temporary expedient until the matter is settled. To deal with the problem, a proposal for a Council Directive was adopted by the Economic and Social Committee of the E.E.C. in February 1970.[4] This proposal is limited in its scope for it purports to regulate the right to consultation service, access to courts' files, visits to a person in detention, presence at a preliminary enquiry and oral conduct of defence. The Directive, when adopted, shall be binding upon the member states as to the result to be achieved though each state is free to chose its own method of implementation. However, this is an important step towards a Community legal profession as such lawyers would be members of the profession both in their native country and the country of their operation. In litigation they would have a limited right of audience though they would work together with local lawyers. Pending the adoption and implementation of the Directive, the legal profession has been left to its own devices though, as we have observed earlier, in some important aspects of the application of art. 52 the Community Court has given a definite guidance.

As for the future, it is clear that the same rules as those applying in a

---

[4] Directive of 17 April 1969, J.O. 1969, C. 78/1; De Croyencour, [1970] R.M.C. 158; see also proposal for a Council Directive of 9 March 1973; text Campbell, Supplement 1975, p. 739 *et seq.*

federal state must be aimed at. It means that a lawyer admitted to practice in one state ought to have an equal right in another state and this is something the legal profession in the member states will have to work out in due course. One can, of course, envisage difficulties, e.g. in France and Germany only specially appointed lawyers may appear before the Supreme Court; in England the position is rather complicated because of the relations between the two branches of the profession and the existence of Queen's Counsel and Juniors. To face these problems the Bar Council[5] has recently relaxed the rules by allowing a barrister to accept a brief from a foreign lawyer directly without the intermediary of an English solicitor and a Queen's Counsel to act without a Junior in Community matters. However these rules apply only to "foreign work" and are not meant to change the nature of the practice at the Bar in England and Wales or allow the barrister to do the solicitor's work. A barrister may enter into any association including partnership with any lawyer (except solicitors practising in the U.K.) for the purpose of sharing any office or services abroad but in the U.K. cannot undertake work not normally performed by a practising barrister in England and Wales, receive or handle client's money or accept the status of an employee or of a commercial agent or business agent.

In December 1975 an agreement[6] between the Paris Bar and the English Bar was made to the effect that members of one may appear and plead before the Courts of the other provided they are led by members of the local Bar. In England and Wales this rule applies to all courts where only barristers may plead. This arrangement may well lead to similar bi-lateral agreements between the English Bar and the corresponding branches of the profession of the remaining member states of the Community.

Practice before the Community Court presents its own problems. The Court was set up largely on the pattern of the French Conseil d'Etat. Its jurisdiction includes supervision over the execution of the Treaties, adjudication of disputes between member states, control of legality of the acts of the Community Institutions and the interpretation of the Treaty and Community legislation. Its procedure is French with some German admixtures imported recently. In the main the proceedings are conducted in writing and this emphasises the importance of the art of "written advocacy" as a feature of the continental legal style. It is unlikely that the existing practice will be changed to accommodate

---

[5] *Law Society's Gazette*, Vol. 68 (1971), pp. 187, 193, 194; Vol. 70, p. 1568; Vol. 71, p. 378; *Guardian Gazette*, 27 April 1974, p. 114.

[6] *The Times*, December 1975; the relationship between the Paris Bar and the Law Society of England and Wales is governed by an Agreement signed on 12 April 1976.

British lawyers, so new skills will have to be learned and unusual difficulties overcome unless we prefer to leave it to others. The case law approach of the Court in developing the Community Law is a hopeful sign but should not lull us into a sense of false security.

As for the right of audience before the Community Court—some rules have been laid down in art. 17 of the Protocol on the Statute of the Court of Justice. This provides that parties must be represented by a lawyer entitled to practise before a court of one of the member states and this includes also university teachers if, as in Germany, they have the right of audience before the national courts. The operative words are not very clear: the French version refers to "avocat inscrit à un barreau de l'un des Etats membres"; the German to "ein Anwalt, der in einem Mitgliedstaat zugelassen ist". This is echoed by the draft Directive mentioned earlier, the formula in the Directive being "inscrit auprès d'une organisation professionelle de droit public". This would mean that English solicitors could appear before the Court during the whole process, written and oral, provided they have the right of audience before the courts in this country. Since their audience is limited at present, the question appears still open.

THE LANGUAGE OF COMMUNITY LAW

Language is the main tool in the legal workshop and it is common ground that each legal system has its own technical language. So it is with Community Law. Within the Community of the Six the problem of the legal language was magnified sixfold as lawyers from the six countries tried first to frame the Treaty and then establish a common interpretation of the texts of Community Law. In the enlarged Community the problem has been further magnified and has been complicated through the accession of two common law countries. The language of the law will provide a clue to the formidable task of making the best British legal traditions available to the Community.

The problem of language has a special bearing upon the legislative process, the interpretation and administration of the law and harmonisation of national laws. It will be considered in relation to these three areas.

The Treaty and Community Legislation

The Treaty of Rome was drawn up in a single document in the German, French, Italian and Dutch languages, all four texts being equally authentic.[7] By contrast the E.C.S.C. Treaty is in one authentic version in the French language.

The Treaty of Brussels concerning the accession of Denmark, Ireland, Norway and the United Kingdom was also drawn up in a single document in the Danish, Dutch, English, French, German, Irish, Italian and Norwegian languages, all eight texts being equally authentic.[8]

This is an accepted form of a multilateral, multi-lingual treaty for which the United Nations Charter is one of the outstanding precedents. The effect of the formula "equally authentic" is that all texts, having an equal status, can be cited as the authoritative statement of the law and that no one text takes precedence over the others. This does not solve the problem of the discrepancies in the various texts which *inter se* are nothing but translations. With the greatest care and skill expended on the formulation of treaties discrepancies are inevitable because the translation of a legal text is not merely a matter of language. The question of interpretation of authentic texts which reveal a discrepancy in the meaning of words attributable to legal concepts and institutions resolves itself into the question of the intention of the parties. The rule of international law, which has evolved to deal with this problem, is that there is a presumption against an interpretation which is contrary to any one of the equally authentic texts. It follows that it is necessary to find a meaning which is compatible with all the texts. In order to achieve this object it is necessary first to establish the meanings of each text and then select the meaning which is not contrary to any particular text. A practical illustration of the application of this role is the *Mavrommatis* case,[9] in which the Permanent Court of International Justice explained that "when considering two equally authentic texts, one of which appears to have a wider meaning than the other it is the duty of the Court to apply the narrower text since such an interpretation is compatible with both texts and, no doubt, corresponds to the common intention of the parties".

In *Fédération Charbonnière de Belgique* v. *High Authority*[10] the Community Court considered the argument that the E.C.S.C. Treaty being an international treaty was subject to restrictive interpretation and broadly agreed with the principle, though it considered that rules of interpretation used in both international law and national laws were

---

[7] Art. 248; the languages are listed in alphabetical order in accordance with the French nomenclature of the four countries.

[8] Art. 3; the languages are listed in alphabetical order according to Cmnd. 4862, I but since Norway failed to ratify the Treaty there are in the Community six official languages; see Adaptation Decision, art. 2.

[9] [1927] P.C.I.J. Rep. Ser. A, No. 2, p. 12.

[10] Case 8/55; 2 Rec. 151 at p. 199.

perfectly acceptable. However, in later cases a broader formula has evolved. In *Milchwerke Heinz Wöhrmann & Sohn K.G.* v. *E.E.C. Commission*[11] Advocate-General Roemer submitted that where three texts revealed a clear meaning but the fourth was inconsistent with them the latter should follow suit. In *Bosch* v. *de Geus*[12] Advocate-General Lagrange submitted that where all four texts conveyed different meanings the Court should decide the issue according to the spirit of the text. In *Mij. P.P.W. Internationaal N.V.* v. *Hoofdproduktschap voor Akkerbouwprodukten*[13] the Court held that no argument could be drawn either from any linguistic discrepancies between the various texts or from the number of the verbs used in one or other version because the meaning of the relevant provisions had to be determined in the light of their objectives.

Since the Treaties of Paris, Rome and Brussels are "self-executing" there is no need of their being "transformed" by statute into the domestic law of the member states. Consequently, as far as the authentic texts are concerned, the Treaties have to be taken as they stand. The danger of producing a different text for the purpose of legislation, not uncommon in the process of translation of international conventions, has been excluded. This does not solve the problem of Community Law in the countries whose language has not been included in the authentic texts or, as in the case of the United Kingdom, countries which have subsequently adhered to the Treaties. The general rule of international law may be too narrow and so the spirit rather than the letter of the Treaty should prevail.

In their endeavour to give effect to the common intention of the parties comprised in a multi-lingual treaty the draftsmen try to exclude discrepancies and potential conflicts of interpretation but this is quite an impossible task. The end product must be a compromise if not a synthesis of the systems involved. Where this is impossible they have to choose consciously the technical language which seems most appropriate or most commonly used or the language of the legal system which has the greatest influence in the deliberations. The Treaties unmistakably bear the imprint of French Law.

Whilst the Treaty is a "once and for all" exercise the Community legislation is a continuous process. The techniques have already been perfected through common effort of the Community lawyers and here, perhaps, the lawyer no longer feels a champion of his own system (which, as every lawyer knows, is the best system in the world!) or

---

[11] Case 31 and 33/62, [1963] C.M.L.R. 152; 8 Rec. 965.
[12] Case 13/61, [1962 C.M.L.R. 1 at p. 23; 8 Rec. 89.
[13] Case 61/72, [1973] E.C.R. 301 at p. 310.

suffers under the limitations of his national training and the inhibitions acquired from his legal language becoming his second nature. The newcomers to this task are at a certain disadvantage and their contribution initially must perforce be rather limited. This is a special practical challenge to the British civil servant joining the legal service of the Community.

Article 191 (1), (2) of the E.E.C. Treaty provides that "regulations shall be published in the Official Journal of the Community" and that "directives and decisions shall be notified to those to whom they are addressed". At first the *Official Journal* was published in Dutch, French, German and Italian but art. 155 of the Act of Accession, as amended by the Adaptation Decision, provided that "the texts of the Acts of the Institution of the Community adopted before the accession and drawn up by the Council or the Commission in the Danish and English languages shall, from the date of accession, be authentic under the same conditions as the texts drawn up in the four original languages. They shall be published in the Official Journal of the European Communities if the texts in the original languages were so published".[14]

Since directives and decisions have to be "notified" but, apparently, need not be "published" difficulties arose in the past[15] and these prompted the Community Court to suggest that publication be improved. As a result directives and decisions are now, as a rule, published in the *Official Journal*.

Let us turn now to some specific pitfalls of the technical language of Community Law, problems known only too well to British translators of the Community texts who soon discovered that "corresponding" legal terms in two languages seldom correspond *exactly*.[16]

In the drafting of conventions the generalisations about the civil law system are brought to the test and, usually, to grief. Illusions of the oneness of the system based on Roman Law and codes are quickly exposed and we are left with a vague notion of a common core of the law, a common historical heritage, and a similarity of styles. As in a large family there are traces of common genes but also manifestations of mutations and acquired differences. As in a family the stronger members prevail and so one can trace in multi-lingual texts the influence of a

---

[14] Reg. 857/72 of 24 April 1972 establishing special editions of the Official Journal; *J.O.* L. 101, 1972.
[15] Joined Cases 73 and 74/63: *Internationale Crediet-en Handelsvereniging "Rotterdam" N.V.* v. *Minister van Landouw en Visserij*, [1964] C.M.L.R. 198; 10 Rec. 1, at p. 28; Case 69/69 *Alcan* v. *E.E.C. Commission*, 16 Rec. 385 (submission at p. 397); [1970] C.M.L.R. 337 at p. 340.
[16] Hall, D. F., "Translating the Treaties", *European Review*, Spring Issue 1972.

particular system. It is not surprising that the French legal language provides a starting point for the consideration of the problems of language in the Community texts.

The student of Community Law must from the start familiarise himself with the problem of language known only too well to the student of comparative law. Examples from the E.E.C. Treaty, given below, have already tested translators and commentators of the texts and in some cases exercised the minds of judges because they present linguistic as well as conceptual teasers.

Parallel French and English Official Texts
(Figures in brackets refer to articles of the Treaty)

mission (2)	task[17]
action (3)	activities
tâches (4)	tasks
buts (5)	objectives[18]
règlementation (7)	rules
a le droit (8)	shall be entitled
instance d'arbitrage (8)	arbitration board
marchandises (9)	goods[19]
produits (9)	products[20]
en provenance (9)	coming from[1]
ristourne (10)	drawback
arrêtant (10)	adopting
droits de douane (11)	customs duties
perception (15)	collection
perception douanière (17)	customs receipts
faculté (17)	right
réduction des entraves aux échanges (18)	lowering of barriers to trade[2]
mise en place (23)	introduction

---

[17] Case 6/72: *Europemballage Corporation and Continental Can Co. Inc.* v. *E.C. Commission* [1973] E.C.R. 215 at p. 244.

[18] Case 2/73: *Riseria Luigi Geddo* v. *Ente Nazionale Risi*, [1973] E.C.R. 865, at p. 878; Case 34/73: *Variola SpA* v. *Amminisrtazione Italiana delle Finanze*, [1973] E.C.R. 981, at p. 991.

[19] Case 8/73: *Hauptzollamt Bremerhaven* v. *Massey-Ferguson GmbH*, [1973] E.C.R. 897 at p. 907.

[20] *Geddo etc., op. cit.; Variola etc., op. cit.*

[1] Case 39/73: *Rewe-Zentralfinanz GmbH* v. *Direktor der Landwirtschafts-kammer Westfalen-Lippe*, [1973] E.C.R. 1039 at pp. 1043–1044.

[2] Cases 37–38/73: *Sociaal Fonds voor de Diamantarbeiders* v. *N.V. Indiamex and Association de Fait de Belder*, [1973] E.C.R. 1609 at pp. 1622–1623.

contingents (25)	quotas
concurrence (29)	competition
moralité publique (36)	public morality
ordre public (36)	public policy
securité publique (36)	public security
monopoles nationaux (37)	state monopolies[3]
formation professionnelle (41)	vocational training[4]
vulgarisation agronomique (41)	dissemination of agricultural knowledge
règlements (43)	regulations[5]
directives (43)	directives[6]
décisions (43)	decisions[7]
marché national (43)	national market
restrictions quantitatives (44)	quantitative restrictions
prix minima (44)	minimum prices
échanges (44)	trade
marché commun (44)	common market
majorité qualifiée (44)	qualified majority
régime (44)	system
accords ou contrats (45)	agreements or contracts
marché intérieur (45)	domestic market
marché mondial (45)	world market
organisation nationale du marché (46)	national market organisation
règlementation interne (46)	internal rules
taxe compensatoire (46)	countervailing charge
sortie (46)	export
rétablir l'équilibre (46)	redress the balance
recours (46)	measures
travailleurs (48)	workers[8]
libre circulation (48)	freedom of movement[9]
discrimination (48)	discrimination

[3] Case 6/64: *Costa (Flaminio)* v. *ENEL*, [1964] C.M.L.R. 425.

[4] Case 2/74: *Reyners* v. *The Belgian State*, [1974] E.C.R. 631 at p. 648; [1974] C.M.L.R. 305 at p. 324; Case 33/74: *J. H. M. van Binsbergen* v. *Bestuur van der Bedrijfsvereniging voor de Metaalnijverheid*, [1974] E.C.R. 1299; [1975] 1 C.M.L.R. 298, Case 39/75: *Coenen et Al* v. *Sociaal Economische Raad*, [1976] C.M.L.R. 30.

[5] Cases 16–17/62: *Confédération Nationale des Producteurs de Fruits et Légumes* v. *E.E.C. Council*, [1963] C.M.L.R. 160 at pp. 173–174; 8 Rec. 901 at pp. 916–918; *Rewe-Zentral A.G.* v. *Hauptzollamt Kehl*, [1973] E.C.R. 1175 at p. 1190.

[6] Case 156/65: *Molkerei-Zentralle Westfalen/Lippe GmbH* v. *Hauptzollamt Paderborn*, [1969] C.M.L.R. 300 at p. 312.

[7] Case 25/62: *Plaumann* v. *E.E.C. Commission*, [1964] C.M.L.R. 29 at p. 46–47 9 Rec. 197 at pp. 222–224.

[8] Case 61/65: *Vaasen-Göbbels* v. *Beambtenfonds voor bet Mijnbedrijf*, [1966] C.M.L.R. 508 at p. 521; 13 Rec. 377; Case 152/73: *Sotgiu* v. *Deutsche Bundespost*, [1974] E.C.R. 153 at pp. 162–165.

[9] Case 41/74: *Van Duyn* v. *Home Office (No. 2)*, [1975] 3 All E.R. 190; [1975] C.M.L.R. 1 at pp. 14–19.

santé publique (48)	public health
dispositions législatives (48)	law
dispositions règlementaires (48)	regulations
dispositions administratives (48)	administrative action
administration publique (48)	public service
administrations ... du travail (49)	employment ... services
niveau de vie (49)	standard of living
sécurité sociale (51)	social security[10]
leurs ayants droit (51)	dependants[11]
totalisation (51)	aggregation[12]
droit aux prestations (51)	right to benefit
liberté d'établissement (52)	freedom of establishment[13]
agences (52)	agencies
succursales ... filiales (52)	branches ... subsidiaries
ressortissants (52)	nationals[14]
activités non salariées (52)	activities as self-employed
gestion d'entreprises (52)	manage undertakings
sociétés (52)	companies
travailleurs salariés (54)	[wage-paid] workers
travailleurs non salariés (54)	self-employed persons
propriétés foncières (54)	land and buildings
organes de gestion ou de surveillance (54)	managerial or supervisory posts
à titre occasionnel (55)	occasionally
autorité publique (55)	official authority
prescriptions (56)	provisions
régime spécial (56)	special treatment
siège statutaire (58)	registered office
but lucratif (58)	profit-making [object]
prestaire (60)	person providing a service
libre circulation des services (61)	freedom to provide services[15]
localisation du placement (67)	place where capital is invested
emprunts (68)	loans
investissement (68)	investment
restriction de change (71)	exchange restriction
marché des capitaux (73)	capital market
domaine des prix (78)	[transport] rates

---

[10] Case 75/63: *Hoekstra-Unger* v. *Bestuur der Bedrijfs-vereniging voor Detailhandel en Ambachten*, [1964] C.M.L.R. 330 at p. 33; 10 Rec. 362 at pp. 362–364.
[11] *Vaasen-Göbbels, op. cit.*
[12] Case 92/63: *Moebs* v. *Bestuur der Sociale Verzekeringsbank*, 10 Rec. 557 at pp. 572–574; [1964] C.M.L.R. 338 at pp. 346–347.
[13] *Reyners, op. cit.*
[14] Case 19/74: *Donato Casagrande* v. *Landeshauptstadt Münich*, [1974] E.C.R. 773 at pp. 778–779; [1974] 2 C.M.L.R. 423; Case 68/74: *Angelo Alaimo* v. *Préfet du Rhône*, [1975] E.C.R. 109.
[15] Case 36/74: *Bruno Walrave and Norbert Koch* v. *Association Union Cycliste Internationale, Koninklijke Nederlandse Wielen Unie, etc.*, [1974] E.C.R. 1405.

taxes ou redevances (81)	charges or dues
frais réels (81)	costs actually incurred
navigation maritime et aérienne (84)	sea and air transport
entreprises (85)	undertakings[16]
prix d'achat ou de vente (85)	purchase or selling prices
répartir les marchés (85)	share markets[17]
partenaires commerciaux (85)	trading parties[18]
usages commerciaux (85)	commercial usages
nul de plein droit (85)	automatically void[19]
position dominante (86)	dominant position[20]
pratiques abusives (86)	abuse[1]
non équitable (86)	unfair
conditions de transactions (86)	trading conditions[2]
règlements ou directives utiles (87)	appropriate regulations or directives
contrôle administratif (87)	administration
ententes (88)	agreements[3]
exploitation abusive (88)	abuse
infraction présumée (89)	suspected infringement
décision motivée (89)	reasoned decision
monopole fiscal (90)	revenue-producing monopoly
pratiques de dumping (91)	dumping[4]
état membre lésé (91)	injured member state
libre pratique (91)	free circulation
aides accordées (92)	aid granted[5]
régimes d'aides (93)	systems of aid
saisir . . . la Cour (93)	refer . . . to the Court

---

[16] Case 23/58: *Mannesmann A.G. Hoeschwerke A.G. v. High Authority*, 5 Rec. 253.
[17] Case 56/65: *Technique Minière* v. *Machinenbau Ulm GmbH*, [1966] C.M.L.R. 357 at p. 375; 12 Rec. 337 at p. 359; Case 8/72: *Vereniging van Cementhandelaren* v. *E.C. Commission* (1973) C.M.L.R. 7 at pp 21–24.
[18] Case 48/69: *Imperial Chemical Industries, Ltd.* v. *E.C. Commission*, [1972] C.M.L.R. 557 at pp. 622–623.
[19] *Technique Minière, op. cit.*
[20] Cases 6–7/73: *Istituto Chemioterapico Italiano SpA and Commercial Solvents Corporation* v. *E.C. Commission*, [1974] E.C.R. 223 at pp. 247–255; [1974] C.M.L.R. 309 at pp. 336–346.
[1] Case 127/73: *B.R.T.* v. *N.V. Fonior: SABM* v. *N.V. Fonior; B.R.T.* v. *SABM and N.V. Fonior*, [1974] E.C.R. 313 at pp. 315–319; [1974] C.M.L.R. 269 at pp. 282–285.
[2] Case 1/70: *Parfums Mareel Rochas Vertriebs GmbH* v. *Bitsch*, [1971] C.M.L.R. 104 at pp. 115–118.
[3] *Ibid.*
[4] Case 13/63: *Electric Refrigerators, Re, Italian Government* v. *E.E.C. Commission*, [1963] C.M.L.R. 289 at pp. 311–312; 9 Rec. 355 at 360.
[5] Cases 6–11/69: *E.C. Commission* v. *French Republic*, [1970] C.M.L.R. 43 at pp. 63–67, 15 Rec. 523 at pp. 538–543.

impositions intérieures (95)	internal taxation[6]
taxe sur le chiffre d'affaires (97)	turnover tax[7]
taxe cumulative à cascade (97)	cumulative multistage tax system
droits d'accise (98)	excise duties
exonérations et remboursements (98)	remissions and repayments
rapprochement (100)	approximation[8]
politique de conjoncture (103)	conjunctural policies[9]
matière monétaire (105)	monetary field
balance des paiements (106)	balance of payments
transactions invisibles (106)	invisible transactions
déséquilibre global (108)	overall disequilibrium[10]
devises (108)	currency
moyens (108)	means
concours mutuel (108)	mutual assistance
détournement de trafic (108)	deflection of trade
politique commerciale (110)	commercial policy
commerce extérieur (111)	external trade
droit syndical (118)	right of association
négociations collectives (118)	collective bargaining
unité de mesure (119)	unit of measurement
congés payés (120)	paid holidays
travailleurs migrants (121)	migrant workers
situation sociale (122)	social conditions
Fonds social européen (123)	European Social Fund
organisations syndicales de travailleurs (124)	trade unions
rééducation professionnelle (125)	vocational retraining
indemnités de réinstallation (125)	resettlement allowances
domicile (125)	home
résidence (125)	residence
Banque européenne d'investissement (129)	European Investment Bank
échanges commerciaux (132)	trade
Assemblée (137)	Assembly [Parliament]
pouvoirs de délibération et de contrôle (137)	advisory and supervisory powers
suffrage universel direct (138)	direct universal suffrage
règles constitutionnelles (138)	constitutional requirements

---

[6] Case 57/65: *Alfons Lütticke v. Hauptzollamt Sarrelouis*, [1971] C.M.L.R. 674 at pp. 684–685; 12 Rec. 293 at pp. 301–303; Case 10/65: *Deutschmann v. Aussenhandelsstelle für Erzeugnisse der Ernährung und Landwirtschaft*, [1965] C.M.L.R. 259; 11 Rec. 601.

[7] *Molkerei-Zentrale, op. cit.*, note 6, p. 57.

[8] Case 32/74: *Firma Friedrich Haaga GmbH*, [1975] C.M.L.R. 32 at pp. 43–45.

[9] Case 5/73: *Balkan Import-Export GmbH v. Hauptzollamt Berlin-Packhof*, [1973] E.C.R. 1091.

[10] *E.C. Commission v. French Republic, op. cit.* note 5, p. 59.

réunit de plein droit (139)	[shall] meet without requiring to be convened
règlement intérieur (140)	rules of procedure
suffrages exprimés (141)	votes cast
motion de censure (144)	motion of censure
gestion (144)	activities
abandonner collectivement leurs fonctions (144)	resign as a body
dispose d'un pouvoir de décision (145)	have power to take decisions
recevoir délégation (150)	act on behalf of
statut des comités (153)	rules governing committees
formation des actes (155)	shaping of measures
exerce les compétences (155)	exercise the powers
assure le respect du droit (164)	ensure that . . . the law is observed
séance plénière (165)	plenary session[11]
chambres (165)	chambers
mesures d'instruction (165)	preparatory enquiries
saisie par un Etat membre (165)	brought by a Member State
questions préjudicielles (165)	preliminary rulings
avocats généraux (166)	Advocates-General
conclusions motivées (166)	reasoned submissions
jurisconsultes (167)	jurisconsults
compétences notoires (167)	recognised competence
Son mandat est renouvelable (167)	He may be re-elected
greffier (168)	Registrar
avis motivé (169)	reasoned opinion[12]
pleine juridiction (172)	unlimited jurisdiction
sanctions (172)	penalties
contrôle la légalité (173)	review the legality
incompétence (173)	lack of competence
violation du . . . traité (173)	infringement of . . . treaty
violation des formes substantielles (173)	infringement of an essential procedural requirement
détournement de pouvoir (173)	misuse of powers[13]
nul et non avenu (174)	void
acte contesté (174)	act concerned
s'abstient de statuer (175)	fail to act
personne morale (175)	legal person
faire grief (175)	complain

---

[11] Cases 28–30/62: *Da Costa en Schaake N.V.* v. *Nederlandse Belasting-administratie*, [1963] C.M.L.R. 224 at pp. 237–238; 9 Rec. 59 at pp. 75–77.
[12] Case 45/64: *E.E.C. Commission* v. *Italy*, [1966] C.M.L.R. 97; 9 Rec. 1057 at pp. 1068–1069.
[13] See p. 67 below.

titre préjudiciel (177)	preliminary ruling[14]
recours juridictionnel (177)	judicial remedy
est tenue (177)	shall bring
est compétente (178)	shall have jurisdiction
litige (179)	dispute
agents (179)	servants
connaître des litiges (180)	shall . . . have jurisdiction in disputes
délibérations (180)	measures
violation des formes (180)	non-compliance with the procedure
clause compromissoire (181)	arbitration clause
différend (182)	dispute
compromis (182)	special agreement
soustraits à la compétence (183)	excluded from the jurisdiction
moyens (184)	grounds
effet suspensif (185)	suspensory effect
acte attaqué (185)	contested act
mesures provisoires (186)	interim measures
ont force exécutoire (187)	shall be enforceable
forment titre exécutoire (192)	shall be enforceable
exécution forcée (192)	enforcement
formule exécutoire (192)	order for . . . enforcement
vérification de l'authenticité du titre (192)	vertification of the authenticity of the decision
caractère consultatif (193)	advisory status
règlements financiers (209)	financial regulations
ordonnateurs et comptables (209)	authorising officers and accounting officers
personnalité juridique (210)	legal personality
capacité juridique (211)	legal capacity[15]
ester en justice (211)	[be] a party to legal proceedings
fonctionnaires et agents (214)	officials and . . . servants
responsabilité contractuelle (215)	contractual liability
dans l'exercice de leurs fonctions (215)	in the performance of their duties
régime linguistique (217)	rules governing the languages
double imposition (220)	double taxation
sociétés (220)	companies or firms
décisions judiciaires (220)	judgments
sentences arbitrales (220)	arbitration awards
régime de la propriété (222)	system of property ownership
troubles intérieurs (224)	internal disturbances
à huis clos (225)	in camera
procédure d'urgence (226)	emergency procedure
mesures de sauvegarde (226)	protective measures

[14] See Chapter 10.
[15] Case 22/70: *Re ERTA E.C. Commission* v. *E.C. Council*, [1971] C.M.L.R. 335; 17 Rec. 263.

exemplaire unique (248)	single original
les quatre textes faisant également foi (248)	all four texts being equally authentic
en foi de quoi (248)	in witness whereof

To appreciate the difficulty inherent in the translation of legal texts the student is advised to study the above selection of phrases in their proper context, especially in the light of decided cases and to consider the accuracy of their English version from a literal and contextual point of view.

Language in the Community Court

The Community Court, the single court of the three communities,[16] is a multi-lingual court not only in a linguistic but also a juristic sense.

The requirement that judges must be fit to occupy the highest judicial offices in their respective countries is both an advantage and a handicap. The advantage is obvious in the quality of the judicial body and the potential of having the best legal traditions of the member states in the service of the Community Court. The handicap is that judges, perhaps more than any other lawyers, are conditioned by their own system. However, until truly Community judges emerge the national judges will continue to enrich and shape the Community judiciary with their native skills and characters. Judge Donner thus summarised the position of the national judge: "I remember one of my colleagues saying at the end of a long debate in which he had tried to win us over to his national solution on a particular point, 'Well, gentlemen, if you do not want to adopt my approach, you will at least have to admit that it is the only reasonable one'."[17]

In order to assist the Court with the linguistic problems the Rules of Procedure[18] enabled the Court to set up a language department consisting of experts, combining the knowledge of several of the official

---

[16] Convention relating to Certain Institutions common to the European Communities of 27 March 1957 annexed to the E.E.C. and E.A.E.C. Treaties and amending the E.C.S.C. Treaty.

[17] Donner, A. M., *The Role of the Lawyer in the European Communities* (1968) p. 43.

[18] These Rules were adopted by the Court on 3 March 1959, in succession to the Treaties of the three Communities and the Statutes of the Courts of Justice envisaged by the Treaties; present version O.J. 1974, L 350.

languages of the Court and law (R.P. 22). Originally the official languages of the Court were French, German, Italian and Netherlands (R.P. 29 (1))[19] but with the enlargement of the Community the rules of procedure[20] had to be adapted to include the new official languages. At present the official languages of the Court are: Danish, English, French, German, Italian and Netherlands; but Irish (though not official) may also be used. These changes resulting in an increased number of the official languages will no doubt further multiply the problems involved.

The present position is that only one of the official languages may be used as the procedural language (R.P. 29 (2)). The choice is, in principle, left to the applicant. However, if the defendant is a member state or a person or corporation subject to a member state the procedural language will be the official language of that state. Should there be more than one official language involved the applicant would be able to choose one from these. If the parties to the case so desire, the Court, upon their joint application, may designate the use of another official language as the procedural language. In exceptional circumstances the Court may authorise the total or partial use of another official language as the procedural language if so requested by one of the parties. Such a request has to be considered in the light of the comments by the other party and the advocate-general but is not open to any of the organs of the Community. In the proceedings involving a preliminary ruling under E.E.C. art. 177[1] on matters of the interpretation of the Treaty, the validity and interpretation of the act of the Community organs and the interpretation of the statutes of bodies established by the Council, the procedural language shall be that of the Court or tribunal which requests the preliminary ruling in question.

The procedural language is used to procure written evidence and pleas before the Court. Documents produced in another language must be accompanied by a translation in the procedural language. These documents are regarded as "authentic" which means in practical terms that they cannot be challenged merely on linguistic grounds (R.P. 31).

Witnesses and experts ought to use the procedural language or one of the official languages but, if unable to do so the Court will allow them to use another language. The witness or expert is allowed to speak

---

[19] Dutch, as the language of Holland, is not synonymous with the "Netherlands language" which is also spoken in certain parts of Belgium. Such Belgians enjoy two "official languages": French and Netherlands.
[20] Act of Accession, art. 142 (4); see p. 53, note 8 and p. 55.
[1] E.E.C. Statute, art. 20; E.A.E.C. Statute, art. 21; E.C.S.C. Treaty, art. 41.

through an interpreter or address himself to a judge of his native language[2] but at the end a record will be made under the direction of the Court's Registrar in the procedural language.

The President of the Court, the Presidents of Chambers when directing the proceedings, the Judge-Rapporteur when making his preliminary report and judges and advocates-general when asking questions and the advocates-general when making their submissions may use an official language in preference to the procedural language. However, their utterings will be translated into the procedural language under the direction of the Registrar.

The Registrar will also, on the application of a judge, advocate-general or one of the parties, ensure that a translation into the official languages of his choice is made of what has been said or recorded during the proceedings before the Court or Chamber (R.P. 30), is delivered in the procedural language (R.P. 29 (2)) and then published by the Registrar in all the official languages (R.P. 68).

In spite of the tremendous language problem only few cases have so far involved the technical question of the use of language. In *De Gezamenlijke Steenkolenmijnen in Limburg* v. *Haute Autorité*[3] the Court had to rule on the use of the procedural language by an intervener. The Court held that "it is only as from the moment that he is admitted to intervene that the intervener is obliged to use the language required for the procedure in the main action, without prejudice to the application of R.P. 29 (2) (*c*)".

In *Acciaieria di Roma* v. *Haute Autorité*[4] the admissibility of documents drawn up in languages other than the procedural language was challenged. The Court held that: ". . . The documents in question were deposited with the Registry before the close of the oral procedure and consequently were within the cognisance of the Court before it rendered judgment. By a production of a document drawn up in one of the official languages of the Community it is not only its physical existence but also its content which is brought to the cognisance of the Court. Indeed, like all the institutions of the three Communities, the Court is quadri-lingual by virtue of a presumption *juris et de jure*. The provisions concerning the language of procedure cannot be regarded as being of public policy (*ordre public; zwingendes Recht; openbare orde; ordine pubblico*)—

---

[2] Case 18/63, where the witness and the President of the Court were Italians but the counsel was French, and the President acted virtually as an interpreter.
[3] Case 30/59: (1959), 8 Rec. 94.
[4] Case 1/50: (1950), 6 (I) Rec.

(*a*) because the language of procedure is that of the applicant, unless the defendant is one of the member states of the three Communities or a legal person subject to the jurisdiction of one of the member states;

(*b*) because, both on the joint application of the parties and on the application of a single party and without the consent of the other party being necessary, the Court can authorise the use of an official language other than the language of the procedure.

That, therefore, the first fundamental condition required by E.C.S.C. art. 38 (the discovery of a fact unknown not only to the party that applies for re-consideration, but also to the Court) is not met in the present case. . . .''

The challenge failed.

The rules governing the language of procedure are fairly clear but they do not explain what actually happens when the multi-lingual Court retires for deliberations in private before proceeding to judgment. Judge Donner[5] explained the problems the judges have to face and stressed how difficult it is for a lawyer to shed his second nature acquired in the practice of his national law and to sublimate his experience to a Community concept of law which must perforce savour of a synthesis of the laws of the member states. No doubt the personality of the individual judge and the authority of his national law play a part in the deliberations.

The deliberations are entirely private and in the absence of translators. Practice established French to be *the lingua franca* with the consequent disadvantage to judges whose fluency in French is not as good as might be desired. To get round this difficulty former Judge Riese[6] used to state his position in his native German and then restate it in French. In this way he endeavoured to have his say as best he could first in the legal jargon of his own country, and then give his brethren the benefit of an authentic translation into the "working" language. It is clear that the Court must live with the problem (further aggravated by the enlargement of the Community) until the relevant portion of the law has become uniform and a new generation of truly Community lawyers has replaced the judges schooled in their native lands.

Still more complex is the jurisprudence of the language of the law. On more than one occasion the Community Court had to turn its mind to the interpretation of technical terms only to confirm that similarities conceal divergencies and nuances in the legal systems. The following examples illustrate the point.

---

[5] Donner, *op. cit.*, p. 44.
[6] Riese, O., "Erfahrungen aus der Praxis des Gerichtshofes der Europäischen Gemeinschaft für Kohle und Stahl", *Deutsche Richterzeitung* (1958), 270–272.

1. *Détournement de pouvoir*[7]—A notion of French administrative law to cover a variety of cases of misuse of power has been before the Court on several occasions. In *Associazione Industrie Siderurgiche Italiane (Assider)* v. *Haute Autorité*[8] Advocate-General Lagrange reviewed painstakingly the concept of the misuse of power in each of the six member states. In that case an association of Italian steel enterprises complained of being adversely affected by certain decisions[9] of the High Authority of the Coal and Steel Community which concerned the publication of price lists and conditions of sale by the steel industry. The plaintiffs contended that the general decisions of the High Authority in these matters constituted a threat to Italian steel enterprises, and that they were vitiated by the *détournement de pouvoir*. Moreover, since those enterprises which had infringed the previous regulations were not subjected to any sanction, the plaintiffs considered this to be a manifest injustice, and thus a misuse of power in respect of those enterprises which had observed the Treaty. The Court held that since decision 2/54 was annulled by the judgment in the case of *The French Government* v. *High Authority*[10] and decision 3/54 repealed by the High Authority it was unnecessary for the Court to define *détournement de pouvoir*. Decision 1/54, having been upheld by the Court in the case of *The Italian Government* v. *High Authority*[11] could not be regarded as misuse of power in the absence of new arguments. In the circumstances the Court was able to fall back on the classical dodge of not having to define an awkward concept. The plaintiffs fared no better in their request for an interpretation of the judgment[12] as the Court held that the judgment, being free from obscurities, presented no occasion for interpretation.

The saga of the *détournement de pouvoir* is likely to continue in spite of the attempts by the Court to offer an objective definition of *détournement* as "the use made by a public authority of its powers for an object other than that for which a power was conferred upon it"[13] simply because of the variations of the use and abuse of public power. The procession of cases will continue.

2. *Faute de service*—In several cases the Community Court considered grievances arising from alleged "default of the administration"

---

[7] Ermessemissbrauch, sviamento de potere, misbruik van beveogdheid.
[8] Case 3/54; 1 Rec. 149–169.
[9] Case 1/54, J.O., 13 January 1953, p. 217; Case 2/54, *ibid.*, p. 218; Case 3/54 *ibid.*, p. 219.
[10] Case 1/54; 1 Rec. 7.
[11] Case 2/54; 1 Rec. 73.
[12] Case 5/55; 1 Rec. 263.
[13] Case 8/55: *Fédération Charbonnière de Belgique* v. *High Authority*, 2 Rec. 151 at pp. 253–256.

(*faute de service*). On one occasion a Belgian corporation[14] complained
that it was unable to sell coal in France because of the refusal of a
licence by French authorities which, in effect, impeded the free flow of
coal within the Community. Repeated requests to the Coal and Steel
Community were of no avail and the corporation suffered damage as a
result of inaction of the Community. The Court held that the plaintiff
was entitled to redress for *faute de service* without insisting that the
act complained of had to be annulled first. However, in *Plaumann* v.
E.E.C. Commission[15] damages were refused in the absence of a declaration of nullity but the decision turned upon different considerations.
In subsequent cases[16] the Court recognised the independent nature of
the action in accordance with art. 215 (2) and 178, but considered that
where a claim is made in respect of injury attributable to a legislative
act of the Community involving choices of economic policy the claimant
can succeed only if there is a "sufficiently flagrant infringement of a
superior rule of law protecting the individual".[17]

Several other cases[18] threw light on the concept of *faute de service*
but perhaps the most instructive are the cases involving grievances of
Community employees. It was held[19] that failure to renew a contract of
employment in an irregular fashion constituted *faute de service* and so
did an unlawful activity of an organ of the Community preventing a
person from carrying on his normal occupation and causing him material
and moral damage.[20]

The many aspects of *faute de service* were considered from a comparative point of view in *Algera and Others* v. *The Assembly*,[1] a case of
disputed validity of the re-grading of employees. The Court stated:[2]

"... A study of comparative law reveals that in the six Member
States an administrative act creating substantive rights in a particular
party cannot in principle be revoked, provided that it amounted to a

---

[14] Case 9–10/60 *Antoine Vloebergs S.A.* v. *High Authority* (1960), 7 Rec. 379.
[15] Case 25/62, [1964] C.M.L.R. 29; 9 Rec. 197.
[16] Case 5/71: *Aktien-Zuckerfabrik Schöppenstedt* v. *E.E.C. Council* (1971), 17
Rec. 975; Cases 63–69/72: *Werhahn* v. *E.E.C. Council*, [1973] E.C.R. 1229.
[17] *Werhahn, op. cit.*
[18] E.g. cases 19/60, 21/60, 2–3/61: *Société Fives Lille Cail* v. *High Authority*,
[1962] C.M.L.R. 251 at pp. 281–282; 7 Rec. 559 at pp. 589–590; Cases 5–7/66,
13–24/66, 30/66: *Firma E. Kampff-meyer* v. *E.E.C. Commission*, J.O. 246/1;
[1967] C.M.L.R., 209; 13 Rec. 317; Case 36/62: *Société des Aciéries du Temple*
v. *High Authority*, [1964] C.M.L.R. 49 at p. 56; 9 Rec. 583; Case 3/65: *Espér-
ance Langdoz* v. *High Authority*, [1966] C.M.L.R. 146 at p. 167; 11 Rec. 1321.
[19] In Case 1/55: *A. Kergall* v. *Common Assembly* (1955), 2 Rec. 11.
[20] Case 18/60: *Worms* v. *High Authority*, [1963] C.M.L.R. 1; 8 Rec. 377.
[1] Cases 7/56, 3 and 7/57, (1957), 3 Rec. 81.
[2] Valentine, D. G., *The Court of Justice of the European Communities*, Vol. 2
(1965), p. 757–758.

legal act. In such a case, the substantive right having been acquired, the necessity of ensuring confidence in the stability of the situation thus created outweighs the interest of the administration which might wish to revoke its decision. This applies particularly in the appointment of an official.

If, on the contrary, the administrative act is illegal, the law of all the Member States recognises the possibility of revocation. The lack of an objective legal basis for the act affects the substantive right of the party concerned and justifies the revocation of the said act. It is appropriate to emphasise that this principle is generally recognised and that it is only the conditions for its exercise which vary.

French law requires that the revocation of the illegal act must occur before the expiration of the time limit for bringing an appeal, or if an appeal is brought, before judgement. Belgian, Luxembourg and Dutch Law, with certain differences, appear to follow analogous rules.

On the other hand, German Law does not recognise a time limit for the exercise of the right of revocation unless such a limit is provided by a special provision. Thus, the Federal Law concerning public officials, by art. 13 thereof, allows the withdrawal of an appointment only within a period of six months. However, it is generally recognised that the principle of good faith (*Treu und Glauben*) is opposed to an unduly delayed withdrawal . . .

. . . Italian law is particularly precise upon this question. Any administrative act is vitiated by incompetence, violation of the law or ultra vires (*eccesso di potere*) can be annulled *ex tunc* by the administration which enacted it, independently of the substantive rights to which it might have given rise . . .

The revocability of an administrative act tainted with illegality is, therefore, recognised in all the Member States . . ."

Faute de service was proved and the earlier decision in *A. Kergall* v. *Assemblée Commune* was cited with approval.

3. *Exception d'illégalité*—The defence of illegality, which is often resorted to in order to contest the legality of an administrative act, is well known in the six member states of the Community. It can also be pleaded before the Community Court. In a leading case[3] Advocate-General Lagrange thus summarised the contribution of the six legal systems to the concept of *exception d'illégalité*:

". . . In three of the member states, France, Belgium and Italy, this *exception* is freely admitted, being considered as forming part of the

---

[3] Case 15/57: *Compagnie des Hauts Fourneaux de Chasse* v. *Haute Autorité*, (1958), 4 Rec. 155. See also *Meroni & Co., Industrie Metallurgiche, SpA* v. *High Authority* (1956), 4 Rec. 9; Cases 31, 33/62: *Milchwerke Wöhrmann & Sohn K.G.* v. *E.E.C. Commission* (1963), C.M.L.R. 152; 8 Rec. 965.

normal sphere of application of the claim for annulment. This is due to the fact that in these three countries, rules made by the executive power are considered, as far as the right to appeal against them is concerned, from the formal point of view, that is to say being administrative acts they are liable to be annulled if they are contrary to the law. Given that the direct claim for annulment is possible with regard to them, there is no objection in principle to the [judicial] control of their legality being also exercised when individual claims are made of which they are the object. The advantage is that the *exception* may be set up at any time, even when the time limit for a claim against the regulation or the general decision has expired. On the other hand, if the claim is successful only the individual decision is annulled, which avoids the grave consequences of the annulment of the regulation itself, declared with retrospective effect *erga omnes*.

As far as France is concerned we will cite, among many, two judgments of the Conseil d'État: *Abbé Barthélémy*, 9 July 1926, Recueil 713; *Marcin-Kowsky*, 28 November 1957, Recueil 548. These decisions are interesting because they begin by rejecting as presented out of time the submissions that the rule should be annulled, and, immediately following, pass judgment on the legality of the very same rule in respect of submissions directed against an individual decision applying the rule. Case law shows, however, that the legality of the rule can only be contested in respect of those of its provisions which provided the basis for the individual decision taken in application of the rule (*Dame Denayer*, 18 February 1949, Recueil 80).

In the three other countries of the Community, Germany, Holland and Luxembourg, there is a strong tendency to remain attached to the material criterion, by virtue of which a regulation is a piece of secondary legislation no different in its legal nature from the law itself. Nevertheless the subordination of the rule to the (general) law remains an established legal principle and, if the former conception causes some hesitation with regard to direct claims for annulment of regulations, the second conception, on the other hand, more readily permits the setting up of the *exception d'illégalité*. In criminal law this *exception* is very freely admitted. The principal difficulties in the latter field lie mainly in determining which judge is competent to rule on the question of legality: that happens, particularly, in France, a country in which the principle of the separation of powers is very strictly applied and where, in consequence, a reference to the administrative court for a preliminary ruling on legality is often made in defiance of the principle according to which the judge in the action is also judge in respect of the *exception*, but such considerations do not arise where, as in the instant case, the same judge has competence.

Are there any special reasons for adopting a different solution for the application of the Treaty? We do not think so. On the contrary, article 41, which confers jurisdiction on the Court—without any restriction as to the nature of the grounds which may be put forward, nor as to the nature of the decision against which the claim is made— to give a preliminary ruling as to the validity of resolutions of the High Authority when the question arises in a dispute the subject of litigation before a national court is an added argument in favour of there being no restrictions, for there is no reason which could justify a more restrictive solution in respect of undertakings having direct access to the Court, than in respect of third parties who may on occasion need the Court's judgment with regard to a decision of the High Authority."

Since the study of cases is the best method of studying law the student will, no doubt, find in many cases decided by the Community Court the problems of legal concepts of which the three mentioned above are only examples.

Language and the Approximation of Laws

Under the directions of the Council the member states are committed to a process of approximation of their laws in the fields directly affecting the establishment and functioning of the Common Market. In fulfilling these obligations they are free to resort to their own methods and, what goes with it, their own legal language. However, two points must be borne in mind in this connection: that the direction comes from the Community and should, therefore, contain elements of uniformity; and that the member states, being committed to the ideal of the Common Market, should comply as best as they can with the spirit of the direction, at the expense, if necessary, of the letter of their law. Since approximation is not easy to achieve it requires at the Community level special skills of draughtsmanship and persuasion and, at the member states' level, a resolute Community orientation.

CHAPTER FOUR

Sources of Community Law

The phrase "source of law" can be used in several senses. It can mean the causes of law that is to say the creative elements which contribute to the making of the law and this can be the law itself. These may be historical facts devoid of any authority or political, social and economic conditions of the society which may, or may not, be regarded by the law as authoritative. The European Community owes its existence to international solidarity and the will to create a better Europe through economic cohesion. As "causes", or sources of Community Law they are rather remote and only of a passing interest to lawyers though lawyers ought to make themselves aware of "the 'grand design' underlying the European construction."[1] When considering the sources of the law lawyers look to the author of the law and the place where the law can be found.

I THE ORIGINS OF COMMUNITY LAW

Unlike the International Court of Justice at the Hague, which is directed to apply international conventions, international custom, the general principles of law recognised by civilised nations and judicial decisions and the teachings of the most highly qualified publicists of the various nations,[2] the Community Court is left without specific guidance. Each of the relevant Treaties is content with the direction that "the Court of Justice shall ensure that in the interpretation and application of this Treaty the Law is observed",[3] without actually defining the *law* or its sources. In spite of this the Court has functioned vigorously applying Community Law from a variety of sources.[4]

In the sense of the author or authority from which Community Law is derived we can distinguish between *primary* and *secondary* sources.

---

[1] Pescatore in Bathurst *et al. op. cit.* at pp. 32–34.
[2] Statute of the International Court of Justice, art. 38.
[3] E.E.C. art. 164; Euratom art. 136; E.C.S.C. art. 31—words "and justice" omitted but words "and of the regulations for its execution" added.
[4] See Bebr, G., *Judicial Control of the European Communities* (1962), p. 26.

PRIMARY SOURCES

(a) *The Treaties*[5]

The primary sources of Community Law consist of the three foundation Treaties (E.C.S.C., E.A.E.C. and E.E.C.) with their Annexes, and Protocols, which supplement the Treaties; the Convention on certain institutions common to the European Communities (1957); the Merger Treaty (1965); the Luxembourg Treaty on Budgetary Matters (1970); and the Treaty of Accession and its annexes (1972).

The foundation Treaties are "self executing"[6] treaties which means that, when ratified, they become law automatically within the member states. In contrast with "non-self-executing" treaties (which constitute international obligations but require implementing legislation before they become applicable in internal law), "self-executing" treaties must be applied directly by the municipal courts as the law of the land. A treaty is, by its nature, a contract between two or more states; it is not a legislative act. However, it may be regarded as a legislative act whenever it is designed by the signatory states as a declaration of their understanding of what a particular rule of law is, or an expressly formulated norm of future behaviour, or a constitution of an international organisation. The legislative nature of the E.E.C. Treaty is indicated by its purpose and specific provisions (arts. 227 and 247 (2)) and confirmed by the "Act concerning the Conditions of Accession and the Adjustment of the Treaties" (art. 2).[7] The status of the Protocols is the same as by virtue of art. 239 they "form an integral part" of the E.E.C. Treaty.

The content of the E.E.C. Treaty is complex not only because it creates institutions and defines the objectives of the Community, but also because it provides the basis and authority for Community legislation. It provides for an Executive, a Bureaucracy, a Parliament and a Court and charges these institutions with the execution of the Treaty. The Treaty remains a treaty, that is an agreement between the signatory states, but it differs from a typical treaty not only because it creates supra-national institutions but, more importantly, because, unlike a typical treaty, its execution has been taken out of the hands of the parties. The institutions it creates, notwithstanding their imperfections and limitations, can be likened to the corresponding institutions of the internal law. Their strength lies in the fact that certain important powers have been transferred or delegated by the states to these

---

[5] For a complete list of the Community treaties and related instruments see Appendix to the Treaty of Accession, Cmnd. 4862, I, pp. 137–44.

[6] On self-executing treaties see the judgment of Chief Justice Marshall in *Foster and Elam* v. *Neilson*, 2 Pet. 253 (U.S. 1829).

[7] Attached to the Treaty of Accession.

institutions making them quasi-autonomous. Their weakness lies in the fact that their functioning is contingent upon the continuous discharge of the Treaty obligations by the member states. If a country withdraws from the Community havoc could be caused but the Community would not come to an end and the institutions would not cease to function. But if a number of states withdrew the Community would cease to be a practical possibility. If we apply a juristic construction to the Treaty modelled upon internal law it can be argued that the Treaty is the Constitution of the Community[8] or, to use Judge Donner's phrase, that the member states have undertaken obligations "not simply on a reciprocal basis but primarily towards the new collectivity they set up".[9] The authors of this book subscribe to the constitutional theory in spite of arguments advancing an opposite opinion, namely that the Treaty is merely a bundle of contractual obligations.

In addition to the Constitution of the Community the Treaty contains what continental lawyers would term "ordinary legislation" implying thereby a hierarchy of legal norms.[10] The Treaty "legislation" is quite detailed in some areas, e.g. the customs union, and only in a general outline in others, e.g. taxation. The relationship between "constitutional" provisions and the "ordinary legislation" of the Treaty, obvious to continental lawyers but rather obscure to British lawyers, who are not familiar with the theory of hierarchy of legal norms, is of some practical importance as far as the legislative function of the Community organs is concerned. The point is whether the Treaty alone can provide sufficient authority for legislation by these organs or whether the growth of Community Law must depend on its original source, i.e. the power delegated by the member states. The answer seems to be in the affirmative, assuming, of course, that the Community organs do not act *ultra vires*. The Treaty could not have envisaged all the eventualities but in art. 235 [E.A.E.C. art. 203] provided a wide scope for Community initiatives, safeguarding at the same time the principle of legality through the instrumentality of the Court and the vital interests of the member states through the instrumentality of the Council. Thus, in order to attain the Community objectives the Council by a unanimous decision may take the appropriate measures (which, presumably, include appropriate legal measures) on the recommendation of the Commission and in consultation with the

---

[8] E.g. Wagner, H., *op. cit.*, p. 24 and Pescatore, P., *L'Ordre Juridique des Communautés Européennes* (1971), pp. 36 *et seq.*

[9] "The Constitutional Powers of the Court of Justice of the European Communities", 11 C.M.L. Review, 1974, p. 128.

[10] I.e. the Constitution, Acts of Parliament, legislative acts of the Executive and delegated legislation.

Assembly. These powers are wide but circumscribed by the Treaty and so, it was argued[11] that the provisions of art. 235 constitute no blanket authority for "implied powers". The problem did arise under the E.C.S.C. Treaty and the Community Court considered *ultra vires* the delegation of powers vested in the High Authority to an agency in Brussels set up for the purpose of operating a system of subsidies to equalise the cost of scrap iron.[12]

In order to supplement the powers of the Community organs (and thus, presumably, curtail the temptation to rely on "implied powers") a practice under the E.C.S.C. Treaty was established whereby a certain amount of law-making power was exercised by assembled representatives of the member states.[13] The practice spread to the E.E.C., the most interesting example of this being the decisions which resulted in the acceleration of the setting up of the customs union.[14] The legal nature of these devices (described as "acts of representatives"[15]) is obscure. They are regarded as "international agreements in simpled form"[16] and "borderline of International Law and Community Law".[17] These "acts of representatives" no doubt contribute to the development of Community Law and in a sense provide a substitute for the revision of the Treaty. A further dynamic application of art. 235 can be seen in the implementation of the Dublin agreement of 1975 on the adoption of the correcting mechanism in respect of the budgetary obligations of the member states.[18] Whilst unopposed use is made of art. 235 in order to bring about minor adjustments only a major re-structuring of the Community should necessitate a revision of the Treaty. However a substantial amendment of the Treaty through the backdoor of art. 235 seems unthinkable. Moreover an anticipated use of art. 235 as, e.g. in

---

[11] Wohlfarth, E., Everling, H., Glässner, H. J., Sprung, R., "Die Europäische Wirtschaftsgemeinschaft", *Kommentar zum Vertrage* (1960), comment (7) on art. 235.
[12] Case 9/56: *Meroni & Co., Industrie Metallurgiche, S.P.A.* v. *High Authority* (1958), 4 Rec. 9 at pp. 40–47.
[13] E.C.S.C. art. 69, concerning free movement of skilled labour (J.O. 586/55 and 1647/63); E.C.S.C. art. 70, concerning international railroad tariffs, (J.O. 607/55, 701/55, 130/56 and 431/59); see Kaiser, "Die im Rat vereinigten Vertreter der Regierungen der Mitgliedstaaten", *Festschrift Ophüls* (1965), pp. 107–24.
[14] J.O. 1217/60 and 1284/62.
[15] Brinkhorst, L. J., "Implementation of (non-self-executing) Legislation of the European Economic Community, including Directives", *Legal Problems of an Enlarged European Community*, edited by Bathurst, M. E., and Others (1972), p. 72.
[16] Pescatore, "La personalité internationale de la Communauté", *Les relations extérieures de la Communauté européenne unifiée* (Liège 1969), p. 585.
[17] Resolution following the parliamentary report by Burger (E.P. doc. 215/1968–69) concerning collective acts of the member states of the Community, J.O. 1969, C.
[18] *Bulletin of the European Communities* 1975, No. 3, p. 6.

the Draft Regulation on Company Mergers of 1973 may well precipitate difficulties already reflected in certain cases.[19] In the circumstances only a major re-structuring of the Community would necessitate, it seems, a revision of the Treaty.

The view that the Treaty provides the Constitution of the Community is fortified by the fact that so far recourse has been taken to the Community Court and Community Law rather than international law sources for the purpose of the interpretation of the Treaties and legislative acts made under the Treaties. The Court itself, through the Advocate-General Lagrange,[20] considered the role of general International Law as a source of Community Law rather limited because:

"... our Court is not an international tribunal, but is concerned with a community which has been created by six states and which resembles more a federation than an international organisation ... The Treaty ... although concluded in the form of international treaties and undoubtedly being one, nevertheless also constitutes, from a substantive point of view, the character of the Community and as a consequence the legal provisions derived from the Treaty must be viewed as the internal law of the Community. As for the sources of this Law, nothing prevents that in a given case they may be sought in international law, however normally, and most frequently, they are found in the municipal law of the Member States. ..."

An international treaty creating rights and obligations of states may be regarded as special law within the general compass of international law. The point which concerns the E.E.C. Treaty as a source of law is whether the obligations contained therein can be derogated from by reference to general principles of international law. One of such general rules (albeit discredited through abuse) is the doctrine of necessity,[1] which suggests that states in cases of extreme emergency may resort to breaches of international law. As states are rather prone to resort to legal subterfuge under the guise of real or imagined emergency[2] art. 226 of the E.E.C. Treaty provides a specific procedure to deal with such situations within the complexity of the Common

---

[19] *Continental Can Co. Inc.*, *op. cit.*, at pp. 32, 52, 273, 275. Cases 160–161/73 R: *Miles Druce & Co., Ltd.* v. *E.E.C. Commission*, [1974] E.C.R. 281; [1974] 1 C.M.L.R. 224; [1974] 2, C.M.L.R. D.17.

[20] In Case 8/55: *Fédération Charbonnière de Belgique* v. *High Authority* (1956), 2 Rec. 151, at p. 263.

[1] Oppenheim, L., *International Law*, Vol. 1 (8th edn. 1955), pp. 297 *et seq.*, and Brownlie, I., *International Law and the Use of Force by States* (1963), pp. 40–44.

[2] Cf. the measures taken by the Labour Government when coming to power in 1967 which resulted in breaches of several treaties.

Market. Accordingly, as decreed by the Community Court,[3] the plea of necessity cannot succeed in face of art. 226. Furthermore, having safeguarded certain state interests (e.g. arts. 36, 56 (1), 108, 223) the Treaty has reduced[4] the scope of arbitrary "emergency" action states may be tempted to take in protection of their "sovereign rights".

There is, however, no reason why a rule of International Law recognised by the member states as a general rule of law should not be applied in the Interpretation of the Treaties or Community legislation. Thus, e.g., in *Van Duyn* v. *Home Office*[5] the Community Court upheld the principle of International Law that, whilst a state has a duty of receiving its own nationals, it has no such duty in respect of the nationals of another state. In *Nold* v. *E.C. Commission* 'the Court considered that "international agreements in which the member states have participated or to which they have adhered contain indications which have to be taken into account within the framework of Community Law" but in an earlier case[7] the Court held that "the validity of acts of the institutions within the meaning of art. 177 of the Treaty cannot be tested against a rule of International Law unless that rule is binding on the Community and capable of creating rights of which interested parties may avail themselves in a court of law".

In the light of the above it seems that the Community, being an autonomous organisation created within the framework of International Law, is governed by its own law and its Court will apply the rules of International Law only if such rules are relevant to the definition of Community rights.[8]

As far as the pre-membership treaty obligations are concerned the Community respects these (art. 37 (5)) but expects the members states to eliminate any incompatibilities (art. 234) so that each member state is in line with the others and its Community obligations. As regards future treaty obligations, membership of the Community entails a certain limitation of their treaty-making power (art. 113) whilst the treaties made by the Community in its autonomous capacity shall be binding upon the Community and the member states as well (art. 228

---

[3] Case 7/61: In *Re Quantitative Restrictions on Italian Pork Imports*, [1962] C.M.L.R. 39 at pp. 52, 56; 7 Rec. 633.
[4] Commission decision of 23 July 1968, No. 68/301/EEC, authorising the French Government to take certain measures under art. 108 (3).
[5] *Op. cit.*, p. 57.
[6] Case 4/73: [1974] E.C.R. 491 at p. 507; [1974] 2 C.M.L.R. 338 at p. 354.
[7] Case 9/73: *Schlütter* v. *Hauptzollamt Lörrach*, [1973] E.C.R. 1135 at p. 1157.
[8] *Van Duyn, op. cit.*; Cases 21–24/72: *International Fruit Co.* v. *Produktschap voor Groenten en Fruit* (1972), 18 Rec. 1219 at 1227.

(2)). It follows that whilst the member states are free to enter into treaties with third parties they must bear in mind their Community obligations when doing so (art. 234).[9]

(b)   Conventions Between Member States

As each country remains sovereign and retains its own legal system it has become necessary to enter into separate conventions between the member states. All this is but a stage in the harmonisation of municipal laws and the elimination of conflicts in the field of commercial laws with which the Common Market is particularly concerned. According to art. 220 member states ought to negotiate conventions to secure for the benefit of their nationals the protection of rights, abolition of double taxation, mutual recognition of companies and reciprocal recognition and enforcement of judgments of municipal courts and arbitration awards. It goes without saying that such conventions shall have the force of treaties and be binding accordingly. By these conventions the member states can create new laws and, in view of the sovereign power of states, these laws can go far beyond the scope of the foundation Treaties. Should this be the case the Community Court might have to rule whether such laws, being in excess of the foundation Treaties, are cognisable by the Court as a source of Community Law. Rules seem to be devolving both by the Community Court and the national courts of the member states. Thus it was held by the Paris Court of Appeal that Community Law superseded rights and obligations arising from previous bilateral social security conventions between member states inconsistent with the foundation Treaty,[10] though the Community Court[11] held that Community Law would not prevent additional social benefits arising under municipal law.

Conventions between member states subsequent to the foundation Treaty were held by the Community Court unable to alter the existing Community Law[12] though doubts were cast on the position in the submissions of Advocate-General Roemer in *Re Tariff Quota on Wine*.[13]

Since the position is somewhat uncertain, a cautious approach should be adopted to the problem of conventions between member states as a source of Community Law. If they are consistent with the Treaty no

---

[9] Cf. Case 22/70: *Re E.R.T.A., E.C. Commission* v. *E. C. Council*, [1971] C.M.L.R. 335; 17 Rec. 263.

[10] *Nani* v. *Caisse d'Assurance Vieillesse des Travailleurs Salariés de Paris*, [1964] C.M.L.R. 334; 4 C.M.L.Rev. 70–71.

[11] Case 92/63: *Moebs* v. *Bestuur der Sociale Verzekeringsbank*, [1964] C.M.L.R. 338 at p. 347; 10 Rec. 557.

[12] Case 33/64: *Krankenkasse der Heseper Torfwerk GmbH* v. *van Dijk*, [1966] C.M.L.R. 191 at p. 208; 11 Rec. 131.

[13] Case 24/62, [1963] C.M.L.R. 347 at pp. 361–362; 9 Rec. 129.

problem should arise but inconsistency *per se* would not, it seems, necessarily import a breach of the Treaty. Inconsistency with the letter of the Treaty furthering nevertheless the objectives of the Treaty should be acceptable as the law willed by the member states but inconsistency distorting in effect the concept of the Community could not be regarded as binding the Community and the Community Court, though they may well create rights and obligations enforceable under the general rules of international law.

The scope of the conventions envisaged in art. 220 is wider than the scope of the approximation of laws under arts. 100–102. However, so far little progress has been achieved and we can record Conventions on the Jurisdiction and Enforcement of Civil and Commercial Judgments (1968), signed in 1969, and in force in the original six member states as from 1 February 1973, and Mutual Recognition of Companies and Bodies Corporate (1968), signed in 1969, Trade Marks, Patents (1963), Know-How (1967), Bankruptcy (1970) and Merger of Companies (1973) but still in draft form. As a result of these conventions a new body of law will come into being, a law broadly founded upon the Treaty but in fact emanating from direct legislation by sovereign states within the Community. In view of the part taken by the Commission in the drafting of these conventions inconsistencies with the spirit of the Treaty should not occur. As a drafting exercise they present a challenge to Community lawyers as they ought to reflect the best elements of the laws of the member states and produce a working compromise.

We have observed earlier that the Community, as a legal person, enjoys treaty-making powers. The question which has to be considered is whether, and if so in what circumstances, conventions between the Community and the outside world are binding upon the member states and thus become a source of Community Law. The treaty-making powers of the Community, unlike that of a state, is not unlimited for by virtue of art. 228 the Community can enter into agreements with the states and international organisations where so provided by the Treaty. It provides further that such agreements shall be binding upon the member states if concluded in accordance with the procedure laid down in art. 228.

Accordingly such conventions shall be negotiated by the Commission and concluded by the Council after consulting the Assembly. In order to ensure that the convention is consistent with the Treaty the Council, the Commission and any member state may seek the opinion of the Community Court.[14] It follows that by submitting to the Treaty the

---

[14] See Opinion 1/75, Re the O.E.C.D. Understanding on a Local Cost Standard, [1976] 1 C.M.L.R. 85.

member states delegate to the Community an important portion of their sovereign power to create international obligations and new laws in as far as the Convention may be a source of law.[15] The delegation is not absolute for it is exercised subject to the participation of each member state in Council and the recourse to the Court. However, the Court acts as the watchdog of the Community legality but not of the interests of the member states.

So far a number of conventions have come into being resulting in a network of relations between the Community and the outside world.[16] These bind the Community with states which have a special interest in West European co-operation as well as states which, being the former dependencies of the member states of the Community, retained their economic ties with them. The result is a trade preference scheme now to be extended to a number of under-developed countries.[17] Further developments in this direction have led to free trade agreements with the E.F.T.A. countries (Austria, Switzerland, Iceland, Norway, Finland, Sweden and Portugal) and may also lead to a trade platform between the Community and the East European Council for Mutual Economic Co-operation (the Comecon). In the seventies the volume of trade between the E.E.C. countries and the East European People's Democracies has increased considerably and by the end of 1975 most of the long-term trade agreements with these countries will have expired. In 1974 the E.C. Council announced that it would enter into Community trade agreements with each of the Comecon countries which already had trade treaties with the member states of the E.E.C. and elaborated a pro forma agreement in this respect. As direct discussions between the E.E.C. and the Comecon with the object of regularising trade relations between the two organisations have not produced any tangible results the present pattern of bi-lateral treaties subject to some E.E.C. Regulations[18] shall continue for the time being.

All these conventions, in so far as they shape the trade pattern between the Community and the outside world and thereby affect both the internal arrangement of the Community and the legal obligations of the member states, can be regarded as a source of Community Law.

---

[15] Cf. Sir Gerald Fitzmaurice, "Some Problems Regarding the Formal Sources of International Law", *Symbolae Verzijl*, p. 160, quot. by Durand, p. 16.

[16] See pp. 37 *et seq.*, above.

[17] *Ibid.*

[18] See Council Reg. No. 109/70 of 19 December 1969 establishing common rules for imports from State-trading countries and updated version of the Annex to the Reg. O.J. Vol. 18, C. 287/55, 15 December 1975 and Council Decision on uni-lateral import arrangements in respect of State-trading cou n tries No. 75/788; O.J. Vol. 18, No. L332, 29 December 1975.

SECONDARY SOURCES

By the secondary sources of Community Law we understand the law-making acts of the Community organs which result in a body of law generated by the Community itself in its quasi-autonomous capacity. The importance of the law-making power of the Community cannot be overemphasised because, as stated by a distinguished jurist, "the first and most essential means by which a supra-national organisation endeavours to carry out its objectives . . . resides in the law-making power".[19] In brief we are concerned with Community legislation.

Legislation denotes rules of law made deliberately in the prescribed form by some competent authority. The founding Treaties carefully avoid the term *legislation* and refer instead to *regulations*,[20] apparently, as has been suggested,[21] to ward off the wrath of the national parliaments likely to be provoked by the suggestion that an outside body shall usurp their legislative function. The Community Court also preferred to refer to *pouvoirs réglementaires*,[1] although on another occasion[2] references were made to *compétence réglementaire* (p. 687), *normative* (p. 688) and *légiférante* (p. 692). Without going into semantic niceties[3] the law-making power of the Community organs can be identified as one corresponding to a generally accepted notion of legislation. This means that it results in rules of conduct addressed to subjects of Community Law which emanate from a definite organ, are made in a set form and by virtue of the authority vested in the organ have a compulsory character.

The Community legislation consists of administrative and judicial acts emanating from the respective organs:

(1) *Administrative Acts*

These consist of regulations, directives and decisions made by the Council or the Commission in order to carry out their task in accordance with the Treaty (E.E.C. art. 189).

(a) *Regulations*—Regulations have a general scope, are "binding in their entirety" and are "directly applicable" in all member states

---

[19] Guggenheim, P., "Organisations économiques supranationales, independance et neutralité de la Suisse", *Rev. de droit suisse*, Vol. 82 (1963) II, p. 247.

[20] E.E.C. art. 182 (2), E.A.E.C. art. 161 (2), E.C.S.C. arts. 31 and 35 (1) and (2).

[21] Pescatore, P., "Les aspects fonctionnels de la Communauté économique européenne", *Les aspects juridiques du marché commun* (1958), p. 67; cf. Catalano, N., "La fusion des voies de droit", *Colloquium at Liège* (1965), p. 284.

[1] Case 15/57 (1958), 4 Rec. 190.

[2] Case 20/59 (1960), 4 Rec. at pp. 687, 688, 692.

[3] Morand, C. A., *La législation dans les Communautés Européennes* (1968), pp. 7–17.

(art. 189 (2), but under E.C.S.C. art. 14 "decisions" correspond to E.E.C. regulations). It follows that, apart from their applicability without the intermediary of the state, regulations are meant to be an instrument of uniformity within the Community. Uniformity is the desired aim but cannot always be achieved and so it may be necessary to leave implementation to the member states. The agricultural regulations illustrate the point and the problem, for they leave it to each state to execute in its own fashion the system of levies and restitutions, to establish the necessary procedures and impose sanctions. In some cases, e.g. the free movement of workers[4] and social security of migrant workers,[5] the regulations are too general to be applied directly without the necessary detailed rules which have to be worked out nationally. The regulation authorising Germany to accept the import of cattle from Denmark is a further variation on the theme as it concerns one country only and simply gives leave to take measures appropriate to the situation in hand.[6]

In order to constitute a regulation the act of the Community organ must comply with certain conditions. In the first place regulations must rest upon the authority of the Treaty which means that they are made where so provided by the Treaty; if not so provided by the Treaty that act cannot have the character of a regulation.[7] Regulations have to be reasoned (*motivés*) (art. 190) which in the submission of Advocate-General Lagrange[8] means that they indicate in general terms the aims pursued by the regulations, the reasons which justify the regulations and the outlines of the system adopted. The degree of motivation depends, of course, on the type of regulation in hand. The Community Court[9] has pointed out that the requirements of motivation differ as to whether the act is of a general or specific character. The former require a more detailed motivation than the latter but it is not necessary to give reasons for each provision of the text, assuming that the provisions are clear and fall into the general pattern of the system. The specific type of regulation, as in the case of the German import of cattle from Denmark, need not be spelt out in any great detail though it has to be based on the Treaty as it concerns a matter of interest to the Common Market. The justification for motivation is clear for it is a safeguard against arbitrary decisions on the part of both the Community and the member states.

---

[4] Reg. 1612/68, J.O. 1968, No. L. 257/2, art. 4 (12) (13) (15).
[5] Reg. 3, J.O. 56/58, art. 52 (2).
[6] Reg. 15/64, J.O. 573/64.
[7] This can be inferred from the judgment of the Community Court in Case 14/57: *Soc. des Usines à Tubes de la Sarre* v. *High Authority* (1957), 3 Rec. 222, referring to "decision" under the E.C.S.C. Treaty.
[8] Case 18/62: *Barge* v. *High Authority* (1963), 9 Rec. 578.
[9] *Ibid.*

Regulations have to be published in the Official Journal of the Community. They become binding on the date specified or, in the absence of a commencing date, on the twentieth day following their publication (art. 191). However, neither the publicity nor the form of the act will be decisive in determining the nature of the act, that is whether or not it is a regulation. The Community Court took the view that it was necessary to consider the contents rather than the form of the act to determine its legal nature[10]. Should this be otherwise, improper acts dressed up as regulations would enable the Community organs to exercise their powers arbitrarily and so would erode the legal protection under the Treaty.

As we have observed earlier, regulations have a mandatory effect. They bind the states and have the force of law in their territories without the need of transformation or confirmation by their legislatures. Thus it was held by the Community Court[11] that Council Regulation 1975/69 and Commission Regulation 2195/69, which provided for the payment of a premium in respect of slaughtered dairy cows, were "directly applicable" and required no domestic provisions to make them effective in Italy. The position of regulations *vis-à-vis* the municipal law has been firmly established by the Community Court ruling in another case that a regulation cannot be overriden by subsequent national legislation inconsistent with it.[12]

Since both the Council and the Commission are empowered to make regulations, a theoretical and practical question of precedence between these two organs may arise. Indeed Advocate-General Roemer argued in a case[13] concerning regulations issued by the Council that they should override regulations issued by the Commission. Theoretically there should be no conflict, practically a conflict can arise if powers are delegated as seems possible under art. 87. The problem resolves itself into a question of interpretation. Thus it was held[14] that under art. 155 (4) (exercise of powers conferred on the Commission for the implementation of the rules laid down by the Council) there can be

---

[10] Cf. Cases 16 and 17/62: *Confédération nationale des producteurs des fruits et légumes* v. *E.E.C. Council*, [1963] C.M.L.R. 160 at pp. 173–174; 8 Rec. 901 at pp. 917–918.
[11] Case 93/71: *Orsolina Leonesio* v. *Italian Ministry of Agriculture*, [1973] C.M.L.R. 343; 18 Rec. 287.
[12] Case 6/64: *Costa* v. *ENEL*, [1964] C.M.L.R. 425 at p. 456; 10 Rec. 1141 at p. 1143; Case 43/71: *Politi S.A.S.* v. *Italian Ministry of Finance*, [1973] C.L.M.R. 60; 17 Rec. 1039 at p. 1049.
[13] Case 32/65: *Italian Government* v. *E.E.C. Council and E.E.C. Commission*, 32/65, [1969] C.M.L.R. 39 at p. 46; 12 Rec. 563.
[14] In cases 11/2–79/67: *Re Export of Oat Flakes*, [1969] C.M.L.R. 85.

no delegation of powers by the Council and that, consequently, art. 235 could not be relied on in order to justify delegation of discretionary power to the Commission in respect of export security.

Over the years regulations have been mounting steadily indicating that this is a measure favoured by the Community organs. In view of their impact upon the municipal laws the newcomers to the Community have been warned accordingly.[15]

(b) *Directives*—As compared with regulations which are, in principle, "binding in their entirety", directives issued by the Council and the Commission are "binding as to the result to be achieved, upon each Member State to which it is addressed" and the choice of the method is left to the state concerned (art. 189 (3), but under E.C.S.C. art. 14 recommendations correspond to directives). We can see that, unlike regulations, directives are not meant to be an instrument of uniformity even if the same objective is aimed at when a directive is addressed to several states simultaneously. In practice, therefore, directives are used to effect approximation of national laws as testified by the Community activity in this field.[16]

Directives must be addressed to states, they cannot be addressed to individuals.[17] This does not preclude creation of rights for individuals or pleading the directive before the municipal courts.[18]

Whilst the choice of the method is left to the addressee the Community usually sets a time limit upon the implementation of the directives which, like regulations, emanate either from the Council or the Commission. The reason for this is that time is needed in order to adapt the municipal law accordingly. Even so states are not always able to comply promptly. The speed with which the Value Added Tax was introduced in Italy is a good example of this, showing, incidentally, that a directive is probably less effective than a regulation.

Like regulations directives have to be reasoned or "motivated" and based on the Treaty (art. 190). They have to be notified to the

---

[15] Brinkhorst, L. J., "Implementation of (non-self-executing) Legislation of the European Economic Community, including Directives", *Legal Problems of an Enlarged European Community*, edited by Bathurst, M. E., and Others (1972), p. 74.
[16] See *Third General Report of the Communities* (1970), para. 63.
[17] Cases 56–58/64: *Consten and Grundig* v. *E.E.C. Commission*, [1966] C.M.L.R. 418 at p. 468; 12 Rec. 429.
[18] E.g. directive 64/221/EEC, J.O. 850/64, art. 4 (3): "The member states cannot introduce new measures or acts which are of a more restrictive nature than those in force at the time of notification of this directive"; cf. Case 28/67: *Molkerei-Zentrale* v. *Hauptzollamt Paderborn*, [1968] C.M.L.R. 187; 14 Rec. 211; see also Case 9/70: *Grad* v. *Finanzamt Traunstein*, [1971] C.M.L.R. 1; 16 Rec. 825 (directives on turnover tax); Case 41/74: *Van Duyn* v. *Home Office (No. 2.)*, [1975] 3 All E.R. 190; [1975] E.C.R. 337; [1975] 1 C.L.M.R. 1 (directive 64/221 on the freedom of movement).

addressees and will take effect upon such notification (art. 191). They may be addressed in the language of the addressee state.[19]

As a source of Community Law directives appear less prominent than regulations but their potential should not be underestimated. Their direct effect in the member states, i.e. whether they create rights which the citizen can vindicate in his national courts, has been subject to controversy. The Belgian Counseil d'Etat held[20] that a directive purporting to co-ordinate the rules of deportation of foreign nationals had such effect in Belgium, but a distinguished Italian jurist[1] considers that they have no direct effect. Being addressed to the states and having to be implemented by the states in whatever manner they deem appropriate, directives, by their designation appear to have an indirect effect. However, in substance they may well be sufficiently explicit and detailed to make transformation a mere formality. In such a case, if inconsistent with municipal law, they should have an overriding effect. This seems to be the tenor of the decision of the Belgian Conseil d'Etat cited above. The Community Court was more definite in this respect. In *Grad* v. *Finanzamt Traunstein*[2] the Court stated that "if, in accordance with art. 189, regulations are directly applicable and consequently are, by their very nature, capable of producing direct legal effects, it does not follow that the other acts mentioned in this article can never have similar effects" and concluded that "the provisions of the decision and of the directives, taken together, produce direct effects in the relations between the member states and their citizens and create for the latter the right to enforce them before the courts." In a later case[3] the Court restated its position saying that "if, in respect of member states to which it is addressed, the provisions of a directive have no less binding an effect than that of any other rule of Community law, such an effect applies all the more to provisions relating to the time limits for implementing the measures provided for." It follows that the potential of directives as a source of law is quite considerable, the exploitation of this potential depending largely upon the skill of the Community draftsmen. In practice the clear-cut distinction between regulations and directives implied in the wording of art. 189 has been blurred.

---

[19] Council Regulation 1/58, art. 3, J.O., 6 October 1958, p. 385/58 (5th Edn. 1952–1958, p. 59).

[20] *Corvelyn* v. *Belgium*, 7 October 1968; [1969] Cahiers de droit européen 343, at pp. 345–46.

[1] Catalano, N., *Manuel de Droit des Communautés Européenes* (2nd Edn. 1965), p. 135.

[2] *Op. cit.*, p. 84, note 18; 16 Rec. 825 (at p. 838).

[3] Case 79/72: *E.C. Commission* v. *Italy, Re Forestry Reproductive Material*, [1973] E.C.R. 667 at p. 672; [1973] C.M.L.R. 773 at p. 781.

(c) *Decisions*—A decision of the Council or the Commission is binding in its entirety upon those to whom it is addressed (art. 189 (4)). It may be addressed either to member states or to individuals or corporations. It must be reasoned (art. 190) and notified to whom it is addressed though no particular form of notification is needed[4]. It takes effect upon notification.

Unlike a regulation a decision is binding upon the addressee only, but, unlike a directive, it is "binding in its entirety" leaving no discretion in the manner in which it is to be carried out. However, a decision may be the result of an obligation imposed on the Commission by a regulation.[5] The term "decision" has of course a special meaning to denote one of the sources of Community Law. It is not, therefore, a mere conclusion of a process of reasoning or settlement or solution of a problem. Furthermore it is not a mere repetition of an established rule,[6] or a stage in internal procedure,[7] or an instruction to an agency set up by the Community.[8] The many cases under art. 14 of the E.C.S.C. Treaty provided an opportunity for the Community Court to define the meaning of "decision" and the definition in one of such cases seems apposite to the position under the E.E.C. Treaty. The Court held that "a decision must appear as an act originating from the competent organisation intended to produce judicial effects, constituting the ultimate end of the internal procedure of this organisation and according to which such organisation makes its final ruling in a form allowing its nature to be identified".[9]

Whether an administrative act of the organs of the Community is a regulation, directive or decision is determined not by its form but by its content and object,[10] or, as put by the Advocate-General Roemer,[11] it is the function of the act rather than the process of its formation which should be primarily examined.

Under art. 33 of the E.C.S.C. Treaty a distinction is made between

---

[4] Case 6/72: *Continental Can Case*, [1973] E.C.R. 215 at p. 221.
[5] Case 16/65: *Schwarze* v. *Einfuhr- und Vorratsstelle für Getreide und Futtermittel*, [1966] C.M.L.R. 172; 11 Rec. 1081.
[6] Case 9/56: *Meroni* v. *High Authority* (1958), 4 Rec. 9.
[7] Cases 53–54/63: *Lemmerzwerke GmbH* v. *High Authority*, [1964] C.M.L.R., 384 at p. 399; 9 Rec. 487.
[8] Case 21/58: *Fetten und Guilleaume Carswerke Eisen- und Stahl A.G.* v. *High Authority* (1958), 5 Rec. 211.
[9] Case 54/65: *Compagnie des Forges de Châtillon, Commentry et Neuves Maisons* v. *High Authority*, [1966] C.M.L.R. 525 at p. 538; 12 Rec. 265.
[10] Case 16–17/62: *Confédération Nationale des Producteurs de Fruits et Légumes* v. *E.E.C. Council*, [1963] C.M.L.R. 160 at pp. 173–174; 8 Rec. 901 at pp. 916–918.
[11] Case 40/64: In *Sgarlata* v. *E.E.C. Commission*, [1966] C.M.L.R. 314 at p. 318; 11 Rec. 279.

general and individual decisions depending on the manner in which the addressees are affected.[12] General decisions are "quasi legislative acts made by a public authority and having a rule-making effect *erga omnes*".[13] Individual decisions were held to be decisions in which the competent authority had to "determine such concrete cases as are submitted to it".[14] In the cited case the High Authority had to determine the principles concerning the calculation of contribution towards compensation due from certain undertakings.

The problem under the E.E.C. Treaty is one of "mixed acts" that is to say acts with the character of regulations[15] and decisions or directives[16] and decisions. Such mixed measures seem impossible under the E.C.S.C. Treaty[17] but they came to light under the E.E.C. Treaty. Assuming that such measures are valid *per se* the practical question of the scope of their application arises or, more precisely, whether they affect individuals apart from states and whether they can give recourse to individuals under art. 173 (2). It was held[18] that a measure which could be classified as a regulation could contain provisions applicable to individuals and thus enable them to take action under art. 173 (2). On the other hand, a Commission decision merely to reject a claim for amendment of a regulation will be treated as analogous to a regulation[19] with the result that an individual may not have the necessary *locus standi* under art. 173 (2) which provides that "any natural or legal person may . . . institute proceedings against a decision addressed to that person or against a decision which, although in the form of a regulation or a decision addressed to another person, is of direct and individual concern to the former".

The problem[20] of a directive and decision was raised by the *Finanzgerichte* (Finance Courts) of Munich (Case 9/70), Baden-Würtemberg (Case 20/70) and Düsseldorf (Case 23/70) which moved the Community Court to rule whether art. 4 of *Decision* 65/271/EEC, J.O.

---

[12] Case 18/57: *Nold* v. *High Authority*, 5 Rec. 89, 112; Cases 55–59/63, 61–63/63: *Modena* v. *High Authority*, [1964] C.M.L.R. 401 at p. 413; 10 Rec. 413.
[13] *Nold*, 5 Rec. 89 at p. 113.
[14] Case 20/58: *Phoenix-Rheinrohr* v. *High Authority*, 5 Rec. 192–193.
[15] E.g. *Plaumann*, *op. cit.*, p. 68.
[16] E.g. *Consten* v. *Grundig*, *op. cit.*, p. 74, note 17.
[17] *Nold*, above, and Case 8/55: *Fédération Charbonnière de Belgique* v. *High Authority*, 2 Rec. 151 at p. 206; also Advocate-General Lagrange in Case 30/59: *Gezamenlijke Steenkolenmijnen in Limburg* v. *High Authority*, 7 Rec. 1 at p. 68.
[18] In Case 30/67: *Industria Molitovia Imolese* v. *E.E.C. Council*, (1968) 5 C.M.L. Rev. 480; 14 Rec. 171.
[19] Case 42/71: *Firma Nordgetreide GmbH* v. *E.E.C. Commission*, [1973] C.M.L.R. 177.
[20] Brinkhorst, L. J., *op. cit.*, p. 75; and Mitchell, J. D. B., "Community Legislation", *ibid.*, p. 100.

1500/65, read together with art. 1 of the first *Directive* on Turnover Tax, J.O. 1301/67 "are directly binding in the relations between Member States and private persons and create individual rights which can be invoked before municipal courts". The Community Court ruled that art. 189 does not prevent private individuals from founding their actions before municipal courts upon *Directives* and *Decisions* addressed to member states. Concluding that these measures can have, in appropriate cases, an internal effect, a learned jurist remarked that, as a result, an important barrier against the legal protection of private parties against these Community measures has been removed.[1]

(d) *Recommendations and Opinions*—It is debatable whether recommendations[2] and opinions[3] can be regarded as sources of Community Law. These are listed in art. 189 of the E.E.C. Treaty as attributes of the power of the Council and Commission necessary for the execution of their task but, unlike regulations, directives and decisions, are said to have "no binding force". Unfortunately there is a certain terminological confusion resulting from the interaction of the three foundation treaties as the basic sources of Community Law. The law-making acts of the E.C.S.C. (art. 14) differ from those of the E.E.C. (art. 189) and E.A.E.C. (art. 161). The High Authority of the E.C.S.C. can make *decisions* which are mandatory in all their aspects and *recommendations* within the scope defined by the Treaty, the choice of the methods of executing recommendations being left to those to whom they are addressed. In this way *decisions* of the E.C.S.C. correspond to both *regulations* and *decisions* of the E.E.C. whilst *recommendations* of the E.C.S.C. correspond to *directives* of the E.E.C. and the E.A.E.C. The High Authority of the E.C.S.C. can promulgate opinions which are not binding.

Taking the binding force as a criterion of the authority of the acts of the Community organs *opinions* cannot be regarded as a source of Community Law but *recommendations* can only in so far as they are made under the E.C.S.C. Treaty. *Recommendations* under the E.E.C. Treaty have no force of law. The existence of "non-binding" acts is not exclusive to the European Community. Such acts are typical of international organisations of sovereign states,[4] which in theory cannot

---

[1] Brinkhorst, L. J., *op. cit.*, p. 76.
[2] E.g. Re Luxembourg Agricultural Policy 65/300/E.E.C. 26 May 1965, (1965) C.M.L.R. 355.
[3] E.g. Case 7/61: *Re Quantitative Restrictions on Italian Pork Imports*, 7 Rec. 633 at p. 654; (1962) C.M.L.R. 39 at p. 50.
[4] Cf. Sloan, B., "The Building Force of a 'Recommendation' of the General Assembly of the United Nations", (1948), 25 B.Y.B.I.L. 1; Johnson, D. H., "The Effect of Resolutions of the General Assembly of the United Nations", (1955–56), 32 B.Y.B.I.L. 97.

take orders from outside. The European Community, in spite of some measure of cohesion, still remains a community of sovereign states and so it has to be recognised that the Community organs have to carry out a variety of functions, some of which call for legislation, others for guidance.[5] Therefore, neither recommendations nor opinions of the Council and Commission should be disregarded. Their role is persuasive and constructive in the formulation and execution of the policies of the Community. Though they cannot be formally cited as sources of Community Law they ought to be regarded, in the light of their potential, as auxiliary elements of the law making process of the Community.

(e) *Control of the Community Legislation*—All the acts of the Community organs are subject to the principle of legality as is the case with the executive and administrative acts of a law-abiding state. This principle imposes a certain limit upon the Community organs as they have to operate within the scope of their organic powers (*infra legem*) or within the scope of their delegated powers. The Treaties are quite explicit in this respect. Article 4 of the E.E.C. Treaty provides that the functions of the Community shall be carried out by the Assembly, the Council, the Commission and the Court of Justice and that "each institution shall act within the limits of the powers conferred upon it by the Treaty".

If we accept the analogy of the E.E.C. Treaty to a state constitution we can construe a system of control of the acts of the Community organs parallel to that of the acts of state organs. In most systems we can note a triple form of control: constitutional, political (or parliamentary) and judicial, to which we can add for good measure the control by what passes for "public opinion".

Thus the constitution (Treaty) sets up the system and defines the functions and powers of the state (Community) organs. The constitutional control is a strictly legal control in so far as it rests upon the assumption that the state itself is governed by law (*Rechtsstaat*, see Bracton on the Rule of Law) and that the machinery of the state operates according to law. Since all the member states of the Community subscribe to the notion of the *Rechtsstaat* there is no reason to suppose that the Community would be different.

Political or parliamentary control of the executive takes various forms: debate, questions, censure. The legislative acts of the executive are subject to parliamentary scrutiny and where breaches of the constitution are alleged the matter may be considered by a constitutional tribunal or (as in the case of the United Kingdom) parliament itself.

---

[5] Cf. Community Court judgment in joint Cases 1/57 and 14/57: *Société Usines à Tubes de la Sarre* v. *High Authority*, 3 Rec. 201 at p. 223.

This does not preclude a judicial review. The Assembly of the European Community can hardly be regarded as a parliament in the accepted sense of the word. It is a deliberative body and in a limited sense a controlling body. Its control is confined to the control of the Commission as the chief bureaucratic body but, not being a fully-fledged parliament, it neither legislates nor controls the legislative acts of the Community organs.

In the Community the control of legality is in the hands of the Community Court (E.E.C. arts. 164, 173, 177). Thus, apart from the duty of ensuring that the law is observed in the interpretation and application of the Treaty, the Court has the power of judicial review of the legality of acts of the Council and the Commission. These include regulations, directions and decisions which are "binding" but exclude recommendations and opinions which are "not binding". The legal status of the Community acts determines the scope of judicial control. It follows that only the "binding acts" may, in accordance with the Treaties (E.C.S.C. art. 33; E.E.C. art. 173; E.A.E.C. art. 146), be subject to judicial control.

The making, the notification and the publication of the binding acts are subject to the Court's scrutiny from the point of view of legality, form and publicity of these acts. The Court has jurisdiction in actions brought by a member state, the Council or the Commission and may pronounce nullity of the act concerned on grounds of "lack of competence, infringement of an essential procedural requirement, infringement of the Treaty or of any rule of law relating to its application, or misuse of powers" (E.E.C. art. 173 (1)).

A natural or legal person can also institute proceedings for the annulment of a decision addressed to that person or a decision which, "although in the form of a regulation or a decision addressed to another person, is of direct and individual concern to [the complainant]" (art. 173 (2)).

(2) *Judicial Legislation*

The Court has the duty of ensuring observance of the law and whilst doing so may explain and complement the Treaties and subordinate Community legislation. This gives the Court an opportunity of exercising a law-making power. The powers and functions of the Court will be analysed elsewhere[6] and it will suffice here to investigate the ways in which the Court may contribute to the sources of Community Law.

---

[6] See Chap. 9, below.

The Court, as a fully-fledged judicial body, has the power necessary to carry out its duties as specified in the Treaties. Its jurisdiction is exceptional in the sense that it is not a substitute for the national courts of the member states, and that its jurisdiction is circumscribed by the Treaties. In all respects it is the internal Court of the Community and as far as legal style is concerned it is a continental court modelled upon the French Conseil d'Etat.

The powers of the Court include:

(a) the power of annulment which is the instrument of legality of the acts of the Community organs (E.E.C. arts. 173, 174, 175, 184);

(b) the power of adjudication (*contentieux de pleine jurisdiction*) (E.E.C. arts. 169, 170, 171), which enables the Court to put pressure upon the member states in order to make them carry out their obligations;

(c) the power of repression (E.E.C. art. 172), which enables the Court to enforce Community Law;

(d) the power of arbitration (E.E.C. art. 181);

(e) the power to decide disputes between the member states (E.E.C. art. 182); and

(f) the power of interpretation of the Treaties, the acts of the Community organs and of the constitutions of bodies established by the Council (E.E.C. art. 177).

In so far as the Court has to ensure observance of the law it acts as an instrument of sovereignty; in so far as it has to ensure the correct interpretation and application of the law as regards both the functioning of the Community and the development of the Community Law, it exercises a law-making function appropriate to a judicial body. We shall address ourselves to the latter.

It is axiomatic that, given the requisite power, the lesser the precision of the law the greater the scope for judicial legislation. The Community Treaties are far from being precise and tightly drafted. In so far as they represent the Community framework it is the task of the Court to complete the system and fill the gaps.

Interpretation is the principal method, and since the Court is a continental court it has adopted what might be termed the "continental style".[7] In the civil law systems the court has no law-making power and precedent is not regarded as a source of law. However, through the instrumentality of interpretation judges are in the position of filling the gaps in the legal system and through the definition of rights and duties

---

[7] See pp. 43 *et seq.*, above.

in judgments they create a body of rules which, without any statutory authority, has a persuasive force. The Community Court is in a unique position: it is a court of first and only instance, it has the power to review the legality of the acts of the Community organs, has no parliament to look up to as a sovereign source of law and, above all, has to interpret Treaties which comprise general policies alongside precise rules of law.[8] In the circumstances the Community Court cannot help contributing to the growth of Community Law.

In the absence of any canons of interpretation the Court is free to draw on rules evolved in the member states and will do so not only in the spirit of the Community but also for practical reasons, because Community Law, in order to command general respect and acceptance has to be a synthesis of the laws of the member states and, at every stage of its growth, has to draw strength from the practices and principles already well established.

Literal, or grammatical, interpretation is always the basic method and where the meaning of the text is clear there is no need of interpretation for *clara non sunt interpretanda.* However, in the Community set-up Community legislation must conform to the relevant Treaty so much so that the clear language of an act of a Community organ must not be allowed to prevail if, in the light of the Treaty, it leads to absurdity.[9]

On the question of linguistic differences and inconsistencies between the different provisions of the Treaty, Advocate-General Roemer submitted in *Internationale Crediet- en Handelsvereniging 'Rotterdam'* v. *Ministry of Agriculture and Fisheries*[10] that the same standard of draftsmanship as that in the national legislation cannot be expected in Treaties.[11] Literal interpretation must take this into account.

Next to literal interpretation comes the logical interpretation which requires the Court to consider the text within the context of the system. In *Simon* v. *Court of Justice of the European Communities*[12] the Court held that where the text is ambiguous the most reasonable solution must be sought, and in *Technique Minière* v. *Maschinenbau Ulm GmbH*[13] the Court restricted prohibitions in the Treaty to matters which it considered detrimental to the aims of the Community. In

---

[8] Cf. submissions of Advocate-General Roemer in Case 13/60: *Ruhrkohlen Verkaufs-GmbH* v. *High Authority,* [1962] C.M.L.R. 113 at pp. 125, 128; 8 Rec. 165.

[9] Case 14/63: *Forges de Clabecq* v. *High Authority,* [1964] C.M.L.R. 167 at p. 176; 9 Rec. 719; Case 2/67: *De Moor* v. *Caisse de Pension des Enployés Privés,* [1967] C.M.L.R. 223 at pp. 230–31, 235; Rec. 255.

[10] Cases 73–74/63, [1964] C.M.L.R. 198 at p. 206; 10 Rec. 1.

[11] Cf. Lord Denning MR in *H. P. Bulmer, Ltd.* v. *J. Bollinger S.A.,* [1974] 2 All E.R. 1226 at pp. 1231–1232.

[12] Case 15/60 (1961), 7 Rec. 225 at p. 245.

[13] Case 56/65, [1966] C.M.L.R. 357 at pp. 371, 376; 12 Rec. 337.

Re Import Duties on Sweet Oranges[14] Advocate-General Roemer submitted that the Court should be guided by considerations which make good sense both politically and administratively, and in *Costa v. ENEL*[15] Advocate-General Lagrange stated that excessive formalism should give way to the Community spirit in relations between the Community and the member states. In a more technical sense Advocate-General Lagrange put in a nutshell the purpose of logical interpretation when he stressed in *Bosch v. de Geus*[16] that the Court must not be defeated by obscurities or contradictions in the wording of the text for the real meaning can be deduced from the context or spirit of the text. In this vein several cases have been decided illustrating both the technique and law-making potential of logical interpretation.[17]

Courts are notoriously reticent about the use of teleological interpretation which, though basically literal, brings out the intention of the legislature in the light of the conditions prevailing at the time of the judgment. The Treaties have not existed long enough to have, in the absence of revision, their lives extended by interpretation, but references to the spirit or the aims of the Treaties[18] enable the Court to fill the gaps in the system and so "up-date" the text.

---

[14] Case 34/62, [1963] C.M.L.R. 369 at p 380; 9 Rec. 269.

[15] Case 6/64, [1964] C.M.L.R. 425 at p. 448; 10 Rec. 1141.

[16] Case 13/61, [1962] C.M.L.R. 1 at p. 23; 8 Rec. 89.

[17] E.g. Case 10/61 : *Re Italian Customs Duty on Radio Valves*, [1962] C.M.L.R. 187 at pp. 201–202; 8 Rec. 1, ref. to arts. 12, 14 (1) and 19 (2) (III); Case 75/63 : *Unger v. Bestuur der Bedrijfsvereniging voor Detailhandel en Ambachten*, [1964] C.M.L.R. 319; 10 Rec. 347, ref. to art. 51 ; Case 24/62: *Re Tariff Quota on Wine*, [1963] C.M.L.R. 347 at pp. 366–367; 9 Rec. 129, ref. to arts. 25 (3) and 29; Case 10/65: *Deutschmann v. Aussenhandelsstelle für Erzeugnisse der Ernährung und Landwirtschaft*, [1965[C.M.L.R. 259; 11 Rec. 601, ref. to arts. 13 and 95; Case 27/67; *Fink-Frucht GmbH v. Hauptzollamt München*, [1968] C.M.L.R. 228 at p. 299; 14 Rec. 327, ref. to arts. 30 and 95; Case 29/68: *Milch- Fett- und Eierkontor GmbH v. Hauptzollamt Saarbrücken*, [1969] C.M.L.R. 390; 15 Rec. 165, ref. to arts. 9, 12, 13; case 13/72: *Re Food Aids : Netherlands v. E.C. Commission*, [1973] E.C.R. 27 at pp. 40–42; see also the opinion of A. G. Roemer in Case 5/71: *Aktien-Zuckerfabrik Schoppenstedt v. E.E.C. Council*, 17 Rec. 975 at p. 997 and A. G. Warner in Case 81/72: *Re Civil Service Salaries E.C. Commission v. E.C. Council*, [1973] E.C.R. 575 at pp. 595–596; [1973] C.M.L.R. 639 at pp. 652–653.

[18] E.g. Case 56/65: *Technique Minière v. Maschinenbau Ulm GmbH*, [1966] C.M.L.R. 357; 12 Rec. 337; Case 34/62: *Re Import Duties on Sweet Oranges*, [1963] C.M.L.R. 369; 9 Rec. 269; Case 6/64: *Costa v. ENEL*, [1964] C.M.L.R. 425; 10 Rec. 1141; Case 13/61: *Bosch v. de Geus*, [1962] C.M.L.R. 1; 8 Rec. 89; Case 6/54: *Royal Government of the Netherlands v. High Authority*, 1 Rec. 201 at p. 232; Case 6/60: *Jean E. Humblet v. The Belgian State* (1960) 6 (II) Rec. 1125 at pp. 1154, 1156; Case 8–11/66: *Re Noordwijks Cement Accoord*, [1967] C.M.L.R. 77 at pp. 104–105; 13 Rec. 93; Case 8/55: *Fédération Charbonnière de Belgique v. High Authority* (1956) 2 Rec. 151 at pp. 302–305; Case 16/61: *Modena v. High Authority*, [1962] C.M.L.R. 221 at p. 241; 8 Rec. 547; Continental Can, *op. cit.* [1973] E.C.R. at pp. 243–245; [1973] C.M.L.R. at pp. 223–225, 233–235; Case 151/73: *Ireland v. E.C. Council*, [1974] 1, C.M.L.R. 424 at pp. 446–447.

The Court does not act arbitrarily but judicially, which means that it has to see that its interpretation reflects the intention of the parties to the Treaties and the *ratio legis* of the text.[19] In tracing the intention the Court is free to consult materials extraneous to the Treaty. These consist of the *travaux préparatoires* leading to the conclusion of Treaties and statements on behalf of the Community. The former are the various publications which reflect the substance of the negotiations and the attitudes of the negotiating parties from the inception to the conclusion of the Treaties. One could single out in this context official communiques and minutes of meetings, should these be available, and the official views of the negotiating governments. In view of the nature of the negotiations and the way governments work in their international relations the materials available are not abundant. They have, according to a learned jurist,[20] "a certain value, though their precise juristic meaning is arguable". So far the Court does not seem to have taken much notice of the *travaux préparatoires* though the advocates-general have referred to these in their submissions.[1]

Statements on behalf of the Community may[2] elucidate the Community legislation but the views of the Community officials on the interpretation of the Treaties are hardly relevant.[3] They are equally ineffective as far as the interpretation of the Community legislation is concerned.[4]

It follows that *travaux préparatoires*, as explained by Advocate-General Lagrange[5] have no compulsory place in the interpretation of

---

[19] Case 6/60 (1960), *op. cit.* at p. 1154.

[20] Reuter, P., *La C.E.C.A.* (1953), p. 30.

[1] Cf. Lagrange in Case 8/55: *Fédération Charbonnière de Belgique* v. *High Authority* (1956), 2 Rec. 151; Roemer in Case 6/54: *Netherlands Government* v. *High Authority* (1955), 1 Rec. 201 at p. 247; Cases 90–99/63: *Re Import of Milk Products*, [1965] C.M.L.R. 58 at p. 65; 10 Rec. 1217; Case 13/60: *Ruhrkohlen-Verkaufs-GmbH* v. *High Authority*, [1962] C.M.L.R. 113 at p. 146; 8 Rec.165; Cases 73–74/63: *Internationale Crediet- en Handelsvereniging "Rotterdam"* v. *Ministry of Agriculture and Fisheries*, [1964] C.M.L.R. 198 at p. 207; 10 Rec. 1; Case 26/68: *Caisse Régionale de Securité Sociale du Nord* v. *Torrekens*, [1969] C.M.L.R. 377 at pp. 382–383; 15 Rec. 125 at p. 140; Gand in Case 38/69: *Re Customs Duties on Lead and Zinc*, [1970] C.M.L.R. 77 at p. 85; 16 Rec. 47 at p. 65; Case 47/72: A. G. Roemer in *Alfons Lütticke GmbH* v. *Hauptzollamt Passau*, [1973] E.C.R. 57 at p. 74–75; [1973] C.M.L.R. 309 at pp. 316–317.

[2] Cases 2–10/62: *Societa Industriale Acciaierie San Michele* v. *High Authority*, [1964] C.M.L.R. 146 at p. 165; 9 Rec. 661.

[3] Roemer in Cases 90–91/63: *Re Import of Milk Products*, [1965] C.M.L.R. 58 at p. 65; 10 Rec. 1217; Cases 8–11/66: *Re Noordwijks Cement Accoord*, [1967] C.M.L.R. 77 at p. 87; 13 Rec. 93.

[4] Cases 53–54/63: *Lemmerzwerke GmbH* v. *High Authority*, [1964] C.M.L.R. 384 at p. 398; 9 Rec. 487.

[5] Case 8/55: *Fédération Charbonnière de Belgique* v. *High Authority* (1956), 2 Rec. 151.

Treaties, but it is universally accepted that judges may turn to them for information in order to clarify the thoughts of the legislator. The judges are entirely free in their evaluation of these materials.

In addition to interpretation in a technical sense further elements play an auxiliary part in the development of Community Law. Of these we shall mention briefly references to the municipal laws of the member states, references to general principles of law and references to learned writings.

The Treaties, like the rules of public international law, are influenced by the rules of municipal law. More than that they are derived from the laws of the six founding states. It is natural, therefore, that the Community Court should turn for guidance to the laws of the member states. As submitted by Advocate-General Roemer[6] the Court has to "call upon the law of the different Member States in order to arrive at a meaningful interpretation of our Community Law". As a result some cases comprise a detailed comparative study. Perhaps the best examples are the cases involving misuse of power[7] and withdrawal, with retrospective effect, of an illegal administrative act.[8]

In the latter case the Court came to the conclusion that "a study of comparative law shows that whenever an administrative act is wrong in law, the laws of the Member States admit the possibility of revocation", and in accordance with this finding decreed that such an act was revokable with a retrospective effect. It does not follow, however, that the laws of all the member states must be consulted. If the problem is peculiar to two countries a consideration of the two systems will be sufficient,[9] and on occasions reference to one country only may suffice.[10] The other extreme, which the Court is free to adopt, is that sometimes a national system cannot be regarded as apposite.[11] More intriguing is the possibility of reference to the law of a non-member state, but this

---

[6] Case 6/54: in *Netherlands Government* v. *High Authority* (1955), 1 Rec. 201 at p. 232.
[7] See p. 67, above.
[8] See also cases 7/56 and 3–7/57: *Alegra* v. *Common Assembly* (1957), 3 Rec. 81 at pp. 114–115; Case 14/61: *Hoogovens* v. *High Authority*, [1963] C.M.L.R. 73 at pp. 90–91, 96; 8 Rec. 485; further examples: Campbell, A., *Common Market Law* (1969), Vol. I, 7.258, pp. 531–532.
[9] Lagrange in case 5/55: *Associazione Industrie Siderurgiche Italiane* v. *High Authority* (1955) 1 Rec. 263 at p. 288.
[10] French law: Cases 7 and 9/54: *Groupement des Industries Siderurgiques Luxembourgoises* v. *High Authority* (1956) 2 Rec. 53 at p. 120; Case 12/74: *E.C. Commission* v. *Federal Republic of Germany*, [1975] E.C.R. 18 at p. 209; German law: Case 18/57: *Nold* v. *High Authority*, Rec. (1959), 5 Rec. 89 at pp. 110–111; Cases 17 and 20/61: *Kloeckner Werke und Hoesch* v. *High Authority* (1962), Rec. 815 at pp. 650–651; E.C.R. 325 at pp. 351–353.
[11] E.g. case 1/64: *Glucosiéries Réunies* v. *E.E.C. Commission*, [1964] C.M.L.R. 596 at p. 599; 10 Rec. 811.

must be regarded as a special case. Indeed the Community Law of monopolies and restrictive practices, being modelled upon American Law, invites such a reference.[12] Before the British accession the English law of estoppel[13] was considered whilst recently Advocate-General Warner made a significant British contribution to the discussion of natural justice.[14]

Echoing art. 38 of the Statute of the International Court of Justice the Community Court also refers to "general principles of law". These can be traced to doctrines developed within the context of public international law[15] or the municipal law of the member states, but others remain untraceable.[16] No doubt the reference to "general principles of law" has a certain scope as such principles may mean general doctrines of the law, e.g. justice, the right to be heard, etc., or rules of law expressed in general terms, e.g. contractual freedom, liability for wrongful act, non-discrimination, etc. Learned commentators[17] recognise the competence of the Court to take recourse to "general principles of law". Their views have been summarised as follows: "il semble que lorsqu'une notion juridique existe, identique, dans le droit interne de tous les Etats membres, celle-ci s'impose aux organes de la Communauté comme un principe général qui doit être appliqué sous peine de la violation d'une règle de droit relative à l'application du traité".[18]

Finally we should note the contribution of learned writers (the so called *doctrine*) to the *Jurisprudence* of the Community Court. Here again an analogy to art. 38 of the Statute of the International Court of Justice comes to mind where reference is made to "the teachings of the most highly qualified publicists". Continental courts are familiar with the contribution of learned writers to the development of the law and

---

[12] Case 13/60: Roemer in *Ruhrkohlen-Verkaufs-GmbH* v. *High Authority*, [1962] C.M.L.R. 113 at p. 141; 8 Rec. 165; Case 16/61: *Modena* v. *High Authority*, [1962] C.M.L.R. 221 at pp. 229–230, 232; 8 Rec. 547.

[13] Roemer in Cases 41 and 50/59: *Hamborner Bergbau A.G. and Another* v. *High Authority* (1960), 6 (II) Rec. 989 at p. 1049. Cf. Case 48/72: *Brasserie de Haecht* v. *Wilkin (No. 2)*, [1973] E.C.R. 77 at p. 87; [1973] C.M.L.R. 287 at p. 302.

[14] Case 17/74: *Transocean Marine Paint Association* v. *E.C. Commission*, [1974] E.C.R. 1063; [1974] 2 C.M.L.R. 459.

[15] E.g. on equality and discrimination, Lagrange in *Re Electric Refrigerators*, 13/63, 13 July 1963; [1963] C.M.L.R. 289, at p. 303; 9 Rec. 335, on the status of international administrative tribunals; Roemer in Case 1/56: *Bourgaux* v. *E.C.S.C. Common Assembly* (1956); 2 Rec. 451.

[16] E.g. on the meaning of "discrimination" and "comparable price conditions to consumers in comparable circumstances" in *Barbara Erzbergbau and Others* v. *High Authority*, Cases 3–18 and 25–6/58, 10 May 1960; 6 (I) Recueil 367.

[17] Reuter, P., "Le recours de la Cour de justice des Communautés européennes à des principes généraux de droit", in *Mélanges Henri Rolin* (1964), p. 263.

[18] Mathijsen, P., *Le droit de la C.E.C.A.* (1958), p. 142.

these, to command authority, need not necessarily be dead. Community Law is still a relatively undeveloped system, a law in books rather than fully entrenched in life and, therefore, offers a challenge and scope for creative comments. *Doctrine* represents, of course, well founded opinions on what the law should be, not any piece of "creative writing", by those who have established a reputation in their field. Its influence should not be exaggerated but viewed from the perspective of the standing of the academic lawyer in the civil law countries and the closer affinity of continental judges to the academic world rather than the Bar. The fact that, in spite of the, abundance of academic writings on Community Law, the Court only in few cases, albeit through the advocates-general,[19] referred to juristic writings indicates both the scope and limitations of their contribution.

To sum up the contribution of the Community Court to the development of Community Law we have to distinguish between the *Jurisprudence* of the Court which alone can be regarded as a source of Community Law and the judicial processes as well as the factors taken into account in these processes which have only an auxiliary function.

Since *Jurisprudence* represents the body of case law evolved through interpretation of the texts a few comments on the role of precedents in the Community system seem necessary. The judgment of the Court can be divided into two parts: the *motifs* (reasons) and the *dispositif* (the ruling). From the parties' point of view the ruling is of a primary interest because, after all, it decides the issue. Indeed, under the doctrine of *res judicata* the judgment is binding upon the Court where there is an identity of parties, cause and object.[20] Apart from *res judicata* the Court is not bound by its previous decisions but this does not mean that precedents are ignored.

In the eyes of the continental lawyer precedents have only a persuasive force in the sense that they reflect the application of the law in practice.

---

[19] Roemer in Case 13/60: *Ruhrkohlen-Verkaufs-GmbH* v. *High Authority* [1962] C.M.L.R. 113 at p. 159; 8 Rec. 165, on oligopoly by a "noted author"; in Cases 106–107/63: *Toepfer K.G.* v. *E.E.C. Commission*, [1966] C.M.L.R. 111 at p. 118; 11 Rec. 525, on the power of intervention of the Council of Ministers by Wohlfart, E., Everling, U., Glaesner, H. J., and Sprung, R., "Die Europäische Wirtschaftsgemeinschaft", *Kommentar zum Vertrag* (1969); Lagrange in Case 67/63: *Sorema* v. *High Authority*, [1964] C.M.L.R. 350 at p. 352; 10 Rec. 293, on the definition of an association of undertakings by Reuter, P., *La Communauté Européenne du Charbon et de l'Acier* (1953); Warner in Case 31/74: *Filippo Galli, Preliminary Ruling*, [1975] E.C.R. at p. 70 on the direct applicability of regulations by J. A. Winter in 9 C.M.L. Rev., 1972 p. 425 at pp. 435–436; Reichl. in Case 72/74: *Union Syndicale, Service Public Européen* v. *E.C.C. Council*, [1975] E.C.R. 401 at p. 416 cites several writers on Administrative Law.
[20] Cases 28–30/62: *Da Costa en Schaake N.V.* v. *Nederlandse Administratre der Belastingen*, [1963] C.M.L.R. 224 at pp. 229, 237; 9 Rec. 59.

Under the doctrine of separation of powers the judges have no law-making function and indeed by art. 5 of the French Civil Code they are prohibited from deciding cases in a general or stereotyped manner. Their decisions must be based on the law, not on previously decided cases. Should the latter be the case the decision in France would probably be quashed by the Cour de Cassation because of *défaut de base légale*.[1] However, there is no harm in considering cases and citing precedents in the *motifs* of the judgment. Judges who study reports of cases cannot fail to notice the interpretation adopted by the Courts. They have the benefit of learned comments and opinions expressed in the *doctrine*, and during oral arguments counsel do not neglect the opportunity of impressing upon the Court the fact that a certain decision was reached on similar facts in previous cases. However, by tradition, when deciding a case judges must arrive at the particular interpretation by themselves just in case the Court which decided the previous case made a mistake. Therefore, judgments are substantiated by reference to the law comprised in codes and statutes. In the absence of a code or statute the case will be decided according to custom and in the absence of custom according to "equity, reason, justice, tradition", but never according to "precedent".[2]

The scope for the persuasive influence of precedent is very great indeed in the uncodified areas of the law, notably Administrative Law. Here in addition to statutes the "general principles of the law" play a considerable part and these, in turn, can often be found applied in precedents. The French Conseil d'Etat not only administers a body of law derived from precedents but also endeavours to relate its decisions to the pattern of case law.

The Community Court, modelled upon the Conseil d'Etat, fulfils a similar function and relies on its own decisions in a similar manner. On several occasions it either followed or referred to its previous decisions[3] in the *motifs*, which correspond to the *ratio decidendi* of the Common

---

[1] David, R., *Le Droit Français* (1960), p. 161.
[2] *Ibid.*, p. 162.
[3] Cases 28–30/62: *Da Costa en Schaake N.V.* v. *Netherlands Revenue Department*, [1963] C.M.L.R. 224; 9 Rec. 59; Case 44/65: *Hessische Knappschaft* v. *Maison Singer*, [1966] C.M.L.R. 82; 11 Rec. 1191; Case 28/67: *Mölkerei-Zentrale Westfalen-Lippe GmbH* v. *Hauptzollant Paderborn*, Case 28/67: [1968] C.M.L.R. 187 at pp. 216–219; 14 Rec. 211; *Filippo Galli, op. cit.*, p. 97; Case 68/74; *Angelo Alaimo* v. *Préfet du Rhône*, [1975] E.C.R. 109; Case 12/74: *E.C. Commission* v. *Federal Republic of Germany*, [1975] E.C.R. 181; Case 67/74: *Bonsignore* v. *Oberstadtdirektor der Stadt Köln*, [1975] E.C.R. 297; *Union Syndicale, op. cit.*, p. 97; Case 94/74: *IGAV-Industria Gomma, etc.* v. *Ente Nazionale, etc.*, [1975] E.C.R. 699 at pp. 701, 705, 708; Case 7/75: *Mr. & Mrs. F.* v. *Belgian State*, [1975] E.C.R. 679 at p. 684; Case 21/75: *Schroeder K.G.-Hamburg* v. *Oberstadtdirektor, Köln*, [1975] E.C.R. 905 at p. 910.

Law doctrine of precedent. There is a growing tendency of citing precedents not only by the Court but also, and to a greater extent, by the Advocates General.[4]

Advocate-General Roemer thus stated the position in the Community Court:[5] "it is in the nature of the development of the Common Market that facts appear, which, by reason of their novelty and the impossibility of foreseeing them, may bring about a revision of well established legal opinions" and concluded that previous decisions cannot have the binding force of precedents. In another case[6] involving the interpretation of E.E.C. art. 85 in which the parties abundantly cited previous decisions, he said: "It is, therefore, appropriate . . . to resort to these decisions with discretion, even where the general terms of propositions suggest their application to problems not arising in the case before the Court when they were formulated."

It is clear that through the interpretation of the texts a body of Community Law supplementing the Treaties and the Community legislation has emerged. The Court has proved an instrument of cohesion and uniformity. From an early stage the Court advanced the idea of a functional unity of the three Communities[7] which, in the jurisprudence of the Court, meant that one foundation Treaty should be interpreted with the aid of the others.[8] Of these cases one involving a Community official merits a special attention.[9] Sr. Campolongo, who was employed by the High Authority of the Coal and Steel Community was discharged and took up an appointment with the European Investment Bank instituted under the E.E.C. Treaty. He claimed various benefits including a re-installation allowance, but the Court decreed that he was not entitled to it because the "functional unity" of the Communities does not permit accumulation of payments due on the termination of employment with one and commencement of employment with another institution of the Communities. The Court recognised the

---

[4] *Fillipo Galli* at p. 68; *Angelo Alaimo* at p. 113; *E.E.C. Commission* at p. 206 *et seq.*; *Bonsignore* at p. 310; *Union Syndicale* at p. 708; Case 7 9/74: *Berthold Küster* v. *European Parliament*, [1975] E.C.R. 725 at p. 734; *IGAV-Industria Gomma etc.* v. *ENCC.-Ente Nazionale, etc.* at p. 715; *Mr. & Mrs. F.*, *op. cit.* at p. 692; Case 8/75: *op. cit. Caisse Primaire d'Assurance, etc.*, [1975] E.C.R. 739 at p. 757; *Schroeder K.G.*, *op. cit.* at p. 915.

[5] In Case 1/64: *S.A. Glucosiéries Réunies* v. *E.E.C. Commission*, [1964] C.M.L.R. 596 at p. 598; 10 Rec. 811.

[6] Case 23/67: *Brasserie de Haecht* v. *Wilkin*, [1968] C.M.L.R. 26; 13 Rec. 525.

[7] Colin, J.-P., *Le gouvernement des juges dans les Communautés Européennes* (1966), pp. 74 *et seq.*

[8] Case 6/60: *Humblet* v. *Belgium* (1960), 6 Rec. 1156 at p. 1157; Case 30/59: *Gezamenlijke Steen Kolenmijnen in Limburg* v. *High Authority* (1959), 7 Rec. at pp. 60–70; Case 9/59: (1959), 6 Rec. 27.

[9] Cases 27/59 and 39/59: *Alberto Campolongo* v. *High Authority* (1960), 6 (II) Rec. 795.

separate legal personalities of the Communities according to arts. 6, 210 and 184 of the Treaties which founded the E.C.S.C., E.E.C. and E.A.E.C., respectively, but emphasised that the Treaties of Rome created a strong legal bond between the Communities through the Convention on certain common institutions, i.e. the Court and the Assembly. Advocate-General Roemer, whose submissions in this respect were followed by the Court, stated that "the European Treaties are nothing but a partial implementation of a grand general programme, dominated by the idea of a complete integration of the European States".

II WHERE TO FIND COMMUNITY LAW

(A) TREATIES AND RELATED INSTRUMENTS

The authentic and official English texts of the Community Treaties are available in a variety of forms:

1. *Treaties establishing the European Communities: Treaties amending these Treaties: Documents concerning the Accession* (European Communities Office for Official Publications, 1973). This volume contains all the Treaties and their annexes as amended by the accession of Denmark, Ireland and the United Kingdom and adjusted by Norway's decision not to accede.

2. H.M. Stationery Office editions of the Treaties are also available as follows:

    (i) *Treaty establishing the European Coal and Steel Community, Paris 18 April 1951* (Cmnd. 5189). The sole authentic text of this Treaty is in French which is printed together with an English translation; the latter has no official standing.

    (ii) *Treaty establishing the European Economic Community, Rome 25 March 1957; Treaty establishing the European Atomic Energy Community, Rome 25 March 1957; Treaty establishing a Single Council and a Single Commission of the European Communities, Brussels 8 April 1965; Treaty amending certain Budgetary Provisions of the Treaties . . ., Luxembourg 22 April 1970* (Cmnd. 5179–II). This volume also contains the annexes to these Treaties.

    (iii) *Treaty concerning the Accession of the Kingdom of Denmark, Ireland, the Kingdom of Norway and the United Kingdom of Great Britain and Northern Ireland to the European Economic Community and the European Atomic Energy*

Community and Decision of the Council of the European Communities concerning the Accession of the said States to the European Coal and Steel Community, Brussels 22 January 1972 (Cmnd. 5179–I).

(iv) *Treaty establishing the European Economic Community, Rome 25 March 1957* (text in force on 1 January 1973). This very useful edition incorporates into the text all amendments made to the Treaty at the time the United Kingdom became a member. The original provisions of the Treaty are conveniently set out in an appendix.

3. The texts of all the Treaties and of some other Community instruments are also available in Sweet & Maxwell's *European Community Treaties* (2nd Edn., 1975).

4. Annotated texts of the Treaties and of related Community instruments are to be found in *Halsbury's Statutes of England* (3rd Edn.), Volume 42A, European Continuation Volume 1, 1952–72 and in Sweet and Maxwell's *Encyclopedia of European Community Law*, Volumes BI and II. Both of these works are kept up to date by Supplements.

(B) SECONDARY LEGISLATION

The secondary legislation of the Communities, i.e. decisions and recommendations in the case of the E.C.S.C. and regulations, directives and decisions in the cases of the E.E.C. and Euratom, are published in the *Official Journal of the European Communities*. This appears, almost daily, in each of the official languages of the Communities. An English edition has been published since 9 October 1972. Since 1968 the *Official Journal* has appeared in two series: one devoted to secondary legislation, the other containing non-normative communications and information.

Authentic English texts of pre-accession secondary legislation have been published in *Special Editions of the Official Journal of the European Communities* covering the period 1952–72. The same texts have also been published by H.M. Stationery Office in 42 volumes arranged under subject headings under the title *Secondary Legislation of the European Communities: Subject Edition*. Annotated texts of Community secondary legislation are to be found in *Halsbury's Statutes of England* (3rd Edn.), Volume 42A and in the *Encyclopedia of European Community Law*, Volume C (as yet incomplete). Community and national legislation relating to economic activities is summarised in *European Law Digest* (1973 and continued).

(C) CASE LAW

The texts of its judgments and opinions with the submissions of the advocates-general are published in periodical parts by the Court of Justice in each of the official languages of the Communities. The version in the procedural language in respect of a particular case is the only authentic version. The French version, which has been commonly used in the United Kingdom is entitled *Recueil de la Jurisprudence de la Cour*. An English version entitled *European Court Reports* has been published in periodical parts since 1973. English translations of the pre-accession volumes of reports of cases before the Court are in the process of publication; volumes for the years 1962 to 1970 have appeared to date.

Since 1962 English translations of the judgments of both the Court of Justice and of some of the courts of the member states on points of Community Law and decisions of the Commission on restrictive practices have been published under the name *Common Market Law Reports*. Since 1970 these Reports have also included the texts of the judgments in the procedural language. English translations of the judgments of the Court of Justice prior to the commencement of the *Common Market Law Reports* are to be found in Volume 2 of Valentine's *Court of Justice of the European Communities* (1965).

English translations of the judgments of the Court of Justice are also to be found in *Common Market Reports* published by the Commerce Clearing House Inc. of Chicago and, since May 1972, in the *Times* newspaper. Community and national case-law relating to economic activities is summarised in *European Law Digest* (1973 and continued).

(D) SUBSIDIARY SOURCES

(i) *Official papers of Community institutions.* There is a vast amount of such material covering all the activities of the Communities. It ranges from general reports and journalism to highly specialised monographs on detailed aspects of Community activity. Most of this material appears in all the official languages and some of the pre-accession papers are also available in unofficial English versions. From the lawyer's point of view the most significant and informative include the following:

Reports and opinions of the Commission and the consultative committees published in the *Official Journal*.

The Debates and Working Documents (*Documents de Séance*) of the Assembly. The Debates are published as an annexe to the *Official Journal* and the Working Documents are published individually by the Assembly itself.

The Bulletin of the European Communities published in periodical parts by the Secretariat of the Commission. In addition to giving an account of current activities and developments the Supplements to the *Bulletin* are convenient sources of the texts of important reports, such as the Commission's Opinions on the enlargement of the Communities. The annual *General Report on the Activities of the Communities* submitted by the Commission to the Assembly.

European Community a monthly journal published by the London Office of the Commission.

(ii) *Journals.* There are three English language journals devoted to Community matters. Both the *Common Market Law Review* (1963/1964 and continued) and the *European Law Review* (1975/1976 and continued) contain articles, notes and surveys of case law and literature. *The Journal of Common Market Studies* (1962 and continued) is not exclusively legal and also covers economic and political aspects of Community activities. Articles on Community legal topics are also to be found in the *International and Comparative Law Quarterly*, the *British Yearbook of International Law* and the *Journal of Business Law*.

(iii) *Treatises.* Campbell's *Common Market Law* in three volumes and kept up to date by periodic supplements was the first major British treatise to be published. It is written by and intended for practitioners and sets out to avoid what the Preface to the second supplement called "the Faery field of conceptual analysis". It has an abundance of detailed information arranged in an encyclopaedic manner and the authors of this book have frequently referred to it. A full and scholarly treatment of Community law will be found in both Lipstein's *Law of the European Economic Community* (1974) and Kapteyn and Verloren Van Themaat's *Introduction to the Law of the European Communities* (1973). Collins' *European Community Law in the United Kingdom* (1975) is a valuable study of structural and procedural aspects of Community law in the context of the law of the United Kingdom, and so is the E.E.C. prize winner: "Die Vereinbarkeit des Vertrages zur Grundung der Europäischen Wirtschaftsgemeinschaft mit der britischen verfassung," by K. Thelen, *Kölner Schriften zum Europarecht*, 1973, Vol. 21.

Among the large quantity of continental literature Gide, Loyrette and Nouel's *Dictionnaire du Marché Commun* in four large loose-leaf volumes and Megret's *Le Droit de la Communauté Economique Européenne* (6 volumes published to date) are particularly valuable.

PART II

The Law of the Institutions

CHAPTER FIVE

The Commission of the European Communities

I INTRODUCTION

It has already been pointed out that the European Communities were brought into existence by means of multilateral treaties between sovereign states signed and ratified in accordance with their customary constitutional procedures. These original treaties, subject to subsequent amendments,[1] are the source of the constitutional law of the Communities. They set out the objectives and purposes of the Communities, create the institutions of the Communities, define the powers of those institutions and regulate their relations both *inter se* and with the member states. In superficial form the Communities are cast in the classic mould of international organisations which has been so frequently used in modern times: the creation, by means of a multilateral treaty, of an organisation which possesses a distinct legal personality and which acts through the agency of institutions set up and regulated under the terms of the constituent treaty. In possessing these characteristics the European Communities fall within a recognisable and well-defined pattern. But despite this superficial identity which the European Communities have with other international organisations both universal and regional, the Communities may also be said to be unique; this uniqueness lies in their institutions. Not, it is true, in the existence of those institutions as bodies independent and autonomous of the member states for such institutions are commonly and necessarily found in international organisations. Nor does this uniqueness lie in the capacity of the institutions to impose obligations on the member states for that is a power possessed, for example, by the Security Council of the United Nations. The uniqueness of the Communities stems from the deep involvement of their institutions in matters traditionally

---

[1] Notably by the Merger Treaty 1965, the Treaty of Luxembourg 1970 concerned with budgetary matters and the powers of the Parliamentary Assembly and the Treaty of Accession 1972 and its annexes concerning the accession of Denmark, Ireland and the United Kingdom.

within the exclusive control of each individual state and their capacity to make rules directly and automatically binding not only on the member states themselves but also on individuals and corporate bodies within those states. Thus the unique character of the Communities lies in the degree of their penetration into the internal legal relations of the member states, whereas classical international organisations tend to be involved merely with the external legal relations of their members.

The institutions of the European Communities fall into two main categories. In the first place there are institutions vested with a variety of political, executive and administrative functions and powers. These are the Commission, the Council and the Assembly, assisted by a number of ancillary organs. Institutions in this category defy more precise classification for two main reasons. One is that these institutions cannot be said to be wholly executive, administrative or political but each possesses more than one of these attributes. The other is that in functional terms the Treaties conceive of these institutions not only co-operating but indeed working as a team so that one cannot fully appreciate the role and significance of any one of them in isolation. In the second place there is the Court of Justice, the judicial organ of the Communities.

The institutions will be treated in the above order.

II THE COMMISSION OF THE EUROPEAN COMMUNITIES

(A) COMPOSITION AND APPOINTMENT

The Commission of the European Communities is composed of thirteen members chosen on the grounds of their general competence.[2] The present Commission, like its predecessors, is made up of a mixture of lawyers, economists, ex-ministers, ex-members of parliament and ex-diplomats. The Treaties provide that the Commissioners must be persons whose independence can be fully guaranteed. They are required to act with complete independence in the performance of their duties solely in the interests of the Communities and they must neither seek nor take instructions from any national government or other body. Each member state, for its part, pledges to respect the independence of the Commissioners and not to seek to influence them in the performance of their duties. During their term of office Commissioners may not engage in any other occupation, paid or unpaid.[3] When entering upon

---

[2] Merger Treaty, art. 10 (1), as amended by the Council Decision of 1 January 1973 altering the number of members of the Commission.
[3] *Ibid.*, art. 10 (2).

their duties they give a solemn undertaking before the Court of Justice of the Communities that they accept the obligations of their office.

The Commissioners must be nationals of the member states. Each member state must have at least one but may not have more than two of its nationals on the Commission.[4] The present practice is for each of the larger member states, viz. France, Germany, Italy and the United Kingdom, to have two Commissioners and for the Benelux countries, Denmark and Ireland to have one each. The Commissioners are appointed by mutual agreement between the member states. They hold office for renewable periods of four years.[5] The President and the five Vice-Presidents of the Commission are appointed by the same process and hold office for renewable periods of two years.[6]

A Commissioner's term of office may be terminated by death in office or by resignation. A Commissioner may resign voluntarily; but if he no longer fulfils the conditions required for the performance of his duties or if he has been guilty of serious misconduct he may be compulsorily retired by the Court of Justice upon the application of either the Commission itself or the Council.[7] The whole Commission may be compelled to resign if the Assembly passes a motion of censure upon it by a two-thirds majority of the votes cast, representing a majority of the Assembly's members.[8] These powers of compulsory retirement and parliamentary censure have yet to be invoked.

Prior to the accession of Denmark, Ireland and the United Kingdom the Commission was composed of nine members. The enlargement of the Communities raised the question of the representation of the new member states on the Commission by persons of their nationality. In strict law, since the Commissioners are not national representatives but independent individuals, there was no necessity to increase the membership of the Commission to accommodate new member states. In reality it would have been impractical to adopt such a legalistic approach. The negotiations over the membership of Denmark, Ireland, Norway and the United Kingdom appear to have proceeded on the basis that if new members were admitted the membership of the Commission would be increased so as to accommodate the new members and maintain the existing level of representation of the original mem-

---

[4] Merger Treaty, art. 10 (1).
[5] *Ibid.*, art. 11.
[6] *Ibid.*, art. 14, as amended by Act of Accession, art. 16. In his Report on European Union Mr. Leo Tindemans, the Belgian Prime Minister, has proposed that the President of the Commission, appointed by the "European Council" with the approval of the European Parliament, should appoint the remaining members of the Commission in consultation with the Council; see *Bulletin of the European Communities*, Suppl. 1/76, at pp. 31, 32.
[7] *Ibid.*, art. 13.
[8] E.g. E.E.C. Treaty, art. 144.

bers.[9] This was in fact done by the Council exercising its power under art. 10 (1) of the Merger Treaty to increase the number of members of the Commission.[10]

Some voices, notably that of Professor Hallstein, a former President of the E.E.C. Commission, were raised against an increase in the size of the Commission on the grounds that experience had shown nine to be the optimum number and a larger Commission would be unwieldy and less effective.[11] But it would have been invidious to exclude persons of the nationality of new member states from the ranks of the Commissioners, at least for the early years of the life of the enlarged Communities. The Commission also expressed this view in 1969 in its revised *Opinion on the Applications for Membership from the United Kingdom, Ireland, Denmark and Norway*.[12]

(B) ORGANISATION

The Commission functions as a collegiate body in the sense that the Commission collectively and not the Commissioners individually bears responsibility for the acts of the Commission.[13] The Commission acts by a majority vote.[14] Its rules of procedure provide that the quorum of members is seven and that the conclusions of the Commission shall be final when they receive at least seven votes in support.[15] There is, nevertheless, an inevitable degree of subject specialisation as far as individual Commissioners are concerned. It is now an established practice for special responsibilities to be allocated to each Commissioner.[16] There is a temptation to compare these responsibilities, by analogy, with the portfolios given to members of a national government.

---

[9] See the Commission's report on the negotiations entitled *The Enlarged Community* (1972), para. 36 and the White Paper, *The United Kingdom and the European Communities* (Cmnd. 4175), para. 71.

[10] By a Decision of 1 January 1973.

[11] In *Problems of British Entry into the E.E.C.*, Chatham House/P.E.P. European Series, No. 11, p. 101. Also see R. Berthoud, *The Times*, 28 April 1972.

[12] See *Bulletin of the European Communities* (1969), Supplement No. 9/10, at p. 36. There is also a precedent for a Commission of 14 during the first three years after the entry into force of the Merger Treaty; see art. 32 (1).

[13] See *Règlement Intérieur de la Commission*, 63/41/CEE, art. 1, J.O., 31 January 1963, and the Commission's Provisional Rules of Procedure, 67/426/ E.E.C., art. 1, O.J. 147, 11 July 1967.

[14] Merger Treaty, art. 17 (1).

[15] Provisional Rules of Procedure, 67/426/EEC, art. 2, as amended by Decision 73/1/E.C.S.C., E.E.C., Euratom, O.J. L7, 6 January 1973, p. 1. Many decisions of the Commission are in fact unanimous.

[16] See Vacher's *European Companion*, No. 14, p. 20.

However, the analogy is imperfect since unlike a member of a national government a Commissioner bears no personal responsibility for his portfolio.

Although the Commission is collectively responsible for its acts, it may authorise its members to take agreed action on its behalf. This practice is provided by art. 27 of the *Règlement Intérieure de la Commission*[17] and was approved by the Court of Justice in *Re Noordwijks Cement Accoord* (1967).[18] Further, to prevent the principle of collective responsibility from imposing unnecessary delays on the Commission's work, considerable use is made of the so-called written procedure in accordance with the terms of art. 11 of the *Règlement Intérieure*. By this procedure draft decisions are circulated among the Commissioners and if no amendments or objections are made within a fixed period the draft is deemed to have been adopted by the Commission as a whole. Where amendments or objections are made or where a Commissioner specifically requests further discussion drafts will be considered at a full meeting of the Commission. This written procedure was not questioned by the Court in *Re Noordwijks Cement Accoord* and so its legality appears to have been accepted.

Each Commissioner is assisted by a *cabinet* in the French sense of a private office or departmental staff whose members tend to be of the same nationality of the Commissioner they serve.[19] A *chef de cabinet* or principal private secretary may deputise for his Commissioner at Commission meetings. In addition to the *cabinets* of the Commissioners the Commission has a staff of some 6,700 divided between the various departments and auxiliary services of the Commission. Each department is presided over by a Director-General who is responsible to the Commissioner whose "portfolio" includes that department.[20] The Directors-General are always of different nationality from the Commissioners they serve. On the lower levels of the administrative hierarchy the aim is to have an equitable representation of all the nationalities of the Communities. In view of the multilingual nature of the Communities with six official languages, viz. Dutch, French, German, Italian, Danish and English, linguists play a vital role in the

---

[17] *Loc. cit.* in note 13 above. Also see Decision 72/2/E.C.S.C., E.E.C., Euratom, O.J.L. 7, 6 January 1972, p. 2 on delegation of signature and Decision 74/55/E.E.C., O.J.L. 34, 7 February 1974, on the exercise of certain powers in respect of Community revenue and expenditure.

[18] Cases 8–11/66: [1967] C.M.L.R. 77; 13 Rec. 93.

[19] A recent exception to this practice was the appointment of a British subject, Mr. C. Layton, as *chef de cabinet* to Sr. Spinelli, an Italian Commissioner; see *European Community*, No. 11 (1971), p. 7.

[20] There are 20 Directorates-General in addition to the Secretariat-General, the Legal Service, the Spokesman's Group, the Statistical Office and some other general services: see Vacher's *European Companion*, No. 14, pp. 21–35.

activities of the Communities; there are over 700 translators and interpreters on the Commission's staff.[1] In recruiting its staff the Commission relies heavily on secondment from the national civil services of the member states.

(C) FUNCTIONS AND POWERS

The Merger Treaty provides in art. 9 that the Commission shall exercise the powers and competences bestowed by the Community Treaties upon the High Authority of the E.C.S.C. and the Commissions of the E.E.C. and Euratom. The functions and powers of the Merged Commission thus vary from Treaty to Treaty. But despite these differences it is possible to categorise the functions and powers of the Commission into three broad groups: it is an initiator and co-ordinator of Community policy; it is the executive agency of the Communities; it is the guardian of the Community Treaties.

As an initiator of policy the scope of the Commission differs in relation to the E.C.S.C. and Euratom on the one hand and the E.E.C. on the other. The E.C.S.C. and Euratom Treaties are *traités-lois* in that they lay down codes of specific rules relating to the relatively limited fields of concern of those Communities. In such a context the opportunities for formulating policy are limited since the policy decisions and the rules implementing them were largely taken at the time those Treaties were negotiated and were incorporated into the Treaties themselves. But the E.E.C. Treaty with its more wide ranging concern with the entire economies of the member states is a *traité cadre* and sketches in bolder strokes the main lines which are to be followed in achieving an economic union. Thus the E.E.C. Treaty leaves the details of the policies to be followed in the attainment of that goal to be worked out by the institutions of the Community and in this task the Commission plays a major and perhaps its most significant role.

In assisting in the formulation of policy the Commission first engages in consultations with interested parties at the political, civil service and trade union levels. Then, with the assistance of its own specialist departments, it proceeds to the consideration, often prolonged, of policy proposals until it reaches its final position which is submitted to the Council. It was in this way, for example, that the Commission prepared

---

[1] The official languages of the Communities are determined by Regulation 1 of 15 April 1958, O.J. 17, 6 October 1958, p. 385/58 (S. Edn. 1952–1958, p. 59) as amended by Act of Accession, art. 29 and Annex I, point XIV, para. 1 and the Adaptation Decision of 1 January 1973, O.J.L. 2, 1 January 1973, p. 1.

its opinion on United Kingdom membership of the Communities and its proposals on the agricultural policy of the Communities. After the main lines of policy have been finally agreed the Commission embarks on a consideration of the practical details of the implementation of that policy. The departments of the Commission concerned with a particular policy convene meetings with experts from the member states for the purpose of working out the practical implications of the policy. The experts are invited from the national civil services of the member states and although they have no brief to commit their respective governments they will be aware of their wishes and so will be in a position to advise the Commission on the acceptability of the Commission's proposals to the governments of the member states.[2] By this process the Commission formulates its proposals for submission to the Council. As an indication of the scale of this aspect of the Commission's work, during 1974 it sent 500 proposals to the Council plus 304 drafts, memoranda, recommendations and communications.[3]

The merged Commission is also the co-ordinator of policy as between the three Communities. Prior to the merger such co-ordination was virtually impossible because the Communities were institutionally separate. Since the merger the Commission has been able to take steps towards the formulation of common policies in such fields as industry, energy, research and technology which cut across the boundaries of the individual Communities. This co-ordination of policy may be regarded as a further stage in the process leading to a complete merger of the three Communities.

The Commission as the initiator and co-ordinator of policy also gives expression to the interests of the Communities; in this role we see the Commission as the conscience of the Communities. The member states despite their acceptance of the obligations of membership are apt to be deflected by national interests. Thus it is for the independent Commission to constantly remind both the Communities and the member states of the fundamental objectives of the Communities and to seek the achievement of those objectives to the fullest extent.[4] This was clearly expressed by Signor Malfatti when President of the Commission, in a statement to the Assembly of the Communities in September 1970: "The Commission is, at one and the same time, the guardian of the

---

[2] The Commission is indeed under an obligation not to seek or take instructions from any Government; see Merger Treaty, art. 10 (2).

[3] *Eighth General Report on the Activities of the European Communities* (1975), p. 21.

[4] See *Premier Rapport Général sur l'activité de la C.E.E.* (September 1958), para. 8.

Treaties and the motive force of integration, capable of accepting with courage the dialectic consequences which go with its twofold task—exercising the vigilance that is needed to preserve us from risks run by the venturesome and acting to correct any excess of vigilance which would inevitably lead to stagnation."[5] In this role the Commission's views of the Communities have not infrequently differed from those of the governments of the member states. Over the enlargement of the Communities, for example, the Commission produced a reasoned opinion in 1967 in favour of the admission of the United Kingdom, Ireland, Denmark and Norway to the Communities subject to certain conditions and recommended the opening of negotiations with those countries. That recommendation was not adopted because of the opposition of the French Government to British entry in particular and to the enlargement of the Communities in general.

Secondly, the three Treaties confer upon the Commission a wide range of executive powers and functions.

Under art. 8 of the E.C.S.C. Treaty the Commission has the duty of ensuring "the attainment of the objectives set out in this Treaty, under the conditions laid down herein". This and many other articles of the Treaty gives the Commission wide rule-making powers. For example, art. 60 of the E.C.S.C. Treaty gives the Commission the power to define practices which come within the prohibition on unfair competitive prices which might tend towards the creation of a monopoly. Similarly art. 155 and art. 125 of the E.E.C. and Euratom Treaties respectively confer upon the Commission the authority to see "that the provisions of [the] Treaty and the measures pursuant to it taken by the institutions are carried out". Thus, for example, art. 48 (3) (*d*) of the E.E.C. Treaty enables the Commission to make regulations laying down the conditions under which workers have a right to live in a member state in which they have been employed.

In addition to such executive powers specifically conferred upon the Commission by the Treaties the Commission may also be invested with powers to ensure the enforcement of decisions made by the Council. This is of particular significance in the E.E.C. where, in connection with the common agricultural policy, the Council has delegated wide rule-making powers to the Commission. In June 1974 the Council declared its intention of making wider use of these powers in future.[6] As a measure of the degree of importance which these powers occupy in the Commission's work, of the 2,590 regulations

---

[5] *Statement to the European Parliament* (15 September 1970), p. 22.
[6] See *Bulletin of the European Communities* (1974), Part 6, p. 122.

made by the Commission during 1972 the vast majority related to the common agricultural policy.[7]

The second type of executive authority vested in the Commission is that of ensuring that the rules of the Treaties are applied to particular cases, whether concerning the government of a member state or a commercial undertaking. Under the E.C.S.C. Treaty the Commission deals directly with coal and steel enterprises. Article 54 of that Treaty, for example, enables the Commission to promote and co-ordinate the capital spending of coal and steel enterprises and it has the power to prohibit the financing of any programme put forward by an enterprise which conflicts with the rules of the Treaty. Under the Euratom Treaty the Commission has responsibilities of a supervisory nature in relation to the protection of the health of workers in the nuclear industry and the supply and use of fissile material.[8] In the E.E.C. Treaty similar powers are conferred upon the Commission particularly in relation to the prohibition of restrictive practices and the control of state subsidies.[9]

The Commission is also given a number of representative, financial and administrative functions. The Commission represents the legal *persona* of the Communities.[10] It represents the Communities in negotiations with non-member states and international organisations.[11] The Commission is responsible for the administration of Community funds. In the E.C.S.C. a levy on coal and steel production is paid to the Commission direct.[12] In the E.E.C. and Euratom the Commission is charged with giving effect to the budgets of the Communities as adopted by the Council.[13] The E.E.C. and Euratom were originally financed out of contributions from the member states. But under the terms of a Council Decision of 1970,[14] since 1 January 1971 the Communities have been progressively financed out of their own resources, the main sources of which are customs duties and agricultural levies. From 1 January 1975 it was intended that the budget of the Communities would be financed entirely from the Communities' own resources.[15] The Commission also administers four special funds

---

[7] Noel, E., *Working Together: The Institutions of the European Community* (1975), p. 9.
[8] See Euratom Treaty, Title Two, Chapters 3 and 6.
[9] See E.E.C. Treaty, Part Three, Title 1.
[10] E.g. E.E.C. Treaty, art. 211.
[11] E.g. E.E.C. Treaty, arts. 228 *et seq.*
[12] E.C.S.C. Treaty, art. 49.
[13] E.E.C. Treaty, art. 205; Euratom Treaty, art. 179.
[14] Decision 70/243, O.J. L94, 28 April 1970, p. 19 (S. Edn. 1970 (I) p. 224). Also see Council Regulation 2/71 applying that Decision, O.J. L3, 5 January 1971, p. 1 (S. Edn. 1971 (I), p. 3).
[15] This aim was achieved subject to a failure to settle the means of assessment for revenue from value added tax.

which form part of the Communities' budget: the European Social Fund which is used to redeploy and retrain workers and to promote social welfare;[16] the European Development Fund which makes grants and loans to overseas territories and countries associated with the Communities;[17] the European Agricultural Guidance and Guarantee Fund which is used to cover agricultural market support costs and to assist farm modernisation schemes;[18] and the European Regional Development Fund which has been set up to correct regional imbalances within the Community.[19] Under the terms of art. 18 of the Merger Treaty the Commission is also required to publish an annual general report on the activities of the Communities.

Lastly, the Commission as the guardian of the Treaties acts as a watchdog to ensure that treaty obligations are observed. If an allegation is made that there has been an infringement of Treaty obligations it is for the Commission, as an impartial body, to investigate that allegation, reach a conclusion and notify the action necessary to correct the error. In the case of such an error in respect of the E.C.S.C. Treaty, art. 88 authorises the Commission to take steps to ensure that member states fulfil their obligations under the Treaty. Where a member state will not voluntarily carry out its obligations the Commission may, with the concurring vote of a two-thirds majority of the Council withhold from the defaulting member state sums of money which the Commission may owe that state under the Treaty and authorise the other member states to withhold certain benefits under the Treaty from the defaulting state as a sanction for its wrong doing. If these measures prove ineffective the Commission shall bring the matter before the Council. This procedure may be subject to review by the Court of Justice of the Communities.[20] Also under the E.C.S.C. Treaty the Commission has the power to impose a monetary penalty on any coal and steel undertaking which acts contrary to its obligations under the Treaty.[1]

The provisions of the E.C.S.C. Treaty authorising action to be taken against a member state were found to be complex and cumbersome and have been seldom used in practice. Partly because of this experience the equivalent provisions of the E.E.C. and Euratom Treaties are

---

[16] E.E.C. Treaty, Part Three, Title 3, Chapter 2.
[17] See Implementing Convention of the Association of the Overseas Countries and Territories with the Community 1957, annexed to the E.E.C. Treaty and Lomé Convention, Title IV, *Encyclopedia of European Community Law*, Vol. BII, p. B12489.
[18] This fund was established by Council Regulation No. 25 of 4 April 1962, O.J. 30, 20 April 1962, p. 991/62 (S. Edn. 1959–1962, p. 126).
[19] See Regulation (E.E.C.) 724/75, O.J. L73, 21 April 1975, p. 1.
[20] See Chap. 9, below.
[1] E.g. arts. 64–66.

simpler and more effective. Article 169 of the E.E.C. Treaty lays down a general procedure for dealing with breaches of treaty obligations by member states. It provides that where "the Commission considers that a member state has failed to fulfil an obligation under the Treaty, it shall deliver a reasoned opinion on the matter after giving the state concerned the opportunity to submit its observations. If the state concerned does not comply with the terms of the opinion within the period laid down by the Commission, the latter may bring the matter before the Court of Justice."[2] To date well over 500 alleged infringements of the Treaty have been challenged by the Commission under this procedure. In earlier years most of the infringements concerned customs duties and quotas but latterly the cases have involved a wider range of Treaty provisions, notably in the field of the common agricultural policy. With the advent of further common policies this is likely to remain an important part of the Commission's activities. In addition to this general procedure the Treaties also confer authority on the Commission to deal with special infringements. For example art. 89 of the E.E.C. Treaty authorises the Commission to investigate suspected infringements of the Community's rules of competition. If the suspicion is well founded and if the infringements are not brought to an end the Commission may direct the member states to take the steps necessary to remedy the situation.

---

[2] Also see Euratom Treaty, art. 141 and Chap. 9, below.

CHAPTER SIX

The Council of the European Communities

(A) COMPOSITION

The Council is made up of one representative of the government of each of the member states.[1] The natural and usual minister who represents a member on the Council is its Foreign Minister. But the composition of the Council may vary depending upon the subject matter to be discussed and so Ministers of Agriculture, Finance, Industry and Transport, for example, may represent a member on the Council upon occasion.[2] In practical terms the Merger Treaty had very little effect on the working of the Council. Because of the common identity of membership there had been virtually a *de facto* merger of the separate Councils since 1958. The Merger Treaty formalised this arrangement and provided for unified rules of procedure.[3] The office of President of the Council rotates among the members for terms of six months in strict alphabetical sequence: Belgium, Denmark, Germany, France, Ireland, Italy, Luxembourg, Netherlands and the United Kingdom.[4] Meetings of the Council are held upon the initiative of the President or at the request of either a member or of the Commission.[5]

(B) THE POWERS OF THE COUNCIL AND ITS RELATIONSHIP WITH THE COMMISSION

As in the case of the Commission, the Council exercises the powers conferred by the Community Treaties upon the former separate

---

[1] Merger Treaty, art. 2.

[2] E.g. during the second half of 1973 the Council was variously under the chairmanship of the Danish Ministers of Agriculture, Public Works and the Environment, Foreign Economic Affairs, Economic and Social Affairs, and Labour; see *Seventh General Report on the Activities of the European Communities* (1974), p. 57.

[3] Merger Treaty, art. 5. These rules have not been published; for the text of original rules see Gide *et al.*, *Dictionnaire du Marché Commun*, Vol. 4, pp. 24–26.

[4] *Ibid.*, art. 2 as amended by the adjusted Act of Accession, art. 11.

[5] Merger Treaty, art. 3.

Councils.[6] One of the most interesting features of the constitution of the Communities is the relationship between the Council and the Commission. This has already been adumbrated in an earlier reference to the role of the Commission in the formulation of policy and as the exponent of the interests of the Communities. There is, however, a noticeable difference in this relationship between the E.C.S.C. and Euratom on the one hand and the E.E.C. on the other. The E.C.S.C. and Euratom Treaties, at arts. 26 and 115 respectively, stress the Council's harmonising and co-ordinating role in relation to the policies of the member states; the E.E.C. Treaty at art. 145 specifies in addition a power to take decisions. In general terms, under the E.C.S.C. Treaty it is the Commission which has the power to take decisions subject to consultation with the Council; under the E.E.C. Treaty the power of decision largely lies with the Council usually acting upon a proposal from the Commission. These differences appear to indicate that the Commission has more power under the E.C.S.C. Treaty than it has under the E.E.C. Treaty and that the supra-national character of the Commission in the E.C.S.C. is not enjoyed in relation to the E.E.C. In fact, the importance of these formal differences is more apparent than real. We have already seen that in the E.C.S.C. the opportunities for the Commission to initiate policy are limited because of the essential character of the treaty as a *traité-loi*. This gives the Commission powers of a largely executive character to give effect to the rules already laid down in the Treaty. The Commission has similar but less extensive powers under the E.E.C. Treaty itself. But that Treaty's essential character is that of a *traité cadre* which, as we have seen, gives the Commission an important role in initiating and formulating policy, subject to the final decision of the Council. Once such a policy decision has been taken, as in the case of agriculture for example, the Council confers upon the Commission the necessary executive powers to implement such policy. Further, whilst the Commission under the E.C.S.C. Treaty has in law wide powers of independent decision, in practice it has made a point of seeking the opinion and approval of the Council even in cases in which this was not strictly necessary.[7] Bearing in mind the different character of the E.C.S.C. and E.E.C. Treaties, the powers of the Commission are broadly of the same order in each with the important addition that under the E.E.C. Treaty the Commission has a vital role in the formulation of policy.

The Commission's initiative in policy-making is enhanced by the fact that in exercising its power of decision under the E.E.C. Treaty the

---

[6] Merger Treaty, art. 1.

[7] See von Lindeiner-Wildau, K., *La Supranationalité en tant que Principe de Droit* (1970), pp. 104, 105.

Council can in general act only upon a proposal from the Commission. The Council may only amend a Commission proposal by unanimous vote.[8] Failing that it can accept it, reject it or return it to the Commission for reconsideration. Thus the text of a Commission proposal tends to go through many drafts passing between the Council and the Commission until a final version is agreed. The Commission's position in this process is further strengthened by the rules of voting in the Council. Whilst the normal rule of voting in the Council is by a simple majority,[9] in fact most of the law-making powers of the Council have to be exercised by a qualified majority. For this purpose a system of weighted voting is employed: France, Germany, Italy and the United Kingdom have ten votes each, Belgium and the Netherlands have five, Denmark and Ireland have three and Luxembourg has two.[10] Where a Council decision is required to be taken upon a proposal from the Commission, for example under art. 94 of the E.E.C. Treaty for the application of the rules concerning aids granted by states, a qualified majority of any 41 of the available 58 votes will suffice. In such a case France, Germany, Italy and the United Kingdom who together command a total of 40 votes could not impose their will on the other five members. But any two of the larger members voting together have a power of veto. Since the three new member states can only muster 16 votes they could be outvoted if the other six members voted together.[11] In other cases in which the Council can act on its own initiative the qualified majority of 41 must be cast by at least six member states, for example under art. 154 of the E.E.C. Treaty where the Council may determine the salaries of the Commissioners and the Judges and officers of the Court of Justice. Here again the four larger members cannot dictate to the other members and a clear majority of members is required. Thus the Treaty introduces a system of checks and balances into the decision-making powers of the Council.

(C) THE COMMITTEE OF PERMANENT REPRESENTATIVES

The common experience of European organisations set up since 1945 has been that where they have institutions made up of ministerial representatives of governments which, because of other demands on

---

[8] E.E.C. Treaty, art. 149; also Euratom Treaty, art. 119.

[9] E.E.C. Treaty, art. 148 (1); also Euratom Treaty, art. 118 (1).

[10] E.E.C. Treaty, art. 148 (2) and Euratom Treaty, art. 118 (2) as amended by the adjusted Act of Accession, art. 14.

[11] If Norway had joined the Communities she would have been allocated three votes and the qualified majority would have been 43 out of 61; in such a situation the four new members with a voting strength of 19 would have been able to veto any concerted move by the six original members. For the original text of the Accession documents see Cmnd. 4862.

their time and attention, can only meet infrequently, a permanent representative body of ambassadorial rank is necessary not only to carry out routine matters of administration but also to undertake preparatory work for meetings of the ministers. This has been the experience of the O.E.E.C., the Council of Europe, the Western European Union and N.A.T.O.[12] In view of this experience it is somewhat surprising to find that the E.C.S.C. Treaty made no provision for the Special Council of Ministers to be assisted by a committee of permanent representatives. But by 1953 the need for such assistance had become apparent and the Special Council used its general power to establish committees to set up the so-called Co-ordinating Committee made up of senior officials of the national administrations of the members to prepare material for Council meetings and to undertake *ad hoc* tasks at the Council's request.[13]

This practice prompted the incorporation in the E.E.C. and Euratom Treaties of provisions to the effect that the Council's Rules of Procedure "may provide for the setting up of a committee consisting of representatives of member states" the tasks and powers of which shall be determined by the Council.[14] This power was used to establish a Committee of Permanent Representatives, who were in practice the ambassadors of the member states accredited to the Communities, to carry out work preparatory to Council meetings and any other specific tasks.[15] The Merger Treaty institutionalised this arrangement providing, in art. 4, that "a committee consisting of the Permanent Representatives of the member states shall be responsible for preparing the work of the Council and for carrying out the tasks assigned to it by the Council". Thus in effect the E.C.S.C.'s Co-ordinating Committee was abolished and the E.E.C./Euratom Committee of Ambassadors extended to the E.C.S.C.

The Permanent Representatives were originally regarded as merely the servants, the eyes and the ears of their governments.[16] But in the course of time the Committee has acquired a Community character and has come to play a distinctive and important role in the affairs of the Communities. At first the establishment and institutionalisation of this Committee was treated with suspicion. Its German title *Ständige Vertreter* (Permanent Representatives) was for a time parodied as

---

[12] See the account of these organisations in Palmer, M., *et al.*, *European Unity* (1968).

[13] See *Les Novelles: Droit des Communautés européennes* (1969), pp. 241 *et seq.*

[14] E.E.C. Treaty, art. 151; Euratom Treaty, art. 121.

[15] See Noel, E., "The Committee of Permanent Representatives", 5 *Journal of Common Market Studies* (1967), pp. 219, 220.

[16] See Noel, E., *op. cit.* in note 16, above, at p. 223.

Ständige Verräter (Permanent Traitors) because it was feared that they might endanger the Community's institutional balance.[17] The specific fear was that the Commission/Council dialogue might become gradually replaced requiring the Commission to deal with a group of subordinate Permanent Representatives rather than with the ministers themselves. This would erode the supra-national role of the Commission and would effectively place more power in the hands of the Council. In 1958 when the E.E.C./Euratom Committee of Permanent Representatives was set up the Commission asked the Council for an assurance that there was no intention of delegating the Council's powers of decision to the Permanent Representatives. This assurance was unanimously given by the Council.[18] The Committee of Permanent Representatives is not a Committee of Minister's Deputies. The power of decision and responsibility for decisions remains where the Treaties put it with the Council and the institutional balance resulting from the dialogue between Commission and Council appears to have been preserved.[19]

This assurance paved the way for the establishment of a fruitful relationship between the Permanent Representatives and the Commission. This has resulted in the settlement of problems which would otherwise waste the time of Ministers and the joining of support for Commission proposals in the face of initial hesitation on the part of the governments of the member states. In practice the functions and services of the Committee of Permanent Representatives fall into three main categories:

(*a*) liaison between national administrations and Community institutions and the mutual supply of information;

(*b*) participation in the working out and co-ordinating of national attitudes; and

(*c*) direct involvement in work of the Community institutions.[20]

(D) THE COUNCIL'S WORKING METHODS

When the Council receives a memorandum or proposal from the Commission the invariable procedure is to refer it, in the first instance, to an appropriate committee or working party made up of civil service

---

[17] See Mayne, R., *The Institutions of the European Community* (1968), p. 37.

[18] See Noel, E., *op cit.* in note 16, above, at pp. 228, 229.

[19] The limited role of the Committee is confirmed by the *Règlement Intérieur Provisoire du Conseil*, art. 16; see Gide *et al.*, *Dictionnaire du Marché Commun*, Vol. 4. But cf. Salmon, J. J. A., "Le rôle des representations permanentes", *La Décision dans les Communautés Européennes* (1969), pp. 57 *et seq.*

[20] See Noel, E., *op. cit.* in note 15, above, at pp. 223 *et seq.* and Noel, E. and Etienne, H., "The Permanent Representatives Committee and the 'Deepening' of the Communities", 6 *Government and Opposition* (1971), p. 447.

experts. Each of the fields of activity of the Communities is covered by such committees and working parties who advise the Council and whose work is co-ordinated by the Committee of Permanent Representatives. The Commission is represented at these preparatory meetings and may amend its proposals in the light of the discussion, although it is under no obligation to do so.

When the Council meets to consider Commission proposals its agenda is divided into so-called 'A' items and 'B' items, a procedure based on the practice of the French Council of Ministers. 'A' items are those upon which provisional agreement has been reached in the course of the preparatory meetings and 'B' items are those on which there is still disagreement. 'A' items have of course to be formally approved by the Council but they are usually settled quickly. 'B' items occupy most of the business of Council meetings.[1] Members of the Commission take part as of right in Council meetings. The role of the Commissioners at these meetings is that of mediator and honest broker. Whilst the Commission is anxious for an agreement which is in tune with Community interests it can also amend its proposals at any time and may thus be able to suggest a compromise which may be acceptable to all sides.

At the Paris Summit Meeting in October 1972 the Heads of State or Government of the enlarged Community pledged themselves to improve the Council's decision-making procedures and the cohesion of Community action.[2] As a result, during 1973 and 1974 the Council adopted a number of measures designed to achieve those objectives.[3] These measures are largely of a practical nature and do not introduce any new matters of principle. They include: advance planning of the timetable for Council meetings; co-ordination of national cabinet meetings so as to make ministers available for Council meetings; the circulation of papers at least a week before a meeting; more careful planning of the agenda in consultation with the President of the Commission; an agreement that the instructions of the Permanent Representatives should give them wider scope for negotiation so that wherever possible agreement may be reached at the level of the Committee of Permanent Representatives.

The solution of particularly difficult problems has been achieved as a

---

[1] See Torrelli, M., *L'Individu et le droit de la C.E.E.* (1970), p. 60; Noel, E. and Etienne, H., "Quelques aspects des rapports et de la collaboration entre le Conseil et la Commission" and Salmon, J. J. A., *op. cit.*, both in *La Décision dans les Communautés Européennes* (1969), at pp. 43 and 67 respectively.
[2] See *Sixth General Report of the Activities of the Communities* (1973), pp. 15, 16.
[3] See *Bulletin of the European Communities* (1973), Part 7/8, p. 76, (1974), Part 2, pp. 103, 104 and Part 6, p. 122.

result of the famous marathon sessions of the Council.[4] The longest of these concerned the making of regulations to implement the agricultural policy; it took place during December 1961/January 1962 and lasted almost three weeks. During the course of these marathons the Council may attempt to reach the unanimity necessary to amend the Commission's proposal. The Commission will suggest its own counter amendments. Adjournments may be granted in an attempt to enable the Commission to work out a package-deal which may be acceptable to the Council, and so on.

Although most decisions of the Council are reached by the process described above and are based on an initiative of the Commission, in a significant number of cases in recent years the Council has sought to exercise a power of initiative of its own. In so doing it has claimed that it is acting in accordance with art. 152 of the E.E.C. Treaty which provides that "the Council may request the Commission to undertake any studies which the Council considers desirable for the attainment of the common objectives and to submit any appropriate proposals". On the face of it this is an innocuous provision which was probably intended to provide a safeguard in two senses. First, to enable the Council to spur the Commission to action should it appear to be neglecting its duty in any respect and, secondly, to enable the Council to suggest possible lines of enquiry to the Commission. In either case provided the actual terms of any proposal inspired by art. 152 emanate from the Commission itself the basic relationship between Commission and Council will be preserved. But when the Council purports to act under art. 152 it tends to go far beyond making a general request to the Commission to consider a particular matter, but it has indicated to the Commission the precise terms its proposal should take.[5] This is quite clearly a distortion of the relationship between Commission and Council as established by the Treaties and an abuse of art. 152.

In practice the Commission has co-operated with the Council in such cases and has supplied proposals in the terms suggested. It has probably done this for two reasons. In the first place when the Council resorts to art. 152 it presents a united front to the Commission and so the matter is cut-and-dried and the Commission has little, if any, room to negotiate.[6] Secondly, whereas during the early years of the existence of the Communities the Treaties themselves laid down programmes and

---

[4] See Alting von Geusau, F. A. M., "Les sessions marathons du Conseil des ministres", *Le Décision dans les Communautés Européennes* (1969), pp. 99 *et seq.*

[5] On this use of art. 152 see Torrelli, *op. cit.*, pp. 42, 43, and Louis, J. V., *Les Règlements de la Communauté Economique Européenne* (1969), pp. 6–8 and notes.

[6] Clearly if the Council is unanimous it would be able to amend any counter proposal from the Commission.

timetables within which the Commission could function as an independent force, now that these transitional periods have passed the Commission has no preconceived programme and has tended to yield to the political ascendancy of the Council.[7] But whilst a Council of six was able to present a united front to the Commission it may not be as easy for an enlarged Council to do so. Further the infusion of new blood as a result of the admission of new member states may revive the independent powers of initiative of the Commission with which it is endowed by the Treaties.[8]

(E) THE CONSTITUTIONAL CRISIS OF 1965

In some cases the problems facing the Communities have proved insoluble, even after recourse to a marathon session. Intransigence on the part of one or more of the member states may provoke a constitutional crisis in the Communities as in 1963 resulting from the French veto on British membership[9] and again in 1965. The latter crisis has had a significant effect on working relations between the Council and the Commission and on the Council's voting procedure.

The 1965 crisis arose in the following way.[10] After the 1963 crisis, relations between France and the other members remained strained and instead of all members working harmoniously to solve problems in the light of the interests of the Communities each side was only prepared to reach agreement if its own interests were safeguarded. In 1965 the Commission, in an attempt to solve a number of outstanding problems at one blow suggested a package-deal embracing three unconnected items: (i) the completion of the farm price regulations, which was sought by France in particular; (ii) a Commission proposal for the independent financing of the Communities out of their own resources instead of relying on contributions from the member states; and (iii) the granting of greater budgetary powers to the Parliamentary Assembly, which was being demanded by the Assembly itself with the support of the Netherlands. This package deal was opposed by France ostensibly on the ground that the Commission had made the details of its proposals known to the Assembly before the French Government had had an opportunity to consider them.

---

[7] See Berthoud, R., *The Times*, 28 April 1972.
[8] On the importance of those powers for the development of the Communities see Hallstein, W., "The E.E.C. Commission: a new Factor in International Life" (1965), 14 I. & C.L.Q. 727. The Tindemans' Report on European Union also stresses the importance of the Commission's freedom of action; *Bulletin of the European Communities*, Suppl. 1/76 at p. 31.
[9] See *Sixth General Report on the Activities of the E.E.C.* (1963), introduction.
[10] See *Ninth General Report on the Activities of the E.E.C.* (1966), Chapter 1.

The other member states were willing to consider the package deal as a whole, but France insisted that only the farm finance question should be settled. A deadline of 30 June 1965 had been fixed by the Council for the settlement of this issue and when no agreement had been reached by midnight on that date the French Foreign Minister, who happened to be the current President of the Council, refused to over-run the time-limit and, despite protests, brought the meeting to an end. Thereafter for seven months France refused to take part in any meeting of the Council designed to advance the purposes of the Communities whilst continuing to observe existing Community policies and regula- · tions. The Council continued to meet in the absence of the French representative and called upon France to resume her place. The French Government urged the *révision* of the institutional structure of the Communities. Both sides in the dispute maintained their positions and eventually France was induced to attend a special private meeting of the Council held in Luxembourg, partly, no doubt because of the possibility that the five might use their power of decision in the absence of France.

The formula worked out at the Luxembourg meeting and known as the *Accords de Luxembourg* was really little more than an agreement to disagree.[11] On the one hand the five whilst refusing to permit any restriction on the Commission's powers under the Treaties accepted a number of relatively minor points concerning Council/Commission relations designed to facilitate their co-operation without compromising their respective competences and powers. It was agreed that before adopting any particularly important proposal the Commission should establish appropriate contacts with the Permanent Representatives without compromising the Commission's right of initiative. And that proposals and any other official acts which the Commission submits to the Council and to member states should not be made public until the recipients have had formal notice of them and are in possession of the texts.[12] On the question of voting in the Council it was agreed that, where a decision may be reached by the qualified majority vote on a proposal of the Commission, the Council should endeavour to reach such a decision unanimously in all cases where very important interests of one or more of the member states are involved. France further insisted that where very important interests are involved the discussion should be continued until unanimous agreement is reached; but the Council failed to produce any agreed policy on what should be done in the event of a failure to reach a unanimous agreement.

---

[11] *Ninth General Report on the Activities of the E.E.C.* (1966), pp. 31–33.
[12] This met the French complaint that the Assembly was informed of Commission proposals before the Council and member states.

This crisis brought to the surface the latent conflict between opposed views on the form which economic union should take: the advocates of integration and ultimate political union on the one hand (represented by the five) and the advocates of national sovereignty and looser political links on the other (represented by France). This conflict is yet to be finally resolved.[13] The 1965 crisis and its resolution illustrates the interdependence of the member states within the Communities. This is an example of what has been called the process of *engrenage*. Literally this term means "gearing" or "meshing" but in this usage it refers to the process whereby as soon as a state becomes involved in the machinery of economic integration it is progressively drawn further into the machine so that matters which in the past were within the sole competence of national governments gradually and irrevocably became part of the Community's decision-making process.[14] This is perhaps the beginning of the replacement of traditional international diplomacy by European constitutional law.

In constitutional terms the legal validity of the *Accords de Luxembourg* is highly suspect. They cannot be regarded as an amendment of the E.E.C. Treaty. Article 236 lays down the procedure for such amendment; that procedure, which was followed in the cases of the Merger Treaty and the Treaty of Luxembourg 1970, was not followed in this case, nor have the *Accords* been ratified in accordance with the constitutional processes of the member states. Equally, the *Accords* cannot be regarded as resolving disputed questions of treaty interpretation, for under art. 219 of the E.E.C. Treaty the member states undertake not to submit a dispute concerning the interpretation or application of the Treaty to any method of settlement other than those provided for therein, in other words such disputes must be referred to the Court of Justice of the Communities. Thus, in so far as the *Accords de Luxembourg* require the Council to be unanimous in cases in which the Treaty, in accordance with the terms of art. 148, merely requires a majority, the *Accords* are constitutionally invalid. They are in direct conflict with the obligation imposed by art. 4 (1) of the E.E.C. Treaty that "each institution shall act within the limits of the powers conferred upon it by [the] Treaty".

The Commission, for its part, whilst it has never expressly approved of the *Accords*, has nevertheless acquiesced and co-operated in their implementation. It would be open to the Commission to challenge before the Court acts of the Council taken under the terms of the

---

[13] The British Labour Government, for example, is clearly unsympathetic towards plans for political union; see *Membership of the European Community: Report on Renegotiation* (Cmnd. 6003), paras. 130–132.

[14] Mayne, R., *The Institutions of the European Community* (1968), p. 50.

Accords but it has not done so.[15] This is no doubt largely due to the acceptance of the view that in the light of the attitudes of the Governments of some of the member states further achievement of the aims of the E.E.C. is only possible within the terms laid down by the *Accords*. Treaty amendment is also impracticable because of the lack of unanimity in the Council on this issue.

Although the *Accords* have not affected the legal relations and powers of the Commission and Council, in practice they have had a limiting effect on the life of the Communities. This has been expressed by the Commission in no uncertain terms.[16] In 1969 the Commission expressed its concern in its revised *Opinion concerning the Applications for membership from the United Kingdom, Ireland, Denmark and Norway*.[17] It referred to the efficacy of the Council's decision-making methods as being a major problem in the institutional life of the Community largely as a result of the application of the unanimity rule in cases where the Treaties do not require it. This has had the result of slowing down and sometimes completely blocking the progress of integration. At times more than 300 of the Commission's proposals have been affected by the sluggishness of the Council's procedures and are awaiting a decision.[18]

The Commission has frequently stressed that its own right of initiative, independence and authority are of absolutely basic importance for the efficient functioning of the Community. The conviction was expressed that "it is only by returning to respect for both the letter and the spirit of the institutional arrangements laid down in the Treaty, by ensuring that they operate efficiently and by strenghening them in the light of developments and the requirements of Community life, that the Community will be able to accept in security the risks involved in enlargement".[19] The Commission has drawn attention in particular to the dangers of insisting on unanimity in the Council, with the consequent power of veto, in an enlarged Community. It has urged that these dangers should be obviated by the acceptance and implementation of two principles: (i) that decisions by majority vote

---

[15] Under the terms of E.E.C. Treaty, art. 173.
[16] Cf. *Second General Report on the Activities of the Communities* (1969), pp. 14 *et seq.* Some obstacles have since been overcome as a result of the Hague Conference of December, 1969; see *Fourth General Report on the Activities of the Communities* (1971), pp. x *et seq.*
[17] Reproduced in *Bulletin of the European Communities* (1969), No. 9/10, Supplement, pp. 33, 34.
[18] See Berthoud, R., *The Times*, 1 June 1972.
[19] See *Bulletin of the European Communities*, Vol. 2 (1969), No. 9/10, Supplement, p. 34. Similar recommendations are contained in the *Vedel Report*, Chapters 3 and 7.

should again be the normal practice of the Council except where the Treaties provide otherwise; and (ii) that where unanimity in the Council is required it should only apply to outline policy decisions and majority voting should then be the rule in connection with the decisions necessary to implement such policies.[20]

The improvements in the Council's decision-making procedures which were mentioned earlier clearly do not tackle the root of the problem. The Commission's fears concerning the continued use of the veto in the enlarged Community have been borne out by the claims of both British Conservative and Labour Governments that they have the right to prevent acts which affect vital national interests.[1] But on the other hand there is also some indication of a willingness to depart from the hard line expressed in the *Accords de Luxembourg*. Where there is a substantial majority in the Council member states are sometimes prepared to abstain from voting[2]. Further, the Heads of Government have now declared that "it is necessary to renounce the practice which consists of making agreement on all questions conditional on the unanimous consent of the member states".[3]

(F) THE COUNCIL AND THE POLITICAL FUTURE OF THE COMMUNITY

It is clear that whilst the immediate aims of the Communities are economic, their long term aims are political. The preamble to the E.E.C. Treaty expresses the determination "to lay the foundations of an ever closer union among the peoples of Europe" and art. 2 of the Treaty itself refers to the establishment of closer relations between the member states. During recent years the questions of political co-operation and political union of the member states have been the subject of active consideration.

When, in 1969, it was announced that a Summit Conference of the Heads of State or Government was to be held at the Hague in December both the Assembly and the Commission took the opportunity of

---

[20] Also see *Bulletin of the European Communities* (1974) Part 1, p. 5 and *Eighth General Report on the Activities of the European Communities* (1975), p. 9.

[1] See *The United Kingdom and the Communities* (Cmnd. 4715), paras. 29 and 70 and *Britain's New Deal in Europe* (H.M.S.O. 1974), p. 12.

[2] See *Bulletin of the European Communities* (1974), Part 6, p. 123, para-2506 and Noel, E., *Working Together: The Institutions of the European Community* (1975) p. 18.

[3] Communiqué of the Meeting of Heads of Government, Paris, 9–10 December 1974, para. 6 printed in *Eighth General Report of the Activities of the European Communities* (1975) at p. 298. Also see the Tindemans Report on European Union, *Bulletin of the European Communities*, Suppl. 1/76 at p. 31.

expressing the hope that the Conference would take steps to ensure that progress will be made towards political union.[4] In their Final Communique the Heads of State or Government reaffirmed their belief in the political objectives of the Community and took the modest step of instructing their Foreign Ministers to study and make proposals for the achievement of progress in the matter of political unification in the context of an enlarged Community.[5] The Foreign Ministers requested a Committee made up of senior officials of their Ministries and presided over by M. Davignon, Director of Political Affairs in the Belgian Foreign Ministry, to prepare a draft report on this matter. The resulting document, the Davignon Report, was approved by the Foreign Ministers on 20 July 1970.[6]

In the Davignon Report the desire is expressed to make progress towards political unification through co-operation on foreign policy. The object of this co-operation is to achieve a better mutual understanding on major problems of international policy and to strengthen the sense of common purpose by harmonising ideas, concerting attitudes and taking common action whenever this is possible and desirable.[7] To those ends it was proposed that the Foreign Ministers of the member states should meet regularly at least at six-monthly intervals.[8] Preparations for these meetings should be undertaken by a Political Committee made up of the Heads of the Political Departments of the respective Foreign Ministries, the Committee itself should meet at least four times a year and may set up working groups responsible for specific tasks.[9] The Report also proposed that if the circumstances are sufficiently grave or the subject matter sufficiently important a ministerial meeting may be replaced by a conference of Heads of State or Government[10] These proposals were implemented and a regular pattern of ministerial meetings in May and November of each year was established.[11] At these meetings such matters as East-West relations,

---

[4] See the Assembly's Resolution and the Commission's Memorandum reproduced in an annexe to the *Third General Report on the Activities of the Communities* (1970), at pp. 482 and 484 respectively.

[5] Reproduced *ibid.*, see paras. 4 and 15, at pp. 487 and 489 respectively.

[6] The Report is reproduced in the *Bulletin of the European Communities*, Vol. 3 (1970), No. 11, at pp. 9 *et seq.* Also see the *Report of the Political Affairs Committee on the Political Future of the European Community* (European Parliament Working Document 118/70).

[7] *Davignon Report*, Part Two, sections I and IV.

[8] *Ibid.*, section II.

[9]*Ibid.*[3] sections II (3) and III. In practice the Political Committee meets much more frequently; see Annex to the Second Report on European political co-operation, *Seventh General Report on the Activities of the European Communities* at p. 509.

[10] *Ibid.*, section II (1) (*b*).

[11] Meetings were held in May and November commencing in November 1970.

the European security conference and the middle east were discussed. At the Paris Summit Meeting in October 1972, in the context of their declared aim to achieve European Union by 1980, the Heads of State or Government agreed to intensify the level of political consultation and asked their Foreign Ministers to prepare a further report on methods to improve political co-operation.[12] That report was completed in July 1973 and subsequently approved by the Heads of State or Government.[13] As a result the Foreign Ministers of the nine now meet at least four times a year. The report also confirmed the role of the Political Committee and established the so-called "Group of Correspondents" to assist it in its work.[14] The machinery for political consultation between the member states of the Community has been given a further dimension by a decision of the Heads of Government at their meeting in Paris in December 1974 to meet regularly three times a year accompanied by their Foreign Ministers.[15] These institutionalised summit meetings are known as meetings of the "European Council." In future they will clearly become a regular feature of Community life.

The status and significance of these developments in the context of the institutional framework of the Communities calls for some comment. By the creation of machinery for political consultation distinct from yet parallel to the institutions of the Communities the Governments of the member states are attempting to draw a clear distinction between matters of international politics on the inter-governmental level on the one hand and the activities of the Communities based on legal obligations contained in the Treaties on the other.[16] Matters of mutual political concern to the member states which do not directly relate to the Treaties are discussed by the Foreign Ministers outside the Community structure and assisted by the Political Committee; matters which do directly relate to the Treaties are discussed within the Council of the Communities assisted by the Committee of Permanent Representatives. The newly created "European Council" is a hybrid which if discussing non-Community matters is no more than a Summit

---

[12] See the Declaration issued at the end of the Summit Meeting, paras. 14 and 15, *Sixth General Report of the Activities of the European Communities* (1973) pp. 15, 16.
[13] The Report is printed in *Seventh General Report of the Activities of the European Communities* (1974) at p. 502.
[14] See Part II of the Report, *ibid.* at p. 504.
[15] See the Communiqué issued at the end of the Meeting, para. 3, *Eighth General Report on the Activities of the European Communities* (1975) at p. 297.
[16] See Second Report on European Political Co-operation, *Seventh General Report on the Activities of the European Communities* (1974) at p. 507.

Conference and if discussing Community matters is a manifestation of the Council of the Communities.[17]

This separation of powers clearly has implications for the institutional life of the Communities.[18] Matters of mutual political concern to the member states are almost always on the periphery of Community affairs. Regular extra-Community meetings of Foreign Ministers together with the institutionalisation of Summit Meetings will tend to enhance the ascendancy of the Governments of the member states within the constitutional framework of the Communities and further undermine the Commission's role as an initiator. Both the Davignon Report and the Second Report on European Political Co-operation are to some extent conscious of such dangers.[19] Where "the work of the Ministers is liable to affect the activities of the Commission" the Commission has been invited to express its views and to participate in meetings of the Foreign Ministers and of the Political Committee and of the "European Council". The Commission has in fact been invited to play an increasing role in these activities and is fully involved in most aspects of political co-operation.[20] Equally, steps are taken to keep the Assembly informed of developments in political co-operation. Every six months joint meetings are held by the Foreign Ministers and the Assembly's Political Affairs Committee and an annual report on progress towards political union is given by the President-in-Office of the Council to the Assembly.[1] It is in the interests of the Community that the practical significance of the legalistic distinction between political co-operation and Community activities be minimised. The "European Council" could have a unifying influence and this would be enhanced if Mr. Tindemans' proposal is adopted that the distinction between the Council of the Communities and meetings of the Foreign Ministers of the Nine is abolished.[2]

---

[17] There is no reason why the Council should not be made up of Heads of Government; see Merger Treaty, art. 11.

[18] E.g. the Commission's threat of collective resignation in May 1972; see Berthoud, R., *The Times*, 27 May 1972.

[19] See *Davignon Report*, Part Two, Sections II and V and the Annex to the Second Report, *loc. cit., supra*.

[20] See *Eighth General Report on the Activities of the European Communities* (1975) at pp. 7, 8.

[1] See *Davignon Report*, Part Two, Section VI and the Annex to the Second Report, *loc. cit., supra*.

[2] *Bulletin of the European Communities*, Suppl. 1/76 at p. 31.

CHAPTER SEVEN

The Assembly of the European Communities

(THE EUROPEAN PARLIAMENT)

(A) COMPOSITION AND ORGANISATION

The Assembly, which since 1958 has served the three Communities in common[1] is designed to introduce an element of democratic control into the Communities. Article 137 of the E.E.C. Treaty thus provides that the Assembly shall consist of representatives of the peoples of the member states. At present the Assembly has 198 members made up in the following way: France, Germany, Italy and the United Kingdom have 36 members each, Belgium and the Netherlands have 14 members each, Denmark and Ireland have 10 members each and Luxembourg has 6.[2]

In very general terms the allocation of the numbers of seats to particular member states reflects the size of their population. A strictly mathematical proportional representation is not aimed at and would not indeed be practicable because of the vast difference between the population of the smallest member Luxembourg with 350,000 inhabitants and France with some 50 millions. A strictly mathematical exercise would give a derisory number of delegates to the small states and an overwhelmingly large number to the big states.[3] The figures actually employed represent a compromise so as on the one hand to recognise the relative size of population of the member states, but on the other to ensure that even the smallest member is given a number

---

[1] Common Institutions Convention 1957, section 1.
[2] E.E.C. Treaty, art. 138 (2) as amended by the adjusted Act of Accession, art. 10.
[3] On the basis of the figures quoted if Luxembourg had five delegates France would be entitled to some 700.

large enough to enable it to have a reasonably representative delegation. And, at the same time not to produce an overlarge unwieldy body.

On the question of the procedure whereby national delegates are appointed to the Assembly the Treaties provide, first, that the delegates shall be nominated by the respective national parliaments from among their members in accordance with the procedure laid down by each member state[4] and, secondly, that the Assembly shall draw up proposals for elections by direct universal suffrage in accordance with a uniform procedure in all member states.[5] At the present time there is no election to the Assembly by direct universal suffrage and the delegates are still appointed by the national parliaments from among their own membership for one year renewable terms. The procedures actually followed by the parliaments of the member states differ: Dutch and Belgian members are nominated on a proportional basis from both houses of parliament; German members are nominated on a proportional basis from the Bundestag (the lower house of the German Parliament); the French and Italian members are chosen by a majority vote in both houses; and the Luxembourg members are nominated by the parliamentary committee for foreign and military affairs.[6] There would be nothing to prevent any member state from electing its own national delegation by a direct suffrage but none has chosen to do so.

Article 139 (1) of the Act of Accession required the Parliaments of the new member states, upon accession, to designate their delegates to the Assembly. The United Kingdom Parliament implemented that obligation and, following the precedents of the British delegations to the Assemblies of the Council of Europe, the Western European Union and N.A.T.O.[7] nominated a delegation drawn from both Houses of Parliament so as to reflect broadly the comparative strength of the political parties in the House of Commons.[8] At the end of 1975 the British delegation was made up of 18 Labour members, 16 Conservative members, 1 Liberal member and 1 member of the Scottish National Party. Twelve of the delegates were members of the House of Lords: 7 Labour 4 Conservative and 1 Liberal.[9]

In May 1960 the Assembly, acting in pursuance of the mandate given it by the Treaties, drew up and approved a draft Convention on election to the Assembly by direct universal suffrage and submitted it

---

[4] E.g. E.E.C. Treaty, art. 138 (1).
[5] *Ibid.*, art. 138 (3); but see further below.
[6] See Palmer, M., *et al.*, *European Unity* (1968), p. 177.
[7] See Erskine May's *Parliamentary Practice*, 18th Edn. (1971), Chapter 3.
[8] For the original resolutions creating the delegation see 848 H.C. Deb. 1293 and 337 H.L. Deb. 1114. The Labour Party refused to nominate delegates until the so-called renegotiation of the terms of entry had been satisfactorily concluded.
[9] See Vacher's *European Companion*, No. 14, pp. 42–65.

to the Council whose unanimous approval is necessary for its adoption.[10] The Council made no recommendation concerning the adoption of this draft Convention despite repeated requests from the Assembly. With the exception of the Netherlands the original member states were not very favourably disposed towards the proposal for direct election. This was largely due to the fact that the Convention proposed that the membership of the Assembly should be increased to 426[11] and with an enlarged, directly elected Assembly the arguments for giving such a body increased powers of control over Community affairs would have been enhanced. This was viewed with disfavour by the national governments from their entrenched position in the Council.

In March 1969 the Assembly in a resolution yet again drew the attention of the Council to the fact that it had not yet reached a decision on the draft Convention and had not indeed studied it for six years![12] The resolution urged that the Council take action without delay. The resolution also referred to art. 175 (1) and (2) of the E.E.C. Treaty which empowers the Assembly to take proceedings before the Court of Justice against the Council if it infringes the Treaty by failing to take action provided that the Council has been asked to take action and has failed to do so within two months of the request. Thus the Council was threatened with proceedings before the Court if it continued to take no action on the Assembly's proposals.

During the periods before and immediately after the accession of the new member states no progress on this matter was possible. But more recently the Assembly turned its attention anew to direct elections[13] and received positive encouragement from the Heads of Government at their meeting in Paris in December 1974. They declared that the Treaty objective of direct elections to the Assembly should be achieved as soon as possible.[14] In January 1975 the Assembly submitted to the Council a new Draft Convention introducing elections by direct universal suffrage.[15] An Assembly of 355 members is proposed allocated as follows: Germany 71, United Kingdom 67, Italy 66, France 65, Netherlands 27, Belgium 23, Denmark 17, Ireland 13 and Luxem-

---

[10] The text of this draft Convention is reproduced in *The Case for Elections to the European Parliament by Direct Universal Suffrage* (European Parliament, 1969) at pp. 238 *et seq.*

[11] See art. 2 of the draft Convention.

[12] For the text of the resolution see *op. cit.* in note 10 above at p. 277.

[13] See the Report of the Assembly's Political Affairs Committee, Dec. 368/74.

[14] See *Eighth General Report on the Activities of the European Communities* (1975), p. 299.

[15] For the text of the Draft Convention see *Bulletin of the European Communities* (1975), Part I, p. 95.

bourg 6. Members should be elected for five years and pending the adoption of a uniform electoral system, each member state may use its own system. It is probable that on the basis of these proposals direct elections to the Assembly will be introduced in 1978.[16]

Although, as we shall shortly see, the Assembly is more of a deliberative and consultative body than a parliament in the true sense, it has nevertheless parliamentary pretensions. In the first place although the Treaties still refer to it as the Assembly, since 1962 it has formally adopted the title European Parliament and it is invariably referred to by this name in Community circles and Community documents. Secondly, it has organised itself as if it were a legislative and not a consultative body. The members are not seated in national groups but sit in multinational political groups. Thus in the Assembly we find the nucleus of European political parties made up of individuals of differing nationality linked by common political beliefs. At present there are six political groups in the Assembly: the Christian Democrats; the Socialists; the Liberals and Allies; the European Conservatives; the European Progressive Democrats; and the Communists and Allies.[17] Of the major British parties the Conservative members established their own group, whilst the Labour and Liberal members joined the Socialist and Liberal Groups respectively.

The Assembly is organised in 14 standing committees each specialising in an aspect of the Communities' activities, e.g. Economic and Monetary Affairs, Budgets, External Economic Relations, Legal Affairs, etc.[18] These committees were originally set up to draft reports upon the basis of which the general debate in a plenary session of the Assembly could take place. This is a procedure based on continental parliamentary practice whereby a debate before the whole house is invariably preceded by an examination of the subject of the debate by a committee of the house. The debate then proceeds on the basis of that committee's report.[19] In practice the committees of the Assembly have come to play an independent Community role largely because an international body like the Assembly cannot meet as frequently as a national parliament. Therefore, the

---

[16] As anticipated by the Heads of Government at their meeting in Paris in December 1974 and confirmed by the "European Council" at its meeting in Rome in December 1975; see *Bulletin of the European Communities* (1975), Part II, p. 8.

[17] See Vacher's *European Companion*, No. 14, pp. 40, 41. In addition there are six members of minority parties which include one Scottish Nationalist.

[18] For the basic provisions concerning these Committees see *Règlement du Parlement européen*, Chapter 8, J.O. No. 97, 15 October 1962, p. 2444/62.

[19] See Niblock, M., *The E.E.C.: National Parliaments in Community Decision Making* (1971).

committees have not only prepared reports for debates in the Assembly, but have also maintained contact with the Commission and Council in the interim between parliamentary sessions. Thus the Committees act as a safeguard for the continuity and effectiveness of Parliamentary control. As standing committees they can meet at anytime at the request of their chairman or the Assembly and so by this means the Assembly is kept abreast of developments within the Communities as they occur and not after the event.

One final point concerning the organisation of the Assembly, in which it differs from a national parliament, is that it is not of course divided into government and opposition parties. The Assembly is not organised or run by any particular political group represented within it. Its officers and the composition of its committees reflect both political and national representation.

Practical questions concerning the organisation of the Assembly are in the hands of the Assembly's Bureau which is elected annually and consists of a President and twelve Vice-Presidents.[20] The details of sessions of the Assembly and its agenda are worked out by a Committee of Presidents made up of the Bureau, the Presidents of the Assembly's Committees and the Presidents of the Political Groups within the Assembly.[1] In these administrative and organisational chores the Assembly is assisted by a Secretary-General and a Secretariat of over 500 persons divided into five Directorates-General. The role of the Secretary-General is similar to that of the Clerk of the British House of Commons.[2]

The Assembly holds a number of plenary sessions each year. During 1974 the Assembly held 14 plenary sessions occupying a total of 56 days. For 38 of these days it met in the Assembly Chamber of the Council of Europe in Strasbourg and for the other 16 in Luxembourg where it has its administrative headquarters. It may also meet in extraordinary session at the request of a majority of its members or of the Council or Commission.[3] Between sessions each Committee will meet at least once. The appropriate Commissioners will appear before it to give an account of decisions taken and of proposals referred to the Council. The Committees follow the working of the Council and Commission closely and they are able to keep the Assembly as a whole well informed of activities and developments within the Communities.

---

[20] See *Règlement du Parlement européen*, arts. 6, 7 as amended.
[1] *Ibid.*, arts. 12, 13.
[2] *Règlement du Parlement européen*, Chapter 11.
[3] *Ibid.*, art. 15.

(B) THE FUNCTIONS AND POWERS OF THE ASSEMBLY AND ITS RELATIONS WITH THE COMMISSION AND THE COUNCIL

As has already been mentioned the Assembly is in no sense a legislative body; its functions are of a supervisory and advisory nature. As a supervisory body it possesses a power of censure over the Commission. If a motion of censure is passed by a two-thirds majority of the votes cast, which also represents a majority of the total membership of the Assembly, the entire Commission must resign and be replaced.[4] This power has not yet been used although it has been threatened.[5] On the face of it this is a far reaching power; a power which is found in no other international organisation. The power of censure does have its limitations however. In the first place the Assembly has no direct voice in the nomination of Commissioners to replace a censured Commission. But, more important than that, the power of censure over the Commission is somewhat inappropriate since in general both the Assembly and the Commission share a common European attitude to Community matters and tend to be both ranged against the Council as the exponent of national interests. That is not to say of course that the views of the Assembly and the Commission are naturally identical. They can and do differ particularly in terms of tactics: the Commission may be prepared to make concessions in the face of the views of the Council in an attempt to reach a workable compromise and the Assembly may be inclined to take a harder line. But in any event the mere existence of the power of censure does enhance the authority and influence of the Assembly in that it is a force to be reckoned with and not to be ignored.[6]

Secondly, the Assembly has the means of exercising a degree of supervision over the day-to-day activities of the Communities through its power to ask questions.[7] This is a procedure reminiscent of the British member of parliament's right to question ministers. Written questions can be put to the Commission and to the Council and ample

---

[4] E.g. E.E.C. Treaty, art. 144.

[5] In 1963 the Assembly was highly critical of the policy of the High Authority of the E.C.S.C. and the Socialist Group in the Assembly threatened to propose a motion of censure; see Palmer, M. et al., op. cit., p. 182. In 1972 a motion of censure was tabled alleging a failure on the part of the Commission to propose further budgetary power for the Assembly; the motion was subsequently withdrawn. See Bulletin of the European Communities (1972), Part II, p. 133 and Part 12, pp. 103–105.

[6] Cf. the Vedel Report, Chapter 3, section II (4); see Bulletin of the European Communities, Vol. 5 (1972), Supplement to No. 4.

[7] E.g. E.E.C. Treaty, art. 140. Also see Règlement du Parlement européen, Chapter 9.

use is made of this procedure: during 1974 678 written questions were put to the Commission and 123 to the Council.[8] Written questions and the replies to them are published in the Communities' *Official Journal.* Oral questions may also be put to Council or Commission during a plenary session of the Assembly and these may be followed by debate. During 1974 65 oral questions were put to the Commission and 31 to the Council.[9] In January 1973 the Assembly amended its Rules so that an hour is set aside for oral questions to the Commission and the Council during each part-session of the Assembly.[10] Both the Commission and the Council have accepted this new procedure; Question Time has become a regular feature of the Assembly's proceedings. It provides an opportunity for short, pointed questions to be put followed by supplementary questions thus enabling a dialogue to take place between the members of the Assembly and the members of the Commission and the Council. During 1974 the Commission replied to 90 such questions and the Council to 37.[11]

This right to ask questions enables an eye to be kept on developments in Community policy both generally and in relation to particular topics. Thus the Assembly is able to comment on issues more or less as they arise, rather than becoming involved in the more protracted procedure of the Assembly's Committees investigating a certain matter and then reporting back to the Assembly. A further example of the supervisory powers of the Assembly lies in the debates which the Assembly has on the Commission's Annual Report on Activities in the Communities. This enables the Assembly to discuss and comment upon the whole field of Community activity.[12]

As an advisory body the most important of the Assembly's powers lie in its right to be consulted over major policy proposals in the E.E.C. and Euratom.[13] This process of consultation may take place at either or both of two stages in the decision-making process: the Council may consult the Assembly after it has received a proposal from the Commission; the Commission itself may consult the Assembly when it is in the process of drafting its proposals. The Commission has frequently sent its proposals to the appropriate Assembly committee at

---

[8] *Eighth General Report on the Activities of the European Communities* (1975) at p. 15.
[9] *Ibid.*
[10] See the Report of the Legal Affairs Committee, Doc. 252/72 and the Debates of the European Parliament, O. J. Annex No. 157, 18 January, 1973.
[11] *Eighth General Report on the Activities of the European Communities* (1975) at p. 15.
[12] E.g. E.E.C. Treaty, art. 143.
[13] E.g. E.E.C. Treaty, arts. 43, 54, 56, 87 and Euratom Treaty, arts. 31, 76, 85, 90.

the same time as it has sent them to the Council. It will be recalled that one of the contributing factors to the 1965 crisis was the French accusation that the Commission had made its views known to the Assembly before it communicated them to the governments of the member states. At the Luxembourg meeting in 1966 it was therefore agreed that proposals and other official acts which the Commission submits to the Council and to the member states are not to be made public until the recipients have had formal notice of them and are in possession of the texts.

In this consultative role the Assembly acts largely through its committees. A given proposal will be submitted to the appropriate committee which will produce a report containing a draft opinion. That draft will then be debated by the full Assembly and the final agreed version will be communicated to the Council or Commission as the case may be. This right of consultation is not a power of decision: the Council is not in any way bound by nor is the Commission obliged to pay heed to, an Assembly opinion. In practice the influence of the Assembly has tended to vary depending on the subject matter: on matters of social policy its influence has been quite extensive; in matters of restrictive practices its influence has been moderate; in matters of agricultural policy its influence has been negligible.[14] The explanation of these variations appears to be that the Assembly's influence is greater where matters can be decided relatively quickly and its influence decreases as negotiations between Council and Commission become more prolonged. In the context of a marathon session on agricultural policy, for example, where there is a sharp difference of view between Council and Commission, the object of the marathon is to find a solution which both sides can accept and in such a context it is more likely that the Assembly's opinion will be disregarded.

In recent years, as has already been pointed out, the authority of the Council has tended to increase largely at the expense of the Commission. This imbalance in the relations between Community institutions has also vitiated the role of the Assembly. The Council's reluctance to adopt the majority voting prescribed by the Treaties, backed up by the terms of the *Accords de Luxembourg* of 1966, has increasingly obliged the Commission to draft proposals designed to secure the unanimous approval of the Council. In such a situation in which the initiative of the Commission has been effectively curbed, the influence of the consultative opinions of the Assembly has been equally diminished.[15]

---

[14] See Palmer, M. *et al.*, *op. cit.*, p. 184.
[15] See the *Vedel Report*, Chapter 3, section II (4).

(C) INCREASED POWERS FOR THE ASSEMBLY

The Assembly has long had pretensions towards becoming a truly parliamentary body and it has kept up steady pressure for increasing its powers. The Assembly has been particularly insistent that its control not only over its own budget but also over the budget of the Communities as a whole should be increased.[16] In the first place the Assembly has always had the power to draft its own estimates and to debate the Community budgets. But apart from that the budgetary powers of the Assembly differed as between the E.C.S.C. on the one hand and the E.E.C./Euratom on the other. In the case of the former, where funds were paid direct to the Community in the form of levies, the Assembly had virtually full power over its budget and had in practice (although not by virtue of any Treaty provision) acquired advisory rights over the whole of the E.C.S.C. budget. In the case of the E.E.C./Euratom, where finances derived from contributions from member states, the Assembly had no power at all and it was the Council which had a decisive voice over both the Assembly's budget and the Communities' budgets generally. Since the Assembly received one-third of its budget from each Community this meant that it had no direct control over the allocation of two-thirds of its budget.

The question of enlarging the Assembly's powers was discussed in 1964 in connection with the Merger Treaty but no action was taken. The matter was revived in the following year in connection with the agricultural policy. The Commission urged that the Assembly should be given an effective voice in approving the Community budget on the grounds that the direct revenues which it was proposed to raise as a result of implementing the agricultural policy should be subject to Assembly approval. It will be recalled that this proposal that the Communities be financed independently out of their own resources instead of out of contributions from the member states was part of the proposed package-deal which was the focus of the constitutional crisis of 1965. When the matter was considered by the Council prior to the crisis there was a general consensus in favour of postponing the establishment of direct revenues until 1970 and all members except France were in favour of firmly linking the question of direct revenues with that of increasing the Assembly's powers. After the crisis it was agreed to postpone these matters until the end of the Communities' transitional period.

These matters were resumed at the Summit Meeting of the Six held at the Hague in December 1969. At that meeting it was agreed that

---

[16] On this topic see *Les ressources propres aux Communautés européennes et les pouvoirs budgétaires du Parlement européen* (European Parliament, 1970).

with effect from 1 January 1971 the Communities would progressively draw a greater proportion of finance directly from the revenue of customs duties and levies on agricultural imports. From 1 January 1975 all such duties and levies would be paid direct to the Communities subject to 10% rebate to cover collection costs. The balance of the revenue necessary for the Communities would be made up out of not more than 1% of a Value Added Tax which would then be in force in the member states plus some contributions from the member states.[17] The member states at the Hague Summit also drew up the Treaty of Luxembourg which amended certain budgetary provisions of the Treaties. These included the conferment upon the Assembly of increased budgetary powers over part of the Communities' budget, the so-called non-compulsory part, which deals with the functioning of the Communities' institutions. During the period 1971–74 the Assembly's budgetary powers were strengthened by making it more difficult for the Council to reject amendments proposed by the Assembly. Since 1 January 1975 the Assembly has had complete control over that part of the budget including the power to amend it.[18] It was estimated that this would probably give the Assembly control over not more than 5% of the total budget of the Communities.[19] In fact in 1975, the first year in which the new budgetary procedure was used, the non-compulsory part of the budget amounted to 22·6%.[20] The political importance of this control may be found to outreach the amount of money actually involved. Control over the non-compulsory part of the budget will give the Assembly important powers in relation to the activities of the other institutions of the Communities because he who holds the purse strings can effectively control the means whereby the independent functioning of the other institutions of the Communities is guaranteed.

As far as the remaining part of the budget is concerned the Assembly has not been given the last word in this field. This is called the compulsory part of the budget in that it is the automatic consequence of Community rules, for example, the cost of implementing the agricultural policy, the social policy, the policy to give aid to underdeveloped

---

[17] Council Decision of 21 April 1970, 70/243/ECSC/EEC/Euratom, J.O. No. L94, 28 April 1970, and annexed to the Treaty of Luxembourg 1972, Cmnd. 4867. The V.A.T. element was not in fact included in the 1975 budget because the member states failed to agree on a uniform basis for assessing the tax.

[18] Treaty of Luxembourg 1970, arts. 1–9.

[19] Noel, E., *op. cit.*, p. 9. Cf. *Vedel Report*, Chapter 4, section IV (3).

[20] See Ehlermann, C. D., "Applying the New Budgetary Procedure for the First Time" (1975), 12 C.M.L. Rev. 325. For a description of the new budgetary procedure also see *European Community*, No. 8, November/December 1975, p. 7.

countries, etc. In respect of this part of the budget the Assembly may only propose amendments to the Council which has undertaken to give its reasons to the Assembly if it does not accept such amendments.[1]

At the time the Treaty of Luxembourg was signed in 1970 the Commission undertook to draft proposals to increase further the budgetary powers of the Assembly.[2] After some delay, occasioned by the membership negotiations and the enlargement of the Community, the Commission eventually submitted its proposals in June 1973 in the form of a draft Treaty to amend further the budgetary provisions of the Community Treaties.[3] In the light of consultation with the Assembly and discussion within the Council, agreement has been reached at the Community level on the content of the draft Treaty.[4] In accordance with the procedure for amending the Treaties,[5] this draft must be referred to a conference of representatives of the Governments of the member states for their unanimous approval. The principal amendments contained in the draft are (i) that the Assembly should be given the exclusive authority to give a discharge to the Commission in respect of the implementation of the budget; (ii) the creation of an independent Court of Auditors as a new Community institution to replace the present Audit Board; and (iii) that the so-called "inverted majority rule" be applied to all Assembly proposals concerning the compulsory part of the budget, i.e. that those proposals should be deemed to have been adopted unless expressly rejected by the Council. To complement these amendments the Assembly, the Council and the Commission have instituted a conciliation procedure designed to promote agreement between the Assembly and the Council on financial matters.[6]

The general question of the future role of the Assembly was taken up by the Commission in July 1971. It set up an *ad hoc* Working Party of 14 independent experts to examine the whole corpus of problems connected with the enlargement of the Assembly's powers. The Working Party was under the chairmanship of Professor Vedel, a distinguished French constitutional lawyer, and included experts not only from the existing member states but also from the candidate

---

[1] E.g. Treaty of Luxembourg 1970, art. 4.
[2] *Sixth General Report on the Activities of the European Communities* (1973), pp. 5, 6.
[3] See *Bulletin of the European Communities* (1973), Supplement 9/73.
[4] *Seventh General Report on the Activities of the European Communities* (1974), pp. 45–47 and 497–501 and *Eighth General Report on the Activities of the European Communities* (1975), p. 12.
[5] E.g., E.E.C. Treaty, art. 236. The Convention now awaits ratification by the member states; *Euromarket News*, Vol. 43, No. 30, 29 July 1975.
[6] See *Bulletin of the European Communities* (1975), Part 2, p. 87.

countries.[7] In its wide ranging report the Working Party proposed that the powers of the Assembly should be increased by means of a two-stage plan.[8]

During the first, transitional, stage it was proposed that the Assembly should have a power of co-decision with the Council in four matters referred to as list A, viz. the revision of the Treaties; decisions to give the Communities any necessary new powers; the admission of new members; and the ratification of international agreements concluded by the Communities. In such cases it was proposed that decisions of the Council would only take effect after receiving the approval of the Assembly. Also during this first stage the consultative powers of the Assembly would be extended to cover 18 additional matters, referred to as list B, which would include the common agricultural policy, harmonisation of laws and taxes, the common transport policy and the mutual recognition of diplomas. In connection with these and other matters it was proposed that the Assembly should be given a suspensive veto. In the event of a difference of opinion between the Council and the Assembly on any of these matters it would enable the Assembly to suspend the decision for one month and require the Council to reconsider the matter. The Council's second decision, whether amended or not, would be final. During the second stage, the Assembly's power of co-decision would be extended to all matters in list B. The matters in list A were chosen because they cover questions which materially involve either the constitutive powers of the Communities or their relations with other international persons. The matters in list B are largely those which involve harmonisation measures of one sort or another. Because of the importance of these matters to the life of the Communities and the obligations which they will impose on member states it was thought appropriate to involve the Assembly in their determination initially in the form of consultation supported by the suspensive veto and eventually by co-decision with the Council.

The Working Party also made a number of other recommendations designed to increase the democratic control exercised by the Assembly. The report commented that as European integration extends to include new sectors national parliaments will gradually become less able to exercise their traditional democratic control over legislation affecting their countries. It was suggested that this should be corrected by increasing the powers of the Assembly. In particular the report

---

[7] The British experts were Professor J. D. B. Mitchell, Salvesen Professor of European Institutions in the University of Edinburgh and Mr. Andrew Schonfield, Director of the Royal Institute of International Affairs.

[8] *Vedel Report*, Chapter 4, sections I and II.

recommended (i) the establishment of closer links between national parliaments and the Assembly,[9] (ii) the drawing up of a timetable for election to the Assembly by direct universal suffrage;[10] (iii) the participation of the Assembly in the appointment of the President of the Commission.[11]

In the light of this Report the Commission presented its own proposals to the Summit Meeting of the member states and candidate states held in October 1972. In particular the Commission stressed the importance of enabling the Assembly to participate in the legislative process of the Communities and having the last word on such matters as the approximation of national laws.[12] Although no concrete progress has been made in this direction the Heads of Government have expressed their agreement in principle to increasing the Assembly's powers. At Paris in October 1972 they expressed their desire to strengthen the Assembly's powers of control.[13] This was reiterated at Paris in December 1974 in terms that "the competence of the European Assembly will be extended, in particular by granting it certain powers in the Communities' legislative process".[14] A similar point has been made by Mr. Tindemans in his *Report on European Union*.[15] If the Assembly's powers are indeed increased along these lines then it may be well on the way to becoming a European Parliament in a real sense.

---

[9] *Vedel Report*, Chapter 6.
[10] *Ibid.*, Chapter 5.
[11] *Ibid.*, Chapter 4, section VII.
[12] *Sixth General Report on the Activities of the European Communities* (1973), p. 5.
[13] *Ibid.* at p. 16.
[14] *Eighth General Report on the Activities of the European Communities* (1975), p. 299.
[15] See *Bulletin of the European Communities*, Suppl. 1/76 at pp. 29, 30.

CHAPTER EIGHT

Ancillary Community Institutions

In addition to the subsidary bodies already mentioned there are a number of ancillary institutions which either advise on or otherwise participate in the activities of the Communities. Some of these owe their origin to the Treaties themselves; others have been established in the light of experience.

(1) CONSULTATIVE BODIES

Of all the ancillary institutions, pride of place should perhaps be given to the Consultative Committee of the E.C.S.C. and the Economic and Social Committee which serves both the E.E.C. and Euratom. Both of these advisory bodies consist of representatives of the various sections of economic and social life in the Communities. Thus the Consultative Committee, appointed under the terms of art. 18 of the E.C.S.C. Treaty,[1] consists of not less than 60 and not more than 84 members (81 members at present) including an equal number of producers, workers, consumers and dealers in the coal and steel industries. The Economic and Social Committee, appointed under the terms of arts. 193 and 198 of the E.E.C. Treaty, arts. 165 to 169 of the Euratom Treaty[2] and art. 5 of the Common Institutions Convention, consists of 144 persons representing producers, farmers, carriers, workers, dealers, craftsmen, professional occupations and the general public. The 144 members are allocated on a national basis as follows: France, Germany Italy and the United Kingdom have 24 each, Belgium and the Netherlands have 12 each, Denmark and Ireland have 9 each and Luxembourg has 6.[3]

---

[1] As amended by Act of Accession, art. 22.
[2] As amended by the adjusted Act of Accession, art. 21.
[3] During the period from accession until the referendum in June 1975 British Trade Union representatives refused to participate in the activities of these Committees.

In the case of both Committees although the members are appointed by the Council they are appointed in their private capacity and are expressly forbidden to act on any mandate or instructions from the bodies nominating them. There is also an obligation on the Council to consult the Commission on appointments to the Economic and Social Committee and it may also obtain the opinion of European organisations representing particular economic and social sectors of interest. The role of these Committees is an advisory one. They may be consulted by the Commission or Council whenever it is thought appropriate and in some cases consultation is obligatory. Under art. 60 (1) of the E.C.S.C. Treaty, for example, the Commission may define unfair competitive pricing practices after consulting the Consultative Committee and the Council and similarly under art. 75 of the E.E.C. Treaty the Council, on a proposal from the Commission, may lay down common rules applicable to international transport between or across the territories of member states after consultation with the Economic and Social Committee. Thus these Committees provide a sounding board for informed and general opinion on matters relating to the policies of the Communities, roughly on a parallel with the practice in the United Kingdom of consulting interested parties prior to the making of legislation whether parliamentary or subordinate.

Although the opinions of these consultative committees are in no way binding they are not without their influence. It has been suggested that they may even be more influential than the opinions of the Assembly since they are the informed views of those involved in activities likely to be affected by the policies of the Communities.[4] The Commission appears to treat their views with respect and the Economic and Social Committee has certainly tended to support the Commission's proposals. The Council in the past adopted a more restrictive attitude.[5] But at the Paris Summit in 1972 the Heads of State or Government invited the Community institutions "to recognise the right of the Economic and Social Committee in future to advise on its own initiative on all matters affecting the Community."[6] The Committee's Rules of Procedure have been amended to recognise this new right of initiative[7] and use has been made of it.[8] The Rules of Procedure have also been

---

[4] See Torelli, M., *L'Individu et le Droit de la C.E.E.* (1970), at p. 58, and Zellentin, G., "The Economic and Social Committee" (1962), 1 *Journal of Common Market Studies* 22.

[5] See Palmer, M., *et al.*, *European Unity* (1968), at p. 186.

[6] *Sixth General Report on the Activities of the European Communities* (1973) at p. 16.

[7] See Decision 74/428/EEC, Euratom, O.J. L228, 19 August 1974, p. 1.

[8] *Seventh General Report on the Activities of the European Communities* (1974) at pp. 70, 71.

amended to give formal recognition of the Committee's *de facto* division into three groups each representing particular interests: the Employers' Group, the Workers' Group and the General Interests Group.[9] It has been the experience of the Committee, rather like that of the Assembly and its political groups, that its members tend to vote by group and not by nationality.

(II) TECHNICAL COMMITTEES

There are numerous agencies and committees of experts relating to specific areas of Community activity; some of the more important of these are as follows. A Monetary Committee set up under the terms of art. 105 of the E.E.C. Treaty to keep the monetary and financial position in the member states under review. The Committee appointed by the Council under the terms of art. 111 of the E.E.C. Treaty to assist the Commission in tariff negotiations with non-member states. The Scientific and Technical Committee set up under the terms of art. 134 of the Euratom Treaty.[10] The Administrative Commission for the Social Security of Migrant Workers which supervises the social security arrangements for citizens of community members working in a country other than their own. The Short Term and Medium Term Economic Policy Committees: the former assists in the co-ordination of day-to-day economic policies; the latter studies the likely development of the Community's economy over a five-year period. The membership of these Committees is commonly drawn from the national administrations of the member states and their role is purely advisory.

(III) EUROPEAN INVESTMENT BANK

The European Investment Bank is an independent institution, established by art. 129 of the E.E.C. Treaty and endowed with legal personality. The members of the Bank are the member states of the Community. The task of the Bank, as set out in art. 130, is to contribute, by means of its own resources and access to the capital market, to the balanced and steady development of the Common Market. To that end the Bank, operating on a non-profit-making basis, is empowered to grant loans and to give guarantees to facilitate the financing of three types of project in all sectors of the economy: (i) projects for developing the less developed regions of the Community; (ii) projects for

---

[9] *Ibid.* at pp. 71, 72.
[10] The membership of this Committee was increased by the adjusted Act of Accession, art. 23.

modernising or converting undertakings or for developing fresh activities called for by the progressive establishment of the Common Market; and (iii) projects of common interest to several member states. In the cases of the latter two types of project, the Bank's assistance is limited to projects which are of such a size or nature that they cannot be entirely financed by the various means available in the individual member states.

The organisation, function and powers of the Bank are set out in detail in a separate statute annexed to the E.E.C. Treaty. The Bank was originally set up with a capital of 1,000 million units of account subscribed by the member states, ranging from 300 million subscribed by France and Germany to 2 million subscribed by Luxembourg;[11] 25% of this sum was paid up. A reserve fund of 10% of the total capital was also built up progressively.[12] Upon the enlargement of the Community the total capital of the Bank was increased to 2,025 million units of account; the largest contributions are those from France, Germany and the United Kingdom at 450 million ranging down to Luxembourg at 3 million.[13] Of this subscribed capital 20% shall be paid up;[14] the contributions of the new members will be paid in instalments extending over a period of two and a half years.[15]

The seat of the Bank is in Luxembourg. The Bank is directed and managed by a Board of Governors, a Board of Directors and a Management Committee.[16] The Board of Governors consists of the Ministers of Finance of the member states. The essential role of the Board of Governors is to lay down general directives for the credit policy of the Bank and to ensure that those directives are implemented.[17] The system of voting which is provided for the Council by art. 148 of the E.E.C. Treaty also applies to the Board of Governors.[18] The Board of Directors consists of 18 directors with 10 alternates. They serve five-

---

[11] Statute of the Bank, art. 4 (1). The value of the unit of account is stated to be 0·88867088 grammes of fine gold. This is the equivalent to the gold content of the U.S. Dollar as fixed in 1944.

[12] *Ibid.*, art. 24.

[13] See adjusted Act of Accession, Protocol No. 1, art. 2. The sterling equivalent of the United Kingdom's contribution is £187·5 million of which £37·5 million will be paid up; see *The United Kingdom and the European Communities* (Cmnd. 4715, 1971), para. 135.

[14] Protocol No. 1, art. 3.

[15] For the arrangements for the payment of instalments see the Commission's report, *The Enlarged Community* (1972), para. 42.

[16] Statute of the Bank, art. 8. Privileges and immunities are enjoyed by the members of the organs, the staff of the Bank and the national representatives on the Bank under the terms of the Protocol on Privileges and Immunities 1965, art. 22.

[17] Statute of the Bank, art. 9.

[18] *Ibid.*, art. 10 as amended by Act of Accession, Protocol No. 1, art. 5.

year renewable terms and are appointed by the Board of Governors. Three directors are nominated by each of France, Germany, Italy and the United Kingdom; one director is nominated by each of Belgium, Denmark, Ireland, Luxembourg, the Netherlands and the Commission. Germany, France, Italy and the United Kingdom nominate two alternates each; the Benelux countries by common accord nominate one alternate as does the Commission. It is the task of the Board of Directors to manage the Bank in accordance with the Treaty and Statute and the general directives laid down by the Board of Governors. It has the sole power to grant loans and guarantees and to raise loans and it fixes the interest rates and commission payable on loans and guarantees respectively.[19] The current business of the Bank is in the hands of the Management Committee consisting of a President and four Vice-Presidents. These are appointed for six-year renewable terms by the Board of Governors upon a proposal from the Board of Directors. The Management Committee acts under the authority of the President and the supervision of the Board of Directors. Its functions are to prepare the decisions of the Board of Directors on both the raising of loans and the granting of loans and guarantees and to ensure the implementation of those decisions.[20] The President, or in his absence one of the Vice-Presidents, acts as non-voting Chairman of the Board of Directors.[1]

The Bank obtains its funds primarily from loans floated on the capital markets of the world. Between its foundation and the end of 1974 the Bank has signed no less than 564 loan and guarantee contracts totalling 4,654·4 million units of account. During 1974 alone the Bank signed 84 loan contracts the combined value being 996·4 million units of account[2]. This included nine loans for projects in the United Kingdom totalling 149·5 million units of account (£79·9 million).[3] Although most loans and guarantees are in connection with projects within the territories of the member states, it has also been empowered to assist overseas territories and states associated with the Community.[4]

Under the terms of art. 180 of the E.E.C. Treaty the Court of Justice of the Communities has jurisdiction over certain types of dispute concerning the Bank. In particular the Board of Directors enjoy the

---

[19] *Ibid.*, arts. 11 and 12 as amended by the adjusted Act of Accession, Protocol No. 1, arts. 6, 7 and 8.

[20] Statute of the Bank, art. 13 as amended by adjusted Act of Accession, Protocol No. 1, art. 9.

[1] Statute of the Bank, art. 11 (2).

[2] See the *European Investment Bank's Annual Report for 1974* at p. 15.

[3] For further details see *ibid.* at pp. 50, 51.

[4] See Yaoundé Convention of Association 1963, art. 16 (*b*) and Lomé Convention 1975, art. 42.

powers conferred on the Commission by art. 169 of the E.E.C. Treaty in connection with the non-fulfilment of member states of obligations under the Statute of the Bank; also under the terms of art. 173 of the E.E.C. Treaty any member state, the Commission or the Board of Directors may challenge measures adopted by the Board of Governors and similarly any member state or the Commission may challenge measures adopted by the Board of Directors. No proceedings appear to have been brought under any of these heads. Article 29 of the Statute of the Bank provides that disputes between the Bank and its creditors and debtors shall be decided by the competent national courts unless jurisdiction has been conferred on the Court of the Justice of the Communities.

(IV) MANAGEMENT AND RULE-MAKING COMMITTEES

We have already seen that with the development of the common policies of the Communities into new areas, particularly agriculture, the Council has delegated to the Commission considerable law-making powers. Under the terms of the Treaties the Commission is not in a subordinate position to the Council, and so if this delegation took the form of empowering the Commission to act independently it would remove such matters entirely from the control of the Council. Further, since these powers would have been transferred to the Commission by the Council upon the Commission's proposal, it is believed that the Commission could only be deprived of such powers by the same process, namely on the Commission's initiative. The member governments wished to avoid these consequences of delegation which might prove disadvantageous to themselves. In addition, particularly in the field of agriculture, it was practically desirable that the process of implementing the common policies should be carried out in close consultation with the governments of the member states. The system of Management Committees or *Comités de Gestion* was devised to achieve those objectives.

The management committee procedure was introduced by Regulation 19 of 1962.[5] Article 25 of that Regulation established a Management Committee for Cereal Products made up of representatives of the member states and presided over by a representative of the Commission. Similar management committees have since been set up for each of the main categories of agricultural products. The chairman of a management committee is a member of the staff of the Commission,

---

[5] J.O. No. 30 of 4 April 1962, p. 933/62, since replaced by Regulation 120/67, J.O. No. 117 of 19 June 1967, p. 2269/67.

usually the head of the Department which covers the products dealt with by the Committee. The chairman has no vote. The procedure is for the Commission to submit a draft implementing measure to the appropriate management committee for its opinion. The management committee employs the system of weighted voting used in the Council itself. The management committee's opinion is not binding on the Commission. The Commission may modify its draft in the light of the opinion or adhere to its original proposal. In either event the Commission's decision, after submission of its proposal to the management committee, will have the immediate force of law. But, if there is a conflict between the views of the Commission and the opinion of the Committee and if that opinion has received the qualified majority of 12 votes, the matter must be referred to the Council which may within a period of one month reverse the Commission's decision. If, on the other hand, the Commission's draft is acceptable to the Committee or if the Committee is opposed to it but cannot muster the qualified majority, the Commission's decision is not subject to an appeal to the Council.

It is generally agreed that the management committee procedure works well in practice. In 1974 as a result of some 400 meetings of management committees well over 1,000 regulations and decisions were adopted. A considerable degree of co-operation and mutual confidence between the Commission and the member states has been engendered by this procedure. When the Commission differs from a committee opinion given by a qualified majority, which happens infrequently, the procedure operates as an alarm mechanism and gives a clear indication of a serious problem which can only be effectively resolved by the member states acting through the Council. The original intention was that this procedure should only be resorted to during the transitional period of the Community's development but because of its success it has been expressly continued in existence for an indefinite period.[6]

Another development has been the application of a similar procedure to areas of community activity other than the agricultural, with a result that committees of government representatives have been set up to assist in the implementation of the common customs tariff and in connection with the control of standards in relation to food and animal health.[7] These latter committees, whilst they are manifestations of the

---

[6] See Regulation 2602/69, J.O. No. L324 of 27 December 1969, p. 23.
[7] E.g. the Committee on Origin, established by Regulation 802/68, J.O. No. L148 of 28 June 1968; the Standing Veterinary Committee established by a Council Decision of 15 October 1968, J.O. No. L255 of 18 October 1968; and the Common Customs Tariff Nomenclature Committee established by Regulation 97/69, J.O. No. L14 of 21 January 1969, p. 1.

management committee procedure, are usually distinguished from the management committees properly-so-called and are referred to as rule-making committees. In connection with these committees the powers delegated by the Council to the Commission are more circumscribed. The Commission's proposal only has immediate binding effect if it is approved by the committee. If the committee disapproves of a proposal by an opinion reached by the qualified majority, or if no opinion is forthcoming because of the committee's inability to reach the qualified majority, then the Commission must refer its proposal to the Council for acceptance by a qualified majority vote. There is a final rider to this procedure, however, and that is if the Council in such a case has failed to take a decision within three months then the Commission itself may adopt the proposed measure and it will thereby acquire the force of law. The management committee procedure has also been incorporated into the machinery for administering the European Regional Development Fund.[8]

The constitutional validity of the management and rule-making committee procedures have been questioned in some quarters.[9] The crux of this question is the vagueness of the Treaty provisions relating to the delegation of powers by the Council to the Commission. Article 155 of the E.E.C. Treaty in its final provision states that the Commission shall "exercise the powers conferred on it by the Council for the implementation of the rules laid down by the latter". It has been argued that the force of that provision is to enable the Council to confer upon the Commission powers which are materially identical with the powers possessed by the Council itself. Thus, where under art. 43 (2) of the E.E.C. Treaty the Council has the power to adopt regulations for the implementation of the common agricultural policy, if the Council purports to delegate that power to the Commission it may only do so absolutely and not conditionally. By imposing the management committee procedure upon the powers delegated it has been suggested that the Council is making an unlawful change in the decision-making powers of the Commission. In other words the suggestion is that the management committee procedure depends on political expediency within the Communities rather than on constitutional authority under the terms of the Treaty.

The view taken by both the Commission and Council in support of the management committee procedures is that they are perfectly compatible with the Treaties. The view of these institutions was

---

[8] Regulation (E.E.C.) 724/75, arts. 11–13, O.J.L73, 21 March 1975.
[9] E.g. Schindler, P., "The Problems of Decision-Making by way of Management Committee Procedure in the E.E.C." (1971), 8 C.M.L.Rev. 184.

clearly put by the Commission in its *Second General Report on the Activities of the Communities* (1968).[10] There it is pointed out that whilst art. 155 of the E.E.C. Treaty does not prevent the Council from exercising its implementing powers itself, it is clear that any implementing powers not retained by the Council may only be delegated to the Commission. Further the Council is, in any event, bound to observe the institutional balance of the Communities.

As early as 1958 in the case of *Meroni & Co.* v. *High Authority*[11] the Court of Justice commented on the general concept of delegated powers in the Communities. In its judgment in that case the Court stressed the necessity of preserving the balance of powers which is a characteristic of the institutional structure of the Communities and concluded that any delegation of a discretionary power upon institutions different from those established by the Treaties would be invalid.[12] These principles laid down in the *Meroni* case underlie the judgment of the Court in three cases decided in December 1970 in which the validity of the management committee procedures was directly challenged.[13]

Part of the Community's agricultural policy takes the form of regulations to forestall unexpected movements of agricultural products which, if permitted, would threaten the common organisation of markets in those products. To that end the Commission has made regulations providing for compulsory import and export certificates to be obtained by those who wish to make imports or exports of particular agricultural products. It is further required that such certificates should be supported by the payment of a security which will be forfeit if the imports or exports were not made during the period of the certificate's validity. In these cases the legality of this system of certificates was challenged on the ground, *inter alia*, that the management committee procedure which had been employed in the making of the regulations was contrary to the E.E.C. Treaty.

The arguments against the legality of the management committee procedure were that it permitted the management committees to interfere in the legislative activities of the Commission, that it gives to the member states a right of appeal to the Council against a Commission

---

[10] Paras. 639–42. Also see *Rapport sur les procédures communautaires d'exécution du droit communautaire dérivé* (European Parliament, Document de Séance, No. 115/68).

[11] 9/56, June 1958; 4 Recueil 9; Valentine, D. G., *The Court of Justice of the European Communities* (1965), Vol. 2, p. 457.

[12] Rec. 9, at p. 44; Valentine, *op. cit.* at p. 478.

[13] Cases 25, 26 and 30/70: *Einfuhr-und Vorratsstelle für Getreide und Füttermittel* v. *Köster, Berodt & Co., Henck and Scheer* (1971), 8 C.M.L.Rev. 250; 16 Rec. 1161, 1183 and 1197.

regulation, thus derogating from the role of the Court, and that consequently it disturbs the institutional balance of the Community. The Council expressed the contrary view in terms which have already been outlined above. The Court supported the Council's view. It held that art. 155 which authorises the Council to delegate rule-implementing powers to the Commission must be understood as permitting the Council to lay down provisions and procedures whereby its own policy decisions may be implemented. The management committee procedure was held to come within the modalities upon which the Council is allowed to make such an authorisation of the Commission dependent. Further, the allegation that the management committees interfere in the legislative activities of the Commission was not substantiated since the role of a management committee is merely to give opinions and it has no power to make decisions. Its views may influence the Commission but, subject to one proviso, the power of decision remains with the Commission. As far as the proviso is concerned, which involves the allegation that the management committee procedure gives a right of appeal to the Council from a decision of the Commission, this the Court also held to be unsubstantiated. The management committee procedure merely enables the Council to take action instead of the Commission where the committee hands down a negative opinion. Practice has shown these cases to be exceptional and in any event whether the final decision is made by the Commission or Council the powers of the Court to review such decisions are left unimpaired.

Finally, the Court said that there is no question of this procedure disturbing the institutional equilibrium of the Communities. The Council has in effect delegated powers to the Commission subject to the condition that the opinion of the appropriate management committee is sought. Regardless of the contents of that opinion the Commission has the power to make binding decisions. In the event of an adverse opinion the Commission is obliged to refer its decision to the Council which may then choose to substitute its own decision for that of the Commission. Thus the Council is merely reserving to itself the freedom to use its own rule-making power in circumstances in which there is a substantial difference of opinion between its delegate, the Commission, and the representatives of the member states. Since the role of the management committees is essentially consultative and since, subject to the power to delegate, the rule making powers are conferred by the Treaty upon the Council, the institutional order was held to be unaffected. It is submitted that these conclusions apply equally to rule-making committees.

There is general agreement that the management committee procedure works well. Not only has it been decided to retain it indefinitely but more use is likely to be made of it in future in view of the Council's decision to make wider use of its powers under the last paragraph of art. 155 of the E.E.C. Treaty.[14] In delicate areas of community policy which impinge on individual national interests the management committee procedure has made it possible for considerable progress to be made in the implementation of that policy. As a measure of the value of these procedures the Commission reported in 1974 that in the overwhelming majority of cases Commission decisions have been adopted with the endorsement of the management committees. During 1974 out of 1,653 votes taken in management committees, 1,556 were favourable, none were unfavourable and no opinion was offered in only 97 cases.[15] But for the introduction of management committee procedures which provide a means for close consultation between the Commission and the governments of the member states, the Council would probably have been reluctant to transfer wide-ranging legislative powers to the Commission. As a result the Commission's authority within the E.E.C. has tended to be strengthened. Thus the political significance of the management committee procedures must not be overlooked. As one commentator has observed, it has enabled the wills of the member states to be joined in common activity thus achieving one of the basic aims of the Communities.[16] It is also noteworthy that these procedures appear to be crisis-proof; during the 1965–66 constitutional crisis, whilst Community legislation by the Council came to a virtual standstill as a result of the absence of the French representative, the French continued to participate in management committee activities throughout the crisis.[17]

---

[14] See *Bulletin of the European Communities* (1974), Part 6, p. 122.
[15] *Eighth General Report on the Activities of the European Communities* (1975) at pp. 167, 168.
[16] Bertram, C., "Decision-making in the E.E.C.: the Management Committee Procedure" (1967–68), 5 C.M.L.Rev. 264.
[17] *Ibid.*

CHAPTER NINE

The Court of Justice of the Communities

I COMPOSITION AND PROCEDURE

(A) COMPOSITION AND ORGANISATION[1]

The Court of Justice of the Communities, as we have seen, has its origins in the Court which was originally set up under the E.C.S.C. Treaty. In the words of the E.E.C. Treaty the role of the Court is to "ensure that in the interpretation and implementation of [the] Treaty the law is observed".[2]

The Court is composed of nine judges unanimously elected by the Governments of the member states. This means in practice that each member state has a judge of its nationality on the Court.[3] They hold office for six-year renewable terms. The Treaties provide that the judges must be chosen "from persons whose independence can be fully relied upon and who fulfil the conditions required for the exercise of the highest judicial office in their respective countries or are legal experts of universally recognised ability".[4] In practice the Bench has been made up of a mixture of professors of law, judges, lawyers in private practice and government legal advisers.

The judges enjoy the usual guarantees of independence and impartiality. They enjoy immunity from suit and legal process during their tenure of office and they retain that status after ceasing to hold office in respect of acts done in the performance of their duties. This immunity may, however, be suspended by the Court itself in plenary session.[5] The judges also enjoy privileges and immunities in respect of

---

[1] See E.E.C. Treaty, arts. 165–168 (as amended by the adjusted Act of Accession, arts. 17–19 and the Council Decision of 1 January 1973 increasing the number of advocates-general) and Protocol on the Statute of the Court of Justice, Titles I and II.

[2] Article 164; see also E.C.S.C. Treaty, art. 31 and Euratom Treaty, art. 136.

[3] The United Kingdom judge is Lord Mackenzie Stuart, a former judge of the Scottish Court of Session.

[4] E.E.C. Treaty, art. 167.

[5] Protocol on the Statute of the Court, art. 3.

taxation, currency and exchange regulations. They may not hold any office of an administrative or political nature nor engage in any occupation or profession paid or unpaid, although in the case of the latter in an exceptional case permission may be given by the Council.[6]

Judges may resign or be removed from office. To resign, a judge must inform the President of the Court who in turn notifies the President of the Council which latter act creates the vacancy. A judge may be removed from office if, in the unanimous opinion of his brethren, he no longer fulfils the conditions required or meets the obligations resulting from his office. The Court's decision to remove a judge must be communicated to the President of the Assembly and the President of the Commission and must be notified to the President of the Council. The latter notification produces a vacancy.[7]

The President of the Court is appointed by the judges from among their own number by an absolute majority vote in a secret ballot. A President holds office for a three-year term which may be renewed. The Court may sit for certain purposes in chambers and so there are two Presidents of chambers who each preside over a chamber. They are elected for one-year renewable periods by the same process used to elect the President.[8] The number of judges may, at the request of the Court, be increased by a unanimous decision of the Council.[9]

The judges of the Court are assisted by four advocates-general who must possess the same professional qualifications as the judges and are also appointed for a six-year renewable term by a unanimous decision of the Council.[10] One of their number is designated annually by the Court as First Advocate-General.[11] The office of advocate-general is one which has no precise parallel in the English legal system. The institution of advocate-general, like much of the procedure of the Court itself, is largely derived from French law. The function of the advocate-general is similar to that of the *Commissaire du Gouvernement* at the French *Conseil d'Etat*. It is the role of the *Commissaire du Gouvernement* to act as what Professor Hamson has called "the embodied conscience of the Court".[12] He is required to consider the issues in a case

---

[6] *Ibid.*, art. 4.
[7] Protocol on the Statute of the Court, arts. 5 to 7.
[8] Rules of Procedure of the Court, art. 10.
[9] E.E.C. Treaty, art. 165.
[10] E.E.C. Treaty, arts. 166, 167; as amended by the Council Decision of 1 January 1973 increasing the number of advocates-general, O.J. L2, 1 January 1973, p. 29.
[11] Rules of Procedure of the Court, art. 10. In practice each of the four larger member states nominates an advocate-general; the United Kingdom advocate-general is Mr. J.-P. Warner, Q.C., formerly junior counsel to the Treasury in Chancery matters.
[12] *Executive Discretion and Judicial Control* (1954), p. 80.

impartially and individually and to reach his own personal conclusion as to what in law and justice should be done. Before the Conseil d'Etat considers its judgment the *Commissaire*, orally and in public, states the facts and the law as he sees them and suggests the principles in accordance with which he thinks the case should be decided. The *Commissaire* does not participate in the giving of judgment still less is he the representative of or subordinate to the government. His purpose is to act as an entirely uncommitted and fearless defender of the law and justice. Similarly, in the case of the advocates-general of the Court of Justice of the Communities, the Treaties require them to "make reasoned submissions in open court, with complete impartiality and independence", on cases before the Court.[13] Their task is a threefold one: to propose a solution to the case before the Court; to relate that proposed solution to the general pattern of existing case law; and, if possible, to outline the probable future development of the case law. The advocates-general therefore represent neither the institutions of the Communities nor the public; they function only as the spokesmen of the law and justice in the context of the Treaties.

As in the case of the submissions of the French *Commissaires du Gouvernement* so the submissions of the advocates-general are in no way binding on the Court. But their submissions are invariably published with the judgment of the Court and where, as often happens, the Court agrees with the advocate-general, the advocate-general's full consideration of the wider aspects of the case not only throws valuable light on the Court's comparatively brief judgments, but also act as an indicator of the direction the jurisprudence of the Court is likely to take in the future. In this way the advocates-general are in a position to influence the development of Community law.[14]

As has been said there is no precise parallel in the English legal system to the office of advocate-general. The Attorney-General does have a role as guardian of the public interest or protector of public rights, e.g. as a party in civil proceedings for an injunction or declaration in cases of public nuisance and his appearance before public tribunals of inquiry as a spokesman for the public interest. Similarly, in matrimonial proceedings, the Queen's Proctor has a right of intervention to prevent a decree nisi being made absolute on the ground, for example, that material facts have not been put to the court. A court may also ask the Official Solicitor to instruct counsel to ensure that all points of view on matters of law are fully before the court. But in these

---

[13] E.g. E.E.C. Treaty, art. 166.
[14] See Hamson, *op. cit.*, pp. 79–81; Brown, L. N. & Garner, J. F., *French Administrative Law*, 2nd Edn. (1973), pp. 50, 151; Bebr, G., *Judicial Control of the European Communities* (1962), pp. 24–25.

cases the roles of the Attorney-General, the Queen's Proctor and the Official Solicitor are limited and special whereas that of the advocates-general is unlimited and general.[15] He is in a sense a sort of institutionalised *amicus curiae*. Advocates-general may retire and be removed by the same procedure as in the case of judges and they enjoy similar privileges and immunities. The Treaties are silent on the nationality of the judges and advocates-general but in practice of course they are always of the nationality of one of the member states.

The seat of the Court is in Luxembourg and, subject to public holidays and the usual vacations, it is in permanent session. In case of urgency the President may convene the Court during vacations.

The day to day administration of the Court is in the hands of the Registrar (*Greffier*) and his staff. The Registrar is elected by the judges by majority vote after consultation with the advocates-general. The Registrar's term of office is six years and he is eligible for re-election. The Court may dismiss him if he no longer complies with the obligations of his office.[16]

Each judge and advocate-general has an *attaché* or personal assistant. *Attachés* are of the same nationality as their masters and are required to have legal training. Their main task is to prepare pre-trial studies on the legal questions involved in a case before the Court. They thus provide a service similar to that of the Law Clerks to the Judges of the United States Supreme Court.[17]

In principle the Court sits in plenary session with a quorum of seven, but it is enabled to set up separate chambers and has established two chambers of three judges each presided over by a President of a Chamber. It is the function of these chambers, at the request of the Court, to undertake preliminary examinations of evidence in particular cases. They can hear and decide cases brought by one of the officials of a Community institution against that institution and uncontroversial cases referred for a preliminary ruling may also be assigned to them.[18] Each chamber is assisted by an advocate-general.[19]

(B) PRACTICE AND PROCEDURE

The practice and procedure of the Court are based on a code of Rules of Procedure drawn up by the Court.[20] The procedure of the Court is divided into three stages: a written stage; an *instruction*

---

[15] See Edwards, J. Ll. J., *Law Officers of the Crown* (1964), Chapter 14; *Rayden on Divorce* (12th Edn. 1974), pp. 471–472; *Midland Cold Storage Ltd.* v. *Turner,* [1972] 3 All E.R. 773 at p. 778.

[16] See Rules of Procedure of the Court, Part 1, Chapter 3.

[17] For a critical comment on the *attachés* see Feld, W., *Court of the European Communities* (1964), p. 27. Also Valentine, D. G., *Court of Justice of the European Communities* (1965), Vol. 1, p. 42. [Footnotes 18–20 appear on facing page]

(enquiry) stage, and an oral stage. As soon as a complaint (a *requête*) is filed with the Registrar, the President appoints one of the judges as *juge-rapporteur* (reporting-judge). The task of the *juge-rapporteur* is to prepare a preliminary report on the case for the consideration of the Court.[1]

The written stage takes the form of pleadings. The plaintiff in his *requête* will set out his claim against the defendant and the grounds upon which it is made. The defendant will then be notified of the *requête* and will be given the period of one month within which to prepare and submit to the Court a statement of defence. The plaintiff may make a written reply to the defence and the defendant may then also make a final rejoinder. This exchange of submissions comprises the written stage in the proceedings. It should be pointed out that these written submissions go far beyond the scope and purpose of English pleadings. The arguments of the parties are set out fully together with the nature of the evidence upon which reliance is placed. This has the effect of stressing the written stage at the expense of the other two stages.[2]

The *juge-rapporteur* then examines the pleadings and considers whether the case requires an *instruction*, i.e. an enquiry or proof-taking stage which is a familiar part of continental legal procedure. The *juge-rapporteur* reports to the Court on whether an *instruction* is necessary and after the Court has also heard the advocate-general on this point it will decide whether to proceed to an *instruction*. If the Court decides that an *instruction* is necessary it can be held before the full court, before one of the chambers of the court or it may be entrusted to the *juge-rapporteur* himself. In any event, the *instruction* will take the form of a personal appearance of the parties and their witnesses for oral examination and the production and inspection of documentary evidence. This procedure of *instruction* is principally conducted not by the lawyers representing the parties, but, following continental practice, by the Court, chamber or *juge-rapporteur* as the case may be. The advocate-general may also participate in the *instruction*. The representatives of the parties may only question witnesses "subject to the

---

[18] See Rules of Procedure, art. 95 and Council Decision 74/584/E.E.C., Euratom, E.C.S.C., O.J. L318, 28 November 1974 at p. 22.

[19] See Rules of Procedure of the Court, art. 9.

[20] The Rules require the unanimous approval of the Council; E.E.C. Treaty, art. 188. The present Rules were approved on 26 November 1974; see O.J. L350, 28 December 1974. For descriptions of procedure before the Court see Cohn, E. J., "Luxembourg Days" (1962) 233 *Law Times* 342, and Barber, J. and Reed, B. (Eds.) *European Community : Vision and Reality* (1973), p. 211.

[1] See generally the Rules of Procedure of the Court, Title 2.

[2] In 1971 the Court gave judgment in 60 cases in which the written procedure totalled 18,000 pages; Campbell, *op. cit.*, Vol. 3, para. 7.23.

control of the President."[3] In addition to witnesses who are called at the request of the parties, the Court and the advocate-general also have the power to summon witnesses. Evidence is given on oath sworn either in accordance with the laws of the state of the witness's nationality, or alternatively in the form set out in the Rules of Procedure. The Court has the power to exempt a witness from taking the oath.[4] At the end of the *instruction* the Court may allow the parties to submit written observations on matters which have arisen in the course of the *instruction*.

After the conclusion of the *instruction*, or, if there has been no *instruction*,[5] at the end of the written proceedings, the oral stage takes place before the full court. During the oral stage the *juge-rapporteur* will present his report which will outline the case, summarise the arguments of the parties and make a statement on the facts of the case on the basis of the evidence presented during the written and *instruction* stages. This report will be followed by oral argument on behalf of the parties. There is no hearing of witnesses or oral examination at this stage. The parties must be legally represented during the oral stage.[6]

Members of the Court and the advocate-general may put questions to agents and counsel during the oral proceedings. The Court may also at this stage order further *instruction* to be held either by a Chamber or by the *juge-rapporteur*. At the conclusion of the case the parties' representatives make closing speeches to the Court: plaintiff first, followed by defendant. The advocate-general then makes his submissions which bring the oral proceedings to a close.

The judges withdraw to deliberate in private. In the course of their deliberations they may re-open the oral proceedings if they so wish. These deliberations finally result in the Court's judgment which is drafted by the *juge-rapporteur*. Judgment is delivered in open court. Again, following continental practice, the court renders a single collegiate judgment; separate or dissenting opinions are not permitted. Even if the judgment is based on a majority decision that fact, let alone the nature of the majority, is not disclosed.[7] It has already been pointed out that in the vast majority of cases the Court accepts the

---

[3] Rules of Procedure, art. 47 (4).
[4] Rules of Procedure, arts. 47 (5) and 110.
[5] As is usually the case.
[6] Member states and Community institutions must be represented by an agent who may be assisted by a lawyer entitled to practise before a court of a member state. Corporate bodies and individuals may also have an agent but they must be represented by a lawyer entitled to practise before a court of a member state. See Protocol on the Statute of the Court, art. 20. Cf. Jacobs F.G. and Durard, A., *References to the European Court* (1975), pp. 177, 178.
[7] For comment on the practice of single collegiate judgments see Bebr. *op. cit.*, p. 24 and Feld, *op. cit.*, p. 99.

conclusions of the advocate-general. But in those cases where the Court has not followed the advocate-general, his submissions can in a sense be regarded as a dissenting opinion.[8]

The languages of the Court are the official languages of the Communities, viz. Danish, Dutch, English, French, German and Italian; Irish may also be used although it is not an official language.[9] All documents submitted to the Court must be translated into these languages. Only one of the languages may be used as the procedural language in a given case. The basic rule is that the choice of procedural language is made by the plaintiff where one of the Communities' institutions is the defendant, on the basis that the representatives of the Communities are well versed in all the official languages. But where the defendant is one of the member states or the court of a member state is seeking a preliminary ruling then the procedural language must be the language of that state. The Court's judgments, together with the submission of the advocates-general, are published in each of the official languages; the copy in the procedural language of a given case being regarded as the authentic and definitive version.[10]

The Court's judgments have binding force from the date of their delivery.[11] As far as the enforcement of the Court's judgments is concerned the position varies depending on the outcome of the case and the identity of the defendant. If the Court upholds or declares invalid an act of a Community Institution then either that act may be implemented or not depending upon the decision of the Court; in such cases there is no question of enforcing the judgment in the strict sense. If the Court gives judgment against a member state under the E.C.S.C. Treaty enforcement is achieved by enabling the Commission, acting jointly with the Council, to impose sanctions on the defaulting member. This procedure is not reproduced in the Treaties of Rome which contain no enforcement measures for use against member states. The Rome Treaties merely provide that the member state in question is required to take the measures necessary to execute the Court's judgment. Lastly, if the Court gives judgment against a corporate body or individual in the form of a fine, such judgment debts are enforceable without further formality by the national courts of the member states.[12]

---

[8] A list of the leading cases in which the Court disagreed with the advocate-general is given in Campbell, A., *Common Market Law*, Vols. 1 and 3, para. 6.33.

[9] Rules of Procedure, art. 29 (1).

[10] See Rules of Procedure of the Court, Title I, Chapter 6. On the problems of multilingual judicial deliberations see Feld, *op. cit.*, pp. 100, 101. It is unusual for the time between filing a complaint and judgment to exceed 2 years; the average time is 10 months: Green, A. W., *Political Integration through Jurisprudence* (1969), pp. 47, 48.

[11] Rules of the Court, art. 65.

[12] E.E.C. Treaty, arts. 187, 192.

(C) REVISION AND INTERPRETATION OF JUDGMENTS

The Court of Justice of the Communities is a court of first and only instance. Thus the decisions of the Court are final and are not subject to appeal; it is not open to a national court when called upon to enforce a judgment of the Community Court to challenge that judgment in any way. The only possible course of action open to an unsuccessful litigant is to request a revision of the Court's judgment.[13] Such a request may be made on the ground of the discovery of a fact likely to prove of decisive importance which, before judgment, was unknown both to the Court and to the party requesting revision. Two periods of limitation apply to requests for revision: the request must be made within ten years of the date of the judgment and within three months of the date on which the new fact became known to the applicant. If these conditions are satisfied, and without prejudice to the merits, the Court hears the advocate-general and considers the parties' written submissions before deciding whether the alleged new fact does exist and whether it justifies revision. If the Court decides that the request is admissible then it proceeds to consider the merits of the case and this can, if necessary, involve a completely new trial. In *Feram v. High Authority* (1960) the Court made it clear that the newly discovered fact must have been unknown both to the Court and to the party, and that knowledge of it prior to judgment by either Court or a party will make the request inadmissible. In *Fonderie Aciaierie Giovanni Mandelli v. Commission* (1971), the Court refused an application for revision in a similar case in which a relevant document could have been obtained by the applicant either at the time of the commencement of the original action or at the enquiry stage.[15]

A final point concerning the practice of the court relates to the possibility in case of difficulty as to the meaning or scope of a judgment of asking the Court to interpret its judgment.[16] Such a request may be made by any of the parties to the case or by a Community Institution which can show that it has an interest in the decision. The only part of a judgment which may be the subject of a request for interpretation is the operative part or what we would call the *ratio decidendi*. As the Court itself put it in *Assider v. High Authority* (1955)[17] "the only parts of a

---

[13] See Protocol on the Statute of the Court, art. 41 and Rules of Procedure of the Court, art. 98 to 100.

[14] Case 1/60, 6 Rec. 351; Valentine, *op. cit.*, Vol. 2, p. 661.

[15] Case 56/70: 17 Rec. 1 at pp. 3, 4. Also see Case 57/70: *August Josef van Eick v. Commission*, 17 Rec. 613, *per* Adv. Gen. Dutheillet de Lamothe at p. 620.

[16] See Protocol on the Statute of the Court, art. 40 and Rules of Procedure of the Court, art. 102.

[17] Case 5/55, 1 Rec. 263; Valentine, *op. cit.*, Vol. 2, p. 55.

judgment which can be interpreted are those which express the judgment of the Court in the dispute which has been submitted for its final decision and those parts of the reasoning upon which this decision is based and which are, therefore, essential to it . . . the Court does not have to interpret those passages which are incidental and which complete or explain that basic reasoning".

In the later case of *High Authority* v. *Collotti* (1965)[18] the Court considered the nature of the "difficulty" necessary to justify a request for an interpretation. In the *Assider* case the court had said that it was sufficient for the parties to give different meanings to the judgment. In the *Collotti* case the Court defined the nature of the difficulty more precisely. The Court held: "In order to be admissible, an application for interpretation . . . must not raise the possible consequences of the judgment in question on cases other than the one decided, but only the obscurity and ambiguity of the meaning and scope of the judgment itself in relation to the case decided by the judgment in question."

II THE CONTENTIOUS JURISDICTION OF THE COURT[19]

The Court is the creature of the Community Treaties and so its jurisdiction derives exclusively from those Treaties. Any attempt to attribute other jurisdiction to the Court will fail. In the case of *Schlieker* v. *High Authority* (1963)[20] the plaintiff alleged that through the inactivity of the High Authority she had suffered loss. It was argued on behalf of the High Authority that the right to bring proceedings before the Court based on the inactivity of a Community institution was limited by the Treaty to member states, other Community institutions and undertakings and associations. Frau Schlieker argued in reply, upon analogy with German municipal law, that the Court had a residual jurisdiction to enable it to protect the interests of individuals where the Treaty texts are silent. This view was rejected both by the advocate-general and the Court. The advocate-general observed that "the Treaty system . . . does not in a general clause guarantee legal protection without any gaps. Reference to . . . the Basic Law (*Grundgesetz*) of the

---

[18] Case 70/63 bis; 11 Rec. 352; Brinkhorst, L. J., & Schermers, H. G., *Judicial Remedies in the European Communities* (1969), p. 259.

[19] The Court's jurisdiction to give preliminary rulings at the request of the courts of the member states will be discussed later in connection with the relationship between Community law and municipal law; see Chapter 11.

[20] Case 12/63: [1963] C.M.L.R. 281; 9 Rec. 173.

Federal Republic of Germany cannot lead to any other solution, for the Court can define the limits of its supra-national legal protection only by using the text of the Treaty and not by following national law."[1] The Court agreed with this submission and held that "whatever may be the consequence of a factual situation of which the Court may not take cognizance, the Court may not depart from the judicial system set out in the Treaty". Thus in interpreting the Treaties the Court is bound to adhere strictly to the provisions of the text, and, being the creature of the Treaty, it has no power other than that conferred by the Treaty.

The jurisdictional provisions of the Treaties are somewhat complex; as one commentator has observed "no international tribunal has ever been equipped with so varied a jurisdictional competence as has the Court of the European Communities."[2] The contentious jurisdiction conferred upon the Court by the Treaties falls under two main heads which will be treated in the following order:

(a) Actions against member states; and
(b) Actions against community institutions.

(A) ACTIONS AGAINST MEMBER STATES

Actions against member states take two forms:

(i) Actions by member states against member states.
(ii) Actions by community institutions against member states.

(i) All the Treaties confer upon the Court a compulsory jurisdiction to decide disputes between member states concerning the application of the terms of the Treaties and a permissive jurisdiction, based on the consent of the parties, over disputes between states related to the object and purpose of the Communities in general. Thus the E.E.C. Treaty provides first at art. 170 that "Any Member State which considers that another Member State has failed to fulfil any of its obligations under this Treaty may bring the matter before the Court of Justice."[3] Secondly, the E.E.C. Treaty provides at art. 182 that "The Court of Justice shall be competent to decide any dispute between Member States connected with the subject of this Treaty, if that dispute is submitted to it under a special agreement between the parties."[4] The Court's jurisdiction over both of these types of dispute is exclusive;

---

[1] Unwritten rules of Community law for the protection of fundamental rights may, however, be derived from national law; see Chap. 2, *supra*.
[2] Bowett, D. W., *Law of International Institutions* (3rd Edn. 1975), p. 278.
[3] Cf. E.C.S.C. Treaty, art. 89, and Euratom Treaty, art. 141.
[4] Cf. E.C.S.C. Treaty, art. 89, and Euratom Treaty, art. 154.

recourse by member states to other means of settlement is expressly forbidden by the Treaties. Article 219 of the E.E.C. Treaty provides that "Member States undertake not to submit a dispute concerning the interpretation or the carrying out of this Treaty to any method of settlement other than those provided therein."[5] This insistence on referring inter-state disputes to the Court of Justice underlines one of the major purposes of the Court and that is to guarantee uniformity of interpretation and application of the law of the Communities. No proceedings under this head have so far been brought.[6]

(ii) By virtue of art. 88 of the E.C.S.C. Treaty the Commission is given the power to decide whether a member state has failed to comply with its obligations under the Treaty. If it so decides in relation to a given member state the Commission must invite that state to express its views on the matter. The Commission may then record the state's wrongdoing in a reasoned opinion and give the state a limited time within which to take steps to fulfil its obligations. The purpose of this process is to enable both the Commission and the member state to exchange views in the hope that the issue may thereby be settled. If it is not, it is open to the member state in question to bring proceedings before the Court challenging the Commission's decision. Although such litigation takes the form of a member state bringing proceedings against the Commission, in substance the issue before the Court is an alleged breach of Treaty obligations by a member state; the Treaty places the onus of challenging that allegation upon the member state. In the E.E.C. Treaty by virtue of art. 169 a somewhat different procedure is followed.[7] There if the Commission considers that a member state has failed to fulfil any of its obligations under the Treaties then it shall issue a reasoned opinion after giving the state concerned the opportunity to submit its comments. If the member state does not comply with the terms of such opinion within the period laid down by the Commission the Commission may bring the matter before the Court of Justice. Thus, whilst in the E.C.S.C. the Commission has the power to determine finally a member state's breach of obligations subject to the member state's right to appeal to the Court, in the E.E.C. and Euratom the Commission can only provisionally determine the breach of obligation and it must apply to the Court for that determination to

---

[5] Cf. E.C.S.C. Treaty, art. 87, and Euratom Treaty, art. 193.

[6] On the application of art. 170, see Case 36/62: *van Gend en Loos* v. *Nederlandse Administratie der Belastingen*, [1963] C.M.L.R. 105. Disputes between member states may be at the root of litigation between, say, the Commission and a member state, although the other member state is not a formal party to the action; e.g. Case 13/63: *Italy* v. *E.E.C. Commission*, [1963] C.M.L.R. 289; 9 Rec. 335.

[7] Also Euratom Treaty, art. 141.

be confirmed. Proceedings under art. 169 will lie against a member state for omissions as well as for positive acts, including an administrative failure to implement regulations.[8] In relation to Treaty provisions which have direct effect an art. 169 action will lie where a member state maintains in force national legislation which is incompatible with those provisions, even if in practice the national law is not enforced.[9] Community law must apply in each member state independent of its unilateral will.

The case law on art. 169 of the E.E.C. Treaty throws some light on the nature of the reasoned opinion which the Commission must make concerning the alleged breach of Treaty obligations. In *E.E.C. Commission* v. *Italy* (1961)[10] the Commission wrote a letter to the Italian Government, after giving the Government an opportunity to make its observations, stating that a particular Italian decree was contrary to the Treaty. The Government was asked to end the alleged infringement within one month. This letter did not contain a full review of the situation of the Italian market nor whether that situation justified the decree. Italy did not comply with the Commission's request within the stated period and so the Commission instituted proceedings under art. 169. Italy challenged the admissibility of these proceedings on the ground, *inter alia*, that the Commission's letter was not a reasoned opinion within the meaning of art. 169. The Court rejected that argument and said that an opinion is considered to be reasoned "when it contains, as in the present case, a coherent statement of the reasons which convinced the Commission that the state in question had failed to fulfil one of its obligations under the Treaty". This was also the view expressed by the advocate-general in his submissions where he said that "no formalism is required . . . because . . . the reasoned opinion is not an administrative act, checked by the Court as far as its legal character is concerned. There is no question here of 'insufficient reasons' giving rise to a formal defect. The only purpose of the reasoned opinion is to specify the point of view of the Commission in order to inform the Government and, possibly, the Court." Thus, if a purported reasoned opinion did not coherently express the Commission's viewpoint that would be a ground on which the Court might dismiss the Commission's case.[11]

---

[8] Case 31/69: *E.C. Commission* v. *Italy*, [1970] C.M.L.R. 175; 16 Rec. 25.
[9] Case 167/73: *E.C. Commission* v. *France*, [1974] E.C.R. 359; [1974] 2 C.M.L.R. 216.
[10] Case 7/61: [1962] C.M.L.R. 39; 7 Rec. 633.
[11] Another essential part of the pre-litigation procedure under art. 169 is the giving of a member state an adequate and realistic opportunity to make observations on an alleged breach of treaty obligations; Case 31/69: *E.C. Commission* v. *Italy*, [1970] C.M.L.R. 175 at pp. 180, 188; 16 Rec. 25.

Another of the cases on art. 169 is of more general interest in that it explains the nature of the member states' obligations under the Treaties: *E.E.C. Commission* v. *Belgium & Luxembourg* (1964).[12] By Royal and Grand Ducal Decrees the Belgian and Luxembourg Governments introduced a tax on licences to import certain dairy products. In the Commission's view these taxes were contrary to the E.E.C. Treaty and it followed the art. 169 procedure culminating in action being brought by the Commission against the two Governments. The Governments argued in their defence that a Council Resolution of 1962 which had not yet been implemented would have justified these taxes. This resolution had not been implemented by the deadline of 31 July 1962. Thus the Governments argued that the Commission had no authority to require the abolition of taxes which, but for the failure to implement the Council resolution, would have been part of Community policy. But the Court held that, except for cases expressly covered by the Treaty, member states are prohibited from taking justice into their own hands. Therefore the failure of the Council to carry out its obligations could not excuse the defendants from carrying out their obligations.

In the case of art. 88 of the E.C.S.C. Treaty if the member state does not appeal to the Court or if it loses its appeal, the Commission may, subject to a concurring two-thirds majority of the Council, impose on the member state the sanctions mentioned earlier. In the cases of the E.E.C. and Euratom Treaties no such sanctions are available. Both art. 171 of the E.E.C. Treaty and art. 143 of the Euratom Treaty state that, if the Court of Justice finds that a member state has failed to fulfil any of its obligations under the Treaty, such state shall take the measures required for the implementation of the judgment of the Court.[13] Thus in such cases the Court's judgments are essentially declaratory in nature indicating that in the last analysis the success of the Communities depends upon the good faith of member states. A member state's failure to implement a judgment given against it would also be likely to have an unfavourable political effect on its relations with its fellow members.

(B) ACTIONS AGAINST COMMUNITY INSTITUTIONS

We have already seen that French law has exerted a strong influence on the procedure of the Court of Justice of the Communities. This is also true of the jurisdiction of the Court to exercise control over the

---

[12] Cases 90–91/63, [1965] C.M.L.R. 58 at p. 72; 10 Rec. 1217 at p. 1231.
[13] A failure by a member state to execute a previous judgment of the Court will constitute an infringement of E.E.C. Treaty, art. 171; Case 48/71: *E.C. Commission* v. *Italy*, [1972] C.M.L.R. 699; 18 Rec. 529.

acts of the institutions of the Communities. French administrative law traditionally recognises two main categories of litigation the *recours de la légalité* and the *recours de pleine juridiction*. The former is a kind of judicial review of the legality of administrative acts in which the Court is merely asked to annul, i.e. declare void, an administrative act on one of a number of specified grounds. In such a case if the Court finds that a given act is unlawful on one of those grounds it can merely give judgment to that effect; it cannot substitute its own decision on the merits for that of the institution whose act has been challenged, nor can it award any other remedy such as damages.[14] In addition to *recours de la légalité* French administrative courts may also hear *recours en pleine juridiction*. In such cases those courts are not limited to controlling the legality of acts on specific grounds but they are free to pronounce on the actual merits of the parties' case and to substitute their own decision for that of the administrative authority. Such jurisdiction is *pleine*, i.e. full or plenary, in the sense that when exercising it the court has the complete powers of a civil court to award compensation for damage. These two types of administrative jurisdiction are possessed by the Court of Justice of the Communities and the following discussion will be in terms of that classification:

(i) *Actions Concerning Legality (Recours de la légalité)*

1. *Actions for Annulment (Recours en annulation)*—The acts of the institutions of the Communities take a variety of forms but not all of them are susceptible to challenge. Only those acts which are binding in law are susceptible to challenge. Under the E.C.S.C. Treaty the Commission may act in three forms: decisions, recommendations and opinions. Of these decisions and recommendations are legally binding whilst opinions have no binding force; thus art. 33 gives the Court jurisdiction to hear actions for the annulment of such decisions and recommendations. Under the E.E.C. and Euratom Treaties the acts of the Commission and the Council may take five forms: regulations, directives, decisions, recommendations and opinions; of these the first three are legally binding and are susceptible of an action for annulment. Thus the Court has declined to entertain an action for annulment in connection with any act which is not designed to produce binding legal effects. In *Société des Usines à Tubes de la Sarre* v. *High Authority* (1957)[15] the Court rejected an action challenging an opinion of the High Authority on the ground that the opinion did not lay down a rule

---

[14] Cf. the effect of issuing the prerogative order of certiorari by the English High Court.
[15] Cases 1 and 14/57: (1957), 3 Rec. 221; Brinkhorst & Schermers, *op. cit.*, p. 21.

capable of being applied and was not therefore subject to the control of the Court. The Court is, nevertheless, flexible in its approach and will look to the substance of an act rather than to its form. Thus if an act is in the form normally used for non-binding acts but in fact created binding obligations such an act would be actionable despite its apparent informality.[16]

Actions may be brought not only by member states and by Community institutions but also by private parties. In the first place, art. 173 (1) of the E.E.C. Treaty states that the legality of measures taken by the Council or by the Commission may be challenged in proceedings instituted by a member state, the Council or the Commission.[17] In general terms only a party which can show sufficient legal interest in a case can institute proceedings before the Court, but such is the nature of the Communities that all member states are deemed to have an interest in the legality of all Community acts. Thus, for example, in the *Netherlands* v. *High Authority* (1964)[18] the Netherlands was permitted to challenge a decision of the High Authority which was in fact addressed to some German coal enterprises on the ground that it conflicted with the terms of E.C.S.C. Treaty.

It is clearly possible under the Treaties for one Community institution to challenge an act of another Community institution. To date this has only happened on two occasions.[19] In his submissions in the first of those cases the advocate-general referred to the novelty of the proceedings and attributed this to the fundamental harmony which reigns between these two Institutions. Be that as it may, in that action the Commission challenged certain activities of the Council in the field of the external relations of the Communities. In March 1970 the Council discussed the attitude to be taken by the members of the Communities at a meeting to be held in April of that year to conclude the negotiations for a European Road Transport Agreement (E.R.T.A.) under the auspices of the U.N. Economic Commission for Europe. At that April meeting the members of the Communities negotiated and concluded the Agreement in accordance with the terms of the Council's discussion. The Commission challenged the validity of that discussion on the ground that it involved violation of Treaty provisions, particularly since under art. 228 the Commission is given the task of negotiating

---

[16] See Case 22/70: *Re E.R.T.A. E.C. Commission* v. *E.C. Council*, [1971] C.M.L.R. 355; 17 Rec. 263. Also see Campbell, *op. cit.*, Vols. 1 and 3, paras. 6.92–6.94.

[17] Cf. E.C.S.C. Treaty, arts. 33 and 38, and Euratom Treaty, art. 146.

[18] Case 66/63, [1964] C.M.L.R. 522; 10 Rec. 1047.

[19] Case 22/70: *Re E.R.T.A. E.C. Commission* v. *E.C. Council*, [1971] C.M.L.R. 355; 17 Rec. 263 and Case 81/72: *Re Civil Service Salaries E.C. Commission* v. *E.C. Council*, [1973] E.C.R. 575; [1973] C.M.L.R. 639.

agreements between the Community and non-member states subject to the approval of the Council. The Council challenged this action on the grounds of its admissibility and its merits. On the question of admissibility the advocate-general submitted that, whilst in principle the action was admissible because the discussion in issue was an official discussion of the Council, upon analysis that discussion was not a legally binding act of the Council as defined by the Treaty and so was not susceptible to challenge. The Court disagreed with the advocate-general on this point and held that the action was admissible. The Court pointed out that art. 173 of the E.E.C. Treaty specifically excluded recommendations and opinions from review by the Court. Not only was this discussion neither a recommendation nor an opinion, it had definite legal effects on the member states since during their negotiations on the E.R.T.A. they consistently acted in accordance with the conclusion of the Council discussion. But although the Court differed from the advocate-general on the question of admissibility they both agreed that the action should be rejected on the merits.[20]

Secondly, actions may be brought against acts of Community institutions by private parties, that is to say by individuals or corporate bodies.[1] The *locus standi* of private parties differs somewhat as between the E.C.S.C. on the one hand and the E.E.C. on the other. In the E.C.S.C. undertakings or associations of undertakings may challenge acts of Community institutions where either those acts apply to them individually or, although acts of a general nature, nevertheless involve a misuse of powers affecting them.[2] *Groupement des Industries Sidérurgiques Luxembourgeoises* v. *High Authority* (1956)[3] is a clear illustration of this. The plaintiffs were manufacturers of steel and the main industrial consumers of coal in Luxembourg. They challenged the refusal of the High Authority to declare illegal a Luxembourg levy on coal for industrial use. The Luxembourg government intervened in the proceedings and argued that the plaintiff's action was inadmissible on the ground that they were steel producers and the action was solely concerned with coal. But the Court held that the Treaty did not limit actions relating to coal undertakings and, since *prima facie* this levy was detrimental to the plaintiffs, their right of action could not be denied. In the E.E.C., on the other hand, the right of action is not limited to undertakings but is available to any individual or corporate body against

---

[20] The merits of this case have already been discussed in connection with the external relations of the Communities; see pp. 36, 37, above.

[1] The novelty of this right of audience is fully justified by the fact that Community law applies directly to private parties.

[2] E.g. E.C.S.C. Treaty, arts. 33 (2) and 80.

[3] Cases 7 and 9/54; 2 Rec. 86; Valentine, *op. cit.*, Vol. 2, p. 141.

either a decision directed to him or it or a decision which, although in the form of a regulation or a decision addressed to someone else is of direct and individual concern to him or it.[4]

Certain points of principle concerning the *locus standi* of private parties to challenge acts in the context of the E.E.C. are clear. The Treaty does not recognise an *actio popularis* but requires the party bringing the action to have sufficient legal interest in the issue. This is comparable to the notion of the person aggrieved in English administrative law[5] and to the French maxim *pas d'intérêt, pas d'action*.[6] A right of action is admitted against three types of act: decisions addressed to the party bringing the action; decisions in the form of regulations addressed to other persons; and decisions addressed to other persons. In the last two cases the party bringing the action must be able to satisfy the Court that the decisions affect him directly and individually. Despite certain *dicta* in which a generous interpretation of these provisions has been suggested,[7] the Court has tended to interpret them restrictively and the resulting case law has not yet evolved an entirely consistent line of authority.

Least difficulty arises where the act challenged is a decision expressly addressed to the private party bringing the action, such as in connection with the Community's rules on competition. In such cases there appears to be a conclusive presumption that the plaintiff has *locus standi*.[8] On the question whether a given act is a decision, particularly in the context of decisions in the form of regulations, the Court looks to the object and content of the act rather than to its form.[9] A distinction is drawn between acts which apply to a limited, identifiable number of designees and acts of a normative character which apply to categories of persons envisaged in the abstract and as a whole; the former are decisions, the latter regulations.[10] Thus the Court has held

---

[4] E.E.C. Treaty, art. 173 (2); also see Euratom Treaty, art. 146 (2).
[5] See de Smith, S. A., *Judicial Review of Administrative Action* (3rd Edn. 1973), p. 362 *et seq.*
[6] See Brown, L. N. and Garner, J. F., *French Administrative Law* (2nd Edn. 1973), pp. 86, 87.
[7] See Case 25/62: *Plaumann & Co. v. E.E.C. Commission*, [1964] C.M.L.R. 29 at pp. 46, 47 and Case 69/69: *S. A. Alcan v. E.C. Commission*, [1970] C.M.L.R. 337 at p. 345.
[8] E.g. Case 48–57/69: *Imperial Chemical Industries v. E.C. Commission*, [1972] C.M.L.R. 557; Case 6/72: *Europemballage Corporation and Continental Can Co. Inc. v. E.C. Commission*, [1973] C.M.L.R. 199, and Cases 6 and 7/73: *Istituto Chemioterapico Italiano SpA and Commercial Solvents Corporation v. E.C. Commission*, [1974] C.M.L.R. 309.
[9] Cases 16–17, 19–22/62: *Confédération Nationale des Producteurs de Fruits et Légumes v. E.E.C. Council*, [1963] C.M.L.R. 160 at p. 173.
[10] *Ibid.* at pp. 173, 174.

that a regulation relating to the manufacture of a particular product by a limited number of producers is nevertheless a regulation because of its objective, normative character.[11] Whereas a regulation which was only concerned with import licences which had been sought before that regulation was made was, in fact, a bundle of individual decisions.[12]

This distinction between regulations and decisions also impinges on the requirement that decisions addressed to other persons[13] must be of both direct and individual concern to the party bringing the action. The Court has tended to reverse the order of these two conditions as they are set out in the Treaty on the ground that "it will become superfluous, if the applicant is not concerned individually with the . . . decision, to discover whether it concerned him directly."[14] In *Plaumann & Co.* v. *E.E.C. Commission* (1964) the Court defined individual concern in the following terms: "Persons other than those to whom the decision was addressed can justifiably claim to be concerned individually only if the decision affects them because of certain characteristics which are peculiar to them or by reason of a factual situation which is, as compared with all other persons, peculiarly relevant to them, and by reference to which they may be individually described in a way similar to that of the addressee of the decision."[15] In applying that definition the Court has declined to find individual concern where a decision is addressed to an abstractly defined category of persons even where in reality the decision only affects an ascertainable number of such persons.[16] Such a decision potentially affects an indeterminate number of persons. But where, on the other hand, at the time a decision is made the number of persons affected by it is already finitely determined, i.e. the decision is retroactive, then those persons are individually concerned.[17]

The Court's approach to the question of direct concern appears to depend on whether the party to whom the decision was addressed had a

---

[11] Case 6/68: *Zuckerfabrik Watenstedt GmbH* v. *E.C. Council*, [1969] C.M.L.R. 26.
[12] Cases 41–44/70: *N.V. International Fruit Co.* v. *E.C. Commission* (1971), 17 Rec. 411.
[13] "Other persons" includes member states; see Case 25/62: *Plaumann & Co.* v. *E.E.C. Commission*, [1964] C.M.L.R. 29.
[14] *Ibid.* at p. 47.
[15] *Ibid.*
[16] E.g. Case 1/64: *Glucoséries Réunis* v. *E.E.C. Commission*, [1964] C.M.L.R. 596; Case 38/64: *Getreide-Import Gesellschaft* v. *E.E.C. Commission*, [1965] C.M.L.R. 276; and Case 63–65/69: *Compagnie Française Commerciale et Financière S.A.* v. *E.C. Commission*, [1970] C.M.L.R. 369.
[17] See Cases 106–107/63: *Alfred Toepfer and Getreide-Import Gesellschaft* v. *E.E.C. Commission*, [1966] C.M.L.R. 111; Case 62/70: *Bock* v. *E.C. Commission*, [1972] C.M.L.R. 160; and Cases 41–44/70: *N.V. International Fruit Co.* v. *E.C. Commission* (1971), 17 Rec. 411.

discretion to implement it. If there was no discretion then, subject to the other criteria, the decision is of direct concern; if there was a discretion then it is not. In *Alfred Toepfer* v. *E.E.C. Commission* (1966)[18] the plaintiff's application for a licence to import maize was rejected by the German authorities on 1 October 1963, because of protective measures which they were taking under the terms of the E.E.C. Regulation No. 19. On the same day the German authorities notified the Commission of those measures which were subject to confirmation, amendment or rejection by the Commission within four days of notification. On 3 October the Commission made a decision authorising the German authorities to maintain the protective measures in force between October 1 to 4 inclusive. The plaintiffs challenged that decision. The Court of Justice held that they had the necessary *locus standi*. The decision concerned them directly because it was immediately enforceable and left no discretion with the German authorities; it concerned them individually because the number and identity of the persons affected was determined before 3 October.

On the question of the grounds of action all three Community Treaties mention the same four grounds which are derived from French Administrative law, viz.

    (i) lack of competence, or

    (ii) infringement of an essential procedural requirement, or

    (iii) infringement of the Treaties or of any rules of law relating to their application, or

    (iv) misuse of powers.[19]

(i) Lack of competence, which is an approximation of the French *excès de pouvoir* or *incompétence*, is broadly comparable to the English doctrine of substantive *ultra vires*. If a Community institution acts without authority that act may be declared void on the ground of lack of powers. An action on the ground of lack of powers is so similar to an action on the ground of infringement of the Treaties and regulations that in practice the Court tends to consider them together. Lack of competence and infringement of Treaties cover situations in which the Communities have no power, or in which the Communities have power but it has been exercised by the wrong body. Thus in *Meroni* v. *High Authority* (1958)[20] the plaintiff challenged certain levies imposed by the High Authority on the basis of decisions taken by

[18] *Loc. cit.* in previous note.

[19] E.C.S.C. Treaty, art. 33; E.E.C. Treaty, art. 173; Euratom Treaty, art. 146. It may be questioned whether all these specific grounds are strictly necessary since (i), (ii) and (iv) are subsumed under (iii).

[20] Case 9/56, 4 Rec. 9; Valentine, *op. cit.*, Vol. 2, p. 457.

subordinate bodies to whom the High Authority had purported to delegate certain powers. The Court held that those subordinate bodies lacked the power to take such decisions since the Treaty did not authorise the High Authority to delegate its decision-making power. This is as much a case on infringement of the Treaty as upon lack of competence. This general ground of challenge includes the infringement of rules relating to the application of the Treaties. Such rules not only take the obvious form of Regulations made under the Treaties, but also unwritten rules which the Court regards as generally applicable. One such rule is what the Court has called "the fundamental requirement of legal certainty."[1] That rule operated in *Re Civil Service Salaries E.C. Commission* v. *E.C. Council* (1973) to annul a Regulation made by the Council under its powers to keep the salaries of Community staff under annual review. Some months prior to that Regulation the Council had decided to operate a particular system of review for an experimental period of three years. The challenged Regulation did not comply with that decision, which the Council had said was binding upon it. The Court accepted the Commission's argument that undertakings of such a nature should be respected in order to protect the confidence of the Community's staff.[2]

(ii) Infringement of essential procedural requirements (*vice de forme*) also has an equivalent in English law, viz. procedural *ultra vires*. But, as in the case of both English and French administrative law, the Court of the Communities will not annul an act merely because some minor and unimportant procedural rule has not been observed; an action for annulment on this ground will only be granted when the procedural rule which has been infringed is an essential rule in the sense that it is substantial or basic. Such procedural requirements can be imposed either by the Treaties or by Regulations. An example of the former is provided by the case of the *Federal Republic of Germany* v. *E.E.C. Commission* (1963)[3] Prior to the establishment of the E.E.C. Germany used to import cheap wines for the production of "Brennwein". In 1961 it asked the Commission for a tariff quota of 450,000 hectolitres of wine for this purpose. The Commission granted a quota of only 100,000 hectolitres. Article 190 of the E.E.C. Treaty requires that the Commission's decisions shall be "fully reasoned" and Germany challenged the partial rejection of its request on the ground that that

---

[1] Cases 48–49, 51–57/69: *Imperial Chemical Industries* v. *E.C. Commission*, [1972] C.M.L.R. 557 at p. 621.
[2] Case 81/72, [1973] E.C.R. 575 at p. 580 *et seq.*; Adv. Gen. Warner argued to the contrary, *ibid.*, p. 587 *et seq.* Cf. case 4/73: *J. Nold, Kohlen-und Baustoff-grosshandlung* v. *E.C. Commission*, [1974] E.C.R. 491.
[3] Case 24/62, [1963] C.M.L.R. 347 at p. 367; 9 Rec. 129, at p. 143.

decision was insufficiently reasoned. The Commission had merely said that its decision was based on "information that has been gathered" which indicated "that the production of wines of this nature within the Community is amply sufficient". The Court agreed with the advocate-general that the Commission's decision should be annulled on the ground that it gave inadequate reasons and thus infringed an important procedural rule. The Court said "By imposing upon the Commission the duty to give reasoned decisions, art. 190 does not merely fulfil a formal function, but seeks to give the parties an opportunity of defending their rights, the Court an opportunity of exercising its control and the member states, as well as all interested parties, an opportunity of ascertaining the conditions in which the Commission applies the Treaty. To attain these objects it would be adequate for the Decision to set out, in a concise but clear and relevant manner, the principal points of law and of fact upon which it is based and which are necessary in order to clarify the reasoning which led the Commission to its decision." This the Court held, the Commission's vague statements failed to do. In *Transocean Marine Paint Association* v. *E.C. Commission* (1974)[4] the procedural requirement arose under a Regulation. In 1967 the plaintiff had been granted an exemption from applicability of the Community's rules on competition under the terms of art. 85 (3) of the E.E.C. Treaty. In 1972 the exemption came up for renewal. The Commission refused to renew it on the original terms and imposed additional conditions because of changes which had occurred in the competitive situation. The plaintiff found one of the additional conditions particularly onerous and sought its revocation on the ground that no notice was given of it nor any opportunity to comment. The Court held that the Regulation under which the Commission had acted[5] incorporated "the general rule that a person whose interests are perceptibly affected by a decision of a public authority must be given the opportunity to make his point of view known."[6] That obligation had not been fulfiled in this case and so the Commission's Decision was, to that extent, annulled.

(iii) *Treated under* (i).

(iv) Misuse of powers (*détournement de pouvoir*) provides the basis of an action for annulment when it can be shewn that a discretionary power has been used to achieve some object other than that for which the power was conferred. Thus proceedings for an action on this ground involve the Court in determining the object which the act in question was

---

[4] Case 17/74, [1974] E.C.R. 1063.
[5] Regulation 99/63/E.E.C., especially arts. 5–7.
[6] [1974] E.C.R. at p. 1080.

intended to achieve and then to decide whether that object comes within the purpose for which the power was conferred. As the advocate-general put it in *Fédéchar* v. *High Authority*[7] "it is a matter of discovering what was the object in fact pursued by the author of the act, when he took the decision, in order to be able to compare it with the subject he ought to have pursued and which, unless the contrary is proved, he is deemed to have pursued". The question is, therefore, whether the author of the act really had an illegal or legal object in view at the time he took the act. It is not necessary for an illegal objective to have been actually achieved, it is sufficient that the motive behind the act was illegal. Further, if an act achieves a legal object but also incidentally achieves other illegal objects that will not be a misuse of power, provided that the legal object is the dominant object. In *French Government* v. *High Authority* (1954),[8] for example, the High Authority, purporting to act under art. 60 of the E.C.S.C. Treaty, made a number of decisions authorising steel enterprises to deviate from their published prices provided that such deviations did not constitute discrimination which is forbidden by the Treaty. The French Government challenged those decisions alleging that the High Authority had no power to achieve those particular aims under art. 60 but should have acted under arts. 61 and 65 for the real object of those decisions was to lower steel prices generally and prevent price agreement and this could only be done under those latter articles. Therefore it was asserted that by issuing those decisions under art. 60 it had misused its powers. But the Court held that in fact there has been no misuse of powers, for even if those decisions had in fact been made to achieve an unjustified object the decisions would not be vitiated provided the essential object of the power was achieved. The Court held that was so in this case.

An action for annulment must be brought within limited periods of one month under the E.C.S.C. Treaty and two months under the E.E.C. and Euratom Treaties.[9] These periods are necessarily short since the economic regime set up by the Treaties is a dynamic thing which it would be impossible to alter long after the event by actions against decisions taken. In the case of regulations, which must be published in the Official Journal, time begins to run from the date of publication; in

---

[7] Case 8/55; 2 Rec. 199.

[8] Case 1/54; 1 Rec. 7; Valentine, *op. cit.*, Vol. 2, p. 18. Also see cases 52 & 55/65: *Germany* v. *E.E.C. Commission*, [1967] C.M.L.R. 22; case 34/62: *German Federal Republic* v. *E.E.C. Commission*, [1963] C.M.L.R. 369; case C.M.L.R. 22; case 34/62: *German Federal Republic* v. *E.E.C. Commission*, [1963] C.M.L.R. 369; case 32/64: *Customs Duties on Silk Fabric Italy* v. *E.E.C. Commission* [1967] C.M.L.R. 207.

[9] E.C.S.C. Treaty, art. 33; E.E.C. Treaty, art. 176; Euratom Treaty, art. 146.

the case of directives and decisions, which do not have to be published but must be notified to their addressees, time appears to run from the date of notification or if there has been no notification from the date upon which the decisions or directives came to the knowledge of the addresses.[10]

In general the effect of an annulment is quite simply to declare the Community act in question to be void and this is the basic rule to be found in all three treaties.[11] In the E.C.S.C. the Commission is required to take steps to give effect to the annulment and to compensate for any loss suffered as a result of the annulled act. The E.E.C. and Euratom Treaties simply require the institution whose act has been annulled to take the necessary steps to comply with the Court's judgment. Thus, subject to compensation under E.C.S.C. Treaty, which in any event is awarded by the Commission, annulment has a purely negative effect. But the annulment may not affect the whole of the act against which an appeal has been brought. Article 174 of the E.E.C. Treaty, for example, enables the Court to confirm particular parts of a regulation which it has otherwise annulled. The E.E.C. Treaty itself does not expressly extend this possibility of partial annulment to acts other than regulations, but nevertheless we find the Court in *Consten and Grundig* v. *E.E.C. Commission* (1966)[12] annulling a decision in part. In that case Consten and Grundig entered into a contract whereby Consten became the sole agent for the distribution of Grundig products in France. Other firms selling Grundig products in France complained to the Commission that this contract was contrary to art. 85 of the E.E.C. Treaty, which controls restrictive practices. The Commission issued a decision which stated that the contract did violate art. 85. Consten and Grundig then brought these proceedings challenging the decision and the Court held that certain elements in the contract infringed the Treaty and certain others did not therefore the decision was partially annulled and partially upheld. This is an example of the flexible approach which the Court adopts towards the question whether a particular administrative act is a regulation or a decision. Indeed there would seem to be no reason in principle why a process of partial annulment should not be applied in appropriate cases to acts other than regulations *stricto senso*.[13]

---

[10] See case 31/62: *Milchwerke Heinz Wöhrmann & Sohn K.G.* v. *E.E.C. Commission*, [1963] C.M.L.R. 152; 8 Rec. 965, and case 2/71: *Germany* v. *Commission*, [1972] C.M.L.R. 431.
[11] E.C.S.C. Treaty, art. 33; E.E.C. Treaty, art. 174; Euratom Treaty, art. 147.
[12] Cases 56 and 58/64, [1966] C.M.L.R. 418; 12 Rec. 429.
[13] Also see Case 17/74: *Transocean Marine Paint Association* v. *E.C. Commission*, [1974] E.C.R. 1063.

2. *Actions Against Inactivity (Recours en carence)*—The second main category of actions concerning legality is the action against inactivity. Where the Treaties impose a duty to act on the Council or Commission and they fail to act then an action may be based on a violation of the Treaty through inactivity. The inactivity must first be brought to the attention of the Institution concerned and if it has not taken satisfactory steps to remedy or justify its inactivity an action may be instituted.[14] Under the E.C.S.C. Treaty such actions may be brought against the Commission either by member states, or by the Council or by undertakings or associations of undertakings. Under the E.E.C. and Euratom while the member states and the other Community Institutions have a general competence to challenge the inactivity of either Commission or Council, individuals and corporate bodies may only do so if they can shew that one of those Institutions has failed to address an act (other than a recommendation or opinion[15]) to him or it[16]. An example of such an action under the E.C.S.C. Treaty is *Groupement des Industries Sidérurgiques Luxembourgeoises* v. *High Authority* (1956).[17] The Luxembourg Government imposed a levy on coal intended for industrial use for the purpose of subsidising the price of household coal. The plaintiffs, who were the main users of industrial coal, alleged that this levy was contrary to the E.C.S.C. Treaty and requested the High Authority to use its powers to require the Luxembourg Government to abolish the levy. During the two months following this request the High Authority did nothing and the plaintiffs brought an action under art. 35 of the E.C.S.C. Treaty and the Court held that the action was admissible. However in *Lütticke* v. *E.E.C. Commission* (1966)[18] where the situation was basically the same, the Court held that a similar action was not admissible since during the two-month period the Commission had declared its position and made clear its attitude to the matter in question.[19] The adoption of a position and a clarification of attitude clearly falls far short of compelling the performance of a specific act. The Court has recently confirmed this and has held that art. 175 cannot be used to found an action against a Community institution for an injunction to issue a particular act.[20]

---

[14] E.C.S.C. Treaty, art. 35; E.E.C. Treaty, art. 175; Euratom Treaty, art. 148.

[15] See Case 6/70: *Borromeo Arese* v. *E.C. Commission*, [1970] C.M.L.R. 436.

[16] See Case 103/63: *Société Rhenania Schiffahrts-und Speditiones-Gesellschaft mbH* v. *E.E.C. Commission*, [1965] C.M.L.R. 82 at pp. 82, 84, 87.

[17] Cases 7 and 9/54; 2 Rec. 86; Valentine, *op. cit.*, Vol. 2, p. 141.

[18] Case 48/65, [1966] C.M.L.R. 378, at p. 387; 13 Rec. 27, at p. 39.

[19] It will be recalled that the Assembly threatened to bring art. 175 proceedings in connection with the Council's inactivity over proposals for direct elections to the Assembly.

[20] Case 15/71: *Firma C. Mackprang Jr.* v. *E.C. Commission*, [1972] C.M.L.R. 52. Also see Case 8/71: *Deutscher Komponistverband* v. *E.C. Commission*, [1973] C.M.L.R. 902.

3. *The Defence of Illegality (L'exception d'illégalité)*—We have seen that a restrictive period of limitation is applied to actions for annulment with the general result that if an act is not challenged within that period the act becomes unassailable. But a situation may arise in an action before the Court under some Treaty article other than that which provides for actions for annulment in which the illegality of an unchallenged act may be in issue. If the period of limitation were to be applied strictly such an issue could not be raised outside the period, but to overcome such a possible result all three Treaties make it possible for such a question of illegality to be raised in such proceedings;[1] this again is a form of procedure known to French law. This provision can only be relied upon as a defence; it does not of itself give rise to an independent cause of action.[2] If such a defence of illegality is successfully pleaded its technical effect will not be to declare the act in question illegal in terms of its general application but only in so far as it applies to the plaintiff. This is made clear by the case law. In *Meroni & Co.* v. *High Authority* (1958)[3] the High Authority requested Meroni to pay a levy on the authority of earlier decisions of a general nature which it had taken. Meroni declined to pay and challenged the High Authority's request on the ground that the general decisions on which it was based were illegal. The High Authority argued that such a plea was inadmissible since the time limit for the challenge of those decisions had expired. The question therefore arose whether Meroni could rely on the defence of illegality. The Court held that he could and in its judgment considered the nature of this defence: "The right of a plaintiff to claim, after the expiration of the period [of limitation] in support of an action against an individual decision the irregularity of general decisions upon which the individual decision has been based cannot lead to the annulment of the general decision but only to that of the individual decision based thereon." In view of the limited right which individual and corporate bodies have to sue for the annulment of general decisions this defence of illegality is important since it completes the legal protection of such parties.

Article 184 of the E.E.C. Treaty refers to "any parties" being able to plead this defence and the question has been raised whether this expression includes Community institutions and member states as well as individuals and corporate bodies. As far as Community institutions are concerned it is generally agreed that the defence is not available on

---

[1] E.C.S.C. Treaty, art. 36; E.E.C. Treaty, art. 184; Euratom Treaty, art. 156.
[2] Cases 31 and 33/62: *Milchwerke Heinz Wöhrmann and Sohn K.G.* v. *E.E.C. Commission*, [1963] C.M.L.R. 152 at p. 158.
[3] 9/56, June 1958; 4 Rec. 9; Valentine, *op. cit.*, Vol. 2, p. 457.

both legal and practical grounds. In the first place the defence is designed to protect the private interests of a party which may be affected by an illegal general act, but a Community institution has no private interests only a share in the general interests of the Communities. Further, Community institutions have no restrictions on their right to challenge a general act and so, unlike the case of individuals and corporate bodies, there is no reason to extend the period of limitation in this way. Secondly, it is difficult to envisage in practice a situation in which, say, the Council would direct an individual decision to the Commission requiring it to respect a Council regulation. As far as member states are concerned there are also reasons in principle why the defence should not be available. Member states, as in the case of institutions, have no restrictions on their competence to challenge acts provided they do so within the period of limitation and so in their case also there would appear to be no reason to make the defence of illegality available. Secondly, the member states wield political influence over Community acts through the Council and this influence plus the general right of challenge should give ample protection to their interests.[4]

But it appears that the Court of Justice takes the view that member states may invoke the defence of illegality. In *Italian Government v. E.E.C. Council and Commission* (1966)[5] the Italian Government challenged Council Regulation 19/65 and it invoked, *inter alia*, art. 184 and asked for Council and Commission Regulations made in 1962 to be declared inapplicable. The action was dismissed on the ground that Regulation 19/65 derived from the Treaty and not from the challenged Council and Commission Regulations, and that even if those Regulations were declared inapplicable that would in no way affect the legality of Regulation 19/65. Although the Court's judgment did not turn on the *locus standi* of a member state, that issue was argued before the Court. The Commission maintained that art. 184 was intended to be used by individuals and corporate bodies and pointed out that the Italian Government had not chosen to challenge the 1962 Regulations which it had been within its competence to do. The advocate-general's submission on this point turned on the wording of art. 184 which refers to "any of the parties concerned" being able to plead the defence and because of the general nature of that expression he submitted that it included member states. The advocate-general was also in favour of such an interpretation since he pointed out that the illegality of a general decision may not fully emerge until that decision is applied to particular cases. The Court itself implicitly confirmed this view since it also

---

[4] See Bebr, *op. cit.*, pp. 141 *et seq.*
[5] Case 32/65, [1969] C.M.L.R. 39; 12 Rec. 563 at p. 594.

referred to the words of the article as being general in nature. Further the Court would, apparently, have accepted the plea of the defence of illegality had the Regulation 19/65 been founded on the 1962 Regulations.

(ii) *Plenary Jurisdiction (Pleine juridiction)*

In addition to its jurisdiction to declare actions of Community Institutions to be null and void the Court has a plenary jurisdiction in certain cases. This enables the Court in those instances to go into the merits of the parties' cases and to substitute its own judgments for those of the Communities' institutions. We have in fact already dealt with one example of this plenary jurisdiction in connection with violations of the Treaties by member states. In addition there are three other instances of plenary jurisdiction.

In general the liability of the Communities in contract falls under the jurisdiction of municipal courts, unless in accordance with art. 181 of the E.E.C. Treaty the contracting parties agree to the contrary. Article 183 of the E.E.C. Treaty provides that, subject to the powers of the Court of Justice, there is nothing to prevent a case to which the Community is a party from being determined by the domestic courts of the member states. But jurisdiction over non-contractual liability on the other hand has been conferred upon the Court of the Communities. Under art. 34 of the E.C.S.C. Treaty an action for damages will lie where the Commission fails to comply within a reasonable time with a judgment declaring a decision or recommendation to be void. Article 40 of the E.C.S.C. Treaty provides for liability for wrongful administrative acts in terms that an action will lie in respect of damage resulting from acts or omissions on the part of the Community or its servants. The E.E.C. and Euratom Treaties do not expressly distinguish between legislative and administrative wrongdoing as grounds for seeking damages but provide generally for non-contractual liability in the context of damage caused by the institutions or servants of the Communities in the performance of their duties in accordance with the general principles common to the laws of the member states[6].

Under all three Treaties the extent of this non-contractual liability is in practice in terms of the distinction known to French law as that between *faute de service* and *faute personnelle*.[7] A *faute de service* occurs where damage results from the mal-functioning of Community institutions or Community servants; there is said to be a *faute personnelle* when the damage results from some personal wrongdoing on the part of a

---

[6] E.E.C. Treaty, art. 215 and Euratom Treaty, art. 188.
[7] See Brown, L. N., and Garner, J. F., *op. cit.*, p. 99 *et seq.*

Community official which is in no way linked with his official position. In the case of a *faute de service* the Communities are liable; in the case of a *faute personnelle* the individual wrongdoer alone is personally liable. This distinction is comparable, although not identical, with the distinction well known to English law between a servant acting in the course of his employment and a servant on a frolic of his own. Within those limits actual liability under the E.E.C. Treaty is in accordance with the general principles common to the laws of the member states. This involves the Court in a comparative study of the relevant national laws in order to pick out the decisive elements which may reflect a trend.[8]

The relationship between the action for damages and the actions for annulment and inactivity has caused the Court some difficulty. When first confronted with this question the Court expressed the view that the action for damages was quite distinct both by reason of its object and the grounds upon which it can be brought.[9] But when, later, an action for damages arose out of an allegedly unlawful act which had not been annulled, the Court changed its mind and held that "An administrative act which has not been annulled cannot of itself constitute a wrong causing damage to those subject to that administration. Such persons cannot therefore claim damages merely on account of the act."[10] More recently, against the background of strong criticism,[11] the Court has reverted to its original view. In *Alfons Lütticke GmbH* v. *Commission* (1971)[12] it observed that the action for damages is an independent action having its own special purpose and subject to conditions which were designed for that purpose. It would be contrary to the independence of this right of action if its exercise was made subject to other Treaty provisions designed for different purposes. This view has been reiterated in a series of subsequent cases which appears now to represent the *jurisprudence constante* of the Court.[13]. Where an action for damages is brought in respect of an illegal legislative act the Com-

---

[8] See Case 3/65: *S.A. Métallurgique d'Esperance-Longdoz* v. *High Authority*, [1966] C.M.L.R. 146, *per* Adv. Gen. Roemer at p. 152 and Case 63–69/73: *Werhahn Hansamühle* v. *E.C. Council*, [1973] E.C.R. 1229, *per* Adv. Gen. Roemer at pp. 1259, 1260. Also see Chapter 2 above.

[9] Cases 9 and 12/60: *Société Commerciale Antoine Vloeberghs S.A.* v. *High Authority* (1960), 7 Rec. 391 at p. 424.

[10] Case 25/62: *Plaumann & Co.* v. *E.E.C. Commission*, [1964] C.M.L.R. 29 at p. 48.

[11] E.g. Adv. Gen. Roemer's submissions in case 5/71: *Aktien-Zuckerfabrik Schöppenstedt* v. *E.C. Council*, 17 Rec. 975.

[12] Case 4/69 (1971), 17 Rec. 325 at p. 337.

[13] See case 5/71: *Aktien-Zuckerfabrik Schöppenstedt* v. *E.C. Council* (1971), 17 Rec. 975; cases 9 and 11/71: *Compagnie d'Approvisionnement de Transport et de Crédit S.A. and Grands Moulins de Paris S.A.* v. *E.C. Commission*, [1973] C.M.L.R. 529; case 43/72: *Merkur Aussenhandels GmbH* v. *E.C. Commission*, [1973] E.C.R. 1055.

munity will only be liable if the individual plaintiff can prove that there has been a breach of a superior rule of law protecting him.[14] Such a rule could, presumably, be either a rule in the Treaty such as the prohibition on discrimination or one of the unwritten rules of Community law which the Court draws from the rules of the constitutions of the member states which are designed to protect individual rights.[15] The plaintiff in an action for damages must, of course, establish a causal connection between the injury and the act or omission on the part of the Community and the quantum of damages must be ascertainable and not speculative.[16]

The Court's plenary jurisdiction also extends to the settlement of disputes between the Communities and their employees over contracts of employment. The terms of service are set out in the Communities' Staff Regulations, and art. 179 of the E.E.C. Treaty, for example, provides that the Court shall be competent to adjudicate in any dispute between the Community and its servants within the limits and under the conditions laid down by their service regulations or conditions of employment. Actions concerning contracts of service cannot be lodged directly with the Court of Justice. Claims must first be made to the appointing body via an hierarchial administrative process. If the dispute is not resolved by this process then a right of appeal lies to the Court of Justice which has the power to consider the dispute in its entirety and to settle it by its judgment. This is a fairly fertile source of litigation before the Court but it is somewhat specialist and it is neither appropriate nor practicable to discuss it in the present context.[17]

Lastly the court has plenary jurisdiction to hear appeals against fines and other pecuniary penalties. The Court not only has jurisdiction to quash a penalty of this sort but it may also lower or increase this penalty when in the Court's view it is either unacceptable or inappropriate.[18] An example is provided by article 17 of Regulation 17 which authorises appeals against fines and periodic penalty payments imposed by the Commission for breaches of the Community's rules on competition.[19]

---

[14] E.g. case 153/73: *Firma Holtz and Willemsen* v. *E.C. Council and Commission*, [1974] E.C.R. 675 at p. 692.

[15] See Chapter 2 above.

[16] See cases 5, 7 and 13–24/66: *Firma E. Kampffmeyer* v. *E.E.C. Commission*, (1967), 13 Rec. 317 and case 30/66: *Kurt A. Becher* v. *E.C. Commission*, [1968] C.M.L.R. 169.

[17] For further information, see Campbell, *op. cit.*, Vols. 1 and 3, paras. 6.354–6.369.

[18] E.C.S.C. Treaty, art. 36 (2); E.E.C. Treaty, art. 172; Euratom Treaty, art. 144.

[19] E.g. case 45/69: *Boehringer Mannheim GmbH* v. *E.C. Commission*, 16 Rec. 769 and 7/72, [1973] C.M.L.R. 864.

PART III

The Relationship between Community Law and the Municipal Law of the Member States

CHAPTER TEN

Implementation of Community Law in the Legal Systems of the Member States

I INTRODUCTION

The most intricate and complex aspect of Community Law is its relationship to the municipal law of the member states. Conceptually Community Law, like public international law, feeds upon the internal law of states but once emancipated and worked into a system Community Law emerges as a different, quasi-autonomous body of law.

Volumes have been written on the subject from a theoretical and practical point of view not only because the growth of the Community Law is symptomatic of the growth of the Community but also because of the theoretical and practical consequences of conflicts between Community Law and the municipal law of the member states. To a British student of Community Law the matter is of a particular interest as an empirical experience of the Six and as a pointer to the likely impact of Community Law in the United Kingdom.

At a theoretical level the starting point of a discussion on the relationship between Community Law and the municipal law of the member states, that is between an "external" and an "internal" system of law, is the doctrine of sovereignty; at a practical level it is the Treaty obligation and the resulting status of Community Law in the territory of the member states.

Sovereignty is a conceptual chameleon: it can be seen in different colours and be described in different ways. In classic terms Jean Bodin (1530–96) wrote that "it is the distinguishing mark of the sovereign that he cannot in any way be subject to the commands of another, for it is he who makes law for the subject, abrogates Law already made, and amends obsolete Law. No one who is subject either to the Law or to some other person can do this. That is why it is laid down in the civil law that the prince is above the law, for the word *Law* in Latin implies command of him who is invested with sovereign power . . ."[1] For the

---

[1] *Six Books of the Commonwealth*, Book I, Ch. 8.

purpose of our discussion sovereignty may be described in positive terms as the oneness of the legal system within the territory of a state. Oneness does not exclude plurality of laws within the system (as is, e.g., the case in the United Kingdom or the U.S.A.) but implies one supreme source of law embodied in the constitution of the state; in other words the jurisdiction over the territory is in the hands of one authority (e.g. government in Parliament) which is supreme. In negative terms sovereignty means a system of law and administration of justice which is free from outside interference. Proceeding from the assumption of the oneness of the legal system the member states of the Community are not entirely sovereign for, by Treaty, they have delegated a portion of their law-making power to an external authority (the Community) and at the same time consented to abide by the law so made. In the field of the administration of justice they recognise the authority of the Community Court over matters and persons in their territory falling within the jurisdiction of that Court and also consent to their municipal courts taking judicial cognisance of Community Law. In theory, therefore, as long as the state remains a member of the Community there should be no conflict between the municipal (internal) law of the member states and the Community (external) Law because the latter becomes part of the former. In fact, however, conflicts do arise and this raises the question of the supremacy of the one over the other. Reduced to a practical level sovereignty means the ultimate authority in respect of a particular matter and raises the question whether the Community or the state law governs a particular situation.

Another digression into the theory of relations between external and internal law leads us to the consideration of two rival doctrines dualism (parallelism) and monism[2] which purport to explain the basis of legal obligation. According to the positivist philosophy of law, the relationship between the law of a sovereign state and the law of mankind, reflected in the law generated by agreements between states, has been expressed in the dualist (parallelist) doctrine. In simple terms this doctrine presupposes the existence of two separate systems of law: international and national, co-existing side by side as it were in water-tight compartments. Though international law is the universal law of mankind it stops at the door of the sovereign state and remains outside unless admitted to the territory of the state. It means that international law binds states in their relations with each other but has, subject to few exceptions, no binding force in the territory of the state unless transformed or translated into rules of municipal law. This doctrine,

---

[2] Starke, J. G., "Monism and Dualism in the Theory of International Law" (1936), 17 B.Y.B.I.L. 66.

favouring sovereignty, is still the reigning theory and the United Kingdom is among its adherents.

Monism is the rival doctrine propounding the existence of a single system of norms or legal rules binding states and individuals alike. States are, after all, nothing but forms of organisation or legal fictions whilst the individual is the ultimate subject of law. Both international and municipal law are only parts of the same structure and their rules are interrelated. Consequently monism cuts across sovereignty bringing the individual face to face with international law and relieving the state of the task of transforming it into rules of domestic law. The origins of monism can be traced to the medieval concept of the unity of law as Natural Law was considered to be a reflection of the wisdom of God through the reason of man. It ceased to be fashionable when the theory of Natural Law was superseded by the theory of Positive Law. The 20th century revival of the monist doctrine in its positivist rather than naturalist garb is a reaction against the 19th century apotheosis of the sovereign state degenerating into nationalism which saw international law solely as a product of the "will" of states.

The legal idea of the European Community reflects a monist approach. Therefore, to understand the relationship between the Community Law and the law of the member states it is unhelpful to think in terms of sovereignty (nationalism) *versus* internationalism. We have to formulate instead a functional approach which in practical terms reconciles the need of a Community Law with the aspiration of states to be supreme within their territories. Once this is appreciated the question of the supremacy of one system or the other resolves itself into a division of labour or functions of the respective bodies of rules within a unitary concept of law. Within its respective sphere each system is supreme as stated by the Community Court:[3]

> ". . . The Community is founded on a common market, common objectives, and common institutions . . . Within the specific domain of the Community, i.e. for everything which relates to the pursuit of the common objectives within the common market the institutions [of the Community] are provided with exclusive authority . . . Outside the domain of the Community, the governments of the Member States retain their responsibilities in all sectors of economic policy . . . They remain masters of their social policy; the same undoubtedly holds true for large segments of their fiscal policy . . ."

Ten years later, in the E.R.T.A. Case which was, *inter alia*, concerned with the treaty-making power of the Community and the member states the Court held that

---

[3] Case 30/59: *Gezamenlijke Steenkolenmijnen in Limburg* v. *High Authority*, 7 Rec. 1 at pp. 43–45.

"... By the terms of art. 5, the member states are required on the one hand to take all appropriate steps to ensure the carrying out of the obligations arising out of the Treaty ... and on the other hand to abstain from any steps likely to jeopardise the attainment of the purposes of the Treaty. If these two provisions are read in conjunction, it follows that to the extent that Community rules are promulgated for the attainment of the purposes of the Treaty, the member states cannot, outside the framework of the Community institutions assume obligations likely to affect such rules or alter their scope ..."[4]

These two *dicta* delimit the respective spheres of the Community and the member states both in the "internal" and "external" aspect of sovereignty.

Let us turn now to the foundation Treaties, especially the E.E.C. Treaty, which is a unique treaty. It cannot be compared with traditional international treaties which set out the obligations of the parties and, in most cases, leave the implementation and enforcement of the obligations to the forces which make international law effective. It is a self-executing treaty. The E.E.C. is, by the will of the founding states, a separate legal entity, a new subject of law and, although it takes life from the agreement of states, it has a quasi-independent existence. Being a subject of law it enjoys the treaty-making power and the power of diplomatic representation but, above all, it has its own institutions and a law making power. Community Law is therefore an autonomous legal order binding not only the member states but also their citizens directly and immediately.

The E.E.C. Treaty itself has a legal framework—actually two such frameworks—the constitutional framework which we have already analysed and the economic framework which we shall consider later on. What we must discuss now is the impact of the Treaty and the Community legislation on the legal systems of the member states. In doing so we should bear in mind the doctrine[5] that "... the Community constitutes a novel judicial order of international law, in favour of which the States within certain areas have limited their sovereign rights ..." because it reflects the difficulties inherent in the "dualist" thinking which has so far dominated the European legal scene. Indeed some of the constitutions of the member states had to be amended in order to

---

[4] Case 22/70: *Re E.R.T.A. E.C. Commission* v. *E.C. Council*, [1971] C.M.L.R. 335 at p. 355; 17 Rec. 263 at paras. 21 and 22; see also case 1/75: *Re the O.E.C.D. Understanding on a Local Cost Standard*, [1976] C.M.L.R. 85.

[5] Case 26/62: *N.V. Algemene Transport- en Expeditie Onderneming van Gend en Loos* v. *Nederlandse Tariefcommissie*, [1963] C.M.L.R. 105; 9 Rec. 1 at p. 23; see also Case 6/64: *Costa* v. *ENEL*, [1964] C.M.L.R. 425; 11 Rec. 811.

ease the process of assimilation of international obligations inherent in the Community Treaties into the law of the land. In this respect the United Kingdom is not in a unique position.

II CONSTITUTIONS OF THE MEMBER STATES AND TREATY OBLIGATIONS

The admission of external law to the territory of a state raises a constitutional problem of transmission, on the one hand, and supremacy in the case of a conflict with municipal law, on the other. A further problem, as far as the civil law countries are concerned, arises from the internal relationship between the constitution and the ordinary law of the land. The constitution, as the basic law of the land, consists not only of the rules which organise the political framework of the state but also of the general principles on which rests the whole edifice of law and order. It follows that there is a hierarchy of legal norms or in Pound's rather inelegant phrase, "authoritative starting points for legal reasoning"[6] which, in the event of a conflict with external law, raises the question whether external law is superior/subordinate to the law of the Constitution and the ordinary law of the land alike or whether the hierarchy of legal norms will affect the issue.

In view of the diversity of the legal systems involved it seems necessary to investigate the position in each member state.

1 *Ratification of the E.E.C. Treaty*

According to the constitutions of the original six member states treaties are made and ratified by the Head of State.[7] However in the case of especially important treaties these Constitutions require a parliamentary approval in the form of either a resolution or a special law. In France, Italy, Germany and the Netherlands a special Act enabling the Head of State to ratify and thus commit the country internationally was necessary.[8] Accordingly these laws were passed during 1957.[9] The position in Belgium and Luxembourg is somewhat different. The effect of the law passed by reference to art. 37 (1) of the Constitution of Luxembourg, which enables the Grand Duke to con-

---

[6] Pound, R., "Hierarchy of Sources and Forms in Different Systems of Law", [1933] Tulane Law Review 475, at p. 483.
[7] Belgium, art. 68; France (Constitution of 1946 which was in force at that time), art. 31, Constitution of 1958, art 52; Federal Republic of Germany, art. 59; Italy, art. 80; Luxembourg, art. 37; The Netherlands, art. 50.
[8] France, art. 27; Italy, art. 80; Germany, art. 59 (2); The Netherlands, art. 60.
[9] France, 8 August 1957, Germany, 27 July 1957, Italy, 14 October 1957, The Netherlands, 5 December 1957.

clude treaties, is to exercise parliamentary control over the acts of the executive.[10] The interpretation of the Belgian Constitution is subject to controversy as to the role of Parliament in this matter[11] but Parliament approved the Treaty by the Law of 22 December 1957 and so according to custom the Treaty may "sortir son plein et entier effet".[12]

In the United Kingdom treaties are made and ratified by the Crown[13] so much so that the battle about the membership of the Community was fought in the political arena of the House of Commons rather than the courts of law. Formally the Treaty obligations were implemented by the European Communities Act 1972, which has the effect of both a "constitutional" and an "ordinary" law. In Eire treaties are made by the government and ratified by *Dail Eireann.*[14] However in order to enable the country to accede to the Communities a bill was passed by the *Oireachtas* in 1971 adding sub-s. 3 to art. 29.4 of the Constitution and a Referendum was held in 1972. According to the Danish Constitution of 1953 (art. 19) the Monarch acts in international affairs on behalf of the Kingdom but without the consent of the *Folketing* cannot commit the country to any obligations of importance or for which parliamentary approval is necessary. Therefore in practice treaties are negotiated and ratified by the Executive subject to parliamentary approval. Accession to the Communities was approved by the *Folketing* and a Referendum held in 1972. Attempts to have the procedures leading to the accession declared unconstitutional[15] and the "signatures on the treasonable document declared void and unauthorised whereby our Queen may be saved from the biggest swindle in the history of Denmark"[16] were dismissed by the courts on the ground that the Head of State could not be held to account before her courts.

2 *Incorporation of the Treaty into Municipal Law*

The method of incorporation depends on whether a country follows the monist or the dualist doctrine. Among the Six, France and Italy represent the two extremes: the former is monist the latter is dualist,

---

[10] Law of 30 November 1957; Pescatore, P., *Introduction à la Science du Droit* (1960), pp. 170 and 175.
[11] Constantinides-Mégret, C., *Le Droit de la Communauté Economique Européenne et l'Ordre Juridique des Etats Membres* (1967), pp. 14–15.
[12] Constantinides-Mégret, *op. cit.*, p. 15.
[13] *Blackburn* v. *A.-G.* (1971), 1 W.L.R. 1037 (see Lord Denning M.R. at p. 1040). Also see Chapter 12 below.
[14] Constitution of 1948, arts. 28 and 29.
[15] *Tegen* v. *Prime Minister of Denmark*, [1973] C.M.L.R. 1.
[16] *Aggergen* v. *The Queen and Prime Minister*, [1973] C.M.L.R. 5.

whilst the remaining four occupy a middle position with a distinct dualist leaning. The three new members fall into the dualist category. The French Republic started with a dualist posture but by art. 26 of the Constitution of 1946 reversed the tradition and turned monist. Article 26 provided that Treaties duly ratified by the Head of State and published have the force of law even if they are inconsistent with French law "without there being any need of resorting to any legislative measures other than those necessary to secure ratification". The Constitution of 1958, now in force, not only adopted the position but art. 55, as if to confirm the supremacy of Community Law, provided that Treaties or Agreements ratified or approved "have an authority superior to that of laws". It follows that Treaties are not subject to transformation into the rules of French municipal law but take their place automatically by virtue of the Constitution in the internal legal order, subject to reciprocity and the sovereign will of the French people. However in the case of the E.E.C. Treaty the condition of reciprocity is satisfied in the light of art. 170 which contains Community remedies to enforce it.[17]

The Italian Constitution of 1948 contains no reference to the incorporation of treaties into Italian law. Article 11 permits a delegation of sovereignty to international organisations but fails to deal with the problem of treaties. Accordingly a practice has been established in accordance with the hierarchy of legal rules: if the treaty affects a law the execution of the treaty takes the form of a law, if it affects merely administrative rules a decree of the executive will take care of the situation. Reflecting this formula the law of ratification of the two Treaties of Rome passed on 14 October 1957 provided in art. 2 that "the agreements specified in art. 1 will receive full and complete execution". In this way the act of ratification became the act of execution or incorporation of the Treaties into Italian law. The consequences, as far as supremacy is concerned, are quite significant because, being equal to an internal legislative act, the Treaty, in principle, assumes no higher or lower rank than the corresponding piece of Italian legislation. Conflicts with domestic law are implicitly avoided in accordance with the principle that *lex posterior derogat priori*.[18] In practice, as we shall see later, difficulties arise.

In Germany, the general view is that the act of ratification signifies

---

[17] *Administration des Douanes* v. *Société Cafés Jacques Vabre et J. Weiget et Compagnie Sarl ; Cour de Cassation*, [1975] C.M.L.R. 336.
[18] Cf. the decision of the Italian Constitutional Court of 7 March 1964 in *Costa* v. *ENEL*.

not only approval of the treaty but also incorporation.[19] However, art. 25 of the Federal Constitution provides that the "general rules of international law shall form part of federal law; they shall take precedence over the laws and create rights and duties directly applicable to the inhabitants of the territory of the federation". This has been interpreted restrictively to include the general customary rules of international law but to exclude the conventional rules.[20] It follows that international treaties have the force of a federal law, that is, ordinary *law*, not constitutional law. Being no more than *law* in the hierarchy of legal rules they can derogate from a preceding federal law or the law of the *Länder* but cannot override a constitutional rule of the Federation or (presumably) the *Länder*.

According to a recent amendment of the Constitution of Belgium[1] art. 25 bis provides that "the exercise of powers may be conferred by a Treaty or by Law on institutions of Public International Law". This formula resembles the delegation of powers under the Italian Constitution and certainly confirms the dualist approach to treaties which are denied the authority of superior law. Amidst the discussions[2] on the relations between the constitution and Treaty law the Belgian Cour de Cassation struck a valiant blow for the recognition of the supremacy of the Treaty law in the judgment of 27 May 1971.[3] The Constitution of Luxembourg was amended in a similar way, art. 49 bis providing for a delegation of legislative, administrative powers to international organisations.[4]

The effect of the delegation of sovereignty in these three constitutions seems to provide room for the recognition of the binding force of the Community Law enshrined in treaties whilst retaining at the same time the sovereignty of parliament. It now remains to be seen whether the formula is sufficiently wide to read into it the supremacy of Community Law necessary for the functioning of the Community as a supranational organisation.

---

[19] Seidl-Hohenveldern, I., "Transformation or Adoption of International into Municipal Law" (1963), 12 I.C.L.Q., p. 101 *et seq.*

[20] Bebr, G., "Law of the European Communities and Municipal Law" (1971), 34 M.L.R. 481, at p. 487 quoting Mangeldt-Klein, *Das Bonner Grundgesetz* (1957), 675–677; Carstens, "Der Rang europäischer Verordnuugen gegenüber deutschen Rechtsnormen", *Festschrift für Otto Riese* (1964), 65, 75.

[1] Law of 18 August 1970; Louis, J. V., "L'article 25 bis de la constitution belge", [1970] *Rev. du Marché Commun* 136, 410–416.

[2] Ganshof van der Meersch, W. J., "Le juge belge à l'heure du droit international et du droit communautaire" (1969), 84 *Journal des Tribunaux*, 4671, 537–551; Waelbroeck, M. in Donner, A. M., *et al.*, Le juge devant le droit national et le droit communautaire (1966) at pp. 29 *et seq.*

[3] *Etat Belge* v. *S.A. Fromagerie Franco-Suisse le Ski* (1971), R.T.D.E. 494.

[4] Pescatore, P., "L'autorité en droit interne des traités internationaux selon jurisprudence luxembourgeoise" (1962), 18 Pasicrisie Luxembourgeoise 99–115.

To meet this situation the amendment of the constitution of the Netherlands of 1956[5] provided that international treaties and agreements shall be supreme law of the land (art. 68). However this authority is reserved only to self-executing treaties and the power to determine which treaties are self-executing is vested in the Dutch Courts. So, subject to this qualification, international treaties override the constitution and the ordinary law irrespective of whether they are precedent or subsequent (art. 63).

The new members proceed from a dualist position. In the United Kingdom it was necessary to pass the European Communities Act 1972[6] in order to transform the Treaty obligations into domestic law, to adopt the so-called "enforceable Community rights" and to set up machinery for the implementation of the remaining rules of Community Law. In Eire, too, this object was achieved by the European Communities Act 1972, which provided, *inter alia*, that "from the first day of January 1973, the Treaties governing the European Communities and the existing and future acts adopted by the institutions of those Communities shall be binding on the state and shall be part of the domestic law thereof under the conditions laid down in those Treaties". In Denmark the law of 11 October 1972 expressly adopted the Treaties enumerated therein and made provision for the delegation of sovereign powers to the Communities and for the adoption of Community acts directly applicable by virtue of Community law.

This brief survey of the constitutional scene of the member states shows not only a diverse approach to the status of the Treaties but also indicates a cautious commitment of the majority of these states to the Community rather than a formal and irrevocable abdication of their national sovereignty.

III   INCORPORATION OF THE COMMUNITY LEGISLATION

(1) *Reception of Community Law*

The logic of the acceptance of Treaty obligations demands an unconditional reception not only of the primary but also of the derivative rules of Community Law. Article 5 of the E.E.C. Treaty reminds the member states that they must "take all appropriate measures, whether general or particular, to ensure fulfilment of the obligations arising out of this Treaty or resulting from action taken by the institu-

---

[5] Van Panhuys, H. F., "The Netherlands Constitution and International Law" (1964), 58 A.J.I.L. 88–108; Van Dijk, P., "The Implementation and Application of the law of the European Communities within the Legal Order of the Netherlands" (1969), 6 C.M.L.Rev. 283–308.

[6] See Chapter 12, below.

tions of the Community. They shall facilitate the achievement of the Community tasks. They shall abstain from any measure which could jeopardise the attainment of the objectives of the Treaty". Moreover, the member states must "in close co-operation with the institutions of the Community, co-ordinate their respective economic policies to the extent necessary to attain the objectives of the Treaty" (art. 6 (1)). Since policies are enforced through the instrumentality of the law, the member states must adapt and modify their laws in order to bring about harmony within the Community and, above all, remove the legal barriers to the creation and working of the Community. Since the E.E.C. is concerned with customs duties, movement of goods, persons, services and capital, agriculture and fisheries, transport, competition and restrictive practices, state aid to industry, taxation, and social security, and whilst the E.C.S.C. and Euratom are concerned with coal, steel and nuclear energy industries, the member states undertake a considerable number of specific obligations. These obligations are in many respects regulated by Community legislation whose scope ranges from relatively trivial provisions like the calculation of the compensation for hatching eggs[7] to the most solemn historical provisions regarding the establishment of the Common Market.

In the case of the new members, the accumulated volume of Community Law became the object of a wholesale reception at the time of their accession. By art. 2 of the Act of Accession they became subject to "the provisions of the original Treaties and the acts adopted by the institutions of the Communities" whilst by art. 149 they were considered "as being addressees of and having notification of directives and decisions within the meaning of art. 189 of the E.E.C. Treaty and of art. 161 of the E.A.E.C. Treaty, and of recommendations and decisions within the meaning of art. 14 of the E.C.S.C. Treaty, provided that those directives, recommendations and decisions have been notified to all the original Member States".

The impact of Community Law upon the laws of the member states depends on two principles: the direct applicability and the supremacy of Community Law. The former is relevant to the implementation, the latter to the enforcement of Community Law. Apart from a reference to the direct applicability of regulations, the Treaties do not contain a detailed exposition of these principles, which are essential to the Community, therefore they had to be elaborated by the Court of Justice of the Community.

---

[7] Article 77 (2) of the Act of Accession provides that "the compensatory amount per hatching egg shall be calculated on the basis of the compensatory amount applicable to the quantity of feed grain required for the production in the Community of one hatching egg".

(2) *Directly Applicable Rules of Community Law*

Depending on their nature and function the rules of Community Law are either "directly" or "indirectly" applicable. In this context a distinction should be made between rules which are "directly applicable",[8] that is rules becoming automatically upon their enactment part of the *corpus juris* of the member states and rules "directly enforceable" that is rules having a "direct effect" as far as rights and obligations of the citizen are concerned.[9]

Whilst a rule may be eased into the national system by virtue of its nature (e.g. a regulation), it does not necessarily follow that it will give rise to rights which the national court must uphold. The problem, as pointed out by Advocate-General Warner,[10] is well known in national statutes, "which unquestionably form part of national law, some provisions of which impose obligations on the State or public authorities without conferring rights on citizens".

The principle of "direct effect" can be traced to certain leading cases: in *Van Gend en Loos* v. *Nederlandse Administratie der Belastingen*[11] the Community Court held that there was an unconditional obligation on the part of the state to refrain from introducing new customs duties which, in turn, created a corresponding right in favour of the citizen.

In *Lütticke* v. *Hauptzollamt Sarrelouis*[12] the Court held that a member state must not impose on the products of another member state any internal tax in excess of that applicable to similar domestic products. In *Salgoil SpA* v. *Italian Ministry of Foreign Trade*[13] the Court confirmed that a member state had no discretion in the application of the Treaty provisions governing import quotas within the Community. The message of the Community Court is that certain provisions of the Treaty are by their very nature and purpose directly enforceable in national courts. As they affect private interests they create Community rights which, as a corollary, correspond to Community obligations imposed upon the member states. These, as confirmed by the Community Court, and national courts, include the following:

---

[8] "Enforceable Community rights" according to s. 2 (1) of the British European Communities Act 1972.

[9] See Winter, J., "Direct Applicability and Direct Effect—Two Distinct and Different Concepts in Community Law," [1972] C.M.L. Rev. 425; Wyatt, D., "Directly Applicable Provisions of E.E.C. Law," [1975] 125 New Law Journal, pp. 458, 575, 669, 793.

[10] In Case 31/74: *Filippo Galli*, Preliminary Ruling requested by the *Pretore di Roma*, [1975] E.C.R. 47 at p. 70.

[11] Case 26/62, [1963] C.M.L.R. 105; 9 Rec. 1.

[12] Case 57/68, [1971] C.M.L.R. 674; 12 Rec. 293.

[13] Case 13/68, [1969] C.M.L.R. 181, 14 Rec. 661.

(1) Article 7 which prohibits discrimination on grounds of nationality;[14]

(2) Articles 9 and 11 on the customs union as from the end of the transitional period;[15]

(3) Article 12 which forbids new customs duties or similar charges;[16]

(4) Article 13 (2) on the abolition of charges having an equivalent to customs duties on imports;[17]

(5) Article 16 on the abolition of customs duties on exports;[18]

(6) Article 31 which forbids quantitative restrictions and measures having equivalent effect;[19]

(7) Article 32 (1), (2) on the abolition of quotas in trade between member states;[20]

(8) Article 36 as far as "disguised restrictions on trade" are concerned;[1]

(9) Article 37 (1) and (2) which forbids measures likely to restrict the abolition of customs duties and quantitative restrictions between member states or adjustment of state monopolies;[2]

(10) Article 48 (2) on discrimination between workers on the ground of nationality;[3]

---

[14] Case 14/68: *Walt Wilhelm* v. *Bundeskartellamt*, [1969] C.M.L.R. 100; 15 Rec. 1.

[15] *SAFA* v. *Amministrazione delle Finanze*, Milan Appeal Court, [1973] C.M.L.R. 152, 157, 161–162; Case 33/70: *SACE* v. *Italian Ministry of Finance*, [1971] C.M.L.R. 123 at p. 132; 16 Rec. 1213 at pp. 1221–1223.

[16] *Van Gend, op cit.*

[17] Case 77/72: *Capolongo* v. *Azienda Agricola Maya*, [1973] E.C.R. 611 at p. 622; [1974] I.C.M.L.C.R. 230; Case 63/74: *W. Cadsky SpA.* v. *Istituto Nazionale per il Commerzio Estero*, [1975] E.C.R. 281.

[18] Case 48/71: *Re Export Tax on Art Treasures (No. 2) E.C. Commission* v. *Italy*, [1672] C.M.L.R. 699; *Ministère Public Luxembourgeois* v. *Muller* (1971), 17 Rec. 723.

[19] *Societa B.P. Colusi Milano* v. *Ministerio del Commercio con l'Estere*, decided by the *Consiglio de Stato*, 7 November 1962, No. 778, [1963] C.M.L.R. 133; *Salgoil, op. cit.*; Case 12/74: *E.C. Commission* v. *Federal Republic of Germany*, [1975] E.C.R. 181.

[20] *Salgoil, op. cit.*

[1] Case 78/70: *Deutsche Gramophon GmbH* v. *Metro-S.B.-Grössmärkte GmbH*, [1971] C.M.L.R. 631; 17 Rec. 481; Case 192/73: *Van Zuylen Frères S.A.* v. *Hag A.G.*, [1974] E.C.R. 731; [1974] 2 C.M.L.R. 127; Case 29/72: *Marimex SpA* v. *Ministerio delle Finance*, [1973] C.M.L.R. 486; Case 21/75: *I. Schröder K.G.* v. *Oberstadt-direktor der Stadt Köln*, [1975] C.M.L.R. 312.

[2] Case 6/64: *Flaminio Costa* v. *ENEL, op. cit.*; *Re Shell-Berre* decided by the French *Conseil d'Etat*, [1964] C.M.L.R. 462; Case 59/75: *Pubblico Ministero* v. *Flavia Manghera et al.* (1976), *Times European Law Report*, 6 February.

[3] Case 167/73: *Re French Merchant Seamen; E.C. Commission* v. *France*, [1974], E.C.R. 359 at p. 371; [1974] 2 C.M.L.R. 216 at pp. 229–230, 234–235.

Case 13/76 (unreported; *Europe* March 1976); Reference from Giudloe Conciliatore of Rovigoto Community Court: "Are Italian regulations concerning the nationality of football teams compatible with art. 48?"

(11) Article 48 (3); Regulations 15 and 38/64; Directive 64/221 on the restrictions of the freedom of movement;[4]

(12) Article 52 concerning the right of establishment;[5]

(13) Article 53 which forbids new restrictions on the right of establishment;[6]

(14) Articles 59 and 62 on the freedom to provide services;[7]

(15) Articles 85 and 86 on competition;[8]

(16) Article 90 (2) on revenue-producing monopolies;[9]

(17) Article 93 (3) concerning aids by states;[10]

(18) Article 95 which prohibits internal taxation of products of other member states.[11]

(19) Article 119 on equal pay for men and women.[12]

It goes without saying that the majority of articles 137–248 representing the "organisational law" of the E.E.C. are "directly applicable" though by their nature and function they do not constitute rights enforceable by individuals.[13]

The list is by no means complete as certain provisions of the Treaty remain yet to be considered judicially. As for the criterion of direct enforceability, the Community Court[14] held as follows:

". . . The Treaty's objective of establishing a common market the functioning of which affects the subjects of member states entails

---

[4] Case 1 T.114/63: *Re Expulsion of an Italian National, Landgericht Göttingen,* 23 December 1963; Case 67/74: *Bonsignore* v. *Oberstadtdirektor der Stadt Köln,* [1975] E.C.R. 297; [1975] C.M.L.R. 472; case 41/74: *Van Duyn* v. *Home Office,* [1975] 3 All E.R. 190; [1973] E.C.R. 1337; [1975] C.M.L.R. 1 at pp. 14–15.
[5] Case 2/74: *Reyners* v. *The Belgian State,* [1974] 2 C.M.L.R. 305 at p. 327; Case 33/74: *Van Binsbergen* v. *Bestuur van de Bedrijfsvereniging voor de Metaalnijverheid,* [1975] C.M.L.R. 298.
[6] *Flaminio Costa* v. *ENEL, op. cit.*
[7] *Van Binsbergen, op. cit;* Case 36/74: *Walgrave and Koch* v. *Union Cycliste Internationale,* [1975] C.M.L.R. 320; Case 39/75: *Robert Gerardus Coenen* v. *Sociaal Economische Raad,* [1976] C.M.L.R. 30.
[8] Case 13/61: *Bosch* v. *De Geus,* [1962] C.M.L.R. 1 at pp. 28–29; 8 Rec. 89; Case 127/73: *B.R.T.* v. *SABAM,* [1974] E.C.R. 51; [1974] 2 C.M.L.R. 238; *H. P. Bulmer Ltd.* v. *J. Bollinger, S.A.,* [1974] Ch. 401; [1974] 2 All E.R. 1226; [1974] 2 C.M.L.R. 9; *Application des Gaz* v. *Falks Veritas,* [1974] Ch. 381; [1974] 3 All E.R. 51.
[9] Case 155/73: *Italian State* v. *Sacchi,* [1974] 2 C.M.L.R. 177 at pp. 204–207.
[10] *Lorenz* v. *Federal Republic of Germany,* [1973] E.C.R. 1471.
[11] Cases 28/67; 31/67, 25/67, 13/67, 7/67; 20/67: *Mölkerei-Zentrale Westfalen/Lippe GmbH* v. *Hauptzollamt Paderborn,* see 28/67, [1968] C.M.L.R. 187 at p. 217; 14 Rec. 211 at p. 226; *Lütticke, op. cit.,* [1971] C.M.L.R. 674.
[12] Case 43/75: *Gabrielle Defrenne* v. *S.A. Sabena* (1976), Times, 9 April.
[13] For exceptions, see E.E.C. arts. 173, 184, 215.
[14] Case 28/67: *Mölkerei-Zentrale Westfalen/Lippe GmbH* v. *Hauptzollamt Paderborn,* [1968] C.M.L.R. 187 at 217; 14 Rec. 211 at p. 226.

that the Treaty is something more than an agreement creating obligations between states parties alone. The Community is a new legal system, in support of which the member states have limited their sovereign rights in certain fields, and the subjects of the new legal system are not only the member states but their inhabitants as well. Community Law, being independent of the legislation passed by member states, therefore, creates rights as well as duties for individual persons who are subject to the legal order of member states. These rights and obligations arise not only when they are expressly provided for in the Treaty, but also as a result of the duties imposed by it in a clearly defined manner upon nationals of member states, the states themselves and the institutions of the Community . . ."

The test of direct enforceability is, therefore, primarily the capacity of the text to produce rights and obligations which individuals may seek to enforce against the state. The national law should not bar the enforcement of such rights and obligations,[15] even though the enforcement may in the context of national law present considerable technical difficulties. However, as indicated by decisions arising from the application of E.E.C. art. 85, a text may, even indirectly, give rise to directly enforceable rights and obligations. In this sense the nature of a specific provision may have to be inferred from its purpose and the intention of the authority which brought into being such a provision (i.e. whether the Treaty or Community legislation). To what extent procedures prescribed by the Treaty may give rise to directly enforceable rights and obligations remains to be seen. Procedural law is, in many respects, the guarantor of substantive rights. Where the prescribed procedures are not observed, the individual may suffer and should, in justice, be entitled to relief. This, among other things, seems to have been in the mind of the Giudice Conciliatore Fabbri in *Flaminio Costa* v. *ENEL*[16] when he considered a complaint that the Italian decree nationalising the electricity industry, passed in the absence of consultation with the Commission (arts. 101 and 102), distorted the conditions of competition and infringed the rights of the individual. Although the Community Court held that art. 102 created no directly enforceable rights, the general question seems to remain open.

The principle of direct applicability of Treaty provisions defined by the Community Court applies also to secondary legislation. Regula-

---

[15] *Salgoil SpA*, above.

[16] *The Free Zones Case*, [1932] P.C.I.J. Rep. Ser A/B, No. 46; *The Wimbledon Case*, [1923] P.C.I.J. Rep Ser. A. No. 1; *German Settlers Case*, [1923] P.C.I.J. Rep. Ser. B. No. 6.

tions[17] fall into that category unless they give the member states discretion in their implementation.[18] This means that whilst they are "directly applicable" to the states they do not necessarily produce "direct effects" as far as the private parties are concerned. The question whether a directive or a decision can have a "direct effect" was answered in the affirmative in *Grad* v. *Finanzamt Traunstein*[19] and *SACE* v. *Italian Ministry of Finance*[20] respectively. In the former case a directive on the harmonization of turnover taxes was held as having a direct effect to support objection against a new tax calculated on the basis of distance and tonnage of transport of goods by road. In the latter case the Court held that the time limit by which a member state must give effect to a decision can be relied on as having a direct effect on the rights of a private party.

(3) *Indirectly Applicable Rules of Community Law*

In addition to provisions which contain rules of law directly applicable in the territory of the member states the foundation Treaties comprise a number of policies or general provisions which have to be implemented by state legislation. The former are cognisable by the national courts and for all intents and purposes are regarded as having a direct and immediate effect with regard to persons and things in the territory of the member states. The latter consist of Treaty obligations which by virtue of the Treaty provisions have to be transformed into detailed rules of law. To these we can add the decisions and directives of the Community organs addressed to one or several states which are of a general or mixed character and have to be further elaborated. The rules of law indirectly applicable have this in common that they have to be enacted by the member states to become part of their municipal law and that the member states have a considerable discretion in the choice of the methods. In most cases the member states have merely to adapt their existing laws to the overall strategy of the foundation Treaties, notably the Common Market in the E.E.C. However the intensity of the adaptation and the degree of discretion accorded to member states depend on the Treaty provisions. Thus according to the E.E.C. Treaty three such degrees can be discerned.[21]

---

[17] See p. 81 *et seq.*
[18] E.g. Reg. 15/64/E.E.C. (J.O. 573/64) concerning the import of cattle from Denmark to Germany.
[19] Case 9/70, [1971] C.M.L.R. 1 at pp. 24–25; (1970) 16 Rec. 825 at p. 839. See also *Van Duyn* v. *Home Office, op. cit.*, note 4 above.
[20] Case 33/70, [1971] C.M.L.R. 123 at p. 132.
[21] Sohier, M., and Megret, C., "Le rôle de l'exécutif national et du législateur national dans la mise en oeuvre du droit communautaire", *Semaine de Bruges* (1965), *op cit.*, pp. 108 *et seq.*; Constantinidès-Mégret, *op cit.*, pp. 132 *et seq.*

Firstly, the states may enjoy complete discretion in the implementation of their obligations. Two examples, discussed by a learned writer,[1] illustrate the point. To implement Regulation No. 3 concerning the social security of migrant workers (reference to E.E.C. art. 51) Italy set up a special pension for miners;[2] the Netherlands, on the other hand, considered that their existing law was inadequate and took the opportunity of remodelling the system and adapting it to the problems of migrant workers.[3] To implement the E.E.C. agricultural policy France passed a general statute (*loi d'orientation agricole*),[4] whilst Belgium decided to recast the whole system and so repealed the law of 1931 on import export and transit of goods and substituted for it a new law on agriculture.[5]

Secondly, the states may have a choice of either implementing or not implementing the Community Law, but in the exercise of their option they have to act within the scope of authority accorded to them. The following provisions of the E.E.C. Treaty are relevant in this respect:

Article 25, which enables the Council to grant to the member states, on the recommendation of the Commission, tariff quotas at a reduced rate of duty or duty free;[6]

Article 115, which enables the Commission to authorise the member states to take protective measures in derogation from the general principles of the commercial policy of the Community;[7]

Article 226, which enables the Commission to authorise the member states to take protective measures during the transitional period in derogation from the rules of the Treaty.[8]

Thirdly, there are measures which the member states have to take in order to discharge their obligations. In this respect they act merely as agents of the Community instrumental in the execution of the Community Law. Should they fail to do so they would be guilty of infringement of the Treaty and subject to consequences arising from arts. 169, 170 and 171 of the E.E.C. Treaty.

---

[1] Constantinidès-Mégret, *op. cit.*, p. 133.

[2] Law of No. 5, 3 January 1960, *Gaz. Uff.*, No. 27, 1960.

[3] Law of 13 January 1965; reference to Regulations 15 and 38/64 on the free movement of workers, E.E.C. art. 48.

[4] Law of 8 August 1962, J.O.R.F., 10 August 1962.

[5] Law of 11 September 1962; M.B. 26 October 1962, p. 9491, and Law of 20 July 1962; M.B. 26 July 1962, p. 6218.

[6] E.g. decisions of the Commission of 9 November 1964 (J.O. 1964, p. 3259) and of 12 November 1964 (J.O. 1964, p. 3549) quoted by Constantinidès-Mégret, *op cit.*, p. 134.

[7] E.g. decision of 21 September 1964 (J.O. 1964, p. 2497, *op. cit.*, p. 134).

[8] E.g. decisions of 20 December 1963 (J.O. 1964, p. 145) and of 16 April 1964 (J.O. 1964, p. 1162).

A study[9] of the problem of state legislation turning the rules of Community Law indirectly applicable into the municipal law of the Six reveals not only a diversity of approach, but, above all, a slow progress. Parliaments are far from being eager to act and their procedures are lengthy and cumbersome. As guardians of national sovereignty they seem to resent the intrusion of extraneous law-making authority although they have accepted the Community Treaties. As legislators parliaments, no doubt, do not relish their subordinate position, or having their functions reduced to mere formality, in the matter of Community legislation. As parliamentary debates seem nugatory in view of clear Treaty obligations to execute Community Law, the tendency is to leave the matter in the hands of the executive.[10]

Should parliament turn perverse and pass a law inconsistent with the Treaty obligations, precious little can be done. Evidently the state concerned could be in breach of the Treaty which in turn would enable the Commission to act under art. 169. Should the state be recalcitrant in not heeding the "reasoned opinion" of the Commission, the matter could be brought before the Community Court.[11] If the Community Court decides against the state, the state is bound to "take the necessary measures to comply with the judgment" (art. 171), which means the repeal of the offending legislation. However, in theory, the game could go on for ever if the government concerned were unable to influence its parliament. Although the Community would be in jeopardy, the Community Court could not strike down the municipal legislation it considers "illegal" in the eyes of the Community Law, simply because the Court has no direct authority in the territory of the member state. Rather than putting the Community at risk the member states have evolved a practical, though individualistic, approach to the implementation of Community Law. Their solution of the problem depends on the Constitution.

The French Constitution of 1958 sharply distinguishes between legislation by statute (*loi*) and legislation by decree (*décret*). Whatever is not listed in art. 34 as being subject to legislation by Parliament falls, by virtue of art. 37, into the Government's lap and becomes subject to *pouvoir réglementaire*. In addition the Government may be authorised to make ordinances by statute which is usually of a limited duration but may be renewed. Consequently the French Government appears

---

[9] Constantinidès-Mégret, *op. cit.*, pp. 139 *et seq.*
[10] Reports on Constitutional Laws in France (1964–65) by M. de Grailly (The House of Deputies) and M. Marcilhacy (Senate) quoted by Constantinidès-Mégret, *op. cit.*, p. 145.
[11] Cf. Case 45/64: *Commission v. The Republic of Italy*, [1966] C.M.L.R. 97 at pp. 107–108; 11 Rec. 1057.

well equipped constitutionally to deal with Community legislation, assuming, of course, that politically this is acceptable to Parliament. Two notable examples[12] illustrate the use of this power by the Government: the ordinance of 9 October 1964[13] which put into operation the directive of the E.E.C. Council of 2 April 1963 concerning the exploitation of abandoned and neglected agricultural estates, and the directive of the same date concerning the right of establishment in agriculture of citizens of member states who have worked more than two years in countries other than their own; the ordinance of 29 April 1964[14] which put into operation the directive of the E.E.C. Council of 25 March 1964 concerning the right of establishment and commercial services. More recently, when certain budgetary provisions of the E.E.C. Treaty were modified in 1970, the French government asked the Conseil Constitutionnel to consider whether the new Treaty included any provisions contrary to the constitution or necessitating an amendment to the constitution. The answer was in the negative.[15]

On 10 July 1966 the law "relative to the application of certain treaties" authorised the government to issue ordinances to ensure the implementation of E.E.C. directives. The government used this power on 28 August 1969 to provide for a commercial identity card for E.E.C. nationals and also in relation to the freedom of establishment in agriculture. Another law was passed on 26 December 1969 in relation to the right of establishment and free movement of services. The government ordinances are made by the Council of Ministers after advice from the Conseil d'Etat. They come into force on publication but become void if the bill ratifying them is not submitted to Parliament before the date fixed by the enabling statute.[16] Parliament too makes statutes to harmonize French law with Community law.[17] The result[18] is a very complex and diverse system of implementation based in principle on parliamentary delegation authorised by art. 38 of the Constitution and the government's own power of legislation.

---

[12] Quoted by Constantinidès-Mégret, *op. cit.*, p. 150.
[13] J.O.R.F., 15 October 1964.
[14] J.O.R.F., 7 May 1964.
[15] J.C.P. 1970, II. 16510.
[16] E.g. 24 July 1966 on commercial companies; 3 July 1970 on monopoly overall explosives; 22 May 1971 on forestry reproductive materials; 8 July 1971 on customs bonded warehouses.
[17] E.g. 15 April 1970 on the nationality of public service concessionaries; 11 February 1971 on transport; 22 February 1971 on investments in the Community.
[18] For a complete and up-to-date account, see Bailleux A., *Techniques d'application du Droit Communautaire dans l'ordre juridique français*, unpublished doctoral thesis, Nice, 1975.

Countries in which the executive cannot rely on a direct constitutional authority in this respect, have evolved a system of delegation of powers. This implies parliamentary approval of the acts of the government which, in practice, is often granted retrospectively so much so that parliament appears to exercise a merely formal control. Examples of this practice can be taken from the Benelux countries, notably in the field of customs law and agriculture.[19] In France the Code of Customs Law enables the Government to take certain measures which have to be approved by Parliament. This method was used in order to carry out the Community customs regulations.[20]

In Belgium the Customs and Excise Law of 2 May 1958, having authorised the King to take measures by decree subject to parliamentary approval, has adopted basically the French solution. A similar law was passed in the Netherlands on 25 June 1960 but it does not require parliamentary sanction for measures taken under the authority of the said law.

The execution of the agricultural policy of the Community in the Benelux countries reveals a more complex picture. Without going into details it may suffice to note that in Belgium under the law of 1962, which replaced the law of 1931 on import, export and transit of agricultural produce, powers were delegated to the King to make decrees relevant to the Community agricultural policy. A similar law was passed in Luxembourg.

In the Netherlands, where the agricultural system is quite unique, and complex because it is based on a network of "professional" organisations endowed with a great deal of autonomous power, authority, under the Agricultural Law, is delegated to the Queen to carry out the Community agricultural policy by decree.

Summing up the position in the Benelux countries we can say that their governments put into effect Community Law by virtue of a general delegation of power. A system of general delegation can be said to exist also in the new member states: in Denmark by virtue of the Constitution[1] (art. 20) and in Eire and the United Kingdom by virtue of the European Communities Acts 1972, ss. 2 and 2 (2) respectively.

A system of specific delegation of legislative power operates in Italy and the German Federal Republic.

---

[19] Constantinidès-Mégret, *op. cit.*, pp. 150–154.

[20] E.g. the decision of the E.E.C. Council of 4 April 1962 was incorporated in art. 19 of the French Customs Code by decree, J.O. 1962, p. 999.

[1] Sørensen, M., "Compétences supranationales et pouvoirs constitutionnels en droit danois", *Miscellanea W. J. Ganshof van der Meersch* (1972), Vol. 2, p. 481 *et seq.*

Article 76 of the Italian Constitution provides that the exercise of the legislative power may be delegated to the Government for a specific purpose and only for a limited period. On this principle art. 4 of the act of ratification of 14 October 1957[1] authorises the Government to promulgate by decree having the force of ordinary law, in accordance with the "general principles enshrined in the E.E.C. Treaty", the necessary rules to:

   (i) ensure the execution of the obligations arising from art. 11;
  (ii) carry out measures provided in arts. 37, 46, 70, 89, 91, 107, 108, 109, 115 and 226;
 (iii) carry out dispositions and principles comprised in arts. 95, 96, 97 and 98 of the E.E.C. Treaty.

The original delegation expired in 1961 but has been extended quinquennially. By virtue of this delegation several decrees have been passed. However, before taking any measure the Government has to seek advice of a Parliamentary Commission consisting of 15 Members of the House of Deputies and 15 Members of the Senate.

Article 80 (1) of the Basic Law of the German Federal Republic of 1953 provides for the delegation of legislative power to the Executive by statute which has to determine the context, purpose and extent of the delegation. The law of ratification[2] granted to the Federal Government the power to carry into effect arts. 14, 16, 17 (1), and 23 (2) of the E.E.C. Treaty (Customs Provisions) as well as certain provisions of the protocols on mineral oils and bananas. Such decrees could be made without approval of the Federal Parliament (*Bundestag*) unless the Parliament objected within three weeks from the date when draft decrees were laid before it. No approval of the decrees by the Federal Council (*Bundesrat*) was required though the Council had fourteen days to make comments on the draft decrees.

The Customs Law of 1957[3] made under the above rules was amended by the Law of 1961[4] which enlarged the powers of the Federal Government. Article 77 of the Law of 1961 is particularly relevant to the implementation of Community Law. It concerns measures under E.E.C. art. 103 (short-term economic policy) and, more generally, Community legislation. The former will be studied by the relevant parliamentary committee and submitted to the Bundestag which will accept or reject the decrees. The Bundestag cannot approve these by silence. They will also be submitted to the Bundesrat but merely for

---

[2] See p. 193, above.
[3] Law of 27 July 1957, B.G.B.I. II (1957), p. 753.
[4] Law of 14 June 1961, B.G.B.I. I (1961), p. 758.

opinion. Drafts of decrees for the implementation of the Community legislation are laid before the Bundestag and the Bundesrat and the Bundestag is presumed to have approved the decrees if within three months from this submission they have not been formally abrogated by Parliament. The function of the Bundesrat is purely advisory. Customs laws have been modified on several occasions by this process. In the field of agriculture several laws have been passed. Of these the Law of 1964[5] conferred upon the Federal Government the power of legislating by decree in order to put into effect the regulations, decisions and directives of the Council and the Commission of the E.E.C. governing the marketing of cereals, milk products and rice.

It is clear from this brief survey of the methods of implementing Community Law that the member states have retained a measure of parliamentary control in this matter. The problem is by no means simple and in the interests of the smooth running of the Community as well as the efficacy of the Community Law in the territory of the member states, it ought to be studied in depth with a view to formulating a common approach and a uniform procedure.

IV   INCORPORATION THROUGH THE COMMUNITY COURT

We have already considered the meaning and effect of Community legislation as a source of Community Law;[6] we should emphasise now the role of the Community Court in the process of the incorporation of Community legislation into the municipal laws. The Court has an indirect influence under E.E.C. arts. 173 and 177. Under art. 173 the Court has the power of annulment and indeed, should the action for annulment be well founded, the Court will strike down the offending piece of Community legislation (art. 174). On the other hand whatever is uncontested or declared valid by the Court has the force of law in the territory of the member states. It is important to note that the decisions of the Court in respect of the validity of the Community legislation have a universal application; they are enforceable (*erga omnes* (art. 174 (1)).

However perhaps more significant, from a practical point of view, is the Court's impact through its interpretation of Community Law. Where the national court requests interpretation the impact is direct and instructive. It is equally instructive in other cases, though the impact has to be measured through the doctrine of judicial precedent.

---

[5] Law of 13 August 1964.
[6] See pp. 81 *et seq.*, above.

Here the British judges are out of step with their continental brethren as they lavishly cite the decisions of the Community Court as well as the judgments of national courts.[7] However a rigid application of the doctrine of *stare decisis* must be discounted simply because the Community Court is not bound by its own decisions and a slavish adherence to a precedent no longer honoured on the continent would lead to serious anomalies and distortions of Community Law by British judges.

In spite of the merely persuasive authority of precedents in continental jurisprudence the decisions of the Community Court are gaining prestige in national jurisdictions. They are being cited[8] and some courts occasionally cite decisions of national courts.[9] They do so not in principle or out of habit but because they appreciate the authoritative exposition of Community Law by the Community Court and of the relevant national law by national courts. As for the authority of the Community precedents there is as yet no uniform approach to this matter. Recent reports indicate that the French *Cour de Cassation*[10] considered that French courts are generally bound by the rulings of the Community Court; a German Court[11] felt that the decisions of the Community Court are binding "beyond the instant case", whilst the Milan Court of Appeal applied[12] the Community Court's ruling in one case and considered it binding only *inter partes*, in another.[13] No doubt a trend towards recognition of Community precedents is gaining momentum.

Article 177 gives the Community Court the power of interpretation of the Treaty, of the acts of the Community organs and of the statutes of bodies established by the Council in the form of a preliminary ruling. The Treaty is silent as to the scope of this ruling: is it valid *erga omnes* or only *quoad casum*? Some writers[14] doubt the *erga omnes*

---

[7] E.g. *Esso Petroleum Co. Ltd.* v. *Kingswood Motors*, [1974] Q.B. 142; [1973] 3 All E.R. 1057; *H. P. Bulmer Ltd.* v. *J. Bollinger S.A.*, [1974] Ch. 401; [1974] 2 All E.R. 1226; [1974] 2 C.M.L.R. 91; *Application des Gaz S.A.* v. *Falks Veritas*, [1974] Ch. 381; [1974] 1 All E.R. 51; *R.* v. *Secchi*, Metropolitan Magistrate, London, [1975] 1 C.M.L.R. 383.

[8] *Fiorini* v. *Société Nationale des Chemin De Fer Français* Court of Appeal, [1975] C.M.L.R. 459; *Re Dry Shavers*, [1975] C.M.L.R. 550; *Administration des Douanes* v *Soc. Cafés Jacques Vabres*, Paris Court of Appeal, [1975] C.M.L.R. 336.

[9] *Francesco Cinzano & Cie GmbH* v. *Java Kaffeegeschäfte GmbH*; *Bundesgerichtshof*, [1974] C.M.L.R. 21.

[10] *Garoche* v. *Striker Boats (Nederland)*, *Cour de Cassation*, [1974] C.M.L.R. 469.

[11] Case KZR 7/69: *Re Brewery Solus Agreement*, [1975] C.M.L.R. 611.

[12] *Sirena S.R.L.* v. *EDA S.R.L.*, [1975] C.M.L.R. 409.

[13] *SAFA* v. *Amministrazione delle Finanze*, [1973] C.M.L.R. 152.

[14] E.g. Catalano, N., *Manuel de droit des Communautés Européennes* (1965) (French Translation), p. 88.

effect, others[15] argue that it has this effect. Whether one can go that far, bearing in mind that a national court may repeatedly request a preliminary ruling in similar circumstances and the Community Court, not being bound by its previous decisions, may change its mind, is debatable. However, whatever the effect of the judgment, it is an instrument of integration of Community Law with municipal law and of uniformity throughout the Community. The importance of art. 177 cannot be overemphasised.

Article 177 should be read together with art. 20 of the Protocol on the Statute of the Community Court which provides for the procedure to be applied when a preliminary ruling is sought. Accordingly when any Court or tribunal of a member state decides that it cannot proceed to judgment without the elucidation of a point of Community Law relevant to the case the proceedings are suspended and the Court or tribunal refers the matter to the Community Court. The decision to seek a ruling is notified by the Registrar of the Community Court to the parties, the member states and to the Commission, and also to the Council if the act, the validity or interpretation of which is in dispute, originates from the Council. Within two months of this notification, the parties, the member states, the Commission and, where appropriate, the Council, are entitled to make their submissions or observations to the Court. In this way the matter ceases to be of sole concern to the parties and the adjudicating court; it becomes of common concern to the whole Community. By giving the national judge access to the Community Court, whilst enabling all the member states and the Community organs to make representations, the Treaty sets the stage for an understanding between the municipal courts and the Community Court and for a development towards a common law of the Community. At the same time the Treaty asserts the superiority of the Community Court.

Many cases have been submitted for a preliminary ruling and the Court has developed a certain practice in this field. In the first case[16] under art. 177 the Court advised that the referring court is free to adopt a direct and simple form of reference which will enable the Community Court to rule strictly within the limits of its jurisdiction. Thus formalism was dispensed with but at the same time the Court implied that it would not be politic to decide the issue otherwise than in the terms of interpretation of Community Law. Furthermore the Court

---

[15] E.g. Zuccala, "Di una forma d'intepretazione guirisprudenziale autentica delle leggi", *Guirisprudenzia Italiana* (1959), IV, Coll. 139–144; quoted by Constantinidès-Mégret, *op. cit.*, pp. 39–40.

[16] Case 13/61: *Geus v. Bosch Van Rijn*, [1962] C.M.L.R. 1; 8 Rec. 89.

stressed that whilst two different legal orders are involved (national and Community) the national court is about to administer Community Law albeit under the guidance of the Community Court.

In another case[17] the Court observed that the considerations which may guide the national court in the choice of its questions and their pertinence to the issue to be decided are outside the jurisdiction of the Community Court. In this case a Dutch Administrative Tribunal enquired whether art. 12 of the E.E.C. Treaty "entailed internal legal effects, that is whether or not an individual may directly derive rights which have to be protected by his national courts". Article 12 provides that member states shall refrain from introducing between themselves any new customs duties on imports or exports, or any charges having equivalent effect, and from increasing those which they already apply in their trade with each other. The question raised a constitutional issue, that is whether the Community Court was really interpreting Community Law or whether it usurped the power to interpret the Dutch Constitution (i.e. the power to levy taxes). The Dutch Government was of the opinion that the Community Court had no jurisdiction in matters involving Dutch customs duties. However the Community Court firmly asserted its jurisdiction and the power to rule in the matter, as it pointed out that art. 12 came for interpretation not for application according to Dutch law. In this delicate situation the Court refrained from ruling upon the conflict between Dutch and Community Law but firmly declared that art. 12 had a direct effect though the mode of application was left to the internal process of the Netherlands.

In *Costa* v. *ENEL* the Court held that it had power to select what was relevant from the list of questions imperfectly formulated by the referring court and in this way refused to be drawn into an internal conflict. "Consequently," held the Court, "the decision should be given not upon the validity of an Italian law in relation to the Treaty but upon the interpretation of the above mentioned articles in the context of the points of law stated by the *Guidice Conciliatore*."[18]

In *Schwarze* v. *Einfuhr-und Vorratstelle*[19] the Court had to decide whether, when asked for an interpretation of Community Law, it could also rule upon the validity of an E.E.C. decision. It held that "when it appears that questions asked by a municipal court for the purpose of interpretation in reality concern the validity of a Community act, it is for the Court of Justice to enlighten the national court

---

[17] Case 26/62: *Van Gend en Loos* v. *Nederlandse Administratie der Belastingen*, [1963] C.M.L.R. 105; 9 Rec. 1; see also case 56/65: *Technique Minière* v. *Machinenbau Ulm GmbH*, [1966] C.M.L.R. 357; 12 Rec. 337.
[18] [1964] C.M.L.R. 425 at p. 455; 10 Rec. 1141 at p. 1158.
[19] Case 16/65, [1966] C.M.L.R. 172 at 186–187; 11 Rec. 1081 at p. 1116–1117.

immediately without insisting upon a formalism which would be purely dilatory and which would be incompatible with the true nature of the machinery established by art. 177."

However, no matter how helpful the Community Court is in the process of the elucidation of the points before it, there is a limit to its competence for the scope of art. 177 is limited to answering questions on issues raised by the referring court.[20]

In yet another case[1] involving E.C.C. arts. 30–37 (elimination of quantitative restrictions) the Court ruled that it cannot apply the Treaty to a particular situation or determine the validity of an internal measure in this respect.

In a sense the rulings of the Community Court under art. 177 may be regarded as rulings on abstract points of law because the Community Court, content with the definition of the law, leaves its application to national courts. This indeed is the message of the *Van Gend* case. It is, therefore, necessary to distinguish between "interpretation" and "application"; the former being the task of the Community Court, the latter of the national court involved.[2]

Article 177 is addressed to both the courts and tribunals "against whose decision there is no judicial remedy under national law"[3] and "any court or tribunal".[4] The former include, *prima facie*, the Supreme Courts and the highest specialist courts of the member states, i.e. the *Cour de Cassation* and the *Conseil d'Etat* in Belgium and France; the *Corte di Cassazione*, the *Consiglio di Stato* and *Corte Costituzionale* in Italy; the *Bundesgerichtshof*, the *Bundessozialgericht*, the *Bundesverwaltungsgericht*, the *Bundesdisziplinarhof* and the *Bundesfinanzhof* in Germany; the *Hoge Raad*, the *Tariefcommissie* and the *College van Beroep* in the Netherlands; the Supreme Court in Eire; the *Højesteret* in Denmark; the House of Lords and in some cases the English Court of Appeal, the Scottish Court of Session and the Northern Irish Supreme Court in the United Kingdom. However, in *Flaminio Costa* v. *ENEL*[5]

---

[20] Case 51/72: *Fratelli Grassi* v. *Amministrazione delle Finanze*, [1973] C.M.L.R. 332; 18 Rec. 443.

[1] Case 20/64: *SARL, Albatros* v. *SOPECO* (*Société de Pétroles et des Combustibles liquides*), [1965] C.M.L.R. 159; 11 Rec. 1.

[2] See *dicta* of Stamp and Stephenson, L.JJ., in *Bulmer H.P.* v. *Bollinger J.* [1974] 2 C.M.L.R. 91 at pp. 121 and 124 and Case 183/73: *Osram GmbH* v. *Oberfinanzdirektion Frankfurt*, [1974] E.C.R. 447 at p. 485; [1974] 2 C.M.L. 360 at p. 366.

[3] Dont les décisions ne sont pas susceptibles d'un recours juridictionnel de droit interne; dessen Entscheidungen selbst nicht mehr mit Rechtsmitteln des innerstaatlichen Rechts angefochten werden können; avverso le cui decisioni non possa proporsi un ricorso giurisdizionale di diritto interno.

[4] Une juridiction, ein Gericht, una giurisdizione.

[5] Case 6/64, [1964] C.M.L.R. 425; 10 Rec. 1141.

the Community Court accepted a reference from a *Giudice Conciliatore* of Milan on the ground that because of the small claim involved, the magistrate in question was a court of the first and last instance. The Court's *dictum* that reference can be made from any court whose decisions are final (*sans recours*) has broadened the basis of art. 177 (3). The reference to "any court or tribunal" (art. 177 (2)) includes, presumably, apart from the inferior courts of Law, any adjudicating body or institution which in the domestic jurisdictions exercise judicial functions,[6] including, of course, the English magistrates' courts and tribunals.

Whilst reference from the "final court" is obligatory[7] it is only discretionary from the other courts or tribunals[8] that, is if the court considers it necessary to enable it to give judgment. However, obligatory reference does not mean that the Supreme Court will in every case involving Community Law seek a ruling from Luxembourg. Should it be so the Community Court would become a kind of court of appeal from the national jurisdiction which it was never meant to be, for its jurisdiction under art. 177 is limited to interpretation of Community Law in cases where such interpretation is requested by national courts. There is, therefore, no automatic reference but a judicial reference which implies uncertainty of the law in the opinion of the referring court and this, to use the expression of Advocate-General Lagrange,[9] embodies *une règle de bon sens et de sagesse*.

This rule of common sense will differ, no doubt, according to the style of the national judiciary, their sense of independence and their Community orientation. Since reference under art. 177 involves interpretation, perhaps the most vital factor in the decision whether or not to refer is the confidence of the national court in the art of the interpretation of Community Law. Indeed, if the court is certain of the position it need not, in accordance with the doctrine of *acte clair* or *sens clair*, seek the ruling of the Community Court. *Acte clair* implies that the legal rule in question is clear and, therefore, requires no interpretation in accordance with the maxim *clara non sunt interpretanda*. However, *certainty* may mean literally certainty in an objective and undisputed sense. It may also mean *certainty* as a form

---

[6] See Case 61/65: *Vaassen-Göbbels* v. *Beambtenfonds voor het Mijnbedrijf*, [1966] C.M.L.R. 508; 12 Rec. 377.

[7] "That court shall; cette juridiction est tenue; dieses Gericht ist verpflichted; tale giurisdizione è tenuta."

[8] "That court or tribunal may; cette juridiction peut; so kann; tale giurisdizione può."

[9] In Case 28–30/62: *Da Costa en Schaake* v. *Nederlandse Administratie der Belastingen*, [1963] C.M.L.R. 224 at p. 234; 9 Rec. 59 at p. 89.

of subterfuge applied to avoid the cumbersome machinery of pre-liminary ruling as remarked bluntly by a French *Avocat Général*[10] "bien entendu, la théorie de l'acte clair intervient essentiellement pour mettre un obstacle au renvoi pour interprétation". On the other hand courts, being well versed in the art of interpretation, need not be reminded that reference to Luxembourg should be an exception rather than a rule and that it should be resorted to out of necessity and not out of habit.[11]

The principle of *acte clair* applies to the inferior as much as to the final courts but in this context a practical question of appeals against the reference from the inferior courts arises. This basically is a matter for each individual country and there is no uniform practice among the nine. In Germany and the Netherlands the reference goes forward to the Community Court whilst in Belgium and France the appeal has first to be disposed of. In the United Kingdom appeal has precedence over reference.[12] The Community Court, on the other hand, follows its own guidelines which are determined by its function in the Community. This was succinctly stated in the *Bosch* case:[13]

"In fact, just as the Treaty does not prohibit domestic supreme courts from receiving the appeal for annulment, but leaves the examination of its admissibility to domestic law and to the opinion of the domestic judge, the Treaty subjects the jurisdiction of the Court of Justice solely to the existence of a request within the meaning of art. 177, without requiring the Community judge to examine whether the decision of the domestic judge is appealable under the provisions of its domestic law."

However, the spirit of non-intervention has not solved the problem as in two cases involving the same parties the Court was in effect asked to make a ruling on a conflict of opinion between German courts.[14] This conflict was, in the terms of the reference from the *Bundesfinanz-hof*, reduced to the question whether an inferior court had an unfettered right of reference to the Community Court or whether art. 177 upheld

---

[10] Quoted by Pescatore, P., "Interpretation of Community Law and the Doctrine of 'Acte Clair' ", *Legal Problems of an Enlarged European Community*, ed. by Bathurst, M.E., *et al.* (1972), p. 42.
[11] Cf. Graham, J., in *Löwenbräu München* v. *Grünhalle Lager International Ltd.*, [1974] C.M.L.R. 1.
[12] Order 114 (5); see Chapter 12.
[13] Case 13/61: *De Geus en Uitdenbogerd* v. *Bosch en Van Rijn*, [1962] C.M.L.R. 1 at p. 27; 8 Rec. 89 at p. 103.
[14] *Rhein-Mühlen-Düsseldorf* v. *Einfur- und Vorratstelle für Getreide und Futtermittel*, 166/73, [1974] E.C.R. 33; [1974] 1 C.M.L.R. 523 and 146/73, [1974] E.C.R. 139; [1974] I C.M.L.R. 523.

the hierarchy of national courts with the effect that on points of law an inferior court is bound by the ruling of a superior court. The Community Court, addressing itself to the *Hessisches Finanzgericht*,[15] ruled that art. 177 did not preclude an inferior court making its reference to the Community Court whilst the Community Court had no choice but to attend to the questions put before it. Addressing itself to the *Bundesfinanzhof*[16] the Community Court ruled that the existence of a rule of domestic law whereby a court is bound on points of law by the rulings of the court superior to it cannot of itself take away the power provided for in art. 177 of referring cases to the Court. If inferior courts were bound without being able to refer matters to the Court, the jurisdiction of the latter to give preliminary rulings and the application of Community Law at all levels of the judicial systems of the member states would be compromised. It seems that the problem is basically a domestic one though for the sake of uniformity and in the spirit of the integration of judicial remedies within the Community a common solution should be found.

The relationship between the Community Court and the Judiciary of the member states is delicately poised between the recognition of the independence of the courts of sovereign states and the need for a uniform application of Community Law throughout the Community. It is a problem which, one hopes, will solve itself in the course of time and as a result of the consolidation of the Community, though nuances between the styles of the national judiciaries are bound to remain.

---

[15] Case 146/73, [1974] E.C.R. at p. 147.
[16] Case 166/73, [1974] E.C.R. at pp. 38, 39.

CHAPTER ELEVEN

Enforcement of Community Law

ENFORCEMENT OF TREATY OBLIGATIONS

The E.E.C. Treaty is a self-executing treaty, a well designed instrument of international co-operation. The member states not only assume the duty of carrying out the measures prescribed by the Treaty and the Community organs but also submit to the judicial authority of the Community. In this way the state acts as an intermediary if not a subordinate instrument of the execution of the Treaty.

The enforcement of the Treaty is safeguarded by political, economic and legal means. The most important weapon, which in classic international law states may resort to in order to frustrate a treaty, is interpretation. This weapon has been taken away from the signatories of the E.E.C. Treaty and so they cannot resort to legal subterfuge. Though they can defy the Treaty by breaking it they cannot get round it or, under the guise of sovereignty, flout their obligations with impunity. Moreover they cannot claim, as Italy[1] did, the benefit of an "international agreement" when the Treaty obligations have been further specified by a decision, i.e. decision 66/532 urging Italy to accelerate the reduction of the import rates on the basis of the continued protection of the Italian lead and zinc industry.

The interpretation of the Treaty has been entrusted to the Community Court (arts. 164 and 177) but there is a double check because by art. 219 "the Member States undertake not to submit any dispute concerning the interpretation or application of the Treaty to any method of settlement other than those provided in the Treaty". This, in addition to administrative action, establishes a judicial system of settling disputes, the Community Court having a monopolist position.

Restricted in their classic weaponry the member states may be

---

[1] Case 38/69: *Customs Duties on Lead and Zinc; E.C. Commission v. Italy*, [1970] C.M.L.R. 77 at p. 89–90.

tempted to flout the Treaty overtly but this too was provided for. The Treaty provides for repressive measures, should this occur. The procedure of repression is gentle and well suited to the type of the likely offender. The Commission must first inform itself of the alleged breaches and this the Commission can do under art. 213 which provides that "for the performance of the tasks entrusted to it, the Commission may collect any information and carry out any checks required within the limits and under the conditions laid down by the Council". Several other articles compel the member states to furnish information to the Commission, but under art. 213 the Council has approved Regulation 10[2] which gives the Commission authority to collect information on earnings and conditions of employment in some fourteen industries. The general power to seek information is limited by art. 223 (1) which, safeguarding the sovereign status of the member states, enables them to withhold information they consider contrary to the essential interests of their security. The states themselves determine what is essential in the interests of their security, but security is confined to military matters and should not provide a subterfuge to frustrate the objectives of the Treaty.

Having collected information which indicates a breach of the Treaty the Commission will take further steps to enforce the Treaty. In this connection art. 93 provides a good illustration. If the Commission finds that subsidies granted by a state to producers are incompatible with the common market, the Commission will direct the state to abolish[3] or adjust these subsidies within a prescribed time. If the state fails to comply the Commission or any other interested state may refer the matter directly to the Community Court[4] as being in breach of the provisions of arts. 169 and 170.

If the Court finds the accused state guilty of failing to carry out its obligations such a state must, in accordance with art. 171, "take the measures required for the implementation of the judgment". The Court has no power to impose sanctions but its judgment is a judicial declaration of fact and a reminder of the obligation to comply with the judgment.[5]

Member states can sue one another before the Community Court but before doing so they must bring their complaint before the Commission (art. 170 (2). In practice the task of suing the defaulter is undertaken by the Commission in the light of its duty "to ensure the

---

[2] J.O., 31 August 1960.

[3] E.g. Decision 64/65 addressed to Belgium; see *Re Subsidies to Ford Tractor (Belgium) Ltd.*, 64/651/EEC, 28 October 1964; [1965] C.M.L.R. 32.

[4] Decision 556/EEC addressed to France, J.O. No. 181, 12 October 1966; referred to the Community Court, quoted by Campbell, *op. cit.*, Vol. 2, 2115, p. 85.

[5] Cf. *Humblet* v. *Belgium* (1960), 6 Rec. 1125.

proper functioning and development of the Common Market (art. 155)".
The reluctance of states suing each other is understandable: such
actions are invidious and the plaintiff state of today may well be the
defendant tomorrow. Moreover a suit by the Commission tends to be
technical rather than vindictive and, from a Community point of view,
the Commission has the title to represent the Community's objective
interests. Should, however, the Commission fail to act, the member
state or the other institutions of the Community may bring the action
against the Commission[6] (art. 175 (1)).

Should a state fail to execute the judgment of the Community Court
it may once more be sued this time for breach of art. 171. This procedure has in fact been applied but the member state in question
complied with the original judgment.

Apart from the judicial sanction there is also an administrative
sanction in the hands of the Commission. Thus if an infringement of
Community Law occurs, the Commission will recommend measures to
rectify the position. If these measures are not applied, the Commission will take an appropriate decision to bring the infringement to
an end and, if this fails, will bring an action against the defaulter or,
in some cases, authorise another member state to take counter measures.

The member states undertake to bring public and state-aided
undertakings within the rules of competition as well as services of
general economic interest and revenue-producing monopolies. The
Commission must keep its watchful eye upon such bodies and, if
necessary, remind the member states of their obligations in this respect
(art 90). In order to enforce these provisions of the Treaty the Commission shall deal with infringements by means of decisions (art. 89)
and directives or decisions (art. 90 (3)). Disregard of such decisions
or directives may result in a judicial sanction.

Dumping, prohibited by art. 91 (1), shall be dealt with by the
Commission by the persuasion contained in its recommendations to
rectify the position but, should these prove ineffective, the Commission shall authorise the injured state to adopt protective measures
under the guidance of the Commission. Aids granted by states in
contravention of art. 92 shall be investigated by the Commission and
abolished in accordance with the timetable proposed by the Commission (art. 93). Should such a decision be disregarded, the Commission or any interested member state may bring the matter directly
before the Community Court (art. 93 (2)). This procedure was
followed in several cases. In *Commission* v. *French Republic*[7] the

---

[6] See case 59/70: *Netherlands* v. *Commission*, 17 Rec. 639 brought under
E.C.S.C., art. 35.
[7] Joined cases 6 and 11/69, [1970] C.M.L.R. 43; 15 Rec. 523 at p. 538.

Commission requested France to discontinue a rebate system aiding French exporters as it was incompatible with the Treaties and there was a considerable exchange of communications between France and the Commission between 1964 and 1968. Finally the Commission took decisions authorising France to grant aids to the steel industry (914/68/ECSC) and to provide a preferential rebate rate for export credits (68/301/EEC). However France maintained two rates of rebates which the Commission held contrary to the Treaties (arts. 88 ECSC and art. 169 EEC). A "reasoned opinion" of the Commission recommended France to discontinue the system and when the time allowed expired without result the Commission brought France before the Community Court. The Commission also took a decision in respect of aids to the steel industry against which France appealed.

Another case, also involving France,[8] was concerned with the aids to the French textile industry. The Commission found the aids compatible with art. 92 of the EEC Treaty but objected to the method by which they were financed, i.e. by a special tax on textiles, both national and imported. Thereupon France brought an action for the annulment of the decision.

Following a discussion with the Commission, in 1968 Germany enacted its *Kohlengesetz* to reorganise the German mining industry and the mining regions. This law contained measures for the adaptation of the production and marketing of coal to the changing pattern of the energy sector and to improve the economic structure of the mining regions. These measures involved certain tax provisions. In 1969 a law was passed to provide for investment grants. The *Kohlengesetz* was also amended and the Commission advised Germany in 1970 that in view of the improvement of the economic situation the tax provisions and investment grants were no longer compatible with article 92 (3) of the E.E.C. Treaty. As Germany failed to comply, the Commission brought an action before the Community Court claiming infringements of art. 93 (2). The Court[9] held that

"... Since the aim of the Treaty is to achieve the practical elimination of infringements and the consequences thereof, past and future, it is a matter for the Community authorities whose task it is to ensure that the requirements of the Treaty are observed to determine the extent to which the obligation of the member state concerned may be specified in the reasoned opinions or decisions delivered under articles 169 and 93 (2) respectively and in applications addressed to the Court ..."

---

[8] Case 47/69: *France* v. *E.E.C. Commission*, [1970] C.M.L.R. 351; 16 Rec. 487.
[9] Case 70/72: *EC Commission* v. *Federal Republic of Germany*, [1973] E.C.R. 813 at p. 832; [1973] C.M.L.R. 741 at p. 766.

Alterations of the rate of exchange in a manner inconsistent with E.E.C. art. 104 may also lead to an investigation by the Commission as well as an authorisation of retaliatory measures by the other member states.

The efficacy of the enforcement procedure, whether by judicial or administrative means, has inherent limitations in cases involving states because a recalcitrant state cannot really be forced to abide by the judgment of the Court or the decision of the Commission. This indeed is the last vestige of sovereignty. In this respect the Community differs from a federal state which may have federal means at its disposal for the execution of the judgments of the federal court or the decisions of the federal executive. Therefore the ultimate sanction in the E.E.C. is political and economic. The former consists of the pressure of public opinion within the Community and persuasion by the member states. The economic sanction lies in the common interest inherent in the preservation and improvement of the Community quite apart from any counter-measures which may be taken by the member states individually or collectively. Though the machinery of enforcement is far from perfect there is no reason to believe that states would wantonly act contrary to the accepted obligations. They are only too well aware that the smooth working of the Community depends on their co-operation and that the economic intertwining cannot be disentangled without self-inflicted hardship. They may drag their feet, as e.g. Italy did over the Value Added Tax, or try to assert themselves as France did on occasions or march out of step as the United Kingdom tends to do from time to time, but ultimately the Community spirit prevails.

There is ample provision in the Treaty for member states in difficulty over their obligations during the transitional period. Article 226 provides a general formula in this respect, specific situations are catered for in several other articles. Article 226 provides for safeguards the member states may adopt, not unilaterally[10] but under the Commission's authority. The state making application under art. 226 must submit all the information necessary in order to enable the Commission to determine the measures to be taken in the given situation. Consequently a breach of the Treaty cannot be justified retrospectively.[11] The object of the concessions a member state may obtain when in difficulty is to enable the state concerned to adjust its economy so as to

---

[10] Case 7/61: *Re Quantitative Restrictions on Italian Pork Imports*, [1962] C.M.L.R. 39 at p. 56; 7 Rec. 633.
[11] Cases 2–3/62: *Re Import Duties on Gingerbread*, 2–3/62, [1963] C.M.L.R. 199 at p. 214; 8 Rec. 813.

be better able to play its part in the Community but not to defeat specific provisions of the Treaty.[12]

However the member states are not expected to prolong unduly the transitional period. In a recent case an Italian[13] firm imported manufactured tobacco directly into Italy after 1 January 1970 (Italy should have adjusted her tobacco monopoly by 31 December 1969) and, by doing so, was in breach of the Italian monopoly law of 1942. In its defence the firm pleaded art. 37 (1) of the E.E.C. Treaty whilst the Italian government claimed that the monopoly was justified because of its fiscal character. The Community Court, in its preliminary ruling under art. 177, held that not only was Italy in default but also that art. 37 was, as from the end of the transitional period, directly applicable, conferring rights upon individuals which they can enforce before national courts. The argument that there was a 1972 Council resolution calling upon French and Italian governments to eliminate discrimination arising from national monopolies by January 1976, did not, in the opinion of the Court detract from the direct applicability of art. 37 (1).

Further to the general safeguards under art. 226 the Treaty provides for measures to meet specific emergencies arising from the application of the rules regarding customs duties (art. 17 (4)); customs tariffs (art. 23 (2));[14] tariff quotas (art. 25 (2), (3));[15] state trading monopolies (art. 37 (3));[16] agriculture (art. 44 (5)); movement of capital (arts. 70 (3) and 73);[17] state grants to producers (art. 93 (2) (3)); balance of payments (arts. 108 and 109). These are examples of situations in which the full rigour of the Treaty need not apply provided, of course, the states concerned take the necessary steps to advise the Community of their problems and co-operate in the process of devising the measures to meet the difficulties.

It is clear from the foregoing that the enforcement of the Treaty obligations rests not only on the legal and moral implications of the cardinal rule of international law *pacta sunt servanda*, but above all on self-interest and the Community spirit.

---

[12] *Re Quantitative Restrictions on Italian Pork Imports.*

[13] Case 59/75: *Pubblico Ministero* v. *Flavia Manghera et al.* (1976), *Times, European Law Report,* 6 February.

[14] *In Re Customs Duties on Polythene,* [1964] C.M.L.R. 295.

[15] Case 24/62: *Re Tariff Quota on Wine,* [1963] C.M.L.R. 347; 9 Rec. 129; case 34/62: *Re Import Duties on Sweet Oranges,* [1963] C.M.L.R. 369; 9 Rec. 269.

[16] *Re Shell-Berre,* decided by the French Conseil d'Etat, 19 June 1964; [1964] C.M.L.R. 462.

[17] Cf. Cases 106–1076/3: Advocate-General Roemer in *Toepfer K.G.* v. *E.E.C. Commission,* [1966] C.M.L.R. 111 at p. 118; 11 Rec. 525.

ENFORCEMENT OF COMMUNITY LAW AT COMMUNITY LEVEL

Away from the lofty stage of inter-state conflicts or internal Community disputes, the enforcement of Community Law (including the Treaty) occurs in the more usual setting of disputes in which individuals, corporations and states are involved. Such disputes are decided either at Community or state level bearing in mind that Community Law is state law and, therefore, subject to the judicial notice of municipal courts.

The underlying philosophy of the Community and, indeed, the practical assurance of the Community development in accordance with the Treaty and the Community legislation is the theory of the supremacy of Community Law. It is still a theory because in spite of the constitutional adjustments of the member states there is, generally, a certain amount of hesitation, if not reluctance, to accept the monist doctrine and by-pass national legislatures. At the root of this is not only distrust of the Brussels bureaucrats who are neither directly controlled by nor responsible to the member states but, more importantly, an instinctive aversion to external laws and authorities invading, as it were, the sacred preserve of sovereign states. These states have a long and proud history and a strong sense of national identity. Therefore psychological barriers have to be removed in order to make the legal obligations enshrined in Treaties and subordinate legislation meaningful and acceptable. In the circumstances it is not surprising that the lead in the process of the enforcement of Community Law had to come from the Community Court.

The main difficulty is that apart from art. 189 the E.E.C. Treaty contains no formal and unequivocal assertion of the supremacy of Community Law. Yet, it is common ground that the edifice of the Community would collapse if the Community were to degenerate into a legal Tower of Babel. Thus the Community Court in a number of cases formulated and re-affirmed the principle of supremacy. The Court, as the guardian of legality and instrument of cohesion within the Community has, from the start, been in a strong position to define the status of the Community Law and to give it precedence when in conflict with the municipal law of the member states. Most of these cases were brought under art. 177 (which defines the jurisdiction of the Court to make a preliminary ruling in several matters) and the Court did not hesitate to use its authority in furthering the aims of the Community.

Whilst the Community Court in its judicial capacity has no rival system of law to administer and is only remotely concerned with the political consequences of its decisions, the municipal courts have to face the juristic and practical problems arising from the conflict between domestic law and Community Law forming part of their national system. The theory that Community Law is part of national law does not solve these problems. However, the fact that municipal courts are not only prepared to follow the Community Court but also to assert independently the supremacy of Community Law is quite significant. It shows that they are prepared to follow the rule of law established by the Community Court and in doing so do not hesitate to disregard the possible claim of municipal law or of their national government to confine disputes involving Community matters to domestic jurisdiction and municipal law. The judge sworn to administer the law of his country has to overcome the temptation to give precedence to the law in which he has been trained over the law derived from an external source.

SUPREMACY OF COMMUNITY LAW IN THE DECISIONS OF THE COMMUNITY COURT

The doctrine of supremacy of Community Law was elaborated gradually by the Community Court in the course of its interpretation of the Treaties. The stage was set probably as early as 1963 when in the *Van Gend en Loos* case[18] the Court declared that the Community constituted "a new legal order—for whose benefit the states have limited their sovereign rights, albeit within limited fields, and the subjects of which comprise not only the member states but also their nationals". The case arose out of the imposition by the Netherlands Government of new import duties which, it was argued, were in contravention of art. 12 of the E.E.C. Treaty which prohibited the member states from introducing new customs duties or equivalent charges. The question was whether art. 12 of the Treaty had a direct effect in the Netherlands and, consequently, whether the duties being in contravention of the Treaty were illegal. In other words, the question was whether the Treaty created rights in favour of individuals which had to be protected by their national court. These questions were answered by the Community Court in the affirmative. However a greater issue was involved because these questions raised a constitutional issue, that is, whether the Community Court was really interpreting Community Law or whether it usurped the power to interpret the Dutch Constitution. Indeed the Dutch Government argued that this was an internal matter and that the Community Court had no jurisdiction in matters involving Dutch customs duties. However the Community

---

[18] Case 26/62: *N.V. Algemene Transport- en Expeditie Onderneming Van Gend en Loos* v. *Nederlandse Administratie der Belastingen*, [1963] C.M.L.R. 105; 9 Rec. 1 at p. 5.

Court firmly asserted its jurisdiction and power to rule on the preliminary issue because, as it pointed out, art. 12 came for interpretation, not for application according to Dutch Law. In this delicate situation the Community Court refrained from pronouncing upon the conflict between Dutch and Community Law but declared that art. 12 was to prevail though the mode of its application was left to the Dutch court.

The Court, whilst giving a preliminary ruling, asserted that Community Law was addressed not only to the member states in the fashion of public international law but also to the citizens of the member states in the fashion of a federal law. It had a direct effect and, therefore, one should surmise, was capable of overriding inconsistent municipal law.

In consolidated cases[19] arising from similar circumstances the Community Court confirmed its previous ruling, referring incidentally to the precedent already established and reminding the national courts generally that they are not obliged to seek the Court's ruling if the matter has been previously disposed of.

In the Italian case *Flaminio Costa* v. *ENEL*[20] which can be regarded as the cornerstone of the doctrine of supremacy, the Community Court went much further. In this case an Italian Giudice Conciliatore (a magistrate of a small claims court) asked for a ruling whether or not the Italian law, which nationalised the electricity industry after the entry into force of the E.E.C. Treaty, was compatible with arts. 37, 53, 93 and 102 of the Treaty.[1] The Italian Government objected on the ground that the Italian court had to apply the Italian nationalisation decree. The Community Court, they contended, may interpret Community Law but has no power to pronounce upon the compatibility of municipal law with Community Law. In this way, arguing that the enforcement of Treaties is a matter for the national law and the national authorities but not for the Community Court, the Italian Government challenged the Community Court. The Court not only interpreted the relevant provisions of the Treaty for the benefit of the Italian court but also took the opportunity to lay down general principles which, in the opinion of the Court, were to govern the relations between Community Law and municipal law. The Court declared:

---

[19] Cases 28–30/62: *Da Costa en Schaake N.V., N.V. Schuitenvoerderij en Expeditie-Kantoor v/h Jacob Meijer, en Hoechst Holland N.V.* v. *Nederlande Administratie der Belastingen*, [1963] C.M.L.R. 224; 9 Rec. 59.

[20] Cases 6/64, [1964] C.M.L.R. 425; 10 Rec. 1141.

[1] These articles are concerned with monopolies, restrictions on the right of establishment, state aid to industry and distortion of conditions of free competition.

". . . . [The Treaty] . . . has created its own legal order . . . having real powers resulting from a limitation of competence or of transfer of powers from the States to the Community. . . . [It] would be impossible to assert any internal text whatsoever against the law created by the Treaty . . . without robbing it of its Community nature and without jeopardising the legal foundation of the Community itself. . ."

and further

". . . The incorporation into the legal order of each member state of the provisions of the Community Law and the letter and spirit of the Treaty in general, have as a corollary the impossibility for states to assert against the legal order accepted by them, on a reciprocal basis, a subsequent unilateral measure which could not be challenged by it. . ."

In *Walt Wilhelm* v. *Bundeskartellamt*[2] the Community Court further emphasised the supremacy of Community Law. The case arose from a conflict between the German cartel law and art. 87 (2) (*e*) of the E.E.C. Treaty. The Court held that:

"the E.E.C. Treaty instituted its own legal order, integrated into the legal systems of the member states and which has priority before their courts. It would be contrary to the nature of such a system to accept that the member states may take or maintain in force measures liable to compromise the useful effect of the Treaty. The imperative force of the Treaty and of the acts issued in implementation of it could not vary from state to state by the effect of internal acts without the functioning of the Community system being obstructed and the attainment of the aims of the Treaty being placed in peril . . ."

In the Second *Art Treasures* case[3] the argument that a tax on the export of art treasures could be repealed only by appropriate constitutional measures was held invalid by the Community Court in face of the conflicting provision of art. 16 of the E.E.C. Treaty which had direct effect. The Court observed that:

"The realisation of the objectives of the Community requires that the rules of Community Law . . . apply as of right at the same time and with identical effect on the whole territory of the Community without the member states being able to raise any obstacles.

---

[2] Case 14/68 [1969] C.M.L.R. 100, at p. 119; 15 Rec. 1, at p. 14.
[3] Case 48/71: *Re Export Tax on Art Treasures* (*No. 2*) *E.C. Commission* v. *Italy*, [1972] C.M.L.R. 699 at p. 708; 18 Rec. 529 at pp. 534, 535.

The member states' assignment of rights and powers to the Community in accordance with the provisions of the Treaty entails a definitive limitation of their sovereign rights against which no provisions of municipal law, whatever their nature, can be legally invoked."

As we began this review with a case in which the Community Court refrained from commenting upon the constitutional issues, we may as well conclude with a case in which the Court, no doubt emboldened by its previous decisions, did not hesitate to do so. In the *Internationale Handelsgesellschaft G.m.b.H.* v. *Einfuhr und Vorratstelle für Getreide und Futtermittel*[4] the issue before a German administrative court was whether an agricultural regulation did violate fundamental rights guaranteed by the Constitution. The regulation provided that the grant of export and import licences was conditional upon the payment of a deposit as a guarantee that the facility would be fully used. Failure to do so would result in the forfeiture of the deposit. When the notice of forfeiture was served upon the *Handelsgesellschaft* the company maintained that it was contrary to constitutionally guaranteed rights especially the right of economic liberty and the principle of proportionality (*Grundgesetz*, art. 2 (1) and 14). According to the latter no citizen should be called upon to make unjustified sacrifices which are out of proportion to the other citizens sacrifices for society. Since the validity of the Community regulation was attacked, the Court had to seek a preliminary ruling. The Community Court, in response, upheld the validity of the regulation and refused to accept the argument that the German Constitution should prevail. It concluded that since the validity of Community acts may be reviewed only in the light of Community Law the norms or principles of municipal law should be disregarded. The Court ruled that:

". . . no provisions of municipal law, of whatever nature they may be, may prevail over Community Law . . . lest it be deprived of its character as Community Law and its very legal foundation be endangered. The validity of a Community act or its application in a member state remains, therefore, unimpaired even if it is alleged that the basic rights . . . of the national constitution were violated . . ."

Encroaching upon rights which are said to be fundamental, the Community Court touched on a delicate issue which involves not only a conflict with municipal legal norms of the highest order but also the question of standards within the Community. Whilst in conflicts

---

[4] Case 11/70, [1972] C.M.L.R. 255.

Community Law must prevail, in the interests of a better Europe its standards must be raised and there is no reason why a particular member state should not act as a pacemaker in this respect.

It is clear that the principle of supremacy was deduced from the status of the Community, its purpose and function, as well as the relationship between the member states and the Community. The foundation treaty by its spirit rather than letter ordained a legal order which, though forming part of the municipal law of the member states, transcended the functions of states and curtailed their powers so much so that it would be inconsistent with their obligations to make unilateral measures incompatible with that order.

Considered from the point of view of sovereignty, the doctrine of supremacy is deduced from the pooling of sovereignty in the Community institutions resulting from a partial transfer of sovereign power: legislative, executive and judicial, of the member states. This must have been in the mind of the Community Court when it stated in *Flaminio Costa* v. *ENEL*[5] that "... the transfer by the states from their internal legal system to the Community legal order of rights and obligations to reflect those set forth in the Treaty, therefore, entails a definite elimination of their sovereign rights against which a subsequent unilateral act that would be incompatible with the Community act, cannot be asserted ..."

The logic of supremacy reflects the philosophy of art. 189, which underlines the need for a working system more or less uniform throughout the Community based on a division of functions or labours within the Community. It reflects the need for a federal structure.[6]

ENFORCEMENT OF COMMUNITY LAW AT NATIONAL LEVEL

The corollary to the incorporation of the Treaties and Community legislation into municipal law is the judicial notice of Community Law in the member states. Community Law, being part of the national legal structure, is applicable and enforceable by the municipal courts as the internal law of the states irrespective of its external origin. However, conflicts arise in practice and an analysis of the decisions of the municipal courts shows, at least during the first decade of the operation of the E.E.C. Treaty, a great deal of confusion and erratic jurisprudence. National judges and lawyers had to settle down to the

---

[5] Case 6/64, 15 July 1964; [1964] C.M.L.R. 425, at p. 456; 10 Rec. 1141.
[6] A federalist explanation of the doctrine of supremacy has been favoured on the Continent by several writers, notably Ipsen, H. P., "Rapport du droit des Communautés Européennes avec le droit national", *Le Droit et les Affaires*, (1964), No. 47.

novel experience and assimilate the challenge of Community Law. In this process, the doctrine of supremacy of Community Law elaborated by the Community Court and the lessons drawn from preliminary rulings under art. 177 had a steadying effect. The recognition by national courts of the direct effect of certain rules of Community Law and of its supremacy, is therefore, the most important factor in the process of enforcement of Community Law at the member state level.

We have already observed that, in some cases in which a preliminary ruling under art. 177 was requested, the national courts were involved in conflicts between Community Law and national law. Moreover, conflicts were often made more acute when the Constitution, the highest law of the land, was said to be infringed. The Community Court refrained from entering the lists, confined itself to interpretation of the relevant rule of Community Law, but, nevertheless, albeit indirectly, indicated that Community Law had to prevail, irrespective of whether the conflict was with the Constitution or the ordinary law of the land.

It seems, in the light of the experience of the founder members of the Community, that once the Treaties have been duly ratified and incorporated into their legal systems, allegations of unconstitutionality of these Treaties can hardly be made an issue of litigation. By the same token, the constitutionality of the Community legislation can *ex hypothesi* hardly be raised because, in order to be "unconstitutional", the Community acts would have to be inconsistent with Community Law and this is a matter for the Community Court. In theory, the Community Court could, by upholding the validity of Community legislation, contribute to a constitutional crisis in a member state, the outcome of which cannot be predicted. If the supremacy of Community Law and the authority of the Community Court were to prevail, the state concerned would have to put its own house in order; if, on the other hand, the authority of the Community Court were to be questioned, the matter would develop into a political crisis within the Community which could be solved only by political means. Putting these highly conjectural questions aside, it seems that more typical is the conflict between Community Law and the ordinary law of the member states. Indeed, as far as the United Kingdom is concerned, it is from this type of conflict that lessons can be learned simply because we do not have an hierarchy of legal norms as our Acts of Parliament have the same status whether they are concerned with the reform of the House of Lords or the reform of the law of illegitimacy.

Arising from Treaties the Community Law, notwithstanding its incorporation into the legal systems of the member states, presents certain problems of enforcement by municipal courts when in conflict with municipal law. According to the prevailing doctrine, international law takes priority over municipal law in the jurisprudence of the International Court of Justice[7] but there is no uniformity in state practice. Among the six, France, the Netherlands and Luxembourg admit supremacy of international law over municipal law, but Belgium, Germany and Italy treat the rules of international law on an equal footing with the rules of municipal law and so is the position in the new member states. However Community Law, though generated by Treaties, is not, strictly speaking *International Law* in the traditional sense of the term. Therefore the analogies with International Law which are occasionally raised are not particularly helpful. Being a *sui generis* system it has to be treated as such and its enforcement has to be seen in the light of the practice evolving in the member states. One starts with International Law as far as the Treaties are concerned but secondary Community Law raises specific Community problems.

France

In the light of art. 55 of the French Constitution of 1958, Parliament must refrain from passing legislation inconsistent with the international obligations of France since "a treaty duly ratified has, from the moment of its publication, an authority superior to that of statutes."[8] Should such a bill be presented to Parliament it could be declared unconstitutional by the *Conseil Constitutionnel* (art. 61).[9] The Judiciary and public authorities have to conform. As confirmed by the Conseil d'Etat in the *Kirkwood* case[10] an individual may contest the validity of administrative acts of the state on the ground that they violate international obligations. Case law,[11] even under the previous Constitution, conforms to the rule that international obligations have to be honoured by the courts, and judges, through the instrumentality of interpretation, endeavour to avoid conflicts on the assumption that Parliament did not intended to violate international law.

The existence of the Community Court with its inherent jurisdiction gave rise to the theory that since the Community Court solely administers Community Law, whilst the national courts administer both the municipal law and Community Law, the latter is called upon to

---

[7] *The Free Zones Case,* [1932] P.C.I.J. Rep Ser. A/B, No. 46; *The Wimbledon Case,* [1923] P.C.I.J. Rep. Ser. A. No. 1; *German Settlers Case,* [1923] P.C.I.J. Rep. Ser. B. No. 6.

[8] *Per* Commissaire du gouvernement Mme Questiaux in *Re Syndicat Général des Fabricants de Semoules, Conseil d'Etat,* [1970] C.M.L.R. 395; Daloz 285.

[9] E.g. *Re The Abortion Law* (1975), II. JCP 180 30 *(Conseil Constitutionnel).*

[10] Decided on 30 May 1952, quoted by Constantinidès-Mégret, *op. cit.,* at p. 85.

[11] Cited by Constantinidès-Mégret, *ibid.,* at p. 86.

resolve conflicts between the two systems without reference to the former.[12] In practice French courts have experienced some difficulty, probably because "traditionally French tribunals, at least in the past, regarded foreign legislation and pronouncements of foreign courts with some mistrust".[13] Consequently they were rather reluctant to administer Community Law. Thus in *Re Shell-Berre*[14] the *Conseil d'Etat*, applying the doctrine of *acte clair*, refused to refer to the Community Court the question whether a law of 1928 which enabled the government to exercise control over the import and distribution of oil was incompatible with arts. 3, 7, 30, 35, 37, 59, 62, 85, 92 and 96 of the E.E.C. Treaty. A similar attitude was shown by the first sub-section of the Conseil d'Etat in *Syndicat Général des Fabricants de Semoules*[15] which held that a French decree introducing an import levy on semolina inconsistent with Community regulations was to prevail. It could be said that the case was rather exceptional as it concerned imports from Algeria which, by virtue of French legislation, was to remain within the French customs frontiers but in fact the *Conseil d'Etat* preferred to apply French law to Community law. The breakthrough came in *Re Syndicat National du Commerce Extérieur*.[16] In that case a syndicate dealing in cereals requested the interpretation of the term "any holder" (E.E.C. regulation 1028/68) to be referred to the Community Court as it considered itself to be prejudiced by the narrow interpretation of this term by the ONIC (i.e. the National Cereals Board). The *Conseil* agreed that the Community Court gave a wide interpretation which, in turn, enabled the *Conseil* to annul the decision of the ONIC in this respect.

The Civil Courts appear to be more favourably disposed towards Community Law but they too had their difficulties. In the *Consten*[17] saga involving the validity of an exclusive distribution contract, the Paris Court of Appeal quashed the judgment of a Commercial Court (which effectively denied the application of E.E.C. regulation 17/1962 in this respect[18]) and stayed the action until the Commission had made

---

[12] See *Riff* v. *Soc. Grande Limonaderie Alsacienne*, decided by the Cour de Cassation (Chambre Criminelle), 19 February 1964, [1965] I Clunet 85-90; 2 C.M.L.Rev. 448-449; *Etat Français* v. *Nicolas and Société Brandt*, decided by the Cour d'Appel of Amiens, 9 May 1963; [1963] C.M.L.R. 239, at p. 245; [1964] Clunet 93; upheld on other grounds by the Cour de Cassation (Chambre Criminelle), 22 October 1964; [1965] Clunet 90; 2 C.M.L.Rev. 449.
[13] Simon, M. "Enforcement by French Courts of European Community Law" (1974) 90 L.Q.R., 467 at p. 471.
[14] [1964] C.M.L.R. 462, [1964] Clunet 794.
[15] [1970] C.M.L.R. 395, [1968] Dalloz 285; 6 C.M.L. Rev. 419.
[16] *Rev. Trim. de Droit Européen*, [1971] 503; [1971] Dalloz 576 and 645.
[17] Cases 56-58/64: *Consten and Grundig* v. *EC Commission*, [1966] C.M.L.R. 418, 12 Rec. 429.
[18] *Consten* v. *U.N.E.F.*, [1963] C.M.L.R. 176; [1963] Dalloz 189.

its decision in the matter. Two years later a Court of First Instance dealing with the same problem[19] noted the Commission decision in the previous case and stayed the action to await the outcome of the proceedings before the Community Court. From that time on the French Civil Courts became quite prepared to resort to the proceedings under art. 177, a notable early example being the *Ulm*[20] case. Thus, the Paris Court of Appeal, applying the judgment of the Community Court in the *Beguelin*, case,[1] held art. 85 and regulations 10/1965 and 67/1967 directly applicable in France with the effect that a contract between a French and a Dutch firm, granting the former exclusive distribution rights, was declared invalid. The decision was confirmed by the Cour de Cassation.[2]

The Criminal Chamber of the *Cour de Cassation* also made its contribution. In *Administration des Contributions Indirectes, etc.* v. *Ramel*[3] the Cour de Cassation dismissed an appeal against the acquittal of the respondent on the charge of offering for sale inferior wine imported from Italy. The wine was admitted to France under the E.E.C. regulations although its quality did not comply with French law. In the *Republic* v. *Von Saldern et al.*[4] the Cour de Cassation dismissed an appeal against conviction for breach of exchange control regulations involved in the import of chemicals from the U.S.A. The appeal was based on Community customs regulations concerning the valuation of imported goods which were issued after the alleged offence. Since these regulations were not retrospective the appeal had to fail and the question of conflict with national law did not arise. In the *Guerrini* case,[5] concerning a conviction for an offence under a 1939 law laying down standards for the marketing of eggs, the Court of Appeal at Aix disregarded the relevant E.E.C. regulations (122/67 and 1619/68) as it considered itself bound by the unrepealed statute. However the Cour de Cassation reversed that decision on the ground that the regulations had a direct effect repealing, as it were, the French legislation from the date on which the regulations came into force.

However, perhaps the most significant case is that of *Directeur Général des Douanes* v. *Société des Cafés Jacques Vabre et Société Weigel*

---

[19] *Consten* v. *Willy-Leissner*, Rev. Trim. de Droit Européen (1965), 487.

[20] Case 56/65, *Technique Minière* v. *Maschinenbau Ulm GmbH*, Court of Appeal, Paris, Rev. Trim. de Droit Européen [1965], 495; Community Court, [1966] C.M.L.R. 357; 12 Rec. 337.

[1] *Beguelin Import Co.* v. *S.A.G.L. Import-Export*, [1972] C.M.L.R. 81; 17 Rec. 949.

[2] *Soc. Stricker Boats Nederland* v. *Soc. Enterprises Garoche*, Commercial Chamber, [1974] C.M.L.R. 469.

[3] [1971] C.M.L.R. 315, [1971] Dalloz 211.

[4] (1971) 10 C.M.L. Rev. 223.

[5] *Guerrini Case*, 7 January 1972 (J.C.P., 1972, II), (1973) 10 C.M.L. Rev. 451.

et Cie.[6] The central point of that case was whether importers of instant coffee from Holland were legitimately charged with import duties which put them at a disadvantage as compared with French manufacturers of the product and thus suffered discrimination contrary to E.E.C. art. 95. The French customs authorities claimed that art. 265 of the *Code de Douanes*, being enacted after the French accession to the Community, had to be applied and that art. 55 of the Constitution notwithstanding, French courts had no jurisdiction in the matter of the constitutionality of the Code. In the Court of First Instance and the Paris Court of Appeal these arguments were rejected and finally the Cour de Cassation decided that the E.E.C. Treaty established a separate legal order which prevails in France even over subsequent legislation. The requirement of reciprocity under art. 55 of the Constitution has been satisfied in the Treaty of Rome. It held

> "... the treaty which by virtue of the above-mentioned article of the Constitution has an authority superior to that of statutes, established its own juridical order integrated with that of member states, and by virtue of this special character the juridical system which it has created is directly applicable to the nationals of these states and is binding on their courts; that therefore ... article 95 of the Treaty has to be applied ... to the exclusion of article 265 of the Customs Code, despite the fact that the latter is of a later date."

In the light of that judgment it can be stated with some confidence that the French judiciary has accepted the supremacy of Community Law.

The Netherlands

Since the amendment of the Netherlands Constitution in 1953 and 1956, there seems to be no doubt that, in principle, Community Law should be given precedence before Dutch law. We have already noted the *Van Gend en Loos Case*[7] which, prior to coming before the Community Court for preliminary ruling, unfolded as a case involving a conflict between the Constitution and Community Law. Similarly in *Bosch* v. *de Geus*[8] the argument that only rules of international law of a "universal application" take precedence over national law failed. These decisions had, undoubtedly, a profound effect upon the practice of Dutch courts.

---

[6] Court of Appeal, Paris, 7 July 1973, Dalloz (1974) 159, Cour de Cassation, [1975] 2, C.M.L.R. 336. Also see Simon, M. (1976), 92 L.Q.R. 85.
[7] Case 26/62, [1963] C.M.L.R. 105; 9 Rec. 1.
[8] Case 13/61, [1962] C.M.L.R. 1; 8 Rec. 89.

Of more recent cases *Centrafarm*[9] calls for special mention. In that case the *Hoge Raad*, applying the preliminary rulings of the Community Court, refused an injunction to a trade mark holder and a patentee which would restrain the marketing in Holland of thus protected pharmaceutical products originating from the United Kingdom. In *Officer Van Justitie* v. *Adriaan de Peijper, Managing Director of Centrafarm B.V.*, the *Kantongerecht*[10] at Rotterdam pronounced upon the freedom of movement and parallel imports of pharmaceutical products but left a question open as to whether certain rules of national law regarding the authentication and certification of such products, imposed by another member state, were contrary to the E.E.C. principles of the freedom of movement of goods.

Luxembourg

The Constitution of Luxembourg contains no provision regarding the relationship between international law and municipal law, but the judiciary, in the course of time, has evolved the principle of supremacy of international law.[11] In this process a judgment of the Conseil d'Etat of 1950 and a judgment of the Superior Court of 1954 have a special significance as they established the principle that a rule of international law will prevail over a rule of national law even if the latter is subsequent to the former.[12]

Belgium

The Belgian Constitution of 1831 has been revised, mainly to accommodate Belgian membership of the European Community. Since 1925 Belgian courts gave precedence over national law if inconsistent with a treaty.[13] This rule was broadened by the Cour de Cassation in 1964.[14] The court distinguished between treaties binding the state and treaties creating rights and obligations directly enforceable by individuals. Only the latter, by their very nature, can be in conflict with Belgian domestic law and if they are in conflict they must have precedence over municipal law. This ruling was complemented by a decision of the Conseil d'Etat made a month before the decision of the Cour de

---

[9] *Centrafarm BV and De Peijper* v. *Sterling Drug Inc, Case No.* 10. 712, [1976] C.M.L.R. 1.

[10] [1976] C.M.L.R. 19.

[11] Pescatore, P., "Prééminence des traités sur la loi interne selon la jurisprudence luxembourgeoise", *Journal des Tribunaux*, 1953, p. 445; see also Constantinidès-Mégret, *op. cit.*, p. 88, 89.

[12] Cases cited in *Les Novelles: Droit des Communautés Européennes* (1969), p. 67.

[13] *Ibid.*, p. 63.

[14] *Ibid.*, p. 63.

Cassation.[15] In a case brought against the Belgian Ministry of Agriculture, the Treaty of 1953 between Belgium and France concerning the protection of birds was construed as an obligation binding the state alone and having no direct effect upon the rights and obligations of citizens. It would appear, accordingly, that depending on their classification (i.e. whether binding the citizen or merely the state) some provisions of the E.E.C. Treaty are directly enforceable by Belgian courts, whereas others are not so enforceable. Following this philosophy the Tribunal de Commerce de Bruxelles considered art. 85 (1) of the E.E.C. Treaty directly applicable.[16] Being directly applicable, the Treaty may render void a contract valid when made.[17]

No doubt the process of accommodating Belgian traditions to the problem of Community Law enforcement was influenced by the two famous cases *Flaminio Costa* v. *ENEL* and *Van Gend en Loos* which made a considerable impact within the Community. Their influence can be seen in the decision of the Magistrates' Court of Antwerp[18] which, having lavishly cited authorities and juristic opinion, concluded that, should there be a conflict between the E.E.C. Treaty and subsequent Belgian legislation, the former would prevail.[19] The Belgian Government too agreed that the Treaty should be given precedence over any subsequent legislation inconsistent with the Treaty.[20]

In the field of social legislation the District Court of Tongeren has held that art. 12 of Community Regulation 3 prevailed over Belgian legislation on industrial accidents in accordance with the principle that *lex posterior derogat priori*.[1]

In the *Corveleyn*[2] case the Conseil d'Etat applied the Community directive 64/221 of 25 February 1964 in order to quash a deportation order. But the high water mark of the evolution towards the recognition of the supremacy of Community Law was reached in the decision of the Cour de Cassation in *Minister for Economic Affairs* v. *S.A. Fromagerie Franco-Suisse "Le Ski"*.[3] This case, concerning a claim for money

---

[15] *Ibid.*, p. 64.
[16] *Van Heuvermeiren* v. *Buitoni*, [1967] C.M.L.R. 241 at p. 245; (1966), 1 *Cahiers de Droit Européen* 317.
[17] *Ass. Gén. des Fabricants Belges de Ciment Portland Artificiel* v. *S.A. Carriére Dufour*, [1965] C.M.L.R. 193 at pp. 207–208.
[18] *Sociaal Fonds voor de Diamantourbeiders* v. *Chougol Diamond Co.*, [1968] C.M.L.R. 315 at pp. 320–323.
[19] The Community Court in another context (effects of the introduction of the common external tariff) involving the same parties, implied the same result; cases 2–3/69, [1969] C.M.L.R. 335 at pp. 349–353; 15 Rec. 211 at p. 223.
[20] *SPRL Corn and Food Trading Co.* v. *Etat Belge* (1968), *Cahiers de Droit Européen*, 550 at p. 554.
[1] *N.V. Essimex* v. *J. Jano* (1972), 11 C.M.L. Rev. 48.
[2] See p. 85 above.
[3] [1972] C.M.L.R. 330.

paid by mistake on the ground that, by reason of art. 12 of the E.E.C. Treaty, the duties in question did not apply to the products imported from member states of the Community, gave the Procureur Général Ganshof van der Meersch, an opportunity to discuss the nature of the self-executing provisions of the Treaty, the binding force of Community Law, sovereignty and the relationship between Community Law and the law of Belgium. In his erudite submissions, he reviewed a host of learned writings and 48 cases decided by the Community Court, the Belgian courts and the courts of Luxembourg and Germany.[4] Quoting *Van Gend en Loos* and *Flaminio Costa v. ENEL* he submitted that:

"... Community Law is integrated in the law of member states. From its very nature, it follows that a subsequent measure of state legislation cannot be set against it ... As Professor Pescatore has said: 'One is entitled to think that the fundamental argument is to be found in this last passage: the very existence of the Community is called in question if the Community legal system cannot be established with identical effects and with uniform effectiveness over the whole geographical area of the Community ...'[5]
... The primacy of the rules of Community law is doubly justified on legal grounds. First by their agreement on the transfer of their rights and obligations under the Treaty to the Community legal system, the states definitely limited their 'sovereign rights', or to put it more accurately, 'the exercise of their sovereign powers'. The Community system implies some surrender of sovereignty and Community Law is a specific law which gives effect to this surrender. The integration aim of the Treaties of Paris and of Rome is attained by handing over to the Community institutions powers having as their object and effect the determination of a corresponding limitation of the powers of member states ...
... Thus was created for these states a duty to abstain from action in the fields regulated by the Treaty and a duty to take all complementary steps needed to enforce Community legislation.
... Secondly, Community Law is a specific and autonomous law which is binding on the courts of the member states and makes it impossible to set against it any domestic law whatsoever. The very nature of the legal system instituted by the Treaties of Rome confers that primacy on its own foundation, independently of the constitutional provisions in states.[6] The specific character of Community Law stems from the objectives of the Treaty which are the establishment of a new legal system to which are subject not only

---

[4] See, in particular, *ibid.*, pp. 351–358.
[5] Pescatore, P., *Droit communautaire et droit national* (1969), p. 183, quoting from *Flaminio Costa v. ENEL*, [1964] C.M.L.R. 425, at pp. 455, 456.
[6] Quoting Tallon, D., *Le droit communautaire* (1966), 1 *Cahiers de Droit Européen* 571.

states, but also the nationals of those states. It also stems from the fact that the Treaty has set up institutions having their own powers and especially that of creating new sources of law. From their very structures, these institutions reflect the will of the authors of the Treaty to go beyond the state framework and to impose obligations directly on individual persons and to confer rights directly on them[7] . . . If the Community system is not recognised as superior, rules would not be the same within each member state, and the consequences would be that such a situation would necessarily give rise to forms of discrimination proscribed by the treaties, that obligations would not bear equally on everybody and that not everyone would derive equal benefit from the rights derived from the treaties . . ."

This long passage represents the quintessence of the Belgian and Community *doctrine* and reflects, it seems, the mood within the Community. The Court, on the other hand, in its terse judgment ruled:

". . . Even if assent to a treaty as required by art. 68 (2) of the Constitution, is given in the form of a statute, the legislative power, by giving this assent, is not carrying out a normative function. The conflict which exists between a legal norm established by an international treaty and a norm established by a subsequent statute, is not a conflict between two statutes.

The rule that a statute repeals a previous statute in so far as there is a conflict between the two, does not apply in the case of a conflict between a treaty and a statute.

In the event of a conflict between a norm of domestic law and a norm of international law which produces direct effects in the internal system, the rule established by the treaty shall prevail. The primacy of the treaty results from the very nature of international treaty law. This is *a fortiori* the case when a conflict exists, as in the present case, between a norm of internal law and a norm of Community Law.

The reason is that the treaties which have created Community Law have instituted a new legal system in whose favour the member states restricted the exercise of their sovereign powers in the areas determined by those treaties.

Article 12 of the Treaty . . . is immediately effective and confers on individual persons rights which national courts are bound to uphold.

It follows from all these considerations that it was the duty of the judge to set aside the application of provisions of domestic law that are contrary to this Treaty provision . . ."[8]

---

[7] Quoting his own writings, "Le droit communautaire et ses rapports avec les droits des États membres, in *Droit des Communautés européennes* (1969), Nos. 138–139.

[8] [1972] C.M.L.R. at pp. 372, 373.

Federal German Republic

Judging by the number of cases decided by various German courts and the Community Court, enforcement of Community Law in Germany gave rise to specific problems in the absence of an express provision in the Federal Constitution governing the relationship between international and municipal law. Rules had to be evolved by the courts assisted by learned writers and, in this process, decisions of the Community Court played a significant part. The starting point is the strong dualist tradition of which Triepel[9] was perhaps the most influential exponent. According to this doctrine a rule of international law becomes enforceable only if expressly incorporated into the municipal law. Having been so incorporated, it ranks in the hierarchy of legal norms among the ordinary rules of internal law (statutes) and is subject to the principle *lex posterior derogat priori*. However, in this context, Community Law was soon recognised as having a special status being a *sui generis* law though the courts have, for a while, followed an erratic course.

Learned writers, especially Ophüls,[10] Ipsen[11] and Wohlfart,[12] advocated a departure from the tradition arguing that Community Law ought to have precedence over national law. The courts, on the other hand, had to deduce the rule of supremacy from the provisions of the Federal Constitution which, by art. 24 (1), enables the Federal State to transfer sovereign powers to international institutions and, in art. 25, proclaims that the general rules of international law form an integral part of the federal law creating rights and obligations for the inhabitants of the federal territory. Ipsen[13] called art. 24 the *Integrationshebel* (lever of integration) and Vogel[14] argued that the legislature must contribute towards European integration. The judges must follow the legislature and give precedence to Community Law inconsistent with internal law.[15] The prevailing juristic opinion favoured supremacy of Com-

---

[9] Triepel, H., *Völkerrecht und Landesrecht* (1899); *Rec. de Cours de l'Académie de la Haye*, "Les rapports entre le droit interne et le droit international", 1923, Vol. 1, pp. 76 *et seq.*

[10] Ophüls, C. F., "Zwischen Völkerrecht und staatlichem Recht, Grundfragen des europäischen Rechts", *Juristen-Jahrbuch*, Vol. 4 (1963–64), pp. 137–162.

[11] Ipsen, H. P., "Rapport du droit des Communautés Européenes avec le droit national", *Le Droit et les Affaires*, 1964, No. 47.

[12] Wohlfart, E., "Europäisches Recht, Von der Befugnis der Organe der europäischen Wirtschaftsgemeinschaft zur Rechtsetzung", *Jahrbuch für Internazionales Recht*, Vol. 9, pp. 12–32.

[13] Ipsen, *op cit.*, p. 26.

[14] Vogel, K., *Die Verfassungsentscheidung des Grundgesetzes für eine internationale Zusammenarbeit* (1964), p. 46.

[15] Fuss, E. W., "Rechtsschutz gegen deutsche Hoheitsakte zur Ausführung der Europäischen Gemeinschaftsrechts", *Neue Juristische Wocheinschrift*, 1966, p. 1782.

munity Law but courts were faced with arguments that Community Law was "unconstitutional" in so far as it contravenes "fundamental rights". Under a written constitution which guarantees "fundamental rights" with little ingenuity any question can be raised to a constitutional issue.

The following are the landmarks on the road to the supremacy rule.

In *Re Tax on Malt Barley*[16] the Federal Constitutional Court (Bundesverfassungsgericht) clarified the position of the E.E.C. Treaty Ratification Law and the Community agricultural regulations whose constitutionality was doubted by the Finanzgericht of Rheinland-Pfalz. It held:[17]

". . . Section one of the E.E.C. Treaty Act is based upon the power contained in art. 24 (1) of the Constitution, and is within the limits imposed on the transfer of sovereign rights to international authorities by art. 79 (3) of the Constitution. A balanced system for the co-operation of the Community's Council, Commission and Parliament guarantees a control of power which is institutionally preserved as effective as the traditional separation of powers. It satisfies the most stringent demands of 'the rule of law' . . ."

Turning to the Regulation issued under the E.E.C. art. 189, the Court declared:

". . . Article 189 is of great importance in the framework of the whole Treaty. But it would be wrong to conclude from this that the whole Treaty would be purposeless if article 189 and the regulations passed thereunder were not immediately binding in the Federal Republic. In the Court's opinion, the nullity of one provision does not in principle entail the invalidity of the whole act or law. The whole law would only be void in such a case if on its true construction, the remaining provisions had no significance on their own or if the unconstitutional provisions are part of a self-contained set of regulations which would have no sense or efficacy if one of their constituent parts is taken away.
. . . These provisions apply to Treaty Law too. The effect of their application to section one of the E.E.C. Treaty Act is that, even if this provision were to be held unconstitutional in so far as it relates to article 189 of the Treaty, the E.E.C. Treaty Act would still not become totally invalid; the effectiveness of the remaining provisions in the German Federal Republic would not be disturbed . . ."

[16] III 77/63, [1964] C.M.L.R. 130.
[17] *Re Tax on Malt Barley*, 2 BvL 29/63, [1967] C.M.L.R. 302 at pp. 311, 316.

As a result, a substantial body of case law has confirmed the view that art. 189 and the Treaty are applicable in Germany.[18]

On the question of Community Law being inconsistent with previous German Law the Finanzgericht of Münster held . . .[19]

".... the organs of the Community were given powers of legislation in matters pertaining to the Community and that legislation is binding on the Member States. If those powers are to mean anything Community legislation must have the effect, within its sphere of competence, of amending or repealing, by implication, national legislation which is repugnant to it . . ."

The Courts went further because in a number of cases[20] they held that Community Law superseded subsequent German legislation.

On the specific question of direct application of the E.E.C. Treaty (art. 95) two cases should be specially noted. In the *Mölkerei* case[1] the Court held that the rate of compensatory tax imposed on an imported agricultural product from another state violated the non-discrimination principle. The Court arrived at this conclusion because ".... in so far as the court finds that there is a contravention of that rule of Community Law it must take account of the *precedence* of Community Law. That is the only way in which the immediate effectiveness accorded to art. 95 by the European Court[2] can be interpreted and a corresponding juridical protection be given to the individual subjects of the member states of the Community . . ." In *Re Imported Thai Sand Flower*[3] the Finanzericht of Bremen held that imported products had to be classified for the purpose of customs duties according to the E.E.C. Regulations governing the common organisation of the market for cereals rather than German rules. The Court ruled that ". . . to the extent that the member states have assigned legislative powers in levying tariff matters to the Community in order to ensure the proper operation of the common market for cereals, they no longer have the power to make legislative provisions in this field".

However, in a case[4] involving the validity of export deposits said to be in violation of the German Constitution, the Administrative

---

[18] See cases listed by Campbell, *op. cit.*, Vol. 1, 1.83 and Supplement No. 2, p. 15.

[19] In *Re Import of Pork*, IVc 20–21/63, [1966] C.M.L.R. 491 at pp. 498–499.

[20] See cases listed by Campbell, *op. cit.*, Vol. 1, 1.103, and Supplement No. 2, p. 16, Suppl. 1975, p. 43.

[1] *Mölkerei-Zentrale Westfalen/Lippe GmbH* v. *Hauptzollamt Paderborn*, VII 156/65, [1969] C.M.L.R. 300 at p. 312.

[2] In *Lütticke* v. *EEC Commission* (1966), 5 C.M.L.Rev. 368.

[3] May 1970 (1971), 10 C.M.L.Rev. 521 at p. 523.

[4] *Internationale Handelsgesellschaft mbH* v. *Einfuhr- und Vorratsstelle für Getreide und Futtermittel*, [1970] C.M.L.R. 294.

Court at Frankfurt am Main held that Community Law enjoyed only a limited superiority over national law.

The Court reviewed a substantial body of juristic opinion representing *inter alia* the view that Community Law can be scrutinised against the provisions of the Federal Constitution which the Federal legislature has no power to abrogate or restrict. The Court held that art. 12 (3) of Regulation 120/67 of the E.E.C. Council of 13 June 1967 and art. 9 of Regulation 473/67 of the E.E.C. Commission of 21 August 1967, which require export deposits, constituted an infringement of the Federal Constitution because they infringed the "freedom of development, economic freedom and the principle of proportionality" and were, therefore, unconstitutional. The Court considered that "these regulations are not German statutes but legal provisions of the European Economic Community which constitute neither public international law nor national law of the member states" and concluded that like statutes (Gesetze) operating in Germany they are subject to scrutiny against the fundamental principles of the Constitution. However it referred the matter for a preliminary ruling to the Community Court which rejected its arguments holding that:[5]

> ". . . . The validity of acts of the Community institutions may be assessed only by reference to Community Law since national legal provisions . . . cannot have priority over the law created by the Treaty . . . unless its character as Community Law is to be denied and the legal basis of the Community itself questioned. The validity of a Community act and its applicability to a member state cannot therefore be affected by the claim that fundamental rights . . . or the principles of its constitution have been infringed . . ."

The Administrative Court, not satisfied with the ruling, submitted the case to the Federal Constitutional Court[6] which considered that the contested ruling on deposits did not offend the fundamental rights guaranteed by the German Constitution but affirmed its determination to scrutinise the secondary Community Law in the light of the Grundgesetz. It also expressed the hope that complete integration of the Community and the development of a Community Parliament should bring about a Community Charter of Fundamental Rights. Until this has occurred conflicts between Community Law and German Fundamental Rights are not excluded and in such conflicts the German law may claim priority.[7]

---

[5] Wording taken from a Note to European Parliament, P.E. 37.907 (Directorate for Research and Documentation) p. 5. Also see [1972] C.M.L.R. 255.

[6] [1972] C.M.L.R. 177.

[7] Note to European Parliament, P.E. 37.907, p. 7. Also see [1974] 2 C.M.L.R. 540.

Italy

In Italy's practice, the dualist doctrine, represented by Judge Anzilotti[8] has left a deep imprint on the relationship between Community Law and Italian law. The dualist tradition coupled with a rigid Constitution put the Italian judge in a position which is more difficult than that of the judge in any other country of the E.E.C. The relevant provisions of the Constitution (arts. 10 and 11) state that the Italian legal order conforms to the generally recognised rules of international law and that Italy will agree, on equal terms with other states, to the limitation of sovereignty necessary to establish a lasting peace and justice among nations. This is hardly conducive to the courts being Community minded when confronted with the compelling challenge to obey the Constitution.

Italy's problem is well reflected in the *Flaminio Costa* v. *ENEL* case which, parallel to its career in the Community, had a full run at home. The Constitutional Court, as we have seen, was called upon to decide whether or not the decree nationalising the electricity industry and establishing a monopoly in the shape of the ENEL as well as certain provisions of the E.E.C. Treaty were contrary to the Constitution. According to the Constitution, the constitutional court has the power to review legislation and declare "illegitimate" Acts of Parliament and subordinate legislation which do not conform to the Constitution (art. 136 (1)). Community Law was brought into the contest as it was alleged that arts. 37 (2), 53, 93 (2) and 102 of the E.E.C. Treaty, which were relevant to this case, infringed art. 11 of the Constitution. In terms of the conflict of legislations, the nationalisation decree of 1962 was said to have repealed an earlier (Community) law.

The Court dealt with the problem in a classic dualist fashion: infringement of the Treaty would entail international responsibility of the State of Italy, but would not, necessarily affect the validity of the law enacted in contravention of the treaty. In this way, the Court, in accordance with the dualist doctrine, accorded to the Treaty no higher rank than that of the ordinary legislation. The problem was reduced to a conflict between two "internal" laws where the principle *lex posterior derogat priori* should apply. It appears that the position would have been different[9] if the Treaty had been promulgated as a *constitutional law* in accordance with art. 138 of the Constitution in which case the nationalisation decree would have to be tested in the

---

[8] Anzilotti, D., *Corso di Diritto Internazionale*, Vol. 1 (3rd Edn. 1928), pp. 51 *et seq.*

[9] Neri, S., "Le juge italien et le droit communautaire", *Le juge national et le droit communautaire* (1966), p. 81.

light of the Treaty. However, art. 11 of the Constitution enabled the State of Italy to surrender by treaty some of its sovereign powers to an international institution and this indeed occurred when the E.E.C. Treaty was ratified. The Court recognised this, but concluded that it did not have to discuss the nature of the E.E.C. or the consequences of the ratification of the Treaty, or, indeed, decide whether or not the decree infringed the Treaty.[10]

The decision of the Constitutional Court stimulated the jurists and the lively discussions which followed produced a trend in favour of the supremacy of Community Law when in conflict with Italian law. This has been deduced by Quadri[11] and others from art. 10 of the Constitution. They reasoned in their dualist fashion that, transformed into Italian law, a rule of international law is binding: *pacta recepta sunt servanda.*

The second support of the Italian doctrine of supremacy is derived from art. 11 of the Constitution. The most plausible is the argument of the former judge of the Community Court, Catalano[12] who sees two effects of art. 11: a permissive effect which enables the Italian State to delegate its sovereignty and a dispositive effect which limits the powers of the constitutional organs of the State. He argues further that, although the measure which in effect limits sovereignty may take the form of an ordinary law, it differs nevertheless from ordinary law because it has a constitutional effect. If, therefore, a treaty limits the legislative power of the Italian law-making bodies within certain areas, the legislature, acting within the scope of its authority, can no longer exercise its power in these areas.

In *Soc. Acciaierie San Michele* v. *High Authority*[13] the Constitutional Court recognised the "permissive" effect of art. 11. In this case the appellant, a steel company, contested the constitutionality of a fine imposed by the High Authority of the E.C.S.C. for failure to produce invoices relating to the consumption of electricity by the appellant. The Court, in dismissing the appeal, held: ". . . in recognising the Community order the state was endeavouring not so much to insert the same in its own system, but rather to make way within such system for the international co-operation which the state has as its aim . . . the organs of our internal jurisdiction are not qualified to criticise acts by organs of the E.C.S.C. because the latter are not subject to the sovereign power of the member states of the Community, and cannot be found

---

[10] 24 February–7 March 1964, *Foro Italiano* (1964), I, 465.
[11] Quadri, R., *Diritto Internazionale Pubblico* (1963), pp. 59 *et seq.*
[12] Catalano, N. "La position du droit communautaire dans le droit des Etats membres", *Droit communautaire et droit national* (Bruges 1965), pp. 61 *et seq.*
[13] Case 98/1965, [1967] C.M.L.R. 160; 4 C.M.L.Rev. 81; [1965] *I Foro Italiano* 569.

within the framework of any such state. Therefore, their acts can only
be subject to a legislative qualification on the part of individual member
states albeit within the limits where there may exist an obligation not to
refuse to acknowledge their effects . . ."

Recognising the "right of the individual to his jurisdictional protection" the Court acknowledged the power of the Community Court
to exercise its jurisdiction and of the Italian subject to plead Community Law where appropriate.

The principle of supremacy of Community Law was thus accepted,
but it fell to a body of jurists assembled in Rome in February 1966 to
affirm supremacy not only in respect of previous but also in respect of
subsequent Italian legislation. An important exception to the rule
lex posterior derogat priori was conceded in favour of Community Law.
But, at the same time, the jurists affirmed the power of the Italian
Judiciary, especially the Constitutional Court, to scrutinise Community
acts and determine whether or not they conform to the Italian Constitution.[14]

Developments in the post *San Michele* period testify to general
compliance with the principle. In *Salgoil SpA* v. *Ministry for Foreign
Trade*[15] the Rome Court of Appeal, following the ruling of the Community Court in the same case,[16] held that art. 31 of the E.E.C. Treaty
gave rise to individual rights which can be enforced by national courts,
though such rights have to be regarded as rights within the national
system of law. The Italian attitude is conveniently summarised in
Frontini v. *Ministero delle Finanze.*[17] On a reference from the *Tribunale*
of Turin the *Corte Costituzionale* confirmed the constitutionality of the
Italian E.E.C. Treaty Ratification Act and upheld the supremacy of
Community regulations. By the same token, the supremacy of the
E.E.C. Treaty itself was implicitly recognised. The *Corte Costituzionale*
made a significant reservation in connection with human rights. It
recognised that the European Court was the guarantor of the rights
and interests of individuals in fields of law concerned with economic
relations. But, if ever the legislative power of the E.E.C. were to be
used to violate the fundamental principles of the Italian Constitution
or the inalienable rights of man, then the *Corte Costituzionale* would
reserve the right to control the continuing compatibility of the E.E.C.
Treaty with such principles and rights.

---

[14] French text of the Jurists' Resolution, Neri, S., "Le droit communautaire
et l'ordre constitutionnel italien" (1966), *Cahiers de droit européen* 363 at
pp. 376, 377.

[15] [1970] C.M.L.R. 314 at pp. 335–336.

[16] Case 13/68, [1969] C.M.L.R. 181 at p. 196; 14 Rec. 661.

[17] [1974] 2 C.M.L.R. 372. Cf. the attitude of the German Constitutional
Court discussed above.

New Member States

The experience of the six original member states will, no doubt, influence the practice of the new members of the Community. We shall consider elsewhere[18] the attitude of the British courts to the challenge of Community Law. In Denmark in an action for infringement of a trade mark in which Community Law was introduced at a late stage, the court decided to hear the arguments and give judgment on the points of Danish Law first. Points of Community Law were deferred with the possibility of reference to the Community Court.[19]

We can say, in the light of this review of practice in the members of the Community, that Community Law is enforced as "Community Law", or the "internal law" and that, in the case of conflict with municipal law, whether previous or subsequent, the Community rule prevails. This situation has not come about without difficulty or heart-searching as the dualist tradition entrenched in the national systems of law had to succumb to the challenge of the Community. In this process, the Community Court acted as the pacemaker and, as we have noted, some of its decisions not only settled matters for the given member state, but also set a trend within the Community. The Community Court acted as an agent of cohesion and uniformity. However, without the stimulating contribution of jurists the message of Luxembourg would not have been as effective and successful as it was. Here the *doctrine* came into its own as an auxiliary source of law. Its power and authority on the Continent should not be underestimated.

---

[18] See Chapter 12, below.
[19] *E.M.I. Records, Ltd,* v. *CBS Grammofon A/S,* [1975] 1 C.M.L.R. 572.

CHAPTER TWELVE

Community Law in the United Kingdom[1]

RATIFICATION OF THE TREATIES

By the constitutional law of the United Kingdom treaty-making power is a prerogative power vested in the Sovereign and customarily exercised on her behalf either by her Ministers or by duly authorised plenipotentiaries. Ratification is the formal act whereby the Crown confirms and finally agrees to be bound by the terms of a Treaty. Under the terms of art. 2 of the Treaty of Accession the High Contracting Parties undertook to ratify the Treaty in accordance with their respective constitutional requirements and to deposit their instruments of ratification with the Italian Government by 31 December 1972 at the latest. In the event three of the four applicant states complied with that obligation and the Treaty entered into force on 1 January 1973.[2] By the act of ratification the United Kingdom acceded to the three European Communities. Article 2 of the Act annexed to the Treaty of Accession thus provides that "from the date of accession, the provisions of the original Treaties [as defined in art. 1] and the acts adopted by the institutions of the Communities shall be binding on the new Member States and shall apply in those States under the conditions laid down in those Treaties and in this Act".

In the United Kingdom, the Courts, and for that matter Parliament, have no role to play in the negotiation and ratification of treaties. In a case concerning a treaty of 1842 between the Crown and the Emperor of China Lord Coleridge C.J., stated that the Queen had "acted throughout the making of the treaty and in relation to each and every

---

[1] For a more detailed treatment of this topic, see Collins, L., *European Community Law in the United Kingdom* (1975).

[2] As a result of Norway's decision not to ratify, the Council used its authority under the Treaty of Accession, art. 2, para. 3 to make the necessary adjustments; see Adaptation Decision of 1 January 1973, O.J. L2, 1 January 1973.

of its stipulations in her sovereign character, and by her own inherent authority; and, as in making the treaty, so in performing the treaty, she is beyond the control of municipal law and her acts are not to be examined in her own Courts".[3] Thus when in 1971 a Mr. Blackburn applied for declarations to the effect that by signing the Treaty of Rome Her Majesty's Government would be irrevocably surrendering part of the sovereignty of the Queen in Parliament and by so doing would be acting contrary to law his statements of claim were struck out as disclosing no reasonable causes of action. The Court of Appeal unanimously upheld Eveleigh J.'s dismissal of the plaintiff's appeal against the Master's order. The court applied the dicta of Lord Coleridge, C.J. cited above. In the words of Lord Denning, M.R. "The treaty-making power of this country rests not in the courts, but in the Crown; that is, Her Majesty acting upon the advice of her Ministers. When her Ministers negotiate and sign a treaty, even a treaty of such paramount importance as this proposed one, they act on behalf of the country as a whole. They exercise the prerogative of the Crown. Their action in so doing cannot be challenged or questioned in these courts."[4]

INCORPORATION OF THE TREATIES INTO THE LAW OF THE UNITED KINGDOM

Although, at least since the time of Blackstone, the customary rules of international law have been regarded as part and parcel of the common law and directly enforceable by English judges, the United Kingdom adopts a distinctly dualist approach to treaties. A treaty to which the United Kingdom is a party is, as we have seen, the result of an exercise of the prerogative and as such is not self-executing in the sense that the provisions of such a treaty do not automatically have the force of law in the United Kingdom. The intervention of Parliament is necessary in order to enable the provisions of such a treaty to be enforced in British courts. The classic statement of this doctrine is contained in an Opinion of the Judicial Committee of the Privy Council in 1937:

> "It will be essential to keep in mind the distinction between (1) the formation, and (2) the performance, of the obligations constituted by a treaty, using that word as comprising any agreement between

---

[6] *Rustomjee* v. *R.* (1876), 2 Q.B.D. 69, at p. 74.
[4] *Blackburn* v. *Att.-Gen.*, [1971] 1 W.L.R. 1037, at p. 1040; Salmon and Stamp L.JJ. to the same effect at p. 1041.

two or more sovereign States. Within the British Empire there is a well-established rule that the making of a treaty is an executive act, while the performance of its obligations, if they entail alteration of the existing domestic law, requires legislative action. Unlike some other countries, the stipulations of a treaty duly ratified do not within the Empire, by virtue of the treaty alone, have the force of law. If the national executive, the government of the day, decide to incur the obligations of a treaty which involve alteration of law they have to run the risk of obtaining the assent of Parliament to the necessary statute or statutes. To make themselves as secure as possible they will often in such cases before final ratification seek to obtain from Parliament an expression of approval. But it has never been suggested, and it is not the law, that such an expression of approval operates as law, or that in law it precludes the assenting Parliament, or any subsequent Parliament, from refusing to give its sanction to any legislative proposals that may subsequently be brought before it. Parliament, no doubt . . . has a constitutional control over the executive: but it cannot be disputed that the creation of the obligations undertaken in treaties and the assent to their form and quality are the function of the executive alone. Once they are created, while they bind the State as against the other contracting parties, Parliament may refuse to perform them and so leave the State in default. In a unitary State whose Legislature possesses unlimited powers the problem is simple. Parliament will either fulfil or not treaty obligations imposed upon the State by its executive. The nature of the obligations does not affect the complete authority of the Legislature to make them law if it so chooses."[5]

This doctrine applies equally to the Community Treaties so that the mere accession of the United Kingdom to those Treaties did not give them the force of law within the United Kingdom. Legislation was necessary to achieve that result and in the absence of such legislation, as the Court of Appeal has pointed out, the Community Treaties would fall outside the cognisance of British Courts.[6] Thus one of the aims of the European Communities Act 1972 is to give the force of law to those provisions of the Treaties which are intended to take direct effect within the member states. Section 2 (1) of the Act provides that:

> "All such rights, powers, liabilities, obligations and restrictions from time to time created or arising by or under the Treaties, and all such remedies and procedures from time to time provided for

---

[5] *Att.-Gen. for Canada* v. *Att.-Gen. of Ontario*, [1937] A.C. 326, *per* Lord Atkin at pp. 347, 348. A similar statement was made in *Legal and Constitutional Implications of United Kingdom Membership of the European Communities*, 1967 (Cmnd. 3301), at para. 22.

[6] *McWhirter* v. *Att.-Gen.*, [1972] C.M.L.R. 882, *per* Lord Denning, MR. at p. 886 and Phillimore L.J. at p. 887.

by or under the Treaties, as in accordance with the Treaties are without further enactment to be given legal effect or used in the United Kingdom shall be recognised and available in law, and be enforced, allowed and followed accordingly; and the expression 'enforceable Community right' and similar expressions shall be read as referring to one to which this subsection applies."

Therefore, what the Act terms "enforceable Community rights" are to be given direct effect in the United Kingdom. This provision is strengthened by section 3 (2) which provides *inter alia* that United Kingdom courts shall take judicial notice of Community Treaties, which term is defined by section 1.

IMPLEMENTATION OF COMMUNITY SECONDARY LEGISLATION IN THE UNITED KINGDOM

It has already been pointed out in earlier chapters that Community secondary legislation falls into two categories: that which is and that which is not directly applicable in the member states. As far as the former is concerned, viz. decisions in the E.C.S.C. and regulations in the E.E.C. and Euratom, whilst within the Community legal system they will be binding on the United Kingdom as soon as they are made, they need statutory authority to give them the force of law within the United Kingdom, just as in the case of the provisions of the Treaties themselves. Section 2 (1) of the European Communities Act applies to them also and without further enactment they are to be given legal effect within our domestic legal systems. Thus the entire body of E.C.S.C. decisions and E.E.C. and Euratom regulations in force at the commencement of British membership automatically became part of the law of the United Kingdom on 1 January 1973. Similarly all such decisions and regulations made after the commencement of British membership will also automatically become part of the law of the United Kingdom as soon as they are made.

An important issue in connection with directly applicable Community secondary legislation made after British entry is the role of the United Kingdom Parliament. Whilst the actual making of such secondary legislation will be in the hands of the Council or Commission and outside the direct control of Parliament, in the absence of effective democratic control within the Communities themselves it is vital that Parliament should have an opportunity to consider such legislation. By the time, say, an E.E.C. regulation has been made it will be too late for comment for such a regulation will already be part of United Kingdom law. In order to enable Parliament to examine and comment upon proposed Community legislation and thus express views for the guidance of the British representatives on the Council of the Communities, each House has established a committee to scrutinise Community secondary legislation. Both Committees concern themselves with matters of principle and policy raised by the legislative proposals of the Communities and debates have been held on the Committees' Reports. Although some difficulties have been experienced, particularly in adjusting the process of scrutiny to the Communities' legislative timetable, the committees promise to develop into an effective piece of Parliamentary procedure.[7]

In the case of Community secondary legislation which is not directly applicable, such as E.C.S.C. recommendations and E.E.C. and Euratom directives, but leaves the choice of the means of their implementation to the individual member states,[8] there are two possible courses of action. Such Community legislation could be implemented in the United Kingdom either by statute or by subordinate legislation. Whilst the European Communities Act does not expressly rule out the use of statutes for such purposes its emphasis is on the use of delegated legislation. Thus section 2 (2) of the Act confers extensive authority upon Her Majesty in Council and upon Ministers and Government Departments to make subordinate legislation:

> "(*a*) for the purpose of implementing any Community obligation of the United Kingdom, or enabling any such obligation to be implemented, or of enabling any rights enjoyed or to be enjoyed by the United Kingdom under or by virtue of the Treaties to be exercised; or
> (*b*) for the purpose of dealing with matters arising out of or related to any such obligation or rights or the coming into force, or the operation from time to time, of subsection (1) above."[9]

The wide extent of these delegated law-making powers is confirmed by section 2 (4) which lays down that a provision made under subsection (2) includes "any such provision (of any such extent) as might be made by Act of Parliament". In other words the subordinate legislation made under section 2 (2) to implement Community obligations can be used to repeal or amend any past or future Act of Parliament the provisions of which are incompatible with Community Law.

---

[7] For a detailed account of the work of the Scrutiny Committees, see Bates, T.St.J.N., "The Scrutiny of European Secondary Legislation at Westminster," *European Law Review*, Vol. 1, No. 1, p. 195. Also see Niblock, M., *The E.E.C.: National Parliaments in Community Decision-Making* (1971).

[8] See Chapter 4 above.

[9] Subordinate legislation will also be needed in many cases to provide penalties for the breach of Community law; see Bridge, J. W., "The European Communities and the Criminal Law," *Criminal Law Review*, February 1976, p. 88.

But these powers of making subordinate legislation are not entirely without limitation and are subject to Schedule 2 to the Act. That Schedule provides that the powers conferred by section 2 (2) shall not include the power:

> "(a) to make any provision imposing or increasing taxation; or
>
> (b) to make any provision taking effect from a date earlier than that of the making of the instrument containing the provision; or
>
> (c) to confer any power to legislate by means of orders, rules, regulations or other subordinate instrument, other than rules of procedure for any court or tribunal; or
>
> (d) to create any new criminal offence punishable with imprisonment for more than two years or punishable on summary conviction with imprisonment for more than three months or with a fine of more than £400 (if not calculated on a daily basis) or with a fine of more than £5 a day."

These limitations are also given a measure of entrenchment since section 2 (4) states that they shall remain in force unless and until amended or repealed by a subsequent statute. As far as the form and procedure of such subordinate legislation is concerned Schedule 2 states that the power to make regulations shall be exercisable by statutory instrument and that wherever the power is exercised without a draft having been approved by resolution of each House of Parliament, then it shall be subject to annulment in pursuance of a resolution of either House.[10] This gives the Government a choice as to the procedure to be adopted and that choice will no doubt be exercised in the light of the subject matter of the legislation.[11]

Thus under the provisions of section 2 of the Act ample provision appears to have been made for the implementation of Community secondary legislation in the United Kingdom subject to the important constitutional safeguards in Schedule 2. Community Law is having an immediate and a continuing impact on the law of the United Kingdom and whilst that impact should not be underestimated it also should not be exaggerated. In the words of the White Paper reporting on the negotiations "the English and Scottish legal systems will remain intact. Certain provisions of the treaties and instruments made under them, concerned with economic, commercial and closely related matters,

---

[10] Statutory Instruments made to implement Community obligations are conveniently reproduced in the *Encyclopedia of European Community Law*, Vol. AI, Part A3.

[11] Sched. 2, para. 2.

will be included in our law. The common law will remain the basis of our legal system and our courts will continue to operate as they do at present. . . . All the essential features of our law will remain, including the safeguards for individual freedom such as trial by jury and *habeas corpus* and the principle that a man is innocent until proved guilty as well as the law of contract and tort (and its Scottish equivalent), the law of landlord and tenant, family law, nationality law[12] and land law".[13]

ENFORCEMENT THROUGH THE COMMUNITY COURT

The enforcement of Community Law through the agency of the European Court is achieved by direct and indirect means. The direct means takes the form of actions against member states who fail to fulfil their obligations under the Treaties.[14] By means of such actions the Court can directly influence the enforcement of Community Law in the national legal orders of the member states. Thus if the United Kingdom either legislated contrary to Community Law or failed to legislate as required by Community Law that would amount to a failure to fulfil Treaty obligations and the Commission would be able to bring proceedings against the United Kingdom in the European Court.[15] If judgment were given against the United Kingdom there would arise an obligation to take steps necessary to comply with the judgment.[16] Although no such actions have been brought against the United Kingdom to date they have been threatened on at least two occasions. In July 1973 the Commission complained that grants which Her Majesty's Government proposed to pay towards the building of oil-rigs were contrary to a Council Directive on aids to shipbuilding.[17] It was reported that the Commission had threatened to take the matter to the European Court if the grants were paid.[18] A satisfactory explanation must have been forthcoming because no action was in fact brought.[19] More recently similar action has been threatened against all three new member states for their failure to implement a Council Regulation which requires the installation of certain mechanical recording equip-

---

[12] But on the question of immigration, see Simmonds, K. R., "Immigration control and the free movement of labour: a problem of harmonisation" (1972), 21 I. & C.L.Q. 307.

[13] *The United Kingdom and the European Communities* (Cmnd. 4715), para. 31.

[14] See Chap. 9 above.

[15] E.g. under the terms of E.E.C. Treaty, art. 169.

[16] E.g. by virtue of E.E.C. Treaty, art. 171.

[17] Directive 72/273/E.E.C., O.J. Special Edn., 1972 (III), p. 749.

[18] See *The Times*, 19 July 1973.

[19] No mention is made of this affair in the Commission's *Third Report on Competition Policy* (1974), which covers the relevant period.

ment in road transport vehicles by 1 January 1976.[20] The matter is pending and it is not yet clear whether the Commission's threat to bring proceedings will be implemented.[1]

The European Court also influences the enforcement of Community Law indirectly by means of its competence to give preliminary rulings on points of Community Law at the request of national courts and tribunals. The provisions of the Treaties which give the right, and in some cases impose the duty, to request preliminary rulings became part of the laws of the United Kingdom by virtue of s. 2 (1) of the European Communities Act 1972 which specifically refers to "remedies and procedures" provided for, by or under the Treaties. This right/duty applies not only to the ordinary courts, from lay magistrates up to the House of Lords, but also to tribunals. Thus all courts and tribunals in the United Kingdom have been able to request preliminary rulings in appropriate cases since 1 January 1973 when the European Communities Act came into force. The unfamiliarity of such a procedure in the United Kingdom prompted the drawing up of special rules of procedure for some, but not all, courts. As far as the English courts are concerned[2] rules have been made for the High Court and Court of Appeal, Civil Division;[3] the Court of Appeal, Criminal Division;[4] the County Court;[5] and the Crown Court.[6] No changes have been made to the Judicial Standing Orders of the House of Lords and it is believed that when requesting preliminary rulings the House will make use of the procedure adopted by the Supreme Court.[7] The rules of magistrates' courts have not been changed, but the attention of magistrates' clerks has been drawn to the possibility of seeking a preliminary ruling by a Home Office Circular.[8] In connection with tribunals, consultation with the responsible government departments led to the conclusion

---

[20] Regulation (EEC) 1463/70, O.J. Special Edn., 1970 (II), p. 482 as applied by Act of Accession, art. 133, Annex VII, point III (4).

[1] See *The Times*, 20 January 1976.

[2] For Scottish Courts, see S.I. 1972 No. 1981, and S.I. 1973 Nos. 450 and 543. For Northern Irish Courts, see S.R. & O. 1972, Nos. 317, 354 and 380.

[3] Rules of the Supreme Court (Amendment No. 3) 1972 (S.I. 1972 No. 1898 (L.27)) which added Order 114 to the Rules of the Supreme Court.

[4] Criminal Appeal (References to the European Court) Rules 1972 (S.I. 1972 No. 1786 (L. 25)).

[5] The County Court (Amendment No. 2) Rules 1973 (S.I. 1973 No. 847 (L.13)).

[6] Crown Court (References to the European Court) Rules 1972 (S.I. 1972 No. 1787 (L.26)).

[7] This statement is based on information kindly supplied by the Judicial Office of the House of Lords.

[8] Circular No. 149/1973 (CS 18/1973), dated 4 September 1973.

that adequate procedural machinery exists to deal with references to the European Court.[9]

The Rules which have been made for English courts all follow a particular pattern. Orders referring questions to the European Court may be made before, or at any stage during, the trial or hearing of a cause or matter. Such Orders shall be made by the Court requesting the preliminary ruling and shall normally have the effect of staying proceedings pending the ruling. In all cases the transmission of an Order requesting a preliminary ruling to the Registrar of the European Court is undertaken by the Senior Master of the Supreme Court (Queen's Bench Division). Where such an Order is open to appeal the Senior Master must not forward it to the European Court until the time for appealing has expired, or, if an appeal is brought, until the appeal has been settled. It has been argued by some commentators that both the use of the Senior Master as an intermediary between United Kingdom courts and tribunals and the European Court, and making Orders requesting a preliminary ruling subject to appeal are incompatible with Community Law.[10] As far as the transmission of the request for a preliminary ruling is concerned it is the practice of continental courts to deal directly with the European Court, which does, for this purpose, form an integral part of the legal systems of the member states. On the question of a request for a preliminary ruling being subject to appeal it has already been pointed out that continental practice is not uniform[11] nor has the question been decided conclusively by the European Court.[12] The English rules on appeals may certainly be questioned to the extent that they have the effect of interposing an obstacle between the English courts and the European Court. The use of the Senior Master and the possibility of appeal may also cause unjustifiable delays in the reference procedure.[13]

It has already been pointed out that while courts and tribunals which are not of last instance have a discretion whether to seek a preliminary

---

[9] This statement is based on information kindly supplied by the Council on Tribunals and the Lord Chancellor's Office.

[10] See Jacobs, F.G. and Durand, A., *References to the European Court: Practice and Procedure* (1975) at pp. 164, 165, 171, 172 and Adv. Gen. Warner in case 166/73: *Rheinmühlen-Düsseldorf* v. *Einfuhr-und Vorretsstelle fur Getreide und Futtermittel*, [1974] E.C.R. 33 at p. 47. For a contrary opinion, see Collins, L., *European Community Law in the United Kingdom* (1975) at p. 76.

[11] See Chapter 10 above.

[12] See the case and literature cited in note 10 above.

[13] These factors may have contributed to the inordinate delay in transmitting to the European Court the request for a preliminary ruling in *Van Duyn* v. *Home Office*. The Order requesting a preliminary ruling was dated 1 March 1974 (see [1974] 1 W.L.R. at p. 1118) and it was lodged at the European Court on 13 June 1974 (see [1975] 1 C.M.L.R. at p. 14).

ruling, courts and tribunals of final instance are under an obligation to do so. Some doubts exist in the United Kingdom concerning which courts and tribunals are those "against whose decisions there is no judicial remedy under national law".[14] The position of the House of Lords is clear; subject to the relevant Treaty provisions it will be obliged to request preliminary rulings. But the position of the Court of Appeal is not so clear. The Court of Appeal may be a court of final instance in two situations. The Court of Appeal may be declared by statute to be the final court of appeal as in the case of bankruptcy proceedings initiated in a County Court.[15] If a question of the validity or interpretation of Community Law came before the Court of Appeal in such proceedings then it would clearly be obliged to seek a preliminary ruling from the Community Court. But rather more problematic may be the commoner situation in which despite the possibility of an appeal to the House of Lords the Court of Appeal may be, and indeed usually is, the final court of appeal. Since appeal to the House of Lords is only by leave that leave may either not be sought or may be sought and refused. In such situations it is suggested that the Court of Appeal should be obliged to seek a preliminary ruling in an appropriate case since, although it is not the supreme appellate court, there is no judicial remedy against its decisions in those situations. A similar problem arises in connection with tribunals. Is a tribunal from whose decision there is no appeal but which is open to review by *certiorari* obliged to seek a preliminary ruling? *Certiorari* is a form of judicial remedy under national law. But, it is a discretionary and highly technical remedy and in most cases the decision of such a tribunal would be final. It is therefore suggested that, as in the case of the Court of Appeal, such a tribunal should regard itself as under the obligation to request a preliminary ruling.[16] Thus in terms of the dispute in continental legal circles between the "concrete" and "abstract" theories of art. 177, para. 3 of the E.E.C. Treaty the "concrete" theory is thought to be preferable.[17]

---

[14] This expression replaces "from whose decisions there is no possibility of appeal under internal law" which was used in the earlier unofficial Foreign Office translation. The new translation certainly seems to be closer to the French "dont les décisions ne sont pas susceptibles d'un recours juridictionnel de droit interne".

[15] See Bankruptcy Act 1914, s. 108 (2) (*a*).

[16] Cf. Jacobs, F.G. and Durard, A., *op. cit* at pp. 162, 163. Also see Freeman, Elizabeth, "References to the Court of Justice under article 177" (1975), 28 *Current Legal Problems* 176 at pp. 184–186.

[17] See Donner, A. M., "Les rapports entre la compétence de la Cour de Justice des Communautés Européennes et les tribunaux internes", 115 *Recueil des Cours de la Haye* (1965), at pp. 42 *et seq.* Also see case 6/64: *Flaminio Costa v. ENEL*, [1964] E.C.R. 585 at p. 592.

The initial reaction of English courts and tribunals to this question has not, however, reflected this attitude. In the Court of Appeal no general view has yet emerged. In *Bulmer* v. *Bollinger* Lord Denning expressed the opinion that "short of the House of Lords no other English Court is bound to refer a question to the European Court at Luxembourg."[18] But in the same case Stamp and Stephenson L.JJ. refused to commit themselves on that point in the absence of further argument.[19] Lord Denning's opinion is echoed in a judgment of the National Insurance Commissioner. He held that since his decisions may be set aside by *certiorari*, he did not "constitute a tribunal against whose decision there is no judicial remedy under English law, even though an application for an order of *certiorari* cannot be made without the leave of the High Court."[20] The House of Lords appears to have recognised its obligation to refer issues concerning the applicability and interpretation of Community law to the European Court.[1]

THE QUESTION OF SUPREMACY[2]

It has been repeatedly laid down by the Community Court and is in general accepted by the original six member states that the Community Treaties have established a new and distinct system of law, the rules of which are inherently superior to the rules of the municipal laws of the member states. Thus from the commencement and for the duration of British membership the municipal law of the United Kingdom must yield in cases of conflict to the superior Community Law. To the generations of British lawyers schooled in the Diceyan orthodoxy such a prospect is no doubt unthinkable if not impossible; but nevertheless it is one of the obligations of membership. The implications were clearly summarised in the 1967 White Paper:

---

[18] [1974] Ch. 401 at p. 420.
[19] *Ibid.* at pp. 427, 430.
[20] *Re a Holiday in Italy* (Decision R(S) 4/74), [1975] 1 C.M.L.R. 184 at p. 188 One British commentator has referred to this as "a sensible approach": Collins, L., *op. cit.*, p. 105, n.3.
[1] See *Miliangos* v. *George Frank (Textiles), Ltd.*, [1975] 2 C.M.L.R. 585, *per* Lord Wilberforce at pp. 595, 596.
[2] The increasing volume of literature on this topic from the British standpoint includes the following: Martin, A., "The Accession of the United Kingdom to the European Communities: Jurisdictional Problems" (1968–69), 6 C.M.L. Rev. 7; Hunnings, N. M., "Constitutional Implications of joining the Common Market", *ibid.*, 50; de Smith, S. A., "The Constitution and the Common Market: a tentative appraisal" (1971), 34 M.L.R. 597; Wade, H. W. R., "Sovereignty and the European Communities" (1972), 88 L.Q.R. 1; Mitchell, J. D. B., *et al.*, "Constitutional aspects of the Treaty and Legislation relating to British membership" (1972), 9 C.M.L.Rev. 134; and Trinidade, F. A. "Parliamentary Sovereignty and the Primacy of European Community Law" (1972), 35 M.L.R. 375.

"The Community law having direct internal effect is designed to take precedence over the domestic law of the Member States. From this it follows that the legislation of the Parliament of the United Kingdom giving effect to that law would have to do so in such a way as to override existing national law so far as inconsistent with it. This result need not be left to implication, and it would be open to Parliament to enact from time to time any necessary consequential amendments or repeals. It would also follow that within the fields occupied by the Community law Parliament would have to refrain from passing fresh legislation inconsistent with that law as for the time being in force. This would not however involve any constitutional innovation. Many of our treaty obligations already impose such restraints—for example, the Charter of the United Nations, the European Convention on Human Rights and GATT."[3]

As far as the body of Community Law in force on the eve of British membership was concerned no difficulty was experienced. That law, as we have seen, was given legal force in the United Kingdom by section 2 (1) of the European Communities Act and will have precedence over prior British law by the simple operation of the rule *lex posterior derogat priori*.[4] Certain difficulties may arise, however, in avoiding and resolving conflicts between Community Law and statutes passed after the commencement of United Kingdom membership. The 1967 White Paper stated that Parliament will have to refrain from passing fresh legislation inconsistent with Community Law and remarked this was by no means an innovation because of existing restraints under other treaties. But the critical question is whether our doctrine of Parliamentary sovereignty means that such restraints must always be voluntarily imposed by Parliament or whether they can be compulsorily guaranteed.

The application of the orthodox doctrine of the absolute sovereignty of Parliament to statutes designed to implement treaty provisions into United Kingdom law has meant that such statutes have been regarded as in no way different from ordinary statutes and may be either expressly or impliedly amended or repealed by subsequent inconsistent statutes. It is true that there is a legal presumption that Parliament does not intend to derogate from international law, but such a presumption cannot prevail in the face of an expressly inconsistent subsequent enactment.[5] If this doctrine were to be applied to Community Law

---

[3] *Legal and Constitutional Implications of United Kingdom Membership of the European Communities* (Cmnd. 3301), para. 23.
[4] Certain express amendments are in fact made by Part II of the European Communities Act.
[5] See *Inland Revenue Commissioners* v. *Collco Dealings, Ltd.*, [1962] A.C. 1.

it would hardly satisfy the Communities since there would be no legal guarantee of Parliament's good behaviour.

There are a variety of possible solutions to this problem. Some are suggested in the writings of those contemporary constitutional lawyers who challenge the orthodoxy of Dicey and his followers. Professor Mitchell has argued that the Act of Union with Scotland 1707 is fundamental law which imposes legal restraints on the United Kingdom Parliament and just as a new legal order was established in 1707 so there is no reason why another new legal order in the context of the Communities should not be created in 1972.[6] Professor Heuston, whilst not denying that Parliament is sovereign in terms of the area of her power, maintains that limitations may be imposed on the manner and form by which that power is exercised.[7] Applied to the matter in hand that thesis would involve the imposition of procedural restrictions on Parliament's freedom to legislate inconsistently with Community Law which would not absolutely prevent such legislation but would make it more difficult. But not all of the possible solutions are of such a fundamental nature. It has been suggested that a formal clause be inserted in all statutes,[8] or that the enacting formula of all statutes should be amended,[9] to include a statement that the statute is to be construed as not conflicting with Community Law. Another commentator has drawn on the experience of the Canadian Bill of Rights and has suggested that a strongly worded presumption against anything other than an express derogation from Community Law should be written into the enabling act.[10] Yet others have suggested that reliance should be placed on the gradual emergence of a constitutional convention by which it would be recognised that Parliament could not legislate contrary to Community Law.[11]

In dealing with the problem of the supremacy of Community Law the European Communities Act adopts a subtle approach which does not incorporate any of the fundamentalist or procedural solutions described above nor is it content to rely on the uncertain emergence of conventional limitations. The Act avoids any outright statement of the supremacy of Community Law. It was probably thought that

---

[6] See Mitchell, J. D. B., *et al.*, *loc. cit.* in note 2, above, and Mitchell, J. D. B., *Constitutional Law* (2nd Edn.), Chap. 4. For an even more drastic solution, see Hood Phillips, O., *Reform of the Constitution* (1970), Chap. 7.

[7] See Heuston, R. F. V., *Essays in Constitutional Law* (2nd Edn.), Chap. 1.

[8] See Hunnings, N. M., *loc. cit.* in note 2, above.

[9] See Wade, H. W. R., *loc. cit.* in note 2, above.

[10] See de Smith, S. A., *loc. cit.* in note 2, above, and *R. v. Drybones* (1970), 9 D.L.R. (3d) 473.

[11] See Martin, A., *loc. cit.* in note 2, above, and cf. Lloyd, Lord, *The Idea of Law* (1966) at pp. 169, 170.

this was unnecessary in view of the practice of the original six member states. It would also be contrary to the main stream of British constitutional practice and it would in any event have been politically dangerous to have adopted such an approach. The supremacy of Community Law in the United Kingdom will be effectively guaranteed by the combined operation of provisions of sections 2 and 3 of the Act. As we have seen section 2 (1) gives present and future Community Law legal force in the United Kingdom and creates the concept of enforceable Community rights. Thus since the doctrine of the supremacy of Community Law is part of that law section 2 (1) makes that doctrine part of the law of the United Kingdom. The effectiveness of that doctrine is guaranteed by two further provisions. Firstly, section 2 (4) provides that, subject only to the limitations specified in Schedule 2, "any enactment passed or to be passed, other than one contained in this Part of this Act, shall be construed and have effect subject to the foregoing provisions of this section", in other words, subject to the rule of the supremacy of Community Law which is an enforceable Community right.[12] Secondly, section 3 (1) provides that:

> "For the purposes of all legal proceedings any question as to the meaning or effect of any of the Treaties, or as to the validity, meaning or effect of any Community instrument, shall be treated as a question of law (and, if not referred to the European Court, be for determination as such in accordance with the principles laid down by and any relevant decision of the European Court)."

Thus in all matters of Community Law the courts of the United Kingdom are to defer to the relevant decisions of the Community Court whether or not such matters have been actually referred to the Community Court. This is a very important factor since the doctrine of supremacy has been developed by the Community Court.

The European Communities Act does not therefore seek to guarantee the supremacy of Community Law by forbidding Parliament to enact conflicting legislation. Instead the guarantee is provided by denying effectiveness to such legislation within the legal systems of the United Kingdom to the extent that it conflicts with Community Law. Thus the ultimate sanction remains an extra-legal one. There is nothing to prevent a future Parliament from repealing the European Communities Act in its entirety. If it chose to do so it would indicate that the political will that the United Kingdom should remain a member of the Com-

---

[12] See the statement by the Lord Chancellor, Lord Hailsham, when introducing the Bill in the Lords, *Parliamentary Debates, House of Lords*, Vol. 333, No. 111, 25 July 1972, col. 1230.

munities was lacking and in the last analysis there is nothing which any mere rule of law can do in such a situation. In other words it must be assumed that as long as the United Kingdom is a member of the Communities she will honour the legal and constitutional obligations of membership. The legal guarantees of good faith contained in the Act are adequate, subject to the political will of the member states that the Community system shall succeed.

The question of supremacy has not yet received much attention from the judiciary. In the pre-accession case of *Blackburn* v. *Att. Gen.* Lord Denning observed "we have all been brought up to believe that, in legal theory, one Parliament cannot bind another and that no Act is irreversible. But legal theory does not always march alongside political reality."[13] After referring to the practical impossibility that Parliament would legislate contrary to the statutes emancipating the Dominions and Colonies he added, "Legal theory must give way to practical politics."[14] He then went on to say that if and when Parliament legislated contrary to Community Law "we will then say whether Parliament can lawfully do it or not."[15] Since the accession, the supremacy of Community Law has not yet been a real issue before United Kingdom courts and tribunals; but there is clearly an awareness of the implications of that doctrine. In *Esso Petroleum* v. *Kingswood Motors, Ltd.* Bridge J. observed that where Community Law" is in conflict with our domestic law the effect of the [European Communities] Act of 1972 is to require that the Community Law shall prevail."[16] Similarly in *Aero Zipp Fasteners* v. *Y.K.K. Fasteners*, Graham J. said that the European Communities Act 1972 "enacted that relevant Common Market law should be applied in this country and should, where there is a conflict, override English law."[17] More recently in *R.* v. *Secchi* a Metropolitan magistrate has remarked that the effect of making Community Law part of English law "is to make English law, both statute and common law, subject to Community Law, in those fields in which Community laws have been passed".[18] Whilst these statements are all *obiter dicta* which reveal very little of the grounds on which they were based, they may be taken as reflecting a trend in judicial thinking.

---

[13] [1971] 1 W.L.R. 1037 at p. 1040.
[14] *Ibid.*
[15] *Ibid.*
[16] [1974] 1 Q.B. 142 at p. 151.
[17] [1973] C.M.L.R. 819 at p. 820.
[18] [1975] 1 C.M.L.R. 383 at p. 386.

COMMUNITY LAW BEFORE UNITED KINGDOM COURTS
AND TRIBUNALS

Since the commencement of British membership the courts, tribunals and lawyers of the United Kingdom have been confronted with the "incoming tide" of Community Law.[19] They have been faced with the unprecedented challenge of participating in a novel and unique system of law based on unfamiliar continental legal principles. During the first three years of membership, points of Community Law, of varying degrees of significance, have arisen in sixteen reported British cases. Eleven have come before the English High Court[20] and one each before the Outer House of the Scottish Court of Session,[1] a County Court,[2] a Metropolitan magistrate,[3] a Value Added Tax Tribunal[4] and the National Insurance Commissioner.[5] The County Court case[6] and two of the High Court cases[7] went on to the Court of Appeal. Aspects of Community Law have also been considered *obiter* in a High Court case which ultimately came before the House of Lords.[8] In all of the reported cases, the points of Community Law have arisen out of the E.E.C. Treaty or regulations and directives made under it. Earlier in this chapter reference has been made to the light which these cases throw on the questions of the supremacy of Community Law and the identity of those courts and tribunals which are under the obligation to request preliminary rulings from the European Court. In addition

---

[19] Cf. Lord Denning in *H. P. Bulmer, Ltd.* v. *J. Bollinger S.A.*, [1974] Ch. 401 at p. 418.

[20] *Lerose, Ltd.* v. *Hawick Jersey International, Ltd.*, [1973] C.M.L.R. 83; *Esso Petroleum Co., Ltd.* v. *Kingswood Motors, Ltd.*, [1974] 1 Q.B. 142; [1973] 3 All E.R. 1057; *Minnesota Mining Co.* v. *Geerpres Europe, Ltd.*, [1973] C.M.L.R. 259; *Aero Zipp Fasteners, Ltd.* v. *Y.K.K. Fasteners, Ltd.*, [1973] C.M.L.R. 819; *Lowenbrau Munchen* v. *Grunhalle Lager International, Ltd.*, [1974] 1 C.M.L.R. 1; *Van Duyn* v. *Home Office*, [1974] 3 All E.R. 178; [1974] 1 W.L.R. 1107; *Application des Gaz S.A.* v. *Falks Veritas, Ltd.*, [1974] Ch. 381; [1974] 3 All E.R. 51, *H. P. Bulmer, Ltd.* v. *J. Bollinger S.A.*, [1974] Ch. 401; [1974] 2 All E.R. 1226; and [1975] 2 C.M.L.R. 479; *E.M.I. Records, Ltd.* v. *C.B.S. United Kingdom, Ltd.*, [1975] 1 C.M.L.R. 285; *Sirdar, Ltd.* v. *Les Fils de Louis Mulliez, Ltd.*, [1975] 1 C.M.L.R. 378; *Dymond* v. *G. B. Britton (Holdings), Ltd.*, [1976] C.M.L.R. 133.

[1] *Gibson* v. *Lord Advocate*, 1975 S.L.T. 134.

[2] *Schorsch Meier GmbH* v. *Hennin*, [1975] Q.B. 416; [1955] 1 All E.R. 152.

[3] *R.* v. *Secchi*, [1975] 1 C.M.L.R. 383.

[4] *Processed Vegetable Growers Association, Ltd.* v. *Customs and Excise Commissioners* , [1974] 1 C.M.L.R. 113.

[5] *Re a Holiday in Italy*, [1975] 1 C.M.L.R. 184.

[6] See note 2 above.

[7] *Application des Gaz S.A.* v. *Falks Veritas, Ltd.* and *H. P. Bulmer, Ltd.* v. *J. Bollinger S.A.*, see note 20 above.

[8] *Miliangos* v. *George Frank (Textiles), Ltd.*, [1975] Q.B. 487; [1975] 1 All E.R. 1076; [1975] 1 C.M.L.R. 121. Reversed, [1975] Q.B. at p. 493; [1975] 1 All E.R. at p. 1080; [1975] 1 C.L.M.R. 630, C.A.; affirmed, [1975] 3 All E.R. 801; [1975] 2 C.M.L.R. 585, H.L.

the cases reveal the nature and extent of judicial understanding and assimilation of Community Law in the United Kingdom at present.

The first and obvious question concerns the extent to which the rules of Community Law have become part of the corpus of law which the courts and tribunals of the United Kingdom themselves apply. There seems to be a general acceptance that Community Law can now form part of the law of the United Kingdom.[9] As far as the E.E.C. Treaty is concerned Vice-Chancellor Pennycuick in *Van Duyn* v. *Home Office* was clearly aware that some, but not all, provisions of that Treaty have direct legal effect in the laws of the member states.[10] But other members of the judiciary are not as well-informed and appear to be under the mistaken impression that every provision of the Treaty must now be given legal effect by United Kingdom courts and tribunals. Lord Denning is a proponent of that view.[11] His judgments contain such statements as "the Treaty is part of our law. It is equal in force to any statute. It must be applied by our courts"[12] and the Treaty of Rome "is by statute part of the law of England."[13] As might be expected, the views of such an influential judge are being adopted at humbler levels of the judiciary.[14] In the context of the secondary legislation of the Community there appears to be a general recognition that regulations are directly applicable in the United Kingdom. The circumstances in which an individual citizen may rely upon a provision of a regulation were clearly appreciated by Lord Keith in the Court of Session.[15] To the extent that this question has come before courts and tribunals in England there is a tendency to interpret direct applicability as always implying that every provision of every regulation is necessarily enforceable at the suit of individuals.[16] The case law also reveals a divergence of opinion on the legal effect of directives. The Master of the Rolls appears to regard them all as made up of rules of law to be

---

[9] E.g. *Lerose, Ltd.* v. *Hawick Jersey International, Ltd.*, [1973] C.M.L.R. 83, *per* Whitford, J. at p. 95; *Minnesota Mining Co.* v. *Geerpres Europe, Ltd.*, [1973] C.M.L.R. 259, *per* Graham, J. at pp. 264, 265; *Dymond v. G. B. Britton (Holdings), Ltd.*, [1976] 1 C.M.L.R. 133, *per* Oliver, J. at p. 135.

[10] [1974] 1 W.L.R. at p. 1116.

[11] Also see *Esso Petroleum Co., Ltd.* v. *Kingswood Motors, Ltd.*, [1974] 1 Q.B. 142, *per* Bridge, J. at p. 151.

[12] *Application des Gaz S.A.* v. *Falks Veritas, Ltd.*, [1974] Ch. at p. 393.

[13] *Schorsch Meier GmbH* v. *Hennin*, [1974] 3 W.L.R. 823 at p. 830. Also see *H. P. Bulmer, Ltd.* v. *J. Bollinger S.A.*, [1974] Ch. at pp. 418, 419.

[14] E.g. a Metropolitan magistrate in *R.* v. *Secchi*, [1975] 1 C.M.L.R. 383 at p. 386.

[15] *Gibson* v. *Lord Advocate*, [1975] S.L.T. 134 at p. 136.

[16] *Bulmer* v. *Bollinger, loc. cit.* in note 13 above; *Esso* v. *Kingswood Motors, loc. cit.* in note 11 above; *Re a Holiday in Italy*, [1975] 1 C.M.L.R. 184 at pp. 187, 188.

applied by national courts;[17] at the other extreme the Leeds VAT Tribunal appears to deny that a directive can have any legal effect in the United Kingdom until it has been implemented by legislation.[18] The true middle way between these extremes was adopted by Vice-Chancellor Pennycuick in *Van Duyn* v. *Home Office*;[19] he alone of the judges in the reported cases is aware of the case law of the European Court concerning the conditions subject to which provisions of a directive *per se* are enforceable by national courts. That case law was expounded and applied by the European Court in its preliminary ruling in that case.[20] It is to be hoped that the lesson of that ruling will be learnt in the United Kingdom and that it will help to correct incipient misunderstandings of the legal effect of Community Law in the member states before they become entrenched.

Another matter which emerges from the reported cases is the mode of interpretation of Community Law. The unfamiliarity of the style and format of the E.E.C. Treaty and Community secondary legislation have provoked judicial comment. The Treaty "lays down general principles. It expresses its aims and purposes. All in sentences of moderate length and commendable style. But it lacks precision. It uses words and phrases without defining what they mean. An English lawyer would look for an interpretation clause, but he would look in vain. There is none. All the way through the Treaty there are gaps and lacunae."[1] The ultimate authority of the European Court on the interpretation of Community Law has been acknowledged[2] as also has the necessity of uniform interpretation of that law in all the member states.[3] As aids to interpretation the case law of the European Court and of the national courts of the member states has been invoked and some use has been made of the texts of Community instruments other than those in English.[4] But the generality and apparent incompleteness of the texts of Community Law has led some English judges, notably the Master of the Rolls, to claim the right to play a creative role in interpreting Community Law so as to fill gaps in its formal

---

[17] *Bulmer* v. *Bollinger, loc. cit.* in note 13 above.
[18] *Processed Vegetable Growers Association, Ltd.* v. *Customs and Excise Commissioners*, [1974] 1 C.M.L.R. 113 at pp. 127, 128.
[19] [1974] 1 W.L.R. at pp. 1037, 1040.
[20] Case 41/74, [1974] E.C.R. 1337 at pp. 1348, 1349; also *per* Adv. Gen. Mayras at pp. 1335, 1356.
[1] *H. P. Bulmer, Ltd.* v. *J. Bollinger S.A.*, [1974] Ch. 401, *per* Lord Denning at p. 425. Also see *Application des Gaz S.A.* v. *Falks Veritas, Ltd.*, [1974] Ch. 381 at pp. 393, 394.
[2] *H. P. Bulmer, Ltd.* v. *J. Bollinger S.A.*, [1974] Ch. 401, *per* Lord Denning at p. 419.
[3] *Ibid.* at p. 425. Also see *E.M.I. Records* v. *C.B.S., Ltd.*, [1975] 1 C.M.L.R. 285, *per* Graham, J. at p. 297.
[4] *Re a Holiday in Italy*, [1974] 1 C.M.L.R. 184 at p. 190.

fabric. English courts have been exhorted to "divine the spirit of the Treaty and gain inspiration from it. If they find a gap, they must fill it as best they can. They must do what the framers of the instrument would have done if they had thought about it."[5] This is indeed what the European Court does and what national courts guided by the European Court may do. But if that approach is adopted by English courts and is coupled with a marked reluctance to seek preliminary rulings from the European Court (as will be noted shortly) then the integrity and uniformity of Community Law may be put at risk. This is particularly so in the case of a new member state whose legal traditions differ in many ways from the continental legal traditions upon which the Community legal order is founded.

The reality of this threat to the uniformity of Community Law is represented by an influential body of opinion amongst the English judiciary which broadly takes the following form. Difficulties over the interpretation of Community Law will not often arise; in the majority of cases lower courts and tribunals should have no difficulty in interpreting Community Law; courts and tribunals should not be too ready to request preliminary rulings from the European Court because of the burden that would place on the Court and because of the increased cost and delay for the litigants.[6] This attitude has resulted in English courts and tribunals adopting a generally restrictive approach to requests for preliminary rulings. The judgment of Lord Denning in *Bulmer* v. *Bollinger* represents the high-water mark of this approach.[7] Stress is placed on the complete discretion of all courts other than the House of Lords to decide when a preliminary ruling is necessary. Drawing largely upon the national case law of the six original member states, the Master of the Rolls purports to lay down "guidelines" to assist English courts in deciding whether a reference is necessary and in exercising their discretion. Quite apart from the fact that the practice of national courts on preliminary rulings is not necessarily an accurate representation of Community Law on preliminary rulings, a number of questionable recommendations are contained in the "guidelines", without qualification. These include recourse to the *acte clair* doctrine; that the facts of a case should always be decided before a decision is taken to request a preliminary ruling; that judges' discretion should be influenced by such factors as time, the burden on the European Court,

---

[5] *H. P. Bulmer, Ltd.* v. *J. Bollinger S.A.*, [1974] Ch. 401, *per* Lord Denning at p. 426.

[6] See Lord Diplock, "The Common Market and the Common Law" (1972), 6 J.A.L.T. 3 at pp. 13, 14; Lord Denning in *The Times, Forward into Europe*, Part 1, 2 January 1973 at p. 11; Lord Hailsham in an extract from a speech to magistrates appended to Home Office Circular No. 149/1973 (CS 18/1973).

[7] [1974] Ch. 401, particularly at pp. 420–425.

the nature and importance of the question in issue, expense and the wishes of the parties. All of these "guidelines" are subject to serious reservations.[8] Lord Denning's assumption that the importance of a question of Community Law is directly related to the position in the national judicial hierarchy of the court in which the question arises[9] is not borne out by the experience of the European Court. Questions of fundamental importance to Community Law and its development have not infrequently come before the European Court in the form of references from lowly national courts and tribunals.[10] Whenever there is a risk of divergent views on Community Law it is in everyone's interest, not least that of actual and potential litigants, to seek a ruling from the European Court at the earliest opportunity.[11] There are indications that these "guidelines" are influencing judicial attitudes: in *R. v. Secchi* a Metropolitan magistrate observed that the Master of the Rolls has supplied "the essential guidelines which English courts must follow."[12] Quite apart from the question whether the "guidelines" form part of the *ratio decidendi* in *Bulmer* v. *Bollinger*, it is plainly contrary to Community Law for national rules to impede the inherent right of courts and tribunals to request preliminary rulings.[13]

Some of the reported English cases do, however, reflect a more positive and constructive approach to requests for preliminary rulings. In *Lowenbrau* v. *Grunhalle Lager* Graham J. said that judges should request a preliminary ruling whenever they feel in need of guidance upon the interpretation of Community Law and such guidance is necessary for the decision.[14] That statement of general principle, unhampered by "guidelines", is broadly acceptable. It is not without significance that the application of that principle has resulted in the two requests for preliminary rulings which have so far been made by United Kingdom courts. In *Van Duyn* v. *Home Office* Vice-Chancellor Pennycuick expressly adopted Graham J.'s statement of principle and

---

[8] For critical comments, see Mitchell, J. B. D., "Sed Quis Custodiet Ipsos Custodes?", (1974) 11 C.M.L. Rev. 351; Jacobs, F. G., "When to Refer to the European Court", (1974) 90 L.Q.R. 486; Freeman, Elizabeth, "References to the Court of Justice under Article 177" (1975), 28 *Current Legal Problems* 176.

[9] [1974] Ch. at p. 421.

[10] E.G. Case 6/64: *Costa* v. *ENEL*, [1964] E.C.R. 585; Case 61/65: *Vaasen* v. *Beambtenfonds Mijnbedriff*, [1966] E.C.R. 261; Case 33/70: *SpA SACE* v. *Ministry for Finance of the Italian Republic*, [1970] E.C.R. 1213.

[11] Cf. Case 190/73: *Officier van Justitie* v. *J. W. J. van Haaster*, [1974] E.C.R. 1123, *per* Adv. Gen. Mayras at p. 1136.

[12] [1975] 1 C.M.L.R. 383 at p. 386.

[13] See Cases 146 and 166/73: *Rheinmühlen Düsseldorf* v. *Einfuhr-und Vorratestelle für Getreide und Futtermittel*, [1974] E.C.R. 33 and 139.

[14] [1974] 1 C.M.L.R. 1 at p. 9. He did not request a preliminary ruling because of the existence of clearly defined principles contained in the case law of the European Court; see *ibid.* at pp. 11, 12.

doubted whether such factors as the burden on the European Court could legitimately be taken into consideration in the exercise of the discretion to request a preliminary ruling.[15] The Vice-Chancellor was faced with a doubt concerning the legal effect in the member states of art. 48 of the E.E.C. Treaty and provisions of Directive 64/221/E.E.C., both concerned with free movement of persons. He sought a preliminary ruling because it would otherwise have been impossible for him to give judgment.[16] Mr. Justice Graham himself has since requested a preliminary ruling in *E.M.I. Records v. C.B.S.* In that case the judge commented on the uncertain state of the Community Law on industrial property and the necessity of obtaining clarification from the European Court so as to avoid conflicting decisions being reached by different national courts.[17]

The threat to the uniformity of Community Law posed by national courts and tribunals, when interpreting that law, going on voyages of discovery of their own without taking advantage of the navigational aids provided by the European Court is clearly demonstrated by two of the reported English cases. In *Schorsch Meier v. Hennin*[18] the defendant was indebted to the plaintiffs in a sum of German Marks. The debt was not paid and as a result of a fall in the value of sterling the plaintiffs brought an action in the County Court claiming payment in German Marks. The judge rejected the plaintiff's argument based on art. 106 of the E.E.C. Treaty on the ground that the article had no bearing on English law, and a request that the matter be referred to the European Court was refused. The plaintiffs appealed against both of those rulings. In connection with the first, on the assumption that the E.E.C. Treaty has the status of an Act of Parliament, the Court of Appeal unanimously held art. 106 to be a rule of law for English courts to apply. No consideration was given to the case law of the European Court concerning the direct legal effect of Treaty provisions. In the absence of any European or national case law on the direct legal effect of art. 106, no reference was made to scholarly commentaries on the subject.[19] When interpreting art. 106 the Court of Appeal took the lead of the Master of the Rolls who said "There is no need to refer the

---

[15] [1974] 1 W.L.R. 1107 at p. 1116.
[16] For the text of the preliminary ruling, see 41/74, [1974] E.C.R. 1337.
[17] [1975] 1 C.M.L.R. 285, at pp. 296, 297. Cf. the same judge's decision not to request a preliminary ruling in *Sirdar, Ltd.* v. *Les Fils de Louis Mulliez*, [1975] 1 C.M.L.R. 378 at p. 380.
[18] [1974] 3 W.L.R. 823.
[19] E.g. *Les Novelles : Droit des Communautés européennes*, chap. VI; Campbell, A., *Common Market Law*, Vol. 3, paras. 15.99 to 15.103; Kapteyn, P. J. G. and Verloren van Themaat, P., *Introduction to the Law of the European Communities* (1973) at p. 222.

interpretation to the court at Luxembourg. We can do it ourselves."[20] The Court of Appeal then attempted to divine the purpose and intent of the article. Since it is concerned, *inter alia*, with the obligation of member states to authorise payments connected with the movement of goods in the currency of the member state in which the creditor resides, the Court of Appeal held that the German plaintiffs were entitled to payment in German currency.[1] Beyond that no genuine attempt was made to interpret the article as a whole nor to place it properly in the context of the Treaty. The case raised entirely novel points of some importance and a preliminary ruling from the European Court was manifestly necessary. An equally novel point was raised in *Re a Holiday in Italy*.[2] Regulation (E.E.C.) 1408/71 provides that a worker who is entitled to welfare benefits in one member state and who is authorised to go to another member state to receive treatment which cannot be provided in his state of residence is entitled to continue to receive his benefit during the period of his absence. A British worker sustained a heart attack and was in receipt of sickness benefit. He had arranged a holiday in Italy and his doctor told him that such a holiday would be beneficial for his health. Before setting out on his holiday he consulted his local Health and Social Security Office and was assured that the benefit would be paid in respect of the period of his holiday. Upon his return he was told that payment would not be made. He appealed to the National Insurance Commissioner who, believing himself not to be under the obligation to request a preliminary ruling, proceeded to interpret the regulation himself. Despite the novelty of the question and the apparent lack of consideration of general principles of Community Law, the Commissioner held that a foreign holiday taken on medical advice did not amount to treatment which cannot be provided in the United Kingdom. The point is clearly arguable and a ruling should have been sought from the European Court.

While the United Kingdom cases reported to date reveal no reluctance to consider and apply Community Law, it is clear that some of the basic principles of that law have yet to be fully grasped. Judicial complacency has tended to be compounded with a misguided unwillingness to seek the assistance of the European Court. It would be quite unreasonable

---

[20] [1974] 3 W.L.R. at p. 830.

[1] Since art. 106 appears in the part of the Treaty concerned with economic policy and balance of payments it is probably of public law rather than private law significance, that is concerned with exchange control rather than the currency in which debts may be paid. The relevance of art. 106 to judgment debts has been questioned *obiter* in the House of Lords; *Miliangos* v. *George Frank (Textiles), Ltd.*, [1975] 2 C.M.L.R. 585, *per* Lord Wilberforce at p. 596.

[2] [1975] 1 C.M.L.R. 184.

to expect complete mastery of Community Law overnight. But if the law of the United Kingdom is to be enabled to make its own contribution to the development of Community Law the closest co-operation between United Kingdom courts and tribunals and the European Court must be fostered and actively maintained.[3]

---

[3] On the contribution of English and Scots law to Community Law to date, see Warner, J.-P., "Some aspects of the European Court of Justice" (1976), 14 J.S.P.T.L. (N.S.) 15.

PART IV

The Law of the Economy

(Droit de l'économie; Wirtschaftsrecht; diritto della economia)

CHAPTER 13

The Concept and Scope of the Law of the Economy

I. THEORETICAL CONSIDERATIONS

In *Nold* v. *High Authority*[1] Advocate-General Roemer described the E.C.S.C. Treaty as *öffentliches Wirtschaftsrecht* implying a branch of public law concerned with the economy of the Coal and Steel Community. This remark applies *a fortiori* to the E.E.C. Treaty which set up an economic regime alongside a political regime. The two are like two sides of a coin: the *political* institutional regime is to promote and carry into effect an *economic* regime—the Common Market—in accordance with the theory that economic integration will bring about a political integration of Europe. The task of correlating the political and the economic objectives has been entrusted to Community Law. However, to appreciate the role of Community Law in this field it is necessary to understand the concept of the law of the economy.

It is difficult to render into English the term used by Advocate-General Roemer because in the British system the boundary between public and private law has never been clear or considered important. Moreover, the law of the economy is an unfamiliar concept to British lawyers. Whilst the law of the economy is a novel concept to us, it is by no means novel on the Continent. Its origins go far beyond the antecedents of the European Community to the period between the two wars or even further[2].

If we consider that the law, apart from organising society, is concerned with the personal as well as the material (property) aspects of human activity, we shall have no difficulty in discerning in the latter

---

[1] Case 18/57; 5 Rec. 89, at pp. 119, 142.
[2] E.g. in the distant past a constitution of Emperor Zeno (483 A.D.) prohibiting monopolies in corn trade and handicrafts; Rinck, G., *Wirtschaftsrecht* (3rd Edn.) 1972, p. 321.

an area of activity which has economic connotations. On that factual plane, discussion seems almost superfluous. However, if we consider the impact of economics in the historical and social context of society, the discussion will take a philosophical turn and will pose the question of the law as the regulator of human behaviour in general and of economic forces in particular. In this sense the theory of Natural Law,[3] anxious to secure autonomy of the individual, postulated the inviolability of his rights to property. In a different, though little more definite sense, Proudhon[4] (1809–65) advocated an idea of an "economic law" or a "law of the economy". This law was, in his view, to resolve the contradictions of social life by means of a *conciliation universelle*. As such reconciliation would be impossible without the re-structuring of society, his *droit économique* was to be the organisational law of the new society. Considering that this process could not be accomplished within the compass of either public law or private law, Proudhon suggested a new branch of the law: *un droit économique, complément et corollaire du droit politique et du droit civil.* In his utopian way, Proudhon planned to use his "economic law" to carry out an equitable division of the land and property, to secure independence of the workers, separation of industries, to organise specialisation and promote individual and collective responsibility, to suppress idleness and relieve poverty. As we shall see later, the function of the "economic law" in the 20th century state and the E.E.C. is vastly different from that envisaged by Proudhon. Indeed, practically nothing has been left of his dreams except a notion of the law of the economy.

Whilst France gave rise to the idea of the law of the economy, it fell to the German jurists to elaborate the relationship between law and economy[5]. However, in spite (or perhaps because) of their enthusiasm, no unanimity ensued and so, even in theory, *Wirtschaftsrecht* failed to be recognised as an autonomous branch of the law, but is regarded as a branch of administrative law[6].

In spite of the fact that no uniform theory of the law of the economy emerged on the Continent, it is evident that a certain economic philosophy lies behind the Treaties founding the three European Communities. All three have this in common: supra-national institutions geared to a concept of a common economic purpose (Coal and Steel and Euratom being concerned with the basic industries and energy and

---

[3] Based on the "trilogy" of natural rights of life, liberty and property. Cf. Locke, J., *Of Civil Government* (1924), Bk. II, Ch. VII, sec. 87, Ch. IX, sec. 123.
[4] *De la capacité politique des classes ouvrières* (1865).
[5] Piepenbrock, R., *Der Gedanke eines Wirtschaftsrechts in der neuzeitlichen Literatur bis zum ersten Weltkrieg* (1964).
[6] Huber, H., *Wirtschaftsverwaltungsrecht* (1953); Rinck, *op. cit.*, p. 3.

the European Economic Community embracing virtually the whole spectrum of the economy of the member states), and a federal concept of inter-state co-operation. Since the emerging European Community is supposed to be the quintessence of the collective experience and common will of the member states, we shall consider the trends within the Community in order to appreciate the underlying economic philosophy of the E.E.C. and the role of the law in this field.

Economics and Law

If economics are concerned with the utilisation of resources, production and distribution of commodities and if the law consists of the rules of conduct enforceable by courts, there is a relationship between economics and law. In our system of the market economy an object has no economic value unless it represents enforceable rights. Indeed a concept of property (i.e. objects *in commercio* or services representing a money value) and a concept of ownership (i.e. rights in possession, use and abuse for oneself or to the exclusion of all others) form the basis of market exchange. Through the instrumentality of the law, things and services are controlled as they are put into circulation or retained, as they become subject of sale, barter, hire, use or whatever rights in respect of things and services are created by law or usage. From a legal point of view the "rights" in respect of things and services form the substance of human relations governed by the law. From an economic point of view, the subject matter of these "rights" represents a utility value to which the market attaches a price. The law favours the movement of goods and services and protects rights invested therein by means of civil and criminal sanctions.

The market economy is based on the freedom of contract. The law and the sentiment of this principle is well expressed in art. 1134 of the Code Napoléon, which attaches a force of law to *conventions légalement formulées*. In the English system of law, freedom of contract is subject only to restrictions recognised by the law: statute, morality and public policy.[7]

Modern society is often recognised by the movement from status to contract. Indeed, the contract, in its various forms and refinements, serves the market and activates its operations. The substance of the contract is the transfer of property or services, on the one hand, and of the definition of legally enforceable rights and obligations on the other. Corollary to the freedom of contract is the system of enforcement of obligations which enables the creditor to enforce his rights. Con-

---

[7] Cf. Parry, Sir David Hughes, *The Sanctity of Contracts in English Law* (1959).

sequently one's conduct in the economic sphere becomes a matter of concern to the legal system.

The capitalist system of private enterprise and initiative is not without restraints which appear necessary to preserve the freedom of contract and choice. The system rests upon competition. To ensure competition, abuse of the freedom of contract, which, if left to economic power alone, would lead to monopolies, has to be checked. At the other end of the scale, the law tends to protect the uninformed and even the gullible customer from becoming a prey to the freedom of contract and so insists upon the manufacturer and the seller providing information about the price, quantity and quality of the product offered for sale. Consumer protection involves civil and criminal sanctions. Furthermore, credit sales and hire-purchase agreements are subject to a certain control of the law, which again tends to restrict the freedom of contract and give protection to the purchaser. All in all the freedom and the restraint are part and parcel of the organisation and operation of the market in commodities which have an economic value.

Apart from controlling the operation of the market as between the seller and the purchaser, the state performs a very important function in defining economic policies, controlling manufacturing and commercial activities through the control of the inflow of currency, public spending, taxation, subsidies and social welfare. The state (government) operates through the instrumentality of the law and so, at least in the United Kingdom, the budget is, no doubt, the only piece of legislation which arouses almost universal interest every year.

It would be a crude oversimplification to speak of the economy in terms of supply and demand and of the law in terms of the rules of control and restraint without mentioning values and justice. Manufacturers often distort the interaction of supply and demand through publicity giving rise to an illusion of demand simply in order to sell and produce more. Thus sheer economic efficiency and rationalisation must, in the ultimate analysis, take into account the human factor and social justice. The same applies to the law. Here, the narrow "realist" concept of the law as a "normative system" is clearly insufficient, for the law, as a system of rules of conduct, implies a "system of values"[8] and "inner morality"[9]. Thus the law, apart from efficiency, is concerned with justice. The law is neither the master nor the servant

---

[8] See especially Radbruch, G., "Legal Philosophy", *The Legal Philosophies of Lask, Radbruch and Dabin*, transl. Wilk, K. (1950), pp. 90 *et seq.*

[9] Fuller, L., "Positivism and Fidelity to Law—a reply to Professor Hart", *Harvard Law Review* (1958), Vol. 71, pp. 630–672; *ibid.*, *The Morality of Law* (1964), p. 96.

of the economy, but through its potential as a regulatory force may promote a coherent system of social justice and prosperity. In this sense the law may operate against economic efficiency in order to achieve socially desirable objectives. For example, through a system of subsidies or taxes and advantages economically moribund enterprises enjoy a prolonged life; through the policy of full employment, inefficient enterprises continue to produce at an uneconomic cost. In certain situations the law is rendered impotent when confronted with organised labour or incompetent management who undermine economic efficiency and social justice. In an inverse situation economic efficiency may be impaired through the prohibition of monopolies and restrictive practices.

One of the results of the interaction of law and economics is the expectation that courts will not only administer law *qua* law but will also consider the economic and social consequences of their decisions. This is an unfamiliar strain which may be imposed upon the administration of justice in the economic sphere and the courts may well have to adapt themselves to this new role. This can be observed in some of the decisions of the European Community Court, of which the *Grundig-Consten* case[10] is a good example. In that case the Court had to consider the effect of a trading agreement upon the market, whilst in *Re Export Credits*[11] the Court had to decide whether a preferential rebate favouring exports constituted a state aid distorting competition. A great many cases under the Coal and Steel Treaty were concerned with scrap iron, whilst under the E.E.C. Treaty the Court has to apply itself to a wider range of the economic problems of society projected on a Community scale.

With the ever-increasing control of the economy by the state the courts are given a correspondingly wider function. However they are not expected to administer a system of palm-tree justice. They have to rely on the rule of law even where their decision implies a measure of discretion. It follows that the law comes to its own as a regulatory force though it has to emanate from economic policy. In this context, the role of the state becomes crucial. Historically economic policy has been left to the interplay of private forces, the state exercising a remote control as the *état-gendarme*. In the course of time, the state became more and more involved, leading to intervention and eventually becoming the *état-commerçant*.

The involvement of the state resulted in a certain confusion between

---

[10] Cases 56 and 58/64: *Consten S.A. and Grundig-Verkaufs-GmbH* v. *E.E.C. Commission*, [1966] C.M.L.R. 418; 12 Rec. 429, see p. 276.
[11] Case 6 and 11/69: *E.C. Commission* v. *France*, [1970] C.M.L.R. 43.

the traditional (at least on the Continent) division of the law into public and private. The state involvement took the form of either *dirigisme* or direct participation. In the *dirigist* system, economic planning has taken the place of the spontaneous interplay of economic forces. Economic planning implies the use of public powers at the disposal of the government for the definition of policies and their execution. It means, in effect, the use of the machinery of the law. Since parliamentary machinery is notorious for its slowness and cumbersome ritual, economic planning can hardly be entrusted to it; it has to be done by the executive, which leads to the development of executive legal measures.

In Western Europe, the exercise of public powers has to be supported by private means and private initiative. Perhaps the most important factor in the national economy is the participation of private capital in industrial investment, made possible through private savings. The state can encourage savings not only by propaganda, but mainly by tax incentives and such an arrangement of the economic structure of the country (including the legal structure of enterprise) as to reduce the risk involved in the investments and increase the return and the legal protection of the investor.

The *état commerçant* enters the economic stage as the manufacturer, the merchant, the purveyor of services and the moneylender. It acts through the nationalisation of (so far) "essential" industries; energy, transport, mechanical engineering (e.g. aviation) and, in some countries, insurance and banking. In a technical sense the state acts through public corporations which are, in essence, modelled upon private enterprise, but as the manager of the national economy, whether in the public or private sector, the state exercises influence through the commercial, industrial and fisal policy of the government. The theoretical as well as the practical question which arises in this connection, and remains yet to be answered, is whether all these activities can be controlled by administrative law or by a separate branch of the law: the law of the economy.

II. THE LAW OF THE ECONOMY IN THE MEMBER STATES

France

In France, the country where the modern idea of a law of the economy germinated more than a century ago, the notion of a positive law of the economy developed under the influence of German scholars.[12]

---

[12] Cf. Kiraly, de F., "Le droit économique, branche indépendente de la science juridique", *Recueil d'études sur les sources du droit, en honneur de F. Geny* (1935), Vol. 3, pp. 111 *et seq.*

Today there is no uniform concept[13] and views differ from a narrow one embracing the *"mesures autoritaires d'organisation économique"*[14] to a wide concept of a *"droit de la concentration ou de la collectivisation des biens de production et de l'organisation de léconomie par des pouvoirs privés ou publics."*[15] The former concept, in spite of its narrow scope, comprises all sorts of legal rules concerned with state interventions which affect the production and distribution of goods and services. In particular, writers enumerate in this context the nationalisation decrees, the law which governs public corporation, economic planning, finance, price control, company law and the law of restrictive practices, as well as the rules under which employees participate in the activities of the enterprise they serve. To this catalogue some writers[16] add the rules which govern the various sectors of the economy (e.g. steel and coal, agriculture, transport, insurance, banking, etc.), state monopolies, state aid to export, customs and excise and so on. The latter (wider) concept embraces virtually all aspects of economic life especially the production and circulation of goods.[17] Thus anything which has an economic purpose seems to fall under the rubric of the law of the economy, including the French idea of business law (*droit des affaires*) which comprises the law said to be relevant to businessmen.

The system depends on planning which applies practically to all aspects of the economy. In this process the National Economic Council, set up in 1925, plays a vital role, whilst the government legislates by decrees on the basis of enabling statutes passed from time to time by parliament.

Despite the Declaration of the Rights of Man and Citizen (1789) and the Preamble to the Constitution which guarantee rights in property, economic freedom is not rooted in the Constitution but in art. 544 of the Civil Code. The present Constitution (art. 34), on the other hand, permits restrictions on economic freedom in the national interest. Moreover the Social Security Law of 1968 provides that those who contribute to the social insurance fund must be secured the advantages of the economic growth of the country. France has a market economy system in which private enterprise and nationalised

---

[13] Svoboda, K., *La notion de droit économique. Etude sur les conceptions récentes du droit économique en France et dans les pays socialistes* (Centre Européen, Université de Nancy, 1966).

[14] Houin, R., "Le droit commercial et les décrets de 1953", *Droit social* (1954).

[15] Farjat, G., *Droit Economique* (1971), p. 14; see also Champaud, C., "Contribution à la définition du droit économique", *Dalloz* (1967), Chron, pp. 215 *et seq.*

[16] E.g. Jeannency, J.-M., and Perrot, M., *Textes de droit économique et social Francais* (1957).

[17] Hamel, J., and Lagarde, G., *Traité de droit commercial* (1954), Vol. 1, p. 14.

industries operate within five year plans and subject to government regulations which include, *inter alia*, price control. The accent is on the social aspect of the economy.

Germany

In Germany, the spiritual home of the law of the economy, there is, in spite of the abundant literature on the subject, no comprehensive legislation governing the national economy. *Wirtschaftsrecht* is taught at the universities as a legal discipline; institutes are busy with research and jurists continue to write. Although there is no unanimity among the writers on the precise meaning and scope of *Wirtschaftsrecht* there is a general understanding of the area with which it is concerned. This area comprises the rules which govern the state direction of the economy. More precisely this includes the powers of public authorities to intervene in the running of the economy, the organisation of certain sectors of the economy (e.g. transport and agriculture), the nationalisation of certain industries, foreign trade, subsidies, price control, monopolies and restrictive practices.

Most German writers seem to agree as far as the subdivision of the *Wirtschaftsrecht* into *Wirtschaftsverfassung* and *Wirtschaftsverwaltung* is concerned. The former (organisation of the economy) is concerned with the relationship between the state and private enterprise including private property, freedom of contract, freedom of industrial and commercial activity and the intervention of public powers. The latter (administration of the economy) is concerned with the procedures and machinery necessary for the implementation of public powers. In this way a division between substantive law and procedural administrative law relevant to the economy ensued. This, in turn, led certain writers[18] to a new division between a general law of the economy (*Allgemeines Wirtschaftsrecht*) and a particular law of the economy (*Besonderes Wirtschaftsrecht*). The former is concerned with juristic institutions basic to economic activities (i.e. the law of property, contract and competition), the latter with the various powers and measures used by public authorities as they interfere with the free running of the economy.

Over the years within the broad concept of the law of the economy the writers managed to construct a number of theories, each having a more or less plausible explanation but none commanding universal acceptance. It is clear, however, that in Germany the law of the economy crosses the traditional lines of division between public and private law

---

[18] E.g. Fikentscher, W., *Rechtsfragen der Planifikation* (1967), pp. 81 *et seq.*

and consists basically of the rules which enable the public authorities to intervene in what is considered to be the private preserve of commercial and economic activities.

At the government level administrative functions are apportioned between the *Länder* and the federal authorities with strong federal control. By the law of 1967 to promote stability and growth in the economy, a measure of planning has been introduced. Economic policies of the *Länder* are co-ordinated at the federal level with the object of securing economic growth and balanced regional development.

It is said that Germany has an "Economic Constitution" based on fundamental economic rights and a machinery for their protection. Indeed, as we have noted above,[19] the problem of fundamental rights in the Community has often been raised in Germany. Two further points should be noted as characteristic of the German law of the economy: the powerful position of the *Bundeskartellamt* which furthers healthy competition and the development of workers' participation in the management of enterprises. The latter, in particular, has influenced similar trends in the member states of the E.E.C.

The Netherlands

The closest notion to the law of the economy adopted in the Netherlands is the concept of a "social-economic law" (*sociaal-economisch recht*), which, according to Dutch jurists, is not imprecise. The term *sociaal*[20] serves to emphasise the social ramifications of the economy. Being linked to social welfare the Dutch law of the economy derives primarily from public powers and does not include what can be termed "business law" (*droit des affaires*). More precisely Dutch jurists include in their concept of the law of the economy legislation governing commercial competition, regulation of prices, sales, credits, insurance, transport of persons and goods, external trade and the organisation of commercial and industrial professions, but do not include company law. The list is by no means exhaustive or agreed by all and discussions on the precise meaning and scope of the *sociaal-economisch recht* continue.

Despite the individualistic traits of the Dutch system the government enjoys considerable statutory control of the economy. It is assisted by the Central Planning Office and a Socio-Economic Council consisting of independent experts and representatives of employers and employees. Planning is less prominent than in France whilst the

---

[19] See pp. 227, 228, 240, 241.
[20] Mulder, A., *De handhaving van de sociaal-economische Wetgeving*, quoted by Jacquemin, A., and Schrans, G., *Le droit économique* (1970), p. 68.

regulatory power of the government depends on parliamentary authorisation rather than executive decrees. The management of enterprises has recently moved closer to the German model of workers' participation.

Belgium

In Belgium, the law of the economy was said to consist of the "rules which limit the freedom of commerce and industry and of the autonomy of the will for the purpose of the promotion of an economic policy of the country."[1] Alongside this concept experts in Commercial Law developed another notion of the law of the economy being merely an extension of the traditional commercial law.[2] The theme was further elaborated recently[3] in an attempt to systematise the subject-matter. As a result the law of the economy is considered to consist of the traditional commercial law and the administrative rules which govern the running of the modern economy.

The Belgian system reflects very much that of France. It relies on five year plans and government regulations with a certain measure of decentralisation. Belgium has no Social and Economic Council but the government is assisted by a number of central advisory bodies including certain statutory councils representing employers and employees. The competition law is rather weak.

Italy

Although, since 1955, a special legal journal[4] has been established the Italian notion of the law of the economy has not crystallised to date. In a Report presented in 1966 at the Institute of Comparative Law in Paris[5] the Italian views are shown to reflect three not dissimilar streams. One of these suggests that the law of the economy comprises a number of institutions susceptible to change resulting from the interaction between public and private law. Another view envisages a "public" law of the economy consisting basically of the rules which govern the intervention of the public administration in the field of the economy. The third view postulates that the law of the economy cannot be defined

---

[1] Van Houtte, J., "Les repercussions de l'économie dirigée sur les institutions du droit privé", *Annales de droit commercial français, étranger et international* (1937), No. 4, quoted by Jacquemin and Schrans, *op. cit.*, p. 61.

[2] Jacquemin and Schrans, *ibid.*, p. 61.

[3] By Limpens, J., "Contribution à l'étude de la notion de droit économique", *Il Diritto dell'Economia* (1966), No. 6, quoted by Jacquemin and Schrans, *ibid.*, p. 61.

[4] *Il Diritto dell'Economia.*

[5] Published in *Il Diritto dell'Economia* (1966).

according to its purpose but constitutes a discipline which is both general and particular as it necessitates a study of all sorts of institutions. It means, in effect, integration of law and economics.

The above mentioned Report registers a certain reluctance of Italian jurists to give up the traditional concepts among which the distinction between public law and private law is regarded as fundamental. So far the marriage between law and economics, even on an academic level, has not been consumated.

The Italian Constitution, like the Federal German Constitution, contains a number of provisions relevant to the economy. It guarantees the freedom of private enterprise but also sanctions the nationalisation of industry and services according to a criterion of public interest. Multi-year economic planning is based on the Constitution but plans furthering economic and social objectives have to be voted by Parliament. The implementation of the plans is largely in the hands of regional authorities and decentralised specialist organisations.

Italy has an Economic and Social Council instituted by law which exercises an advisory function and participates in the legislative process. There is as yet no workers' participation in the management of enterprise or indeed a definite economic policy. Attempts to introduce competition law by statute have so far foundered.

United Kingdom

After this brief *tour d'horizon* of the law of the economy in the six members of the E.E.C. we must consider the position in the United Kingdom which is neither blessed nor burdened by any concept of the law of the economy. British lawyers are not normally schooled in the mystique of economics and the economists remain blissfully aloof from the law. The lawyer knows his commercial law which, as the Lex Mercatoria, was during the 18th century absorbed by Common Law. He is now made aware of the existence of business law by the pioneers of this new discipline.[6] However, our business law cannot be regarded as equivalent to the law of the economy considered in the preceding pages because it is concerned merely with the practice of commercial operations. Our business law, is, in a sense, a further extension or rather application of the traditional commercial law in our modern highly commercialised society.

---

[6] Schmitthoff, C. M., "The Concept of Economic Law in England", *Journal of Business Law* (1966), pp. 309 *et seq.*; Lord Wilberforce, "Law and Economics" *ibid.*, pp. 301 *et seq.*

The law of the economy, in the sense discussed above, was considered from a British point of view by Professor C. M. Schmitthoff[7] who thought that it would comprise the regulation of the intervention of the state in commerce, industry and finance. The idea is quite fresh in this country and requires some consideration. Our accession to the Community ought to stimulate interest and lead to a comprehensive review of the impact of the Treaty upon the laws which govern our economy. A lawyer, without knowledge or understanding of economics and sociology, is potentially a social menace.[8]

In the United Kingdom the economy is subject to extensive government control through Acts of Parliament and ministerial orders but, in view of the polarisation of the country caused by the two party system, there is no national economic policy. Depending on the colour of the government, economic policy oscillates between extensive controls and liberal tendencies. The budget is the principal instrument of the government policy.

There is no economic planning on the continental pattern but there is machinery for consultation and advice in the form of the National Economic Development Council, the Economic Planning Councils for each of the eight English regions, Scotland and Wales and Economic Development Committees for the major industries.

Nationalised industries and private enterprise play their part in the national economy, the Labour Party tending to extend the former, the Conservative Party striving to preserve the latter. The Confederation of British Industries speaks for the management, the Trade Unions for the workforce and there is as yet no acceptance of worker participation in the management of enterprises. There is price control but an incomes policy or rather wage restraint depends, at present, on the so-called "social contract" between the Labour Government and the Trades Union Movement rather than law.

Freedom of contract gives ample scope for the interplay of market forces but the relatively strict law against restrictive practices and legal protection of the consumer tend to moderate the system. Despite the tremendous potential for state intervention the British economy suffers from the lack of a national economic policy.

As we have observed, on the Continent the concept of the law of the economy has been under active consideration for quite a while but, in spite of a general understanding of its function, there is no unanimity,

---

[7] Schmitthoff, *op. cit.*, p. 315.
[8] "A lawyer who has not studied economics and sociology is very apt to become a public enemy", by Justice Brandeis, quoted by Goodhart, A.L., *Five Jewish Lawyers of the Common Law* (1949), p. 31.

even in one country, as to its precise meaning or position within the national system of law. The colourful, though imprecise, description by a Belgian jurist, C. del Marmol,[9] in his recipe for a law of the economy fits the picture. He wrote:

"Prenez un shaker. Mettez-y une mesure de droit commercial: colorez par des pigments de droit social; adjoutez une bonne dose de droit fiscal et de droit administratif; assaisonnez par une pincée de droit civil; saupoudrez abandamment de sociologie et d'économie politique; secouez à volonté et servez frais en baptisant ce breuvage juridique d'une appellation: droit économique."

However in spite of their divergencies there are certain common features which dominate the continental economic systems. All reveal the concept of a "directed economy" with the government at the helm. With one exception the original member states of the E.E.C. have an Economic and Social Council; all have advisory and consultative bodies. Economic planning is gaining ground and so does the idea of worker participation in management. Each national system represents a more or less cohesive unit in which the mechanism of direction and control brings law and economics together.

The economic design of the European Community has, no doubt, been inspired by the national systems but since integration is the ultimate object of the Community it is to be expected that in the course of time a certain measure of precision and uniformity will be achieved within the Community. When the E.E.C. Treaty has been fully implemented and the concept of the Common Market developed it will become clear that the law of the European Community can be conveniently divided into two branches: the Law of the Institutions and the Law of the Economy of the Communities.

---

[9] Quoted by Jacquemin and Schrans, *op. cit.*, p. 61.

CHAPTER 14

The Law of the Economy under the E.E.C. Treaty

The three Communities, in their specific ways, advance the idea of an organised economy, so much so that it can be said that each Treaty reflects a political as well as an economic regime. Article 2 (2) of the E.C.S.C. Treaty provides that the Community ought to bring about progressively the conditions necessary for the most rational distribution of the production of coal and steel and art. 5 complements this by saying that the Community ought to carry out its objectives with limited intervention. This implies that the Community ought not to exercise any direct influence upon the production and distribution of coal and steel unless it is necessary in the interest of the Community. The other two treaties have no equivalent provisions, but the E.E.C. Treaty contains the blueprint for a system of economy which, when fully implemented, will make significant changes in the economy of each member state. Since the policies enshrined in the Treaty are enforceable through the instrumentality of the law, the Treaty aims to establish a European Law of the Economy which, according to a learned writer[1] consists of the "rules designed to bring about an economic integration of the Six".

I GENERAL PRINCIPLES

(A) FORMULATION OF THE POLICIES OF THE E.E.C.

According to art. 2 of the E.E.C. Treaty:

"The Community shall have as its task, by establishing a common market and progressively approximating the economic policies of Member States, to promote throughout the Community a

---

[1] Cartou, L., *Introduction à l'étude du droit des Communautés Européennes*, p. 15.

harmonious development of economic activities, a continuous and balanced expansion, an increase in stability, an accelerated raising of the standard of living and closer relations between the States belonging to it."

In greater detail, art. 3 enumerates the activities of the Community which, when carried out according to a set time-table (art. 8), will bring about not only a considerable uniformity of the economic systems of the member states, but will also project the Community as a unit on the world market. These activities include:

(a) the elimination, as between member states, of custom duties and of quantitative restrictions on the import and export of goods, and of all other measures having equivalent effect;

(b) the establishment of a common tariff and of a common commercial policy towards third countries;

(c) the abolition, as between member states, of obstacles to freedom of movement of persons, services and capital;

(d) the adoption of a common policy in the sphere of agriculture;

(e) the adoption of a common policy in the sphere of transport;

(f) the institution of a system ensuring that competition in the common market is not distorted;

(g) the application of procedures by which the economic policies of member states can be coordinated and disequilibria in their balance of payments remedied;

(h) the approximation of the laws of member states to the extent required for the proper functioning of the common market;

(i) the creation of a European Social Fund in order to improve employment opportunities for workers and to contribute to the raising of their standard of living;

(j) the establishment of a European Investment Bank to facilitate the economic expansion of the Community by opening up fresh resources;

(k) the association of the overseas countries and territories in order to increase trade and to promote jointly economic and social development.

Part Two of the Treaty lays down the foundations of the economic community. These include:

(1) free movement of goods which, in effect, transforms the Community into a Customs Union to be achieved through the elimination of customs duties between the member states, the setting up of a common external customs tariff and the elimination of quantitative restrictions between the member states;

(2) common agricultural policy;

(3) free movement of persons, services and capital based on the right of establishment and non-discrimination; and

(4) common transport policy.

Part Three of the Treaty contains certain common rules affecting the economy of the member states. These rules are designed to promote a climate of sound competition between the manufacturers and distributors, do away with the dumping practices and restrict state subsidies likely to distort the conditions under which undertakings compete with each other within the Community. They also include tax provisions and a general pattern of the approximation of laws relevant to the establishment and functioning of the common market. The common rules affect the short-term economic policies of the member states, their balance of payments and their commercial policy. Coupled with the economic and commercial policies are the social provisions of the Treaty aiming generally at an improvement in the standard of living and the working conditions within the Community. The financial implications of all these policies are reflected in the provisions for the establishment of the European Social Fund and the European Investment Bank.

Part Four of the Treaty sets the stage for an association with the Community of the overseas countries and territories having special relations with the member states; Part Five sets up the institutions of the Community and Part Six lays down the general and final provisions of the Treaty.

Parts Two and Three of the Treaty are really pivotal to the law of the economy of the Community and the law of the member states. In these Parts, in accordance with the legislative techniques of codified systems of law, the policies and the methods of their implementation have been laid down in general and, where necessary, in detailed provisions. As parts of a self-executing treaty, these provisions rank as the law of the member states and are according to their nature and purpose, directly or indirectly enforceable by these states and by the Community Institutions.

In the light of Community legislation and the ever-growing number of decisions of the Community Court, the Law of the Economy outlined in the Treaty has expanded considerably. However, in view of the limited objectives of this book, we shall restrict discussion to the rudimentary aspects of the Community Law of the Economy.

(B) ECONOMIC FREEDOMS AS THE BASIS OF THE COMMON MARKET

The Common Market was not established by the Treaty, but by the Economic Community set up by the Treaty (art. 2). The Treaty (art. 8) provided for a transitional period of twelve years during which, by stages, the various policies were to be implemented. The first stage began on 1 January 1958, the pace was accelerated in 1960, and the third and last stage ended on 1 July 1968. A similar time-table in respect of the new members will operate under the Brussels Treaty of Accession. The transitional period is to run from 1 April 1973 to 1 July 1977.[2]

The idea of a common market is not entirely new, for it was, for example, the underlying philosophy of the American Constitution of 1787. It implies a geographical area in which, unhampered by restrictions, the market forces of supply and demand are brought face to face. This means, in practical terms the elimination of the economic frontiers between the member states of the Community and the creation of a customs union where, protected by a common external tariff, the market operates on the basis of a free movement of goods, persons, services and capital. The essence of the Common Market, which has the character of an "internal market" of the Community was described in 1962 by the Fiscal and Financial Committee[3] in the terms of:

> "a free movement of persons, free movement of goods and capital, one monetary system, relatively uniform transport, uniform economic and social policy, *grosso modo* uniform laws and a high supply of commodities".

The economic freedom which the Common Market implies means in the first place the removal of customs barriers between the member states, next the removal of other obstacles to the freedom of movement such as discrimination against foreign goods or persons and the removal of monopolies and restrictive practices. However, mere removal of customs barriers and obstacles to the interplay of supply and demand would be insufficient to promote a homogeneous economic area. To achieve this objective within the Community, the Treaty provides for the approximation of economic (arts. 103–109) and commercial (arts. 110–116) policies and the approximation of laws (arts. 100–102). Moreover, the Treaty, not content with the setting up of the Community, endowed it with appropriate institutions for the implementation, enforcement and policing of the design. In this setting the

---

[2] Act of Accession, art. 32.
[3] *Rapport Neumark*, 7–8 July 1962, p. 12.

correlation of law and economics makes sense. Therefore, when we speak of the law of the economy within the Community, we have in mind the rules which define the economic freedoms (or areas of activity) and provide the machinery for their enforcement.

II FOUNDATIONS OF THE COMMON MARKET

(A) FREE MOVEMENT OF GOODS (ARTICLES 9–37)

1. *Elimination of Customs Duties between Member States*

To ensure a free flow of goods, the Treaty contains quite a detailed scheme for the purpose of dismantling the economic barriers between the member states. Following the principle of art. 3 (*a*),[4] art. 9 states that the Community shall be based upon a customs union covering all trade in goods and comprising both the prohibition, as between member states, of customs duties on imports and exports and of all charges which are equivalent to customs tariffs. The provision is quite comprehensive since it applies to *all goods* which have an economic value (German: *Waren*, French: *marchandises* and *produits*), irrespective of whether they originate from the member states or third countries if, with regard to the latter, the import formalities have been complied with and any customs duties or equivalent taxes have been levied in the importing member state (art. 10 (1)). By art. 10 (2) the Commission has been empowered to lay down the methods of administrative co-operation to be adopted by the member states and, by art. 11, the member states have undertaken to carry out all the appropriate measures necessary to establish the customs union within the Community. In these articles, we have an example of a Treaty obligation imposed upon the member states and a Community Law pursuant to the execution of this obligation.

In subsequent articles, the Treaty lays down further specific measures to execute and speed up this operation. Absolutely crucial in this context is the prohibition of increases in the existing customs duties and the imposition of new customs duties on imports and exports (art. 12). This prohibition extends to all measures which may have the same effect as customs duties, that is leading to discrimination against foreign goods and protection of home produce.[5] Applying this

---

[4] "The elimination, as between member states, of customs duties and of quantitative restrictions in regard to the import and export of goods, as well as of all other measures having equivalent effect."
[5] Cases 2–3/62: see *Re Import Duties on Gingerbread,* [1963] C.M.L.R. 199; 8 Rec. 813.

principle, a German Court held[6] that when goods of German origin are re-imported into Germany for repair, the E.E.C. tariff ought to be applied. A French Court decided[7] that goods imported from a non-member state which are exempt from customs duties because they are to be trans-shipped to another member state are not free of duties or quantitative restrictions. Following this decision, the Cour de Cassation held[8] that, where goods imported into the Community were to be processed within the Community, a national court was competent to determine the country of origin of such processed goods and upheld a conviction for a false declaration of origin. As for the "tax having equivalent effect", this has been defined by the Community Court[9] as a duty whatever its description or technique, imposed unilaterally, applying specifically to a product imported by a member state but not to a similar national product and by altering its price having the same effect upon the free movement of goods as a customs duty.[10] However, of the many cases decided by the national courts and the Community Court in this field perhaps the *Van Gend en Loos* case[11] is the most important since it dealt with the question of "taxes having equivalent effect" but, above all, held that art. 12 of the Treaty is self-executing and has a direct and immediate effect in the territory of the member states.

The principles mentioned above apply to the new members of the Community who, like the founder members, have to adjust their customs laws within the transition period. In the light of this obligation a new Customs Law, implementing the Community legislation, will emerge in the United Kingdom.[12]

2. *Setting up of the Common Customs Tariff (Articles 18–29)*

A corollary to the elimination of customs duties as between the member states is the establishment of a common customs tariff applicable to the outside world. The Common Customs Tariff was gradually introduced during the period of transition and the official scheme was adopted on 28 June 1968 by Council Regulation 950/68.[13] By the

---

[6] In *The French Iron Castings*, [1966] C.M.L.R. 332.
[7] In *The Republic* v. *Cornet*, [1965] C.M.L.R. 105.
[8] In *Lapeyre* v. *Administration des Douanes*, [1967] C.M.L.R. 362.
[9] In Cases 2–3/62: *E.E.C. Commission* v. *Luxembourg and Belgium, Re Import Duties on Gingerbread*, [1963] C.M.L.R. 199; 8 Rec. 813.
[10] See Campbell, *op. cit.*, Vol. 2, pp. 9–12.
[11] Case 26/62: *Van Gend en Loos* v. *Nederlandse Administratie der Balastingen*, [1963] C.M.L.R. 105, 9 Rec. 1 at p. 5.
[12] The European Communities Act 1972, s. 5 and Scheds. 3 and 4.
[13] [1968] J.O. L172; for full details see the Customs Tariff of the European Communities published by the Commission; up-dated version: Regulation 1/74 of 1 January 1974 (O.J.L. 1.1974).

abolition of customs duties between member states and the establishment of the common external customs tariff, the Community has reached the stage of a customs union. The effect for the member states is that they can impose upon goods coming from third states only such duties as are agreed by the Community. Moreover, they cannot act unilaterally for any independent alteration or suspension of duties in the common customs tariff must be decided by the Council unanimously (art. 28).

However the Tariff Union is only a stage on the road to a real Customs Union. The latter requires a "uniform interpretation of the common customs tariff, its continuing administration and Community legislation to replace national legislation in this field.[14] This, to a large extent, has already been done. Uniformity is vital not only in the interest of the Common Market but also in view of the fact that as from 1 January 1975 all revenues of the Common Customs Tariff were to accrue to the Community Budget as "Community own resources" (E.E.C. Art. 201).

The Community Court too made a significant contribution to the interpretation of the customs classification and the clarification of the Customs Law. In the *Deutsche Bakels* case[15] it held that the explanatory notes and tariff notices should be regarded as authoritative sources of information relevant to the interpretation of the tariff headings and confirmed that, subject to Community Law, the member states may make regulations to clarify the obscurities of the Common Customs Tariff. In other cases the Court explained the meaning of certain tariff headings in relation to specific products, e.g. manioc flour,[16] farmyard poultry,[17] chocolate,[18] mayonnaise,[19] sugar content,[20] hominy chop,[1] edible turkey offal,[2] sausage,[3] etc. thus lending its authority to a uniform Customs Law.

---

[14] Second General Report, 1968 para. 1.
[15] Case 14/70: *Deutsche Bakels GmbH* v. *Oberfinanzdirektion München*, [1971] C.M.L.R. 188, 16 Rec. 1001.
[16] Case 74/69: *Hauptzollamt Bremen-Freihafen* v. *Waren-Import Gesellschaft Krohn & Co.*, [1970] E.C.R. 51; [1970] C.M.L.R. 466; 16 Rec. 451.
[17] *Deutsche Bakels*[3] *op. cit.*
[18] Case 51/70: *Firma Alfons Lütticke* v. *Hauptzollamt Passau*, [1971] C.M.L.R. 752, 17 Rec. 121.
[19] Case 30/71: *Firma Kurt Siemers & Co.* v. *Hauptzollamt Bad Reichenhall*, [1972] C.M.L.R. 121; 17 Rec. 919; Case 77/71: *Firma Gervais-Danone A.G.* v. *Hauptzollamt München*, [1973] C.M.L.R. 415; 17 Rec. 1127.
[20] Case 92/21: *Interfood GmbH* v. *Hauptzollamt Hamburg-Ericus*, [1973] C.M.L.R. 562, 18 Rec. 231.
[1] Case 18/72: *N.V. Granaria Graaninkoopmaatschappij* v. *Produktschap Voor Veevoeder*, [1973] C.M.L.R. 596; 18 Rec. 1163.
[2] Case 40/69: *Hauptzollamt Hamburg-Oberelbe* v. *Firma Paul G. Bollmann*, [1970] E.C.R. 69; [1970] C.M.L.R. 141; 16 Rec. 69.
[3] Case 12/73: *Muras* v. *Hauptzollamt Hamburg-Jonas*, [1973] E.C.R. 963.

For the new members, the common customs tariff will be introduced gradually in four stages starting a year after accession (Act of Accession, art. 39). The new tariff will be fully enforced as from the date on which the internal tariffs should disappear, i.e. on 1 July 1977.

3. *Elimination of Quantitative Restrictions* (*Articles 30–37*)

Finally, to achieve a complete liberalisation of trade, the member states must refrain from introducing quantitative restrictions on imports as well as exports or any measures having equivalent effect. This provision, like the fundamental provisions of arts. 2 and 3 of the Treaty, has a direct effect. Thus, it was held by the Community Court[4] that the Italian Government committed a breach of art. 31 (1) of the Treaty by suspending the import of pork products. An attempt to justify the action of the Italian Government by reference to art. 36[5] failed.

The regulation of imports by quotas is a straightforward proposition but indirect regulation by financial means is a little more subtle. In the second *Marimex*[6] case the Community Court considered *inter alia* the effect of charges for sanitary inspection of live cattle and frozen meat imported into Italy as it was alleged that such charges had an equivalent effect to customs duties and, consequently constituted an import restriction. The Italian government contended that under art. 36 the inspection was permitted and the charges were thus justified. The Court held that whilst sanitary controls were justified the extra charge was not and may well result in an additional obstacle for internal Community trade. A similar conclusion was reached in respect of fees for veterinary health inspection[7] and fees for examination of imported oranges.[8]

Still more subtle is the argument that the protection of industrial and commercial property, guaranteed, it seems, by art. 36, impedes the free circulation of goods in the Community and leads, in effect, to "quantitative restrictions". By art. 36 the member states may prohibit or restrict the movement of goods in this respect provided such measures do not "constitute a means of arbitrary discrimination or a disguised restriction on trade between member states". Several

---

[4] In Case 12/74: *E.E.C. Commission* v. *Italian Government, Re Quantitative Restrictions on the Imports of Pork Products into Italy*, [1962] C.M.L.R. 39; 7 Rec. 633; see also Case 12/74: *E.C. Commission* v. *Germany*, [1975] E.C.R. 181.
[5] See pp. 221 above and 312 below.
[6] Case 29/72: *Marimex SpA* v. *Ministero delle Finanze*, [1973] C.M.L.R. 486; 18 Rec. 1309.
[7] Case 21/75: *I. Schröder K. G.* v. *Oberstadtdirektor der Stadt Köln*, [1975] C.M.L.R. 312.
[8] *Re Fees for Examination of Imported Oranges*, [1975] C.M.L.R. 415.

cases[9] have touched upon the subject and it is clear that the problem is unlikely to be solved unless there is unification of national laws governing industrial and commercial property and a more precise definition of quantitative restrictions.

To facilitate the process of the elimination of quantitative restrictions art. 33 (7) authorises the Commission to issue directives establishing the procedure and timetable in accordance with which member states must abolish, as between themselves, any measures in existence which have an effect equivalent to quotas. In response the Commission issued three such directives: one concerned with the import of potatoes into Germany,[10] another concerned with the abolition of legislative and administrative provisions relative to the import of products which ought to be subject to free circulation, export or purchase or sale like any other national product;[11] and one to eliminate discrimination between national products and products envisaged in arts. 9 and 10 of the Treaty (i.e. products from third countries in circulation in the Community).[12]

The policy of elimination of quantitative restrictions applies also to state monopolies of a commercial character. By virtue of art. 37, the member states are bound to adjust such monopolies[13] so as to allow competition from their nationals and other member states.

In order to accelerate the process the Commission[14] recommended the abolition of "exclusive rights" in this respect and, in fact, France and Italy have undertaken to abolish their monopolies by the end of 1975. Considerable progress has been achieved[15] so much so that practically the only monopoly remaining is that in spirits which is to be dealt with by the proposed Common Market Organisation for Spirits.

Although art. 44 of the Act of Accession reminds the new members of their obligations under E.E.C. art 37, there seems to be no problem with these countries as they have no monopolies of a commercial nature.

---

[9] E.g. Case 24/67: *Parke, Davis & Co.* v. *Probel*, [1968] C.M.L.R. 47; 14 Rec. 81; Case 78/70, *Deutsche Grammophon GmbH* v. *Metro-SB-Grössmärkte GmbH & Co. K.G.*, [1971] C.M.L.R. 631; 17 Rec. 481; Case 192/73: *Van Zuylen Frères* v. *Hag A. G.*, [1974] E.C.R. 731; [1974] 2 C.M.L.R. 127. Case 15/74: *Centrafarm B. V.* v. *Sterling Drug Co. Inc.*, [1974] 2 C.M.L.R. 480; *E.M.I. Records Ltd.* v. *C.B.S. Schallplaten GmbH, unreported.*

[10] Directive of 28 July 1964.

[11] Directive of 7 November 1966.

[12] Directive of 22 December 1969, O.J.L. 13/29.

[13] These monopolies included France: tobacco, matches, alcohol, potash, paper for the press, gunpowder and explosives, petroleum products; Italy: salt, tobacco, matches, flints, cigarette papers; Germany: matches and alcohol; the Netherlands: natural gas.

[14] 1970, J.O. L6 and L31.

[15] But see the *Manghera Case, op. cit.*, p. 200 above.

(B) AGRICULTURE (ARTICLES 38-47)

1. *General Principles*

In his report to the Messina Conference which paved the way for the creation of the E.E.C. the Belgian statesman, Henri Spaak, wrote:

"On ne peut concevoir l'établissement d'un marché commun général en Europe sans que l'agriculture s'y trouve incluse. C'est l'un des secteurs où le progrès de productivité qui résulteront du marché commun, c'est-à-dire de la spécialisation progressive des productions et de l'élargissement des débouchés, peuvent avoir les effets les plus importants sur le niveau de vie des producteurs aussi bien que des consommateurs. En outre, cette inclusion de l'agriculture dans le marché commun est une condition d'équilibre des échanges entre les différentes économies des États membres ..."[16]

Agriculture, as an absolutely essential sector of the economy, had to be included in the concept of the Common Market together with industry and commerce. Moreover, because of its nature and role in the economy of the member states, agriculture had to be singled out for a special regime. In view of the conflicting interests of the member states, the problem of agriculture in the Community has proved to be not only special, but also the most difficult to solve.

Having been recognised as "a sector closely linked with the economy as a whole" (art. 39 (2) (c)) and given its "particular nature" (art. 39 (2) (a))[17] the agricultural regime of the Community rests on its own philosophy. This philosophy can be reduced to two principles enshrined in art. 38 of the Treaty, i.e. that the rules governing agriculture derogate from the rules which establish the common market (art. 38 (2)) and that the operation and development of the Common Market for agricultural products[18] must be accompanied by a common agricultural policy (art. 38 (4)).

It follows that there can be no common market for agricultural products without a common agricultural policy. Whilst there is no definition of the agricultural policy in the Treaty, art. 39 enumerates the objectives of this policy and art. 43 gives considerable powers

---

[16] Quoted by Olmi, G., "L'Agriculture", *Les Novelles, op. cit.*, p. 680.
[17] This particular nature "results from agriculture's social structure and from structural and natural disparities between the various agricultural regions": art. 39 (2) (a).
[18] Agricultural products comprise the products of the soil, of stock-farming, of fisheries and products of first-stage processing directly related to the foregoing (art. 38 (1)). For a list of these see E.E.C. Treaty, Annex II.

to the organs of the Community, authorising them to devise and enforce the common agricultural policy. It follows that there is no question of the co-ordination at the Community level of the various national policies but of the one policy for the whole Community.

As for the basic principles of the Common Market in Agriculture, art. 42 provides that "the rules of competition shall only apply to the production of, and trade in, agricultural products, to the extent determined by the Council". The relevant Common Agricultural Policy Regulation 26,[19] art. 2, issued in 1962, exempts agreements essential to an agricultural market organisation or the production and sale of agricultural products from the operation of art. 85[20] (prohibition of agreements between undertakings which may affect trade between member states and are designed to stultify free competition) and art. 86[1] of the Treaty (prohibition of the abuse of a dominant trade position by one or more undertakings). Furthermore arts. 92 and 93 (2) of the Treaty do not apply to agriculture. Article 92 declares state aids incompatible with the Common Market and art. 93 governs the procedure to be followed by the Commission in cases involving alleged breaches of art. 92. It follows that state aids to agriculture are not ruled out as a matter of principle, but, in practice, specific Regulations[2] expressly provide that arts. 92–94 of the Treaty shall not be derogated from unless stipulated to the contrary.

2. *Common Agricultural Policy*

Article 39 (1) sets out the objectives of the common agricultural policy as follows:

> "(*a*) to increase agricultural productivity by promoting technical progress and by ensuring the national development of agricultural production and the optimum utilisation of all factors of production, in particular labour;
>
> (*b*) thus to ensure a fair standard of living for the agricultural community, in particular by increasing the individual earnings of persons engaged in agriculture;
>
> (*c*) to stabilise markets;
>
> (*d*) to provide certainty of supplies; and
>
> (*e*) to ensure supplies to consumers at reasonable prices".

---

[19] J.O. 993/62.
[20] See pp. 314 *et seq.*, below; Case 71/74: *Frubo* v. *E.C. Commission*, [1975] C.M.L.R. 123.
[1] See pp. 323 *et seq.*, below.
[2] E.g. Regulation No. 121/67, 13 June 1967, on the common organisation of the market in pigmeat, art. 21, J.O. No. 103, 2 June 1967, p. 2075/67.

The member states are committed to adopt the common agricultural policy gradually during the transitional period. The new members are equally committed.[3] In order to achieve the objectives of the policy the member states must adopt a common organisation of agricultural markets (art. 40 (2)).

3. *Common Organisation of Agricultural Markets*

The Common Organisation of Agricultural Markets has not been defined in the Treaty, but art. 40 (2) provides that it should take one of the following forms depending on the product concerned:

(*a*) common rules as regards competition;

(*b*) compulsory co-ordination of the various national marketing organisations;

(*c*) a European organisation of the market.

In the light of (*b*) it seems that, if the Community cannot eliminate national organisations, it can at least harmonise them into something resembling a Community concept. The task has been entrusted to the Community Institutions and in the terms of art. 43 (2): "The Council shall, on a proposal of the Commission and after consulting the Assembly acting unanimously during the first stages and by a qualified majority thereafter, make regulations, issue directives, or take decisions, without prejudice to any recommendations it may also make." The Commission's proposals emerged from a conference held in July 1958 at Stresa, which defined the guidelines of the Common Agricultural Policy.[4] In June 1960, the Commission, after consulting the Economic and Social Committee, submitted its proposals to the Council in respect of four main policies: structural, market, commercial and social.[5] Having had the benefit of the views of the Special Committee for Agriculture created in 1960 the Council adopted certain guidelines which were to form the future Common Agricultural Policy, viz. free movement of agricultural products within the Community, a joint commercial and agricultural policy, a common price level for agricultural products within the Community and co-ordination of national structural reform. These guidelines added practically nothing to the existing provisions of the Treaty, but reaffirmed the resolve to tackle the Community agricultural problem and in some respects interpreted the Treaty provisions. The importance of the problem is well reflected in the machinery of Community legislation

---

[3] Act of Accession, art. 50 *et seq.*

[4] See *First General Report*, 1958, ss. 97–101.

[5] See *Third General Report*, 1960, s. 230 and *Fourth General Report*, 1961, s. 103.

which involved the co-operation of the Commission, the Assembly and the Council.

The first regulation issued by the Council concerned the market organisation in cereals[6] and applied during the transitional period to wheat, rye, barley, oats, maize, buckwheat, millet, hardwheat, meal and groats of wheat and rye and processed grain products. It was replaced, in 1967, by a Final Regulation.[7] This Regulation is no longer concerned with the co-ordination of the various national markets, but sets up a single Community market based on a common price system within the Community and regulated trade with third countries. The price system comprises a target price, an intervention price and a threshold price.

The *target price* is determined annually before 1 August by the Council acting on a proposal of the Commission after consulting the Assembly (art. 43 (2)). This is not a fixed price, but a price intended to enable the producers to plan their production for the following year; it provides an expectation of the price the product should fetch during the next marketing year (1 August to 31 July).

The *intervention price*, determined according to the same procedure as the target price, is the price which the national authorities must pay to producers who are unable to sell their product on the market. It forms a guarantee to farmers. However, whilst the target price is uniform within the Community, the intervention price varies as from area to area according to the circumstances of the area. The intervention price is lower than the target price. The basic intervention price has been fixed by the Council in relation to the market conditions in Duisburg (Germany) because the area of Duisburg is considered to have the lowest production of cereals.

The *threshold price* is the price fixed by the Community for cereals imported from third countries. It is fixed in respect of the same standard quality as the target price. It is calculated in relation to cereals, notionally imported through Rotterdam to be sold on the Duisburg market. In other words, the threshold price is the target price less the cost of transport from Rotterdam to Duisburg.

The threshold price is determined by the Council in accordance with the procedure outlined above every year before 15 March. It is fixed in relation to a system of levies imposed on imported cereals, these levies being equal to the difference between the threshold price and the c.i.f. price at Rotterdam. The levies are fixed by the Commission whilst the c.i.f. prices for Rotterdam are calculated on the basis of the

---

[6] Regulation of 14 January 1962, No. 19, J.O. 933/62.
[7] Regulation of 13 June 1967, No. 120/67, J.O. 2269/67.

most favourable purchasing possibilities on the world market. It follows that the threshold prices are lower than the Community prices.

Whilst the price system is designed to ensure production within the Community and to guarantee a fair return to Community producers, the system of levies on imports is designed to protect Community producers against competition from third countries. In a sense, this is a Community preference and an example of the economic barrier round the Community. However, the Regulation requires strict control of the quality of the product to preserve not only a high standard of the market, but also an equitable basis of competition.

Target prices, intervention prices and threshold prices are reviewed monthly to take into account the cost of interest and stockpiling. These reviews result in price increases spread out over the marketing year.

In order to encourage exports, the Regulation provides for refunds to exporters from the Community to third countries. These refunds constitute a form of subsidy which is the same for the whole Community, but varies according to the destination of the products. The refunds are calculated in relation to the difference between the world and Community prices for the given product. This is necessary since world prices are usually lower than Community prices and there is a policy against the accumulation of surpluses within the Community. Exports and imports are under control by means of appropriate certificates.

At the Community level, the system is supervised by a Management Committee set up under the Regulation and consisting of representatives of the member states presided over by a representative of the Commission. The Chairman refers matters to the Commission either on his own initiative or at the request of the representative of a member state. The decisions are implemented by the Commission. If there is a difference of opinion between the Committee and the Commission, the latter must submit the matter to the Council which may adopt a different decision from that proposed by the Commission.[8]

In addition to the Regulation for Cereals, the Community has adopted Regulations in respect of other essential sectors of Agriculture, notably Pigmeat,[9] Eggs,[10] Poultry Meat,[11] Fruit and Vegetables,[12]

---

[8] See Chap. 8, *ante*.
[9] Final Regulation of 13 June 1967, No. 121/67.
[10] Final Regulation of 13 June 1967, No. 122/67; also Regulations issued in 1968, 1969, 1970, 1972.
[11] Final Regulation of 13 June 1967, No. 123/67.
[12] Final Regulation of 28 June 1968, No. 865/68; also Regulation No. 2454/72 and 2455/72.

Wine and Vines,[13] Milk and Dairy Products,[14] Beef and Veal,[15] Rice,[16] Vegetable Oils, Fats, Oil Seeds and Olives,[17] Sugar,[18] Tobacco[19], Wine[20] certain horticultural products[1] and Fisheries.[2]

As a result of these Regulations, several essential sectors of Agriculture have become subject to Community Rules. The organisation of these markets differs as from sector to sector, but, broadly speaking, the pattern of the Regulation for Cereals, which we have considered as an example of a Community Market Organisation, has been followed.

Alongside the Market Organisation the Community postulates a structural re-organisation of agriculture. The problem is by no means simple and has, over the years, focused the attention of the Community. In order to solve it, the Commission in 1968 submitted to the Council a "Memorandum on the Reform of Agriculture in the European Economic Community" (Agriculture 1980)[3] and, in 1971, the Council adopted a resolution[4] based on this Memorandum. The Commission analysed and made recommendations in respect of several aspects of the structural reform of agriculture. In particular it considered the problem of the manpower engaged in agriculture, the size of farms and production methods.

On the first problem, the Commission concluded that in view of high productivity and overproduction fewer people will be needed in the farming industry of the future. This creates a social problem which the Community must alleviate by helping those who wish to leave the land, by assisting farmers over fifty-five years of age who wish to give up their occupation and by providing schemes for re-training and placement of those who wish to find another occupation.

On the second problem, the Commission found that the average farm within the community was too small to engage in profitable

---

[13] Basic Regulation of 28 April 1970, No. 816/70; also Regulation of 24 September 1973 (J.O.L. 269).

[14] Regulation of 27 June 1968, No. 804/68; also Regulations No. 1353/73 (Council) and 1821/73 (Commission) on conversion of dairy farms to beef production.

[15] Regulation of 27 June 1968 No. 805/68; also Regulation No. 1896/73 and 2096/73.

[16] Basic Regulation No. 359/67, amended by Regulation No. 830/68.

[17] Regulation of 22 September 1966, No. 136/66.

[18] Final Regulation of 18 December 1967, No. 1009/67.

[19] Regulation No. 727/70.

[20] O.J. 30, 20 April 1962, 989/62 (Sp. Edn. 1959–62, p. 123).

[1] Hemp and Flax, Regulation of 1 August 1970, No. 1308/70; Flowers, Bulbs and Live Plants, Regulation of 27 February 1968, No. 234/68; Directive on horticultural holdings No. 72/1590/17 April 1972.

[2] Regulation No. 2141/70 on structural policy for the fishing industry; O.J. L236, 27 October 1970, 1 (Sp. Edn. 1970 (III), p. 703).

[6] See *Second General Report*, 1968.

[4] [1971] J.O. C52.

industrial farming and recommended a definite policy for the increase of the size of farms in accordance with the type of production.

On the third problem, the Commission felt that the production methods were not modern enough and that, coupled with the lack of flexibility, this contributed to the relatively low incomes of farmers in the Community. It proposed the modernisation of production methods, greater adaptability to market needs and better marketing.

The Commission costed its recommendation estimating the relative contribution of the Community and the member states to the cost of the reform programme.

The Memorandum and the ensuing discussions in the Assembly and the Economic and Social Committee led to the above mentioned Council Resolution on the subject which, in turn, paved the way for a new set of proposals by the Commission.[3] These proposals were dressed up in the form of directives issued on 17 April 1972 on the modernisation[4] of the farming industry, assistance to farmers leaving the land[5], professional training and advice.[6] Taken together, with the Council Resolution, the emerging picture of agriculture is one of a modernised industry, manned by well-qualified and efficient farmers, organised into a competitive market and catering for the social and human problems involved in the movements of the farming population. In this set-up, state aids and subsidies authorised under arts. 92 and 93 of the Treaty will have to go as the principles of a common market in agriculture will be implemented. However implementation has been delayed and problems continue to arise. To deal with these problems the Commission, in November 1973, submitted a Memorandum to the Council in which the future of the CAP to 1978 has been considered. The objectives include proposals to deal with disequilibria in certain agricultural markets, to simplify the common organisation of markets and to reduce costs.

In connection with agriculture, two further points have to be mentioned: finance and the machinery for implementing the Community Agricultural Policy.

The financing of the common agricultural policy, although germane to agricultural problems, is really part of the Community budget, governed by the Luxembourg Treaty of 1970 which came into force

---

[3] [1971] J.O. C75.
[4] No. 72/159.
[5] No. 72/160.
[6] No. 72/161.

on 1 January 1971,[7] but is now subject to the new budgetary arrangements agreed at the meeting of the Heads of Government of the member states in Dublin in March 1975.[8] Indeed, the European Agricultural Fund figures prominently in the budget, representing, e.g. in 1971, some 86 per cent of the whole[9]. The underlying philosophy of the financing of the agricultural policy is the principle that since there is a common policy and a common price system, the financial responsibility must be undertaken by the Community. Accordingly, on the basis of art. 40 (4) of the E.E.C. Treaty, the European Agricultural Guidance and Guarantee Fund[10] was set up and an elaborate system of Community agricultural finance was established.

As for the machinery to implement the Community Agricultural Policy, we have already observed that, at the Community level, the crucial decisions have to be taken by the Council after consulting the Assembly, whilst the background work and the administrative actions stem from the Commission. Agriculture has the constant attention of the highest Community organs. At the national level, the execution of the decisions of the Council has been left to the machinery of the member states. In particular the member states assume responsibility for the purchase of the agricultural product at the intervention price determined by the Council. They also operate the system of import and export certificates, collect levies and pay out refunds. Their financial liability to the Community forms part of their contribution towards the Community budget.

The new members of the Community had to accept the Common Agricultural Policy as a condition of their accession. They are, therefore, committed to a process of adaptation and integration during the five years' transition period as set out in the Act annexed to the Treaty of Accession.[11] For the United Kingdom, this meant a radical change in the system. To implement the Community Policy provisions have been made in the European Communities Act (s. 6) for the setting up

---

[7] Treaty amending certain budgetary provisions of the treaties establishing the European Communities and of the treaty establishing a Single Council and a Single Commission of the European Communities, of 21 April 1970, [1971] J.O. L2; Cmd. 4867.

[8] *Bulletin of the European Communities*, 1975, No. 3, p. 6.

[9] According to the *Fourth General Report*, 1970, the Community budget of £1,273 million was divided as follows: Agricultural Fund: £1,096 million; Administration: £62 million; Costs of Collecting Levies and Duties: £56 million; Euratom: Aid £8 million. According to the *Eighth General Report*, 1974, the Community Budget of 5,825,283,360 u.a. provided 4,307,805,260 u.a. for Agriculture.

[10] By Regulation No. 25, J.O. 991/62; this was replaced by Regulation No. 130, J.O. 2965/66, which was replaced by the decision of 21 April 1970 now in force; see the Act of Accession, arts. 127–132.

[11] Arts. 50–93.

of an Intervention Board for Agricultural Produce and such consequential changes as appeared necessary.[12]

The implementation of the Common Agricultural Policy means in effect a uniform body of Community Law as contended on behalf of the Commission:[13]

" . . . The integral and exclusive nature of the competence of Community institutions in the agricultural sectors formed into 'European market organisations' derives from the consistent body of case law of the Court of Justice[14] according to which any lacunæ in a system of organising agriculture cannot be filled by Member States since the institution of a European market organisation has deprived Member States of their original legislative power" . . .[15]

(C) FREE MOVEMENT OF PERSONS, SERVICES AND CAPITAL

The freedom of movement of persons, services and capital is regarded as one of the "freedoms" essential for the creation of the Common Market. The member states are, accordingly, bound to abolish "obstacles to the free movement of persons, services and capital" (E.E.C. Treaty, art. 3 (c)).

The free movement of persons is intended to be secured through two expedients: the right of establishment and the principle of non-discrimination. The Treaty makes a distinction between workers (art. 48–51) and others (including liberal professions, merchants, artisans, industrialists and corporations) who are considered under the title of "establishment" (arts. 52–58).

---

[12] The Intervention Board for Agricultural Produce Order 1972 (S.I. 1972 No. 1578); the Common Agricultural Policy (Agricultural Produce) (Protection of Community Arrangements) Order 1973 (S.I. 1973 No. 204); the Eggs (Marketing Standards) Regulations 1973 (S.I. 1973 No. 15); the Imported Food (Amendment) Regulations 1973 (S.I. 1973 No. 1351); the Fishing Boats (European Economic Communities) Designation Order 1972 (S.I. 1972 No. 2026); the Farm and Horticultural Development Regulations 1973 (S.I. 1973 No. 2205); the Vegetable Seeds Regulations 1973 (S.I. 1973 No. 1049).
[13] In Case 31/74: *Filippo Galli* (preliminary ruling requested by the Pretore di Roma), [1975] E.C.R. 1 at p. 54.
[14] Case 159/73: *Hannoversche Zucker*, [1974] E.C.R. 121.
[15] Case 131/73: *State [Italy]* v. *Grosoli*, [1974] C.M.L.R. 40.

1. *Movement of Workers (Articles 48-51)*

"Workers"[16] are not confined to manual workers but comprise all wage-earners (*salariés*) or persons subject to a contract of employment which in one case included an international dance band leader.[17] Their position is governed by the Treaty and several Regulations[18] and Directives. Article 48 defines the freedom of movement and art. 49 provides the machinery of implementation. The freedom of movement implies a right to accept offers of employment, move freely within the territory of member states for the purpose of employment, stay in a member state for that purpose and remain in the territory of a member state after having been employed in that state[19]. It also means equal treatment as regards conditions of work and employment with the nationals of the host country, access to vocational training schemes and the right to join a trade union. The foreign worker is entitled to be considered for housing allocation and may bring with him his spouse, children under 21 years of age and dependant relatives.

The freedom of movement is not without qualification as it is subject to restrictions on the ground of *ordre public*, public safety or security and public health (art. 48 (3), the opening line) and does not apply to employment in the public service (art. 48 (4)). The formula is quite wide as it takes into account not only the sovereign rights of the member states, but also their duty to maintain decent standards in their own communities. This implies the power of control and, where necessary, the power to expel undesirable aliens. However, in accordance with directive 64/221, the measures taken on grounds of public policy or public security cannot serve economic ends and must be based "exclusively on the personal conduct of the individual concerned". This, in effect, limits the discretionary powers of the host state especially that "previous criminal convictions shall not in themselves constitute grounds" for the refusal of admission or expulsion of a foreign worker.

Article 49 gives to the Council the power to make regulations and directives in order to implement the principle of free movement. In

---

[16] Case 75/63: *Unger v. Bestuur der Bedrijsvereniging voor Detailhandel en Ambachten*, [1964] C.M.L.R. 319; 10 Rec. 347.

[17] Case 8/75: *Caisse Primaire d'Assurance Maladie de Selestat v. Association du Foot-Ball Club d'Andlau*, [1975] C.M.L.R. 383.

[18] Regulation 15 of 16 August 1961 (O.J. 1513/61); Regulation 38/64 of 1 May 1964 (OJ. 963/64); Regulation 1612/68 (OJ. L257/2; Sp. Edn. 1968 (II.), p. 475); Regulation 1251/70 (OJ. 1970, L142/24; Sp. Edn. 1970 (II.), p. 402); Directive 64/240 (OJ. 1964, 981/64); Directive 68/360 (OJ. 1968, L257/13; Sp. Edn. 1968 (II.), p. 485; Directive 64/221 of 25 February 1964; Sp. Edn. 1952–66, p. 117.

[19] Art. 49 (3) and Regulation No. 1251/70, [1970] J.O. L142.

particular, the Council should bring about co-operation between national employment services, liberalisation of the national laws affecting migration and employment within the Community and create machinery to correlate the supply and demand of manpower in the Community. The Council must do all this "in such a way as to avoid serious threats to the standard of living and of employment in the various regions and industries".

Most of those provisions have a direct effect, creating rights which can be enforced in national courts. However, there is a growing body of case law arising from references under art. 177 in which the Community Court makes its own distinct contribution to the definition and clarification of migrant workers' rights in the Community.

The *Van Duyn*[20] case clarifies the right of entry into a member state and the power of expulsion of the host state. The Dutch national, who was refused entry into the United Kingdom where she was to work for the Church of Scientology, was unable to vindicate her claim of "free movement" as her prospective employers were engaged in what the British government considered to be a "socially harmful" activity. Her membership of the organisation was "personal conduct" within the meaning of art. 3 (1) of directive 64/221 which enabled the United Kingdom to invoke a principle of International Law according to which a sovereign state can control the influx of aliens into its territory.

The *Bonsignore*[1] case is one of the recent moving examples that a conviction does not in itself constitute a ground of expulsion. The principle was followed by the German Courts[2] with the warning that expulsion "pour encourager les autres" will not be permitted. However deportation of a German couple with criminal records who settled in Holland and built up a flourishing business there, ordered by the Dutch authorities, was justified in the circumstances. It was held by the District Court of the Hague that art. 3 (2) of directive 64/221 "should be interpreted in such a manner that ... the sole fact of previous criminal convictions may not be the only motive but, in addition, regard must be had and certainly may be had, to the number and nature of the offences committed and sentences imposed."[3]

---

[20] Case 41/74, see pp. 77 and 262, *supra*.
[1] Case 67/74, see p. 201.
[2] *Lauricella* v. *Land Rheinland-Pfalz*, [1973] C.M.L.R. 733; *Re deportation of a Belgian national*, [1974] C.M.L.R. 107 but cf. *R.* v. *Secchi*, [1975] C.M.L.R. 383 where a London Metropolitan magistrate ordered deportation of a foreign "drifter" convicted of shoplifting and a sexual offence.
[3] *Diedrichs and Platschke* v. *The State*, [1973] C.M.L.R. 509 at p. 514.

The principle of non-discrimination against foreign workers was upheld in several cases and in one case the Community Court held that the provisions of the French *Code de Travail Maritime*, which restricted the employment of foreigners in the French Merchant Navy were inconsistent with Regulation 1612/68 in particular and with the freedom of movement in general.[4] However the selection of a team for a sporting event is not subject to the rule against discrimination.[5]

The principle of non-discrimination means in effect equal rights in comparable situations. Thus Mr. Ugliola,[6] who had to interrupt his employment in Germany in order to complete his national service in Italy was entitled to resume his work and benefit from the accrued rights arising from continuous employment. He had to be treated like a German doing his national service.

Mr. Sotgiu,[7] who worked for the Federal Post Office, was in receipt of a separation allowance in respect of his family living in Italy. This allowance was available to German workers living away from home. In 1965 the allowance was increased except for workers originally resident abroad for whom it remained the same. Mr. Sotgiu claimed that he suffered discrimination contrary to Regulation 1612/68 and was granted redress notwithstanding the contention that, being employed in the public service, he could have been denied equal treatment under E.E.C. art. 48 (4).

The right to equal treatment also affords protection from dismissal in the case of special provisions in respect of workers disabled by industrial accidents.[8]

In view of the developments in the field of social security and welfare state benefits, the movement of workers makes economic and social sense only if it does not result in disadvantage for the worker and his family. The problem became quite acute in the Coal and Steel Community and in the wake of the ratification of the E.E.C. Treaty a project of a Convention on Social Security, elaborated under the E.C.S.C. Treaty, was signed in Rome on 9 December 1957. In the spirit of the Convention, arts. 15 and 118 of the E.E.C. Treaty and E.E.C. Regulations Nos. 3 and 4 of 1958[9] gave rise to a social security charter for migrant workers within the Community.

---

[4] Case 167/73: *E.E.C. Commission* v. *French Republic*, [1974] E.C.R. 359; [1974] 2 C.M.L.R. 216.
[5] Case 36/74: *Walgrave and Koch* v. *Union Cycliste Internationale*, [1975] C.M.L.R. 320.
[6] Case 15/69: *Würtembergische Milchverwerkung-Südmilch A.G.* v. *Ugliola*, [1970] C.M.L.R. 194 (1969), Rec. 363.
[7] Case 152/73: *Sotgiu* v. *Deutsche Bundespost*, [1974] E.C.R. 153.
[8] Case 44/72: *Marsman* v. *Fa M. Rosskamp*, [1973] C.M.L.R. 501; 18 Rec. 1243.
[9] [1958] J.O. 561 and 597.

This charter rests on art. 51 of the Treaty which, in order to assist the movement of workers, authorises the Council to adopt measures which would eliminate discrimination in the field of social security arising from a move from one country to another. In particular, these measures must ensure the aggregation of rights to social benefits taking into account the qualifying periods under the laws of the countries involved and the payment of benefits to persons resident in the territories of member states. Regulation 3 implemented these principles in detail and Regulation 4 took care of the administrative and financial implications. However, Regulation 3 proved too narrow and has been replaced in 1971 by a wider code[10] which will come into force when Regulation 4 has been brought into line. It should be borne in mind that the Regulations have direct effect in the member states[11] and have to be applied as national law. However, in view of the fact that the social security or welfare state systems are not uniform within the Community, the benefits secured by the Regulations must be regarded as the enforceable minimum. There is nothing to prevent one member state from being more generous than another state, but, if the benefit in question does not fall under the rubric, it may not be available to a foreign citizen. The *French Widow's Pension* case[12] illustrates the point: the plaintiff was in receipt of a widow's pension until her re-marriage when she claimed a gratuity under the German *Reichsversicherungsordnung* in compensation for the cessation of her widow's pension. German law prohibits the payment of this gratuity to persons resident abroad. The widow was a Frenchwoman and her claim was based on the principle that pensions or capital payments in lieu should not cease to be payable merely because the recipient lived in another state. The *Bundessozialgericht*, invoking the *acte clair* doctrine, refused to refer the matter to Luxembourg and held that the gratuity on re-marriage was not a pension and, being governed by German law, could not be claimed in the circumstances.

However the Community Court[13] held that a widow's re-marriage gratuity should be treated as a widow's pension for the purpose of the E.E.C. Regulation and the same conclusion was reached by a Belgian

---

[10] Regulation No. 1408 of 5 July 1971; [1971] J.O. L149; also Regulation 574/72 (O.J. 1972, L74/1) amended by Regulation 878/73 (O.J. 1973 L86/1).

[11] E.g. *Nani* v. *Caisse d'Assurance Viellesse des Travailleurs Salariés de Paris*, Paris Court of Appeal, [1964] Clunet, 642–645; 4 C.M.L. Rev. 70; *Union Regionale des Sociétés de Secours Minières du Nord*, French Cour de Cassation, [1965] Dalloz 723; 4 C.M.L. Rev. 71.

[12] Case 109/69: *Re French Widow's Pension Settlement*, 4 R.J., [1971] C.M.L.R. 530.

[13] Case 130·73: *Vandeweghe* v. *Berufsgenossenschaft für Chemische Industrie*, [1974] C.M.L.R. 449.

Labour Court.[14] In the light of this ruling and in the light of the general proposition that benefits acquired under the legislation of one or more member states shall not be subject to any reduction, modification, suspension, withdrawal or termination on the ground that the beneficiary resides in the territory of a member state other than that in which the paying institution is situated, it would seem that the gratuity should now be payable abroad.[15] Indeed the German case cited above reflects the difficulties but not the Community Law in this respect. Widow's rights have on several occasions been considered by the Community Court,[16] and they shall remain subject to uncertainty as long as there are substantial discrepancies between national laws (e.g. in France a woman is not entitled to a widow's pension if her husband dies before his retirement and she is capable of work).

Problems do arise from the definition of "worker"[17] or beneficiary; qualifications under several national systems;[18] residential qualifications;[19] the nature of the entitlement[20] and so on. However the underlying principle is equality with the nationals of the host state in the treatment of the migrant worker and his dependants. Thus Mr. Frilli[1] was entitled to his old-age pension in Belgium like any Belgian citizen irrespective of any question of reciprocity between Belgium and Italy; the child of a deceased Italian worker living in Germany was entitled to an "educational grant" although under the relevant Bavarian statute the child of an alien was not within the class of persons so entitled[2] and so was a worker's daughter to be admitted to an educational course

---

[14] *Office National des Pensions pour Travailleurs Salariés* v. *Goszkowski*, [1974] C.M.L.R. 303,

[15] Article 10 (1) of Regulation 3 and Regulation 1408/71; Case 51/73: *Bestuur der Sociale Verzekeringsbank* v. *Smieja*, [1973] E.C.R. 1213; [1974] C.M.L.R. 620.

[16] See case 75/63: *Hockstra-Unger* v. *Bestuur der Bedrijfsvereniging voor Detailhandel en Ambachten*, [1964] C.M.L.R. 319, 10 Rec. 347; case 92/63: *Moebs* v. *Bestuur der Sociale Verzekeringsbank*, [1964] C.M.L.R. 338; Case 61/65: 10 Rec. 557; *Vaassen-Göbbels* v. *Beamtenfonds voor Mijnbedrijf*, [1966] C.M.L.R. 508; 12 Rec. 377; *Van der Veen* v. *Bestuur der Sociale Verzekeringsbank*, [1964] C.M.L.R. 548; 10 Rec. 1105.

[17] E.g. case 23/71: *Janssen* v. *Landesbond der Christelijke Mutualiteiten*, [1972] C.M.L.R. 13; 17 Rec. 859—"helper" to a self-employed farmer.

[18] E.g. case 2/67: *De Moor* v. *La Caisse de Pension des Employées Privés*: (1967), C.M.L.R. 223; 13 Rec. 255.

[19] *Smieja Case, op. cit;* Case 19/67: *Sociale Verzekeringsbank* v. *Van der Vecht*, [1968] C.M.L.R. 151 at p. 164; 13 Rec. 446 at p. 455.

[20] E.g. Case 1/72: *Frilli* v. *The Belgian State*, [1973] C.M.L.R. 386; 18 Rec. 457 but see Case 93/75; *Adlerblum* v. *Caisse Nationale* [1976] 1 C.M.L.R. 236 (Compensation for Nazi persecution non-justiciable before Community Court).

[1] *Op cit.*

[2] Case 9/74: *Donato Casagrande* v. *Landeshaupt der Stadt München*, [1974] E.C.R. 773.

under the same conditions as a French girl;[3] handicapped children were
not disqualified from receiving appropriate treatment[4] and the question
whether the Italian mother of a large family was entitled to a reduced
rate card on French Railways as a "social benefit" has been submitted
to the Community Court.[5]

The many cases decided by national courts and the Community
Court show the complexity of the problem and the variety of situations
in which a migrant worker may have to seek legal redress. This suggests
that we have barely crossed the threshold of the development of the law
in this field. However the law has not been static. Moreover the Heads
of Government at their meeting in Paris in December 1974 considered
the creation of a "passport union". A common passport would be the
first step towards Community citizenship. A draft proposal in this
respect should be prepared by the end of 1976.

2. Free Movement of Liberal Professions (Articles 52–58)

Under the title of the "right of establishment" the free movement of
persons other than wage-earners is intended to be established through
the right to engage in and carry on self-employed occupations, to set up
and manage undertakings, firms and companies under the conditions
laid down for its own nationals by the law of the country where such
establishment is effected (art. 52). Therefore, as distinguished from
wage-earners, members of the liberal professions are merely entitled
not to be discriminated against on the ground of their nationality[6],
and, according to the Community Court, residence.

The Treaty envisages a gradual abolition of restrictions on the
freedom of establishment of foreign nationals and to that end prohibits
new restrictions and enjoins the Council, acting on a proposal from the
Commission and after consulting the Economic and Social Committee
and the Assembly, to draw up a general programme for the abolition
of the existing restrictions. However, the practical problems remain
yet to be solved for the exercise of many professions is conditional
upon the approximation and harmonisation of national laws and customs
as far as education, qualifications and professional status are concerned.
The difficulties, as compared with the movement of workers, are understandable not only because of the entrenched position of certain
professions, but also because of their social and professional respon-

---

[3] Case 68/74: *Angelo Alaimo* v. *Préfet du Rhône*, [1975] E.C.R. 109.
[4] Case 7/75: *Fracas* v. *Belgian State*, [1975] C.M.L.R. 442.
[5] *Fiorini* v. *Société Nationale des Chemins de Fer*, Court of Appeal, Paris,
[1975] C.M.L.R. 459.
[6] See: *Reyners* (nationality); *Van Binsbergen* (residence) and *Coenen* (residence)
cases, pp. 49, 57, 201.

sibilities. Whilst essential to the social and economic life of the society, liberal professions cannot be easily harnessed into uniformity across the national borders through the instrumentality of expedients applicable to industry and commerce.

Article 57 provides that the "Council shall issue directives for the mutual recognition of diplomas, certificates and other evidence of formal qualifications" and also "for the co-ordination of the provisions laid down by the law, regulation or administrative action in member states concerning the taking up and pursuit of activities as self-employed persons". So far, little has been achieved in the field[7] but work on the preparation of directives continues whilst certain professions themselves endeavour to discuss their future position in the Community.[8]

Under the principle of the freedom of establishment companies or firms set up in accordance with the law of a member state and having their centre of control within the Community shall be treated like physical persons who are the citizens of member states (art. 58). They too enjoy the right of establishment. A directive concerning companies was issued by the Council in 1968.[9] It purports to govern joint stock companies, publication of particulars and liabilities. Four other draft directives followed suit.[10] In order to facilitate the establishment of companies a Convention was adopted on 29 February 1968 on the mutual recognition of companies and corporations but the concept of a "European Company"[11] is still under consideration. In the meantime yet another proposal on the grouping of enterprises irrespective of their national origin, size or status has been made by the Commission.[12]

3. Services (*Articles 59–66*)

In many respects services are connected with the exercise of liberal professions or activities of self-employed persons. As in connection with the self-employed persons, the Council is enjoined to "draw up a general programme for the abolition of existing restrictions on freedom

---

[7] On the position of the legal profession, see p. 50 above, but a directive on the Medical Profession has been adopted in 1975, O.J. L/167.

[8] See *Barreau et médicins face du droit d'établissement*, Centre d'études européennes, Université Catholique de Louvain (1968).

[9] Directive of 9 March 1968, [1968] J.O. L65/8.

[10] 2nd Draft Directive of 5 March 1970 (1970), J.O.C4 8/8; 3rd Draft Directive of 16 June 1970 (1970), J.O. C89/20; 4th Draft Directive of 10 November 1971 (1972), J.O. C7/11; 5th Draft Directive of 9 October 1972 (1972), J.O. C131/49.

[11] See Renauld, J., *Droit européen des sociétes* (1969); Stein, E., *Harmonization of European Company Laws* (1971); *Eighth General Report*, 1974, p. 73.

[12] (1974) O.J. C14; *Bulletin of the European Communities*, Supp. 1/74.

to provide services within the Community (art. 63 (1)) in order to implement the provisions of art. 59 which envisages a progressive abolition of such restrictions. So far, two such programmes[13] have been propounded and a number of directives have been issued.[14] These directives are concerned mainly with the conditions of entry and the exercise of the freedom to supply services in trade, industry, wholesale trade and handicraft.[15] Apart from re-insurance,[16] insurance (other than life) is subject to two directives[17] and there is also a proposed directive on co-insurance. Banking[18] too is subject to a directive which *inter alia* endeavours to link banking services with capital movements. However these measures are far from comprehensive and it is evident that the process of the harmonisation of services will take some time to accomplish.

Services, according to art. 60, mean services for renumeration, in particular "activities of an industrial character, commercial character, craftsmanship and activities of the professions".

4. Capital (Articles 67–73)

The economic freedoms on which the idea of the Common Market is based would be largely illusory without the corresponding liberalisation of financial operations whether by a migrant worker or a capital investor. The objective is clear: to enable individuals to use their money the way they deem appropriate and to make capital work wherever it can be used. To ensure the flow of capital the member states are committed to "the abolition as between themselves of all restrictions on the movement of capital belonging to persons resident in member states and any discrimination based on the nationality or on the place of residence of the parties or on the place where such capital is invested" (art. 67 (1)). To that end, they must liberalise "the domestic rules governing the capital market and the credit system" (art. 68 (2)) and "avoid introducing any new exchange restrictions" (art. 71 (1)).

In order to implement the principle of the free movement of capital a Monetary Committee was established under art. 105 and the Council, acting upon the recommendations of the Commission and the advice of the Committee, issued directives in accordance with art. 69.

---

[13] J.O. No. 2, of 15 January 1962, 32/62 and J.O. No. 2 of 15 January 1962, 36/62.

[14] For details of the directives see Bontemps, J., *Liberté d'établissement et libre prestattion des services dans le Marché Commun.* (1968).

[15] Bontemps, *op. cit.*; see also Act of Accession, Part II, pp. 50 *et seq.*

[16] J.O. 878/64, of 25 February 1964.

[17] Directive 73/239 of 16 August 1973, J.O. L228/3; 73/240 of 16 August 1973, J.O. L228/20.

[18] Directive 73/183 of 28 June 1973, J.O. L194/1.

The directives of 12 July 1960 and 18 December 1962 were concerned primarily with the movement of capital, i.e. transfers at the exchange rate pertinent to current transactions, transfers of a personal nature, investment in real estate and transfers in connection with the movement of goods and services. These directives also recommended liberalisation of dealings in stock exchange securities with the exception of foreign trust shares and bonds. In 1964, the Council initiated discussions on a Monetary Policy, but no substantial progress had been made until 1969 when the leaders of the member states decided, at The Hague, that an Economic and Monetary Union has to be established. In 1971 the representatives of the member states passed a Resolution to that effect endorsing the work done by the Community institutions and proposing to carry out a programme by stages. The first stage, which commenced on 1 January 1971, should be completed by 31 December 1973. The economic and financial measures proposed in this programme should make the movement of persons, goods, services and capital more effective; should improve the co-ordination of the conjunctural policy and of the monetary and credit policies; should activate the regional policy and bring about a monetary policy in relation to third countries and establish a European Fund for financial operations[19] The Heads of Government, at their meeting in Paris in October 1972 resolved to achieve by stages the Economic and Monetary Union by the end of 1980 but after the change of Government in the United Kingdom objections to the Union were raised during the so-called "fundamental re-negotiations."[20] However the principle was endorsed by the Heads of Government in Paris in December 1974 and confirmed by the British White Paper.[1] In view of the lack of progress the idea seems to have been shelved for the time being.

The Treaty also encourages liberalisation of the movement of capital between the member states and third countries, but proposes co-ordination of the national policies under the aegis of the Council, which is authorised to issue appropriate directives (art. 70).

In order to deal with the balance of payments, art. 73 makes provisions for self-protecting measures which a member state may adopt in consultation with the Commission acting upon the advice of the Monetary Committee. In dire emergency, a state may take self-protecting measures unilaterally, but has to advise the Commission

---

[19] [1971] J.O. L28.
[20] The British Foreign Secretary addressing the Council of Ministers on 1 April 1974; *Bulletin of the European Communities*, Supp. 3/74, item 1104, p. 15.
[1] Membership of the European Community: Report on Re-negotiation (1975) Cmnd. 6003, para. 51.

and the other member states at least by the date when such measures begin to operate.

It is clear that the free movement of capital affects not only individuals but also the states, not only ordinary transfers and investments, but also industrial growth and trade. Therefore, it must be geared to the idea of the Common Market and close co-operation between the member states leading to a common monetary policy and resulting one day in a common currency.

(D) TRANSPORT (ARTICLES 74-84)

A common transport policy is indispensable for the working of the Common Market and, therefore, the member states are bound to adopt such a policy (art. 3 (*e*)). Transport, perhaps like Agriculture, has been singled out as having a special significance to the economy of the Community. Here again, the Council, acting upon a proposal from the Commission and after consulting the Economic and Social Committee and the Assembly, is authorised to lay down common rules applicable to international transport and the conditions under which non-resident carriers may operate transport services within a member state (art. 75).

Although a number of directives, regulations and resolutions[2] dealing mainly with transport of goods by rail, road and inland waters have been issued, today the overall picture is rather patchy and, in spite of the need for a transport policy for the Community, it is as yet premature to speak of such a policy. The effort to galvanise the Community into action resulted in 1973 in a Memorandum from the Commission which defined the objectives of the policy and a new set of guidelines. The blue-print is closely linked with other activities of the Community and takes into account public transport needs and social desiderata. Progress is to be marked by two stages, the first stage to be completed in 1977. However the energy crisis which as from 1974 has affected adversely the industrialist countries may prove to be yet another obstacle to the attainment of the common transport policy.

In some countries (e.g. Belgium) transport is regarded as a service, in other countries (e.g. Holland) it is an industry. Whatever the nomenclature harmonisation of the various laws of the member states governing transport presents a considerable difficulty. Transport plays an important part in the national economy,[3] is in some areas subject to

---

[2] For a full list of the measures and a selection of important texts see Campbell, *op. cit.*, Supp. No. 2 (1971); Vol. 1, pp. 127-133 and pp. 139-152; Supp. No. 1, Vol. 1, pp. 79-125; Supp. 1975, p. 319 *et seq.*

[3] See Bayliss, B. T., *European Transport* (1965).

state monopoly and contributes substantially to the national product. Its diversity and complexity cannot be harnessed easily.

The Treaty and the measures taken so far at Community level aim at harmonisation of transport organisation, termination of discrimination against foreign carriers, sound competition and a freedom of choice for customers. Uniform rates mentioned in several articles of the Treaty (arts. 78, 79, 80 and 81), remain yet to be negotiated.

(E) RESTRICTIONS OF ECONOMIC FREEDOMS

The "economic freedoms" on which the idea of the Common Market is based are not without restraints. However, these restraints are regulated by the Treaty ensuring thereby a certain measure of uniformity within the Community. The restraints are either general, emanating from the concept of the Community as an association of sovereign states, or specific, emanating from the nature and objectives of the Common Market.

In a traditional sense, the Treaty recognises certain fundamental functions of the state, such as keeping peace and order, ensuring a certain level of decency and moral standards, providing social care and security to its citizens and protecting the national cultural heritage and resources. In the light of these duties, the member states may, according to art. 36, restrict the free movement of goods on the ground of "public morality, public policy or public security; the protection of health and life of humans, animals or plants; the protection of national treasures possessing artistic, historic or archaeological value; or the protection of industrial and commercial property". Thus a state may wish to prohibit the export of paintings, sculpture, manuscripts or ancient monuments; it may wish to prohibit the import of pornographic literature or cinematographic materials exhibiting violence or moral degradation; it may wish to prohibit the traffic in arms or drugs. The Community leaves this to the discretion of the member states subject to the proviso that "such prohibitions or restrictions shall not constitute a means of arbitrary discrimination or disguised restriction on trade between member states" (art. 36). Whilst restrictions in good faith are legitimate, art. 36 cannot be used as a legal subterfuge to undermine the free movement of goods.[4]

---

[4] Cf. Case 7/61: *Re Quantitative Restrictions on Imports of Pork Products into Italy*, 19 December 1961; [1962] C.M.L.R. 39; (1965), 4 C.M.L.R. 105; Case 48/71: *Re Export Tax on Art Treasures (No. 2) E.C. Commission v. Italy*, [1972] C.M.L.R. 699; 18 Rec. 529.

Of a more special nature are the restraints implied in arts. 223, 224 and 225 for the "protection of the essential interests or security of the member states which are concerned with the production of or trade in arms, munitions and war material" (art. 223). Whilst the states remain in control of their "essential interests or security", this being their sovereign prerogative, the Council has, in a secret list, enumerated the products involved. If the measures taken by states under arts. 223 and 224 (art. 224 is concerned with civil disturbances and war) distort conditions of competition in the Common Market, the Commission shall, together with the state concerned, look into the matter with a view to adapting the position to the rules of the Treaty (art. 225).

For similar reasons a member state may have to restrict the movement of persons, i.e. refuse admission to citizens of another member state, to known criminals, anarchists and organisers of various forms of disturbance, or expel persons of such dispositions. Article 56 (1) is relevant here because it enables a state to lay down rules for the control of entry and exit of foreign nationals on the ground of "public order, public safety and public health". It follows that a member state may rid itself of undesirable aliens whether they are layabouts,[5] unfit-for-work migrants,[6] persons convicted of crime,[7] carriers of certain disease or political agitators[8] as long as it can be shown that their conflict with the law of the host state is a result of "personal conduct" within the meaning of directive 64/221.

It is apposite to mention at this stage specific restraints of the economic freedom which may have an indirect effect upon the movement of goods, persons, services and capital. To further the objects of the Common Market, the Treaty chose a policy of competition on the assumption that sound competition can be secured by the elimination of restrictive practices and unfair exploitation of economic power. Thus certain practices, possible in the conditions of absolute freedom, have been expressly condemned and restrained because they are considered an abuse of the freedom. These include cartels and monopolies (arts. 85 and 86), dumping (art. 91), state aids (art. 92) and fiscal discrimination (art. 95).

---

[5] Case 427/66: *City of Wiesbaden v. Barulli*, [1968] C.M.L.R. 239.
[6] *Re Expulsion of an Italian National*, [1965] C.M.L.R. 285.
[7] *Re Expulsion of an Italian Worker*, [1965] C.M.L.R. 53.
[8] Case 36/75: *Rutili v. Minister of the Interior*, France, [1976] C.M.L.R. 140.

III POLICY OF THE COMMUNITY

(A) RULES ON COMPETITION (ARTICLES 85–90)

In the Preamble to the Treaty, "fair competition" is recognised as one of the tenets of the European Economic Community. However, although the Treaty purports to institute a "system ensuring that competition in the Common Market is not distorted" (art. 3 (*f*)), competition, fair or otherwise, has not been defined either by the Treaty or the Community Court.[9] It seems to be treated as a self-explanatory term.

The Treaty sets out to establish a system of sound competition based on three sets of rules: rules applying to undertakings, rules against dumping and rules governing state aids.

1 Rules Applying to Undertakings

In the first set of rules, arts. 85 and 86 form the backbone of rules addressed to "undertakings" in general; art. 90 is specifically concerned with "undertakings" of a public nature. Article 85 prohibits as "incompatible with the common market all agreements between undertakings, decisions by associations of undertakings and concerted practices which may affect trade between member states and which have as their object or effect the prevention, restriction or distortion of competition within the common market". This does not import prohibitions of *all* combinations or *cartels* but some of them. Article 86, on the other hand, prohibits "any abuse by one or more undertakings of a dominant position within the common market or in a substantial part of it as incompatible with the common market in so far as it may affect trade between member states". Here again, the "dominant position" *as such* is not condemned, but merely its *abuse*.

Since the Treaty contains merely the bare principles, art. 87 charges the Council with the task of elaborating detailed Community rules by means of directives or regulations to be designed with the assistance of the Commission and the Assembly. Articles 88 and 89 contain transitory provisions to be in force until the measures envisaged in art. 87 have been enacted. The Council has issued a number of Regulations of which Regulation No. 17[10] is the principal one.

The provisions of arts. 85 and 86 are addressed to "undertakings", both private and public. The term "undertakings"[11] has not been

---

[9] See the leading case, Cases 56 and 58/64: *Consten and Grundig* v. *E.E.C. Commission*, [1966] C.M.L.R. 418; 12 Rec. 429.

[10] Of 6 February 1962, J.O. 204/62 (see Campbell, *op cit.*, Vol. 2, pp. 165 *et seq.*), amended by Regulations Nos. 59 (J.O. 1655/62), 118 (J.O. 2696/63) and 2822 [1971] (J.O. L285).

[11] French: *entreprise;* German: *Unternehmen.*

defined in the Treaty, but art. 58 (2) gives a definition of "companies or firms" by enumeration earmarking these, however, as profit-making entities. We can say that by analogy, an "undertaking" means a legal entity, whether a physical person or corporation or an association of legal entities engaged in a profit-making activity. The exact legal status of the entity (which is a matter for the national law concerned) seems of secondary importance as long as there are certain characteristics corresponding to the concept of a natural or juristic person.[12] After all, the entity must have a certain standing under the Treaty which implies capacity to enter into legal agreements, to sue and be sued[13]; and to own property should a punitive sanction be imposed for contraventions of the rules of competition.

The Community Court on several occasions has had to determine the meaning of the term "undertaking" and has stated that "an enterprise is constituted by a unitary organisation combining personal, material and immaterial elements attached to an autonomous juristic subject and pursuing permanently a definite economic objective".[14] It follows that, for the purpose of arts. 85 and 86, an undertaking has to be endowed with a juristic and economic *autonomy* and has to be engaged in the production or distribution of goods or services. It may include a liberal profession within the scope of art. 60 of the Treaty,[15] but not purely personal pursuits.[16]

Unlike art. 80 of the E.C.S.C. Treaty, arts. 85 and 86 of the E.E.C. Treaty are not concerned with the geographical situation of the undertakings. They will come, therefore, under the rules even if situated in, or controlled from a third country.[17]

Some problems have arisen in connection with subsidiaries which, though having a separate legal status from their parent company (*juristic autonomy*), need not be independent (*economic autonomy*). If they are not independent, they cannot be regarded as economic entities in competition with their mother-company. This, in fact, was the conclusion reached by the Commission in *Re Christiani and*

---

[12] Cf. Cases 42 and 49/59: *SNUPAT* v. *High Authority*, [1963] C.M.L.R. 78; 7 Rec. 101, 151.
[13] E.E.C., art. 173 (2): "Any natural or legal person may . . . institute proceedings . . ."
[14] Case 19/61: *Mannesmann A.-G.* v. *High Authority*, 8 Rec. 675 at p. 705.
[15] Deringer, A., *Das Wett-Bewerbsrecht der Europäischen Wirtschafts-Gemeinschaft Wirtschaft and Wettbewerb*, No. 11 (1962), p. 794.
[16] *Id.*, *Les règles de la concurrence au sein de la C.E.E.*, No. 12 (1963), p. 37.
[17] *Re Grossfilex* (decision of the Commission), (1964) 3 C.M.L.Rev. 257; *Re Kodak* (decision of the Commission), 70/332/EEC, [1970] C.M.L.R. D19.

Nielsen,[18] where a Dutch subsidiary, wholly owned by its Danish mother-company, was held unable to engage in independent economic activity. Therefore, held the Commission, "the sharing of markets provided for in the agreement is nothing else but a distribution of tasks within a single unit". In *Re Kodak*[19] the Commission held that a European subsidiary of an American company, acting on instructions from the mother-company, could not behave independently. Therefore, the agreements in question (i.e. between the mother-company and its subsidiaries) could not restrict competition between the parties although they could do so between one of the parties and third parties.

In the light of the above, art. 85 does not apply if the undertakings concerned are in competition with each other or third parties.

Article 85 (1), as we have noted earlier, states what kind of agreements, decisions and concerted practices are prohibited. They must exhibit two characteristics, i.e. they must prevent, restrict or distort competition and they must affect trade between member states. A textual comparison with art. 3 (*f*) which states the general principle reveals that only the word "distort" occurs in both arts. 85 (1) and 3 (*f*). This is the key word and the words "prevent" and "restrict" seem purely subsidiary or explanatory of the key word. Thinking in terms of the English terminology "restrictive practices" may appear narrower than the inelegant phrase "distortive practices". As free competition is one of the underlying philosophies of the Common Market, anything affecting that freedom adversely would constitute "distortion" within the general meaning of the word. However, art. 85 enumerates agreements and practices which, *in particular*, are considered to have that effect, because they:

> "(*a*) directly or indirectly fix purchase or selling prices or any other trading conditions;
> (*b*) limit or control production, markets, technical developments or investments;
> (*c*) share markets or sources of supply;
> (*d*) apply dissimilar conditions to equivalent transactions with other trading parties, thereby placing them at a competitive disadvantage;
> (*e*) make the conclusion of contracts subject to acceptance by the other parties of supplementary obligations which, by their nature or according to commercial usage, have no connection with the subject of such contracts."

---

[18] 69/195/EEC, [1969] C.M.L.R. D36. See also *Re Cartel in Aniline Dyes*, 69/243/EEC, [1969] C.M.L.R. D23.
[19] *Re Kodak* (decision of the Commission), 70/332/EEC; [1970] C.M.L.R. D19.

The list is by no means exhaustive, it simply comprises the most usual types of agreement and practices likely to affect the freedom of competition.

Such agreements and practices have to "affect" trade between member states. Some problems of the interpretation of this word[20] have arisen in practice and Advocate-General Lagrange is on record as saying that one has to approach arts. 85 and 86 in their spirit rather than letter.[1]

The word "affect" has a wide meaning and, it seems, has to be interpreted extensively to give effect to the Community interest in free trade. Indeed, if the Community is to be seen in its federal concept, there is an analogy in this field to the "interstate commerce" of the United States of America[2]. An allusion to this position can be seen in the decision of the Community Court in the *Ulm* case[3]. Several cases decided by the municipal courts and the Community Court explain the position,[4] but the following two decisions of the Community Court provide a good illustration of the present judicial practice.

In the *Ulm* case[5] there was an exclusive dealing agreement between the German company *Machinenbau Ulm GmbH* and the French company *Technique Minière*, whereby the latter became exclusive dealer for the sale of machinery in France and the French overseas territories. The agreement provided that the French company would buy a specified number of levellers at a fixed price, maintain a stock of spare parts, organise repairs, look after the interests of the sellers and refuse to sell competing products unless authorised by the sellers. A dispute arose in France and the French company argued that the agreement was void under art. 85 (1) and (2) of the Treaty, the German company asserted the opposite. The Court of Appeal in Paris sought a preliminary ruling under art. 177. In his submissions, Advocate-General Roemer suggested a middle way between the Commission's view that a perceptible interference with competition must take place in order to bring the matter under the rubric of art. 85 (1) whilst the German

---

[20] French: *affecter*; German: *beeintrachtigen*; Italian: *prejudicare*; Dutch: *ongunstig beinvloeden;* Ellis, J.J.S., "L'interprétation du mot 'affecter' dans l'article 85, par. 1er, du traité de la C.E.E. par rapport aux mots 'empêcher', 'restreindre', ou 'fausser le jeu de la concurrence' " *Recueil Dalloz* (1963), Ch. XXIII, pp. 221 *et seq.*

[1] Case 13/61: In *Société Kledingverkoopbedrigf de Geus en Uitdenbogerd v. Societé de Droit Allemand Robert Bosch GmbH*, [1962] C.M.L.R. 1 at p. 23; 8 Rec. 89 at p. 139.

[2] *Les Novelles, op. cit.,* p. 825.

[3] Case 56/65: *Technique Minière v. Maschinenbau Ulm GmbH*, [1966] C.M.L.R. 357 at p. 375; 12 Rec. 337 at p. 359.

[4] See Campbell *op. cit.,* Vol. 1, pp. 161–164.

[5] [1966] C.M.L.R. 357.

company argued that the application of art. 85 (1) should be excluded "whenever the competition remains in existence notwithstanding the existence of the agreement". He submitted that "it would be excessive to place under the rigorous prohibition of article 85 (1) the slightest interference with competition . . . and only to grant exemption within the context of article 85 (3).[6] He referred to a risk of divergence in the municipal jurisdiction and concluded that national judges "must take account of the real or seriously likely repercussions of the agreement on the market and examine in the particular case whether it has interfered with competition to a noticeable extent and trade between member states been affected to a noticeable extent".[7]

In its judgment the Court examined the purpose of art. 85 (1) and held that an agreement must be considered in its economic context. If the object of the agreement cannot have "a sufficient degree of harmfulness with regard to competition" the Court should consider the possible effect of the agreement, i.e. whether it is likely to prevent, restrict or distort competition "to a noticeable extent". In order to determine the extent the court must take into consideration: (1) the nature and quantity of the product, which is the object of the agreement; (2) the position and size of the parties to the agreement in the particular market; (3) the isolated nature of the agreement or its position in a series of similar agreements; (4) the severity of the clauses which aim at the protection of the exclusive rights or on the possibilities left for other commercial currents upon the same products by means of re-exporting and parallel imports.[8]

In *Consten S.A. and Grundig-Verkaufs-GmbH* v. *E.E.C. Commission*[9] the German firm, Grundig, concluded with Consten, a French firm, an agreement for an indefinite period whereby Consten became the sole representative of Grundig for France, the Saar and Corsica. Consten undertook to buy Grundig products, carry out publicity, set up repairs workshops with sufficient spare parts and to undertake the guarantee and after-sales service. Consten also undertook not to sell similar products or to compete with Grundig. Grundig, on the other hand, undertook to retain sale rights and not to deliver, either directly or indirectly, to other persons within the area covered by the agreement. Grundig authorised Consten to use the name and emblem of Grundig as registered in Germany and other member states. Moreover Consten registered in France, in its own name the trade mark GINT (Grundig International).

---

[6] *Ibid.* at pp. 367, 368.
[7] *Ibid.* at p. 372.
[8] *Ibid.* at p. 376.
[9] Cases 56 and 58/64, [1966] C.M.L.R. 418; 8 Rec. 429.

Since April 1961, the company UNEF had bought Grundig products from German traders who delivered them in spite of the export prohibition imposed by Grundig, and UNEF resold these in France at more favourable prices than those charged by Consten. Consten brought two actions against UNEF, one for unfair competition and one for infringement of the GINT trade mark. The litigation in France led to a decision by the Commission,[10] which held the agreement contrary to art. 85 (1) and concluded that Grundig and Consten "are required to refrain from any measure tending to obstruct or impede the acquisition by third parties . . . of the products set out in the Contract, with a view to their resale in the contract territory".

Both firms brought an action in the Community Court for annulment of this decision and the Governments of Germany and Italy intervened.

The Advocate-General Roemer and the Court considered very fully the implication of the Consten-Grundig arrangement and the several points raised by it. The Advocate-General submitted *inter alia* that to judge the criterion of an agreement capable of affecting trade "account must be taken of the possible repercussions which it is reasonable to expect *on the market* (and this is so even though the Commission must be held correct in declaring that proof of an *increase* in international trade is not enough in itself to show that trade has not been affected)".[11]

The Court, considering the effect of the arrangement on interstate trade, held that:

"... it is necessary . . . to know whether the agreement is capable of endangering, either directly or indirectly, in fact or potentially, freedom of trade between member states in a direction, which could harm the attainment of the object of a single market between states. So the fact that an agreement favours an increase . . . in the volume of trade between states is not sufficient to exclude the ability of the agreement to 'affect' the trade . . . In the present case the contract . . ., on the one hand by preventing undertakings other than Consten importing Grundig products into France, and on the other hand by prohibiting Consten from re-exporting those products to other countries of the Common Market, indisputably affects trade between member states. These limitations on the freedom of trade, as well as those which might follow for third parties, from the registration in France . . . of the GINT trade mark, which Grundig places on all its products, suffice to satisfy the condition under discussion . . ."[12]

---

[10] *Re Grundig Agreement*, 64/599 E.E.C., [1964] C.M.L.R. 489; J.O. 2545/64.
[11] [1966] C.M.L.R. 418 at p. 434.
[12] *Ibid.* at p. 472.

2. *Exceptions to the Rule*

Agreements, decisions and concerted practices prohibited under art. 85 (1) may be saved from the sanctions consequent upon their incompatibility with the common market if they fulfil the conditions laid down in art. 85 (3). The power vested in the Commission appears to be discretionary as, according to art. 85 (3) of the Treaty, and art. 8 of Regulation No. 17, the provisions of art. 85 (1) *may be* declared inapplicable if an agreement, decision or concerted practice contrary to art. 85 (1) "contributes to improving the production or distribution of goods or to promoting technical or economic progress, while allowing consumers a fair share of the resulting benefit".

In addition to these positive criteria, there are also two negative criteria, i.e. that the agreement, decision or concerted practice does not impose on the undertakings concerned restrictions which are not indispensable to the attainment of these objectives"; or "afford such undertakings the possibility of eliminating competition in respect of a substantial part of the products in question".

The practical application of art. 85 puts the undertakings into one of the following positions:

(*a*) if the agreement, decision or practice falls under the rubric of art. 85 (1) and the exemption under art. 85 (3) cannot be claimed, the agreement, etc., must be either terminated[13] or suitably amended;

(*b*) if the agreement, etc., is of the kind envisaged by art. 85 (1) but can be exempted on one of the grounds enumerated in art. 85 (3) the firm cannot remain passive but must apply to the Commission for a declaration that art. 85 (1) is inapplicable. We should recall in this context the wording of art. 85 (3) which makes the exemption a matter of discretion. According to Regulation 17, art. 9 (1), the Commission is the only authority to exercise this power and the application has to be made according to set procedure;[14]

(*c*) if in doubt about the legal position, the firm should apply for "negative clearance" which the Commission will grant if, in the light of all the available information, the Commission is satisfied that there is no ground for intervention. Here again, the set procedure has to be followed.[15]

---

[13] If the agreement existed before 13 March 1962 the procedure laid down by Regulation 17, art. 7 applies.

[14] Regulation 17, art. 9 (1).

[15] Regulation 17, art. 2. On Negative Clearance, see Deringer, A., *The Competition Law of the European Economic Community* (1968), pp. 263 *et seq.*

The Commission will define the period in which its decision shall remain in force, but this can be extended upon further application.[16] The Commission is, of course, free to refuse an extension and it may attach conditions to its decision and stipulate that fines will be imposed in the event of non-compliance.[17]

The Commission may also revoke or amend its decision before the expiry of the specified period, since it is in the nature of the competition law that the position must be under review and changes may be necessary in the light of the general development of the economy and the interplay of the economic factors within the given sector of the economy.

However, the Commission cannot act entirely according to its discretion for it has to follow the guidelines provided in art. 8 (3) of Regulation 17. These are broad enough to give the Commission a considerable margin of appreciation. Accordingly, the Commission may revoke or amend its decision if:

(*a*) the situation has changed with regard to a factor essential to the granting of the decision;

(*b*) those concerned infringe a condition attached to the decision;

(*c*) the decision is based on inaccurate information or has been obtained by deceit;

(*d*) those concerned abuse the exemption from art. 85 (1) granted by the decision.

The decisions of the Commission are subject to appeal under art. 173 of the Treaty which, as we have observed earlier, gives to the Community Court the power of judicial review of the legality of the acts of the Council and the Commission. Apart from this general rule, there is a specific provision to that effect in Regulation 17 (art. 9 (1)).

The exemption or rather the "declaration that the prohibition mentioned in art. 85 (1) is inapplicable" (to use the Treaty terminology) by virtue of art. 85 (3) can be made in respect of either a particular agreement, decision and concerted practice[18] or a category of agreements, decisions or practices. Declarations with regard to the latter (i.e. block exemptions)[19] can only be made by regulations or directives issued in accordance with art. 87 by the Council on a proposal from

---

[16] Regulation 17, art. 8 (1).

[17] *Ibid.*, art. 8 (1) and art. 15 (2).

[18] Case 48/69: *Imperial Chemical Industries* v. *E.C. Commission*, [1972] C.M.L.R. 557; 18 Rec. 619; Case 56/65: *Technique Minière* v. *Maschinenbau Ulm GmbH*, [1966] C.M.L.R. 357; 12 Rec, 337; *Re the European Sugar Cartel*, 72/109/E.E.C., [1973] C.M.L.R. D65; (1973), J.O. L.140/17.

[19] Case 32/65: *Italy* v. *E.E.C. Council and Commission*, [1966] C.M.L.R. 39; 12 Rec. 563.

the Commission and on the advice of the Assembly. A regulation to that effect was adopted by the Council in 1965[20] but instead of specifying the block exemptions the Council delegated the power to do so to the Commission. The Commission, in turn, issued Regulation 67/67[1] which exempts the following agreements and practices between no more than two undertakings (art. 1):

(*a*) where one party undertakes to supply to the other only certain goods for resale within a defined area of the Common Market;[2] or

(*b*) where one party agrees with the other to purchase certain goods for resale only from him; or

(*c*) where the two undertakings have agreed as in (a) and (b) with each other in respect of exclusive supply and purchase for resale.

By art. 3 of the Regulation the exemption will not apply to:

(*a*) agreements between manufacturers of competing goods who arrange for exclusive dealing[3] in those goods;

(*b*) practices whereby the contracting parties make it difficult for intermediaries or consumers to obtain the goods to which the contract relates from other dealers within the Common Market especially where they use their industrial property rights for that purpose.

Originally art. 1 of Regulation 67/67 was to be in force until the end of 1972 but its life has been extended for another ten years.[4]

In 1971 another Council Regulation[5] enabled the Commission to grant exemptions from art. 85 (1) to agreements relating to standardisation, research, development and specialisation.[6] This power was embodied in Commission Regulation 2779/72.[7]

---

[20] 19/65, O.J. (Sp. Edn.), 1965–66, 35; J.O. 533/65.
[1] O.J. (Sp. Edn.), 1967, 10; J.O. 849/67.
[2] *Re Misal S.A.*, 72/397/E.E.C., [1973] C.M.L.R. D37; (1972), J.O. L267/20.
[3] *Ibid.*; *Re Optische Werke G. Rodenstock*, 72/396/E.E.C., [1973] C.M.L.R. D40; (1972) J.O. L 267/17; *Re The European Sugar Cartel, op. cit.*; *Technique Minière* v. *Maschinenbau Ulm GmbH, op. cit.*; Cases 56–58/64: *Costen S.A. and Grundig* v. *E.E.C. Commission*, [1966] C.M.L.R. 418; 8 Rec. 429; Case 23/67: *Brasserie de Haecht S.A.* v. *Wilkin*, [1968] C.M.L.R. 26; 13 Rec. 525; Case 1/71: *Cadillon S.A.* v. *Firma Höss Machinenbau K.G.*, [1971] C.M.L.R. 420; 17 Rec. 351.
[4] O.J. (Sp. Edn.), 1972; J.O. L276.
[5] 2821/71, O.J. (Sp. Edn.) 1971 (III); J.O. L285.
[6] *Re the Agreement of William Prym-Werke K.G.*, 73/323/E.E.C., [1973] C.M.L.R. D250; (1973) J.O. L296/24.
[7] O.J. (Sp. Edn.) 1972; J.O. L292.

Moreover the Commission issued four Communications on the subject of exclusive agency agreements,[8] patent licensing agreements,[9] co-operation between undertakings and agreements of minor importance[10] respectively. The system has become complex and highly technical with the Commission in the centre of power and the Community Court contributing to the development of the law not merely as a *court of law* but as a *court* of *economic law*.

3. *Abuse of a dominant position*

Whilst art. 85 prohibits certain arrangements which may affect interstate trade and are likely to distort free competition within the Community, art. 86 prohibits abuse of a "dominant position" which has a similar effect.

The notion of the "dominant position" is not alien to the Community, as it is well entrenched in the municipal laws of Germany, France, Belgium and the Netherlands.[11] However, it is not defined in the Treaty. A dominant position means, in effect, a monopoly within a sector of the economy. Like cartels, not all the monopolies are prohibited, for they may result from the lack of appreciable competition or from mergers which increase efficiency and do not eliminate competition. On the other hand, as suggested in the *Continental Can* case,[12] market shares in the range of 50% to 55% may constitute a dominant position—a picture somewhat different from a layman's concept of monopoly. "Abuse" is, therefore, the key word. Article 86 enumerates such abuses as consisting in:

"(a) directly or indirectly imposing unfair purchase or selling prices or other unfair trading conditions;

(b) limiting production, market or technical development to the prejudice of consumers;

(c) making the conclusion of contracts subject to acceptance by the other parties of supplementary obligations which, by their nature or according to commercial usage, have no connection with the subject of such contracts".

---

[8] See note 3; *Re Cimbel* 72/474/E.E.C., [1973] C.M.L.R. D167; (1972) J.O. L303/24; *Re Marketing of Potassium Salts*, 73/212/E.E.C., [1973] C.M.L.R. D219; (1973) J.O. L217/3.

[9] Case 24/67: *Parke, Davis & Co.* v. *Probel*, [1968] C.M.L.R. 47; 14 Rec. 81; Case 15/74: *Centrafarm B.V.* v. *Sterling Drug Co. Inc.*, [1974] 2 C.M.L.R. 480; Case 16/74: *Centrafarm B.V.* v. *Winthrop*, [1974] 2 C.M.L.R. 480.

[10] *Re Kodak*, 70/332/E.E.C., [1970] C.M.L.R. D19; J.O. L147; *Re Omega*, 70/488/E.E.C., [1970] C.M.L.R. D49; J.O. L242; cf. *Re Gas Water Heaters*, 73/232/E.E.C., [1973] C.M.L.R. D231; O.J. L217.

[11] *Les Novelles, op. cit.*, p. 837; see also art. 66 of the E.C.S.C. Treaty.

[12] *Re Continental Can Co. Inc.*, [1972] C.M.L.R. D11.

This list of abuses is illustrative rather than exhaustive. Indeed, in its First Report on the Competition Policy of the Community, the Commission gave notice that it intends to apply art. 86 to situations in which consumers are adversely affected as a result of the abuse of a dominant position.[13] In its Third[14] Report on Competition Policy the Commission addressed itself mainly to the problem of "industrial concentration as an obstacle to the open market and effective competition threatening the "unity of the Common Market". To combat this mischief the Commission drafted, in 1973,[15] a proposal for a regulation to provide control of concentrations between undertakings. If adopted the regulation would give the Commission (subject to review by the Community Court) jurisdiction to prevent concentrations (mergers) which it lacks at present unless one of the undertakings is already in breach of art. 86.

The judicial definition of "dominant position" is of a rather recent vintage. The Community Court was urged by the Italian Government to apply art. 86 in the *Grundig* case[16] and in *The Government of Italy* v. *Council and Commission of the E.E.C.*[17] but the Court refused the temptation, contending that "the possible application of art. 85 to a sole agency agreement should not be excluded merely because the grantor and the concessionaire are not competitors *inter se* and not on a footing of equality"[18].

An opportunity to define dominant position arose in the *Sirena* case,[19] where the Community Court held that an undertaking does not enjoy a dominant position by the sole fact of being able to prevent "third parties from selling in the territory of a member state products bearing the same trade-mark; moreover, since art. 86 requires that this position covers at least a 'substantial part' of the common market, it is necessary that it has the power of preventing effective competition within an important part of the market, considering also the possible existence and the position of producers or distributors of similar or substitute products . . ."

This passage was substantially repeated in the *D.G.G.* v. *Metro* case[20] where the Community Court held that a price maintenance scheme operating in Germany not only in respect of good produced

---

[13] *Fifth General Report*, 1971, pp. 99 and 103.
[14] Annexed to the *Seventh General Report*, 1974, pp. 28 *et seq.*
[15] 1973 O.J. C92.
[16] Cases 56 and 58/64, [1966] C.M.L.R. 418; 8 Rec. 429.
[17] Case 32/65, [1969] C.M.L.R. 39; 12 Rec. 563 at p. 592.
[18] [1966] C.M.L.R. 418 at p. 470; 12 Rec. 429 at p. 492.
[19] Case 40/70: *Sirena S.r.l.* v. *Eda S.r.l.*, [1971] C.M.L.R. 260 at p. 275; 17 Rec. 69 at p. 84.
[20] Case 78/70: *Deutsche Grammophon GmbH* v. *Metro-SB-Grossmärkte GmbH & Co. KG*, [1971] C.M.L.R. 631 at p. 658; 17 Rec. 487 at p. 501.

in Germany bearing the same trade mark but also imported from another member state coupled with the control of supplies constituted an infringement of art. 86.

In *Laboratorio Chimico*, etc.[1] the Community Court confirmed the finding of the Commission that a company incorporated in a third country but having a substantial presence in the E.E.C. and enjoying a world monopoly in the supply of certain raw materials used in the production of a drug did abuse its dominant position by refusing to supply the necessary material to one of its users in order to eliminate that user from competition in the manufacture of the drug.

In *B.R.T.* v. *N.V. Fonior*, etc.[2] the Belgian Association of Authors, Composers and Publishers, entrusted with the exploitation, administration and management of all copyrights and kindred rights of its members and associates was held to have abused its dominant position by imposing on its members obligations which encroached unfairly upon the freedom of exercising their rights.

The Continental Can Case,[3] on the other hand, involved take-overs of companies specialising in various kinds of containers and metal lids for glass jars. As a result of the concentration competition in the field would have been practically eliminated. The Commission, in order to prevent this, initiated a procedure under art. 3 (1) of Regulation 17/62 against Continental Can and its subsidiary Europemballage and ordered these companies to divest themselves of the newly acquired control over other companies. The companies applied for annulment of the Commission decision on the ground, *inter alia*, that the Commission was unable to show in which market or markets these companies were supposed to have abused their dominant position. However the Court clarified an important point saying that:

"... Article 86 is not only aimed at practices which may cause damage to consumers directly, but also at those which are detrimental to them through their impact on an effective competition structure, such as mentioned in article 3 (f) of the Treaty. Abuse may therefore occur if an undertaking in a dominant position strengthens such position in such a way that the degree of dominance reached substantially fetters competition, i.e. that only undertakings remain in the market whose behaviour depends on the dominant one ..."[4]

---

[1] Cases 6–7/73: *Istituto Chemioterapico Italiano SpA and Commercial Solvents Corporation* v. *E.C. Commission*, [1974] E.C.R. 223; [1974] C.M.L.R. 309.
[2] Case 127/73: *B.R.T.* v. *N.V. Fonior*; *SABAM* v. *N.V. Fornior*; *B.R.T.* v *SABAM* and *N.V. Fonior*, [1974] E.C.R. 51 and 313; [1974] 2 C.M.L.R. 238.
[3] Case 6/72: *Europemballage Corporation and Continental Can Company Inc.* v. *E.C. Commission*, [1973] E.C.R. 215.
[4] *Ibid.* at p. 245 (para. 26).

Improper practices under art. 86 arising from a dominant position have to affect the trade between member states. They do not come under the rubric if they merely affect the outside world including, presumably, the countries associated with the Community. In this sense and also in the sense of territorial dominance, the geographical area of the undertaking involved is an essential factor in the determination of the dominant position. At any rate, the territory of the common market or a substantial part of it has to be affected and this could be one state or several regions.

As stated in art. 86, abuse can be perpetrated by "one or more undertakings", that is to say entities within the meaning of art. 85. In the case of one such undertaking, the position seems clear, but plurality implies a consideration of the relationship between the undertakings concerned from the point of view of their relative autonomy. However, the form of the collective abuse is immaterial.

4. *Determination of Infringements of Articles 85 and 86*

The Commission, whilst exercising an exclusive authority in respect of exemptions under art. 85 (3) shares, in part, this power with the member states when dealing with infringements of art. 85 (1) and art. 86. In other words, the states may deal with the latter as long as the Commission has not initiated proceedings under arts. 2, 3 or 6 of Regulation 17.[5] This has caused some difficulty in practice and there is no uniformity in this matter in the Community.[6] The disadvantages of concurrent jurisdiction are quite apparent.

The question of the overlap between municipal law and Community Law was considered by the Community Court in *Walt Wilhelm* v. *Bundeskartellamt*[7] and it was held that, in principle, both could apply simultaneously subject to the underlying philosophy that Community Law has to be implemented by the member states and that in the case of conflict, Community Law prevails.

According to art. 3 of Regulation 17, infringements of arts. 85 and 86 are dealt with by Commission either *ex officio* or at the instance of interested parties. The former implies independent investigations of a case which comes to the notice of the Commission informally or in the course of the exercise of its duties as laid down by the Treaty (art. 155) and Regulation 17 (art. 11). The interested parties who put the Commission on enquiry can be either states or undertakings or individuals

---

[5] E.E.C., art. 88 and Regulation 17, art. 9.
[6] *Les Novelles, op. cit.*, p. 844.
[7] Case 14/68, [1969] C.M.L.R. 100; 15 Rec. 1; cf: "new commercial torts": *Application des Gaz S.A.* v. *Falks Veritas Ltd.*, [1974] 2 C.M.L.R. 75.

who have an interest in the matter as being directly or indirectly affected by the alleged infringement. The Commission will use its powers of investigation and follow the prescribed procedure in order to reach a decision.[8]

If an infringement has been proved the Commission will take appropriate steps to have the offending practice terminated, may make recommendations to the offending party and apply sanctions provided by the Treaty and the Regulation.

Before taking a decision, the Commission must give the parties concerned an opportunity to express their views, give them a hearing and, where it intends to issue negative clearance it must publish the essential content of the application or notification, inviting all interested third parties to submit their observations (Regulation 17, art. 19). Finally, it must consult the Consultative Committee on Cartels and Monopolies (Regulation 17, art. 10).

5. *Sanctions for Infringements*

In the case of infringement of art. 85 and art. 86, the Treaty provides for three different sanctions: nullity of the offending practice, fines and penalties.

According to art. 85 (2) any prohibited agreements or decisions are null and void by operation of law. This being a sanction *de plein droit*, there is no discretion in its application. The only exception applies to certain existing agreements, decisions and practices (Regulation 17, art. 7).

The question whether nullity taints all has been answered by the Community Court in the *Ulm*[9] and *Grundig*[10] cases in the negative. Only the bad elements are tainted with nullity and these can be severed from the sound body of the contract or decision.

According to art. 15 of Regulation 17, the Commission may inflict heavy fines upon undertakings guilty of an infringement of art. 85 (1) and art. 86, and also for the supply of false or misleading information, for submission in incomplete forms of the books or other documents required or for refusal to submit to an investigation. This sanction has no criminal or punitive character (art. 15 (4)).

---

[8] Examples: *Grundig* Case, 64/598/EEC, [1964] C.M.L.R. 489; J.O. 2545/64; *Re Quinine Cartel*, 69/240/EEC, [1969] C.M.L.R. D41; [1969] J.O. L129/5; *Re Continental Can Co. Inc.*, [1972] C.M.L.R. D11; [1972] J.O. L7.
[9] [1966] C.M.L.R. 357, at p. 376.
[10] [1966] C.M.L.R. 418, at p. 475.

The Commission has power to inflict penalties[11] under art. 16 of Regulation 17 in order to oblige the offenders to:

(a) put an end to an infringement of art. 85 or 86;
(b) discontinue any action prohibited under art. 8 (3) (c) of Regulation 17;[12]
(c) supply completely and truthfully any information requested under article 11 (5);[13]
(d) submit to any investigation ordered under the investing powers of the Commission.

The penalties, depending upon the severity of the infringement, range from fifty to one thousand units of account per day.

6. *Judicial Control*

The decisions of the Commission do not rank as *res judicata*. Indeed, decisions made under art. 85 (3) may be revoked or amended. However, decisions which impose a pecuniary obligation on persons other than states are enforceable by the authority of art. 192 (1) of the Treaty. The procedure of enforcement is left to the municipal law of the member states.

Decisions of the Commission are subject to judicial review either under proceedings for annulment[14] or the principle of plenary jurisdiction.[15] The former is governed by art. 173 (2) of the Treaty, the latter by art. 172. We should add that there is also a possibility of a *recours en carence* under art. 175 (3) which enables any aggrieved party to complain to the Community Court that the Commission has failed in its duty.[16]

It is clear that whilst the Commission acts in a quasi-judicial capacity, the Court, as the watchdog of legality within the Community, exercises an overall supervision to ensure compliance with Community Law.

7. *Rules Applying to Public Undertakings*

Modern states are involved in trade and industry through the instrumentality of public undertakings. The forms and the degree of government control of these bodies differ considerably as from country to country and so does the area of their operation. They have, however, a common tendency towards monopolies and in that sense enjoy a

---

[11] See *Laboratorio Chimico Farmaceutico Giorgio Zoja SpA.* v. *Commercial Solvents Corporation* 72/457/E.E.C., [1973] C.M.L.R. D50; (1972) J.O. L299/51.
[12] Reference to a decision obtained fraudulently or by false information.
[13] Reference to time-limit for the supply of information.
[14] See pp. 170 *et seq.* above.
[15] See pp. 183 *et seq.* above.
[16] See pp. 180 *et seq.* above.

"dominant position"—the very negation of the idea of the Common Market. The Treaty attacks the problem from two angles. By art. 37 the member states are committed to a policy of progressive adjustment of state monopolies "so as to ensure that . . . no discrimination regarding the conditions under which goods are procured and marketed exists between nationals of member states". Rather than "adjusting" their monopolies the Commission recommended[17] that states should bring about their abolition. Indeed a certain amount of progress has already been made in that direction though the end of state monopolies is not in sight yet. In the same spirit, the Act of Accession (art. 44) urges the new members to deal with their monopolies and authorities the Commission to make specific recommendations as from the beginning of 1973.

The second angle of attack is expressed in art. 90 of the Treaty, which is addressed specifically to two types of undertakings, viz. "public undertakings" and "undertakings to which member states grant special or exclusive rights"—a classification rather difficult to substantiate in the light of the law of the member states, but corresponding to art. 17 of the G.A.T.T. Accordingly, member states are obliged to "neither enact nor maintain in force any measure contrary to the Treaty, in particular article 7 and articles 85 to 94". The gist of the provisions as far as the rules of competition are concerned, is that a state enterprise is, in principle, reduced to an equal status with a private enterprise. This is not without significance in view of the role played by state enterprises in the national economy and the traditional (especially on the Continent) preference accorded to "public" interest. The privilege had to be sacrificed on the altar of the Common Market.

However, not all was sacrificed because art. 90 (2) provides an exception in the case of "undertakings entrusted with the operation of services of general economic interest[18] or having the character of a revenue-producing monopoly". In the first category one can place undertakings procuring public utility services such as water, gas, electricity or transport where the elements of manufacture and trade are, in a sense, in the background and "service" to the public at large (having incidentally an economic value) is the primary function of the undertaking. In the second category fall the revenue-raising undertakings engaged in the manufacture and marketing of certain products of everyday use (e.g. salt in Italy, matches in France and Italy) or luxuries (e.g. alcohol in France and Germany, tobacco in France and

---

[17] [1970] J.O. L6 and L31; see p. 292 above.
[18] See Case 10/71: *Ministère Public Luxembourgeois* v. *Müller*, [1971] E.C.R. 723; Case 127/73: *B.R.T.* v. *SABAM*, [1974] E.C.R. 313 at p. 320.

Italy).[19] However, even these exempted undertakings are subject to the Treaty, notably the rules of competition, in so far as the application of these rules does not obstruct the performance of their specific tasks. And for good measure the Treaty adds: "The development of trade must not be affected to such an extent as would be contrary to the interests of the Community."

(B) DUMPING (ARTICLE 91)

There is no definition of "dumping" in the Treaty. Dumping practices consist of exporting goods unsaleable at high prices in home markets to foreign markets for sale at low prices in order to capture a new market or maintain high prices in the home market. The Commission is authorised to send recommendations to perpetrators of dumping practices, but, if such practices continue, the "injured member state" may be authorised by the Commission to take protective measures under the control of the Commission.

"Boomerang" dumping, whereby products dumped from one member state to another shall be re-admitted to the country of origin free of duties and quantitative restrictions, is provided for in art. 91 (2).

In pursuance of the Treaty, the Council issued in 1968 detailed "Anti-dumping Regulations".[20]

(C) AIDS GRANTED BY STATES (ARTICLES 92–94)

Article 92 (1), in general terms, declares incompatible with the Common Market "any aid granted by a member state or through state resources in any form whatsoever which distorts or threatens to distort competition by favouring certain undertakings or the production of certain goods". We should note that not *all* the aids are prohibited and that the prohibition, applying to selected undertakings and goods, starts from the premise that such aids would affect trade between member states.

As an exception to the rule art. 92 (2) regards certain state aids compatible with the Common Market, viz. those which:

(*a*) have a social character granted to individual consumers without discrimination as to the origin of the products concerned;

(*b*) are intended to alleviate hardship resulting from natural disasters or other extraordinary events;

(*c*) are provided for certain regions of Germany to relieve the hardship resulting from the division of Germany.

---

[19] See p. 292 above.

[20] Regulation 459/68 of 5 April 1968; amended by Regulation 2011/73 of 24 July 1973; O.J. (1973) L206/3. See Case 9/72: *Georg Brunner, K.G., Münich* v. *Hauptzollamt Hof,* [1973] C.M.L.R. 931; 18 Rec. 961.

A further exception to the rule may, in appropriate circumstances, be considered in respect of:

(a) aids intended to promote the development of regions afflicted by low standard of living or serious unemployment;

(b) aids intended to promote an important European project or remedy a serious disturbance in the economy of a member state;

(c) aids intended to facilitate the development of certain economic activities or regions;

(d) aids specified by the Council on a proposal from the Commission.

In the spirit of art. 92 (3) the Commission saw no objection to various measures for the promotion of artisanship in Sicily,[1] modernisation of the French industry[2] or the development of the machine-tools sector in the United Kingdom[3] (subject to reservation regarding stockpiling), but objected to a Belgian project in aid of the production of tractors by the Ford Company.[4]

To examine the aid system and bring about the elimination of aids incompatible with the Common Market, arts. 93 and 94 define the powers of the Commission and the Council and determine the procedure to be followed in such cases. However, it should be borne in mind that these provisions are addressed to the member states and create no rights enforceable by individuals.[5]

As a by-product of the problem arising from state aids, certain Community policies begin to emerge. These are the regional policy[6] and industrial policy.[7]

(D) TAX PROVISIONS (ARTICLES 95–99)

It should be stated from the outset that uniform taxation throughout the Community is not the object of the Treaty, but a Common Market.

---

[1] *Les Novelles, op. cit.,* p. 865.
[2] *Re Aids to Textile Industry: France* v. *E.C. Commission,* 47/69, [1970] C.M.L.R. 351; 16 Rec. 487. *Les Novelles, op. cit.,* p. 865.
[3] *Europe,* No. 1946 (22–23 March 1976), p. 7.
[4] *Re Subsidies to Ford Tractor (Belgium) Ltd.,* 64/651/E.E.C., [1965] C.M.L.R. 32, J.O. 3257/64.
[5] Case 6/64: *Flaminio Costa* v. *ENEL,* [1964] C.M.L.R. 425; 10 Rec. 1141.
[6] *Third General Report,* 1969, p. 277. Draft regulations regarding regional developments: 1971, J.O. C90; 1973, Report on Regional Problems in the Enlarged Community, *Bulletin of the European Communities,* Supp. 8/73; Regional Development Fund, 1973, O.J. C86; *Bulletin of the European Communities,* 12/74; Council adoption of regulation to set up the Regional Fund on 18 March 1975. See *Eighth General Report* 1975, pp. 105 *et seq.*
[7] *Fourth General Report,* 1970, p. 167. Commission memorandum, 1970, *Fourth General Report,* para. 205; Commission communication to Council, 1973, *Bulletin of the European Communities,* 5/73, para. 1101 and Supp. 7/73; *Eighth General Report* 1975, pp. 169 *et seq.*

Therefore the tax provisions of the Treaty should be seen in that perspective, that is, as relative to the free movement of goods, persons, services and capital. In so far as taxation is relevant to these objectives, it is a proper concern of the Community. Thus, with the abolition of customs duties and charges having equivalent effect, it is necessary to ensure that internal taxation will not replace the abolished customs duties.

Article 95 (1), which the Community Court has held to be directly enforceable in the member states,[8] prohibits the imposition on the products of other member states of internal taxation of any kind in excess of the tax imposed upon similar domestic products. Article 95 (2) prohibits any internal taxation intended to afford protection to domestic products. Thus art. 95 imports the principle of non-discrimination into the field of taxation of imported goods. Taxes on such goods can be levied, but only in the same measure as the internal taxes on similar goods.

Article 95 is complemented by art. 96, which provides that "any refund of internal tax in respect of exported goods shall not exceed the internal tax imposed upon such goods whether directly or indirectly". "Direct" taxes are taxes charged upon finished products; "indirect" taxes are charges upon the product at the various stages of production. Article 96 covers, therefore, both eventualities. However, from a practical point of view, a line has to be drawn between taxes affecting the undertaking and those which fall upon the product. The Community Court has held that a refund of taxes which are charged to the undertaking as a taxable entity to encourage exports was inconsistent with art. 96.[9] Should this not be so, the undertaking would enjoy an advantage over another exporter and this, in turn, would affect free competition and trade between member states. This case is also important in so far as it provided an opportunity for an examination of tax refunds. The Community Court found the Italian system incompatible with the Treaty, especially that customs duties were included in the computation of the refunds.[10]

Article 97, which is not directly enforceable,[11] purports to bring about a simplification of the multi-stage turnover tax by introducing a single tax on imports according to products or groups of products. By the same token, tax refunds on exports should be subject to uniform

---

[8] Case 57/65: *Lütticke* v. *Hauptzollamt Sarrelouis*, 16 June 1966; [1971] C.M.L.R. 674; 12 Rec. 293.

[9] Case 45/64: *Re Drawback on Italian Machine Parts, E.E.C. Commission* v. *Italy*, 1 December 1965; [1966] C.M.L.R. 97; 11 Rec. 1057.

[10] Case 45/65: *E.E.C. Commission* v. *Italy*, 15 Rec. 433.

[11] Case 28/67: *Molkerei-Zentrale Westfalen-Lippe GmbH* v. *Hauptzollamt Paderborn*, [1968] C.M.L.R. 187 at p. 221; 14 Rec. 211 at p. 236.

average rates. In order to ensure that there is no infringement of arts. 95 and 96, the Commission is authorised to issue directives or decisions to the state concerned (art. 97). In pursuance of this provision, the Council issued a directive to provide a uniform system of calculating the average rates.[12]

Article 98 purports to control charges "other than turnover taxes, excise duties and other forms of indirect taxation". More specifically, it prohibits exemptions and repayments in respect of exports and the imposition of countervailing duties in respect of imports from member states, unless approved by the Commission.

Taking arts. 95–98 together, we can see the overall concern with the complexities of the national tax systems and the desire to remove the obstacles to free movement of goods concealed in the technicalities of fiscal policies designed to promote export of national products and restrict import of foreign goods on a competitive basis of equality. Rationalisation of the tax provisions necessitates a Community policy in this respect. Since, at this stage, a uniform tax system appears unattainable, a modicum of order appears possible through harmonisation of national tax systems.

A general scheme for the harmonisation of tax systems is provided in art. 99, which enjoins the Commission to study the problem and, in the interests of the Community, find ways and means of harmonising the national legislation governing "turnover taxes, excise duties and other forms of indirect taxation". Harmonisation does not mean uniformity, but a tolerable state of affairs which permits diversity within the ideal of the Common Market.

In this sense, the Council, on the proposals of the Commission, issued a number of directives. The most important are the two directives of 1967 intended to introduce a common value added tax system (V.A.T.).[13] The first directive consists of a general outline of the principles, definition of the value added tax and the time-table according to which it should become part of a reformed tax system of the member states. The second directive elaborates the details and the guidelines of its application. Whilst members are committed to apply the principles, they are free to determine the rates of tax and exceptions.

The value added tax system was to be introduced by 1 January 1970, but the deadline was later extended to 1 July 1972. It has been implemented by all the member states though Italy experienced considerable difficulties when introducing tax reforms. The value added tax system will, of course, be introduced by the new members of the Community.

---

[12] Directive 68/221, 30 April 1968; O.J. (Sp. Edn.), 1968 (I.) 114; J.O. L 115.
[13] 11 April 1967, and 14 April 1967; J.O. No. 71, pp. 1301 and 1303.

The system, based on the French *taxe sur la valeur ajoutée*[14] is said to have distinctive advantages over the various types of turnover tax in so far as it is capable of a relatively high yield, should be simple to administer in the international setting of the Community, and should have little effect on competition. However, perhaps the most important aspect of the tax reform is the movement towards elimination of tax frontiers and liberalisation of international trade.

The process of the harmonisation of taxes continues under the guidance of the Community. In 1969, the Council issued a directive to regulate indirect taxes on the raising of capital[15] and the Commission worked out proposals for directives on company taxation. Quite apart from sorting out the taxation problems of the Community, in the spirit of the free movement of goods, persons and services, the process of approximation has an important contribution to make towards economic integration and monetary union within the Community.

(E) APPROXIMATION OF LAWS (ARTICLES 100–102)

1. *General Principles*

It is considered that the approximation of laws of the member states is necessary for the proper functioning of the Common Market (E.E.C. Treaty, art. 3 (*h*)). This we have already observed since the implementation of the economic freedoms of the Community depends on the degree of harmonisation of national laws affecting trade and the movement of persons and goods. Approximation (*rapprochement, Angleichung*) represents, by definition, a more intense process of integration than harmonisation. The problem was well understood from the inception of the Community and the difficulties of changing laws, like changing the ways of life or forsaking the national heritage, were never underestimated. In spite of the lack of spectacular progress, there is a Community policy in this field and there is no lack of ideas or projects. The aims were thus summarised by the Commission:[16]

> "the object is not the creation of a vast European law of a unique character, but of a system of a federal type which would draw its force and authority of the conviction of history and at the same time of the plurality of the living nature of the laws of the member states, of the common juristic heritage and of the necessity of an economic concentration".

---

[14] Egret, G., *La T.V.A. française* (1963).
[15] 17 July 1969, 69/335; J.O. L249.
[16] *Eighth General Report of the E.E.C.*, 1965, para. 83.

Community law, because of its nature and origin, should reflect the legal philosophy of the member states and their experience. It should, at the same time, contribute towards political and economic integration by building up a federal system of law. In this respect, the objectives are limited for they are centred, at this stage, on the concept of the common market. In other words the mechanism of harmonisation must be used for the removal of obstacles to the establishment of the common market. Whilst there is a challenge to comparative lawyers at the national and Community level, the Community organs, especially the Commission being entrusted with the task, must adopt a functional approach.

The guidelines can be found in arts. 100–102 of the Treaty. Article 100 refers to "such provisions laid down by law, regulation or administrative action . . . as directly affect the establishment or functioning of the common market". This is both a programme and its limitation. Moreover, laws are to be enacted by the member states on the basis of directives[17] issued according to the Community procedures. The power of the Council to issue such directives under art. 100 is limited because unanimity is required and so a member state can veto the proposals of the Commission. Where, however, the Commission finds a distortion of the conditions of competition arising from the laws of the offending state, the Commission shall, through consultation, eliminate such distortion, but should this effort fail, the Council may be called in (art. 101). The Council must be unanimous during the first stage but thereafter may issue appropriate directives by a qualified majority. Where there is reason to fear that a state will create distortions through taking certain legislative or administrative measures, the Commission alone is empowered to act and shall issue appropriate recommendations (art. 102). The sanction for ignoring the recommendation is that the other member states may disregard art. 101 in relation to the offending state.

It appears that the above provisions proceed from the principle of the sovereign law-making power of the member states modified by the Treaty obligation. Under arts. 101–102, this obligation is of a negative character, for it means that the member states must refrain from passing laws or adopting administrative measures contrary to the Treaty. The letter and spirit of the Treaty require a certain degree of co-operation and a Community approach to matters of common concern. Where this is lacking, the Community organs shall intervene,

---

[17] See Case 32/74: *Firma Friedrich Haaga GmbH* v. *Rechtspfleger*, [1975] C.M.L.R. 32, in which for the first time the Court had to interpret an article in a directive (i.e. 68/151 of 9 March 1968 (O.J. L65)) on harmonisation of company law.

not to legislate for the member states as this would mean usurpation of their sovereign power, but to use their authority in order to make the defaulting state mend its ways. In this way, the Community organs can only indirectly bring about the approximation of national laws.

These are the general principles of approximation. By contrast, in some areas, as we have already observed, the Treaty contains specific directions for the approximation of the national laws, e.g. in the field of customs (art. 27), movement of workers (art. 49 (*b*)), establishment (art. 54 (3) (*g*)), liberal professions (art. 57 (1)), taxation (art. 99) and export aids (art. 112). Also, in these areas, the appropriate procedures have to be observed.

Finally, the Council (art. 145) and the Commission (art. 155) may act in accordance with the general provisions of the Treaty to achieve approximation of laws.

2. *The Area of Approximation*

At first sight, arts. 100–102 may appear rather narrow in scope, but, if one considers that they are concerned not only with the "establishment", but also with the "functioning" of the Common Market, the scope widens considerably and is as wide as the concept of the Common Market itself. The same applies to the mechanism of approximation. Although these articles are framed to emphasise the sovereign law-making power of the member states and, if interpreted narrowly, arts. 101 and 102 would suggest that the Community organs will intervene only in a remedial capacity, there is ample authority for positive initiatives. These initiatives have resulted in general programmes of legislation[18] concerning the freedom of movement of persons, establishment, services and recognition of professional qualifications, as well as many directives ranging from industrial production, agriculture, trade, insurance, banking, transport and food, to motor vehicles, measuring instruments, pipe-lines and crystal glass. Recent directives concern public work contracts,[19] whilst the work on the European Patent,[20] Environmental Protection,[1] Criminal Law relating to Economic Transactions and European Officials continues.

---

[18] 18 December 1961, [1962] J.O. 36 *et seq.*; for progress see annual General Reports.

[19] O.J. (Sp. Edn.) 1971 (II), 678 and 682; J.O. L185; O.J. (Sp. Edn.) 1972 (III), 823; J.O. L176, etc.

[20] See European Patent Convention, 1975, J.O. L19 of 26 January 1976.

[1] *Seventh General Report*, 1974, para. 258; *Bulletin of the European Communities*, 11/74, paras. 1203 and 2115; *Bulletin of the European Communities*, 7/8/75, paras. 3239–2243; *Eighth General Report*, 1975, paras. 248–254; *Bulletin of the European Communities*, 1/76, paras. 2219 and 2220.

However, the most challenging is the problem of approximation of Company Law, which has been lingering for years and which has inspired a great deal of learned writing.[2] It is apposite to mention in this connection the approximation of laws through international conventions under art. 220. This article enumerates areas in which the law ought to be regulated by multilateral conventions, viz. protection of nationals of the member states in the territory of another state, abolition of double taxation, recognition of firms or companies and the reciprocal recognition and enforcement of judgments and arbitral awards. So far, two conventions have materialised: the Convention on the Mutual Recognition of Companies and Bodies Corporate, signed on 29 February 1969, and the Convention on Jurisdiction and the Enforcement of Civil and Commercial Judgments, signed on 27 September 1969. The latter came into force in the original six member states on 1 February 1973. The potential for the approximation of national laws within the Community is quite considerable in view of the ever closer ties between the nations forming the Community and the unprecedented, in modern times, opportunities for travel and settlement. The Treaty is hardly concerned with the problems governed by the rules of the Conflict of Laws, and, it appears, these problems can better be solved by approximation of the law than by codification of Private International Law.

(F) ECONOMIC POLICY (ARTICLES 103–109)

The economic policy of the Community, being based on the Treaty, has a legal foundation in the provisions of the Treaty. Article 3 (9) refers to the application of procedures by which the economic policies of member states can be co-ordinated and disequilibria in their balances of payment remedied and arts. 103–116 deal in some detail with three areas falling under the rubric of economic policy, viz. conjunctural policy, balance of payments and commercial policy.

1. *Conjunctural Policy*

As the economy of a country or a group of countries (e.g. the European Community) is subject to fluctuations resulting in booms and depressions, it was thought necessary to deal with the problem on a community basis. In other words, there ought to be a community "conjunctural policy" (*politique de conjoncture, Konjungturpolitik*). Accordingly, art. 103 is addressed to the member states who should

---

[2] *L'harmonisation dans les communautés*, Editions de l'Institut d'Etudes Européennes Bruxelles (1968); Bärmann, J., *Europäische Integration im Gesellschaftsrecht* (1970); Stein, E., *Harmonisation of European Company Laws* (1971).

consult with each other and the Commission in matters affecting economic trends and should regard these problems as Community problems.

In order to assist the member states and the Community, a Committee on Policy relating to Economic Trends has been set up and this Committee meets regularly and acts generally in an advisory capacity.

If it is necessary to take measures, the Council may, on a proposal from the Commission, unanimously decide upon the action to be taken. The Council has also power to issue directives, but for these a qualified majority is sufficient. In several cases before the German courts the validity of Council Regulation 974/71[3] on measures of conjunctural policy to be taken in agriculture as a result of the fluctuation of the currency values in certain member states, and of a number of other Commission Implementing Regulations fixing compensatory rates, was questioned. The Community Court, requested for rulings under art. 177, made several decisions[4] which appear to go beyond the actual scope of the questions involved but contribute to the consideration of the legal aspects of conjunctural policy.

As regards the disputed legal basis of Regulation 974/71, the Court confirmed that the measures were of a conjunctural nature as they were meant to prevent the breakdown of the intervention price system and support the trade in agricultural products. The Court held that the powers conferred upon the Commission in respect of the agricultural policy included the authority to take specific short-term economic measures, so that the Council should have acted under arts. 40 and 43. Had it not been for the urgent need to act and the absence of adequate forecasts, recourse to art. 103 would not have been justified.

It seems that, in the field of short term economic policies, the member states are left to their own devices and, unlike in the field of agriculture, there is, as yet, no Community conjunctural policy.

2. *Balance of Payments*

The realisation that balance of payments problems have a chain reaction and may endanger the working of the Common Market is behind the provisions of the Treaty. Article 104 proceeds from the principle that the member states are responsible for their own balance

---

[3] 1971, O.J. L106.
[4] Case 5/73: *Balkan-Import-Export* v. *Hauptzollamt Berlin-Packhof*, [1973] E.C.R. 1091; Case 9/73: *Schlüter* v. *Hauptzollamt Lörrach*, [1973] E.C.R. 1135; case 10/73: *Rewe Zentrale* v. *Hauptzollamt Kehl*, [1973] E.C.R. 1175; Case 154/73: *Becker* v. *Hauptzollamt Emden*, [1974] E.C.R. 19.

of payments, whilst maintaining a high level of employment and the stability of prices. In order to achieve these objectives, art. 105 counsels co-ordination of the economic policies of the member states and sets up the appropriate machinery. Accordingly, an advisory and co-ordinating body has been established. This is the Monetary Committee consisting of representatives of the governments and central banks of the member states. Its function is "to keep under review the monetary and financial situation of the member states and of the Community and the general payments system of the member states and to report regularly thereon to the Council and the Commission" (art. 105 (2)). It can also deliver opinions at the request of the Council or the Commission or on its own initiative.

Article 106 gives effect to the basic policies of the Common Market as it obliges the member states to remove restrictions on the outflow of currency in connection with the movement of goods, persons, services and capital. Moreover, the member states undertake to refrain from introducing as between themselves any new restrictions on transfers of currency in respect of the invisible transactions listed in Annexe III to the Treaty[5].

Article 107 refers to the rates of exchange which each member state is free to determine for its own currency bearing in mind the interest of the Community and the objectives of art. 104. Should an alteration of its rate of exchange result in distortion of the conditions of competition, the Commission may step in and, after consulting the Monetary Committee, authorise other member states to take appropriate measures.

Article 108 purports to deal with balance of payments difficulties which may endanger the economy of a member state. The underlying philosophy is that no member of the Community should suffer and, in order to alleviate the resulting hardship, the Commission ought to assist the member facing such difficulties. In particular, the Commission is bound to investigate the problem and recommend appropriate measures. If necessary, the Council may authorise mutual assistance recommended by the Commission but, should this prove insufficient, the state concerned may be authorised to take protective measures. Such measures may, in accordance with art. 226, derogate from the Treaty obligations, but should cease when no longer necessary.

---

[5] The list comprises some 60 items including earnings from transport, warehousing, repairs, technical assistance relating to the production and distribution of goods, commissions, travel and tourism, films, repair and maintenance of property, customs duties and taxes, fines, salaries and wages, dividends, interest, rents, royalties, pensions, maintenance, inheritances and dowries.

The French crisis of 1968 provides an illustration of the practical application of art. 108. The Commission investigated the difficulties facing the French economy at that time and recommended that mutual assistance be granted. The Council issued a directive to that effect[6] and the Commission decided that France may adopt emergency measures including exchange controls of certain capital transactions, restrictions of certain imports and aid to exports.[7]

Finally, art. 109 authorises the member states to take provisional emergency measures when faced with a sudden crisis in the balance of payments. These measures must take into consideration, possible repercussions within the Community, they should be appropriate to the emergency and the least harmful to the common market. The Commission and the other member states must be informed. The Commission may then recommend action under art. 108 and the Council may decide, by a qualified majority, that the protective measures be amended, suspended or terminated.

These procedures were in 1974 applied in respect of Italy in order to assist that country to solve its financial difficulties. The Commission authorised[8] Italy to take protective measures, including restrictions on the supply of moneys and agreed that aid should be provided for but the Council opposed the latter.

(G) COMMERCIAL POLICY (ARTICLES 110–116)

A common commercial policy, as one of the basic principles of the Common Market (art. 3 (*b*)) is the necessary corollary to the establishment of a common customs tariff. It means, in effect, a common attitude to the outside world, the Community acting virtually, as one commercial unit. Article 111 regulates the position during the period of transition providing for a co-ordination of the commercial relations of the member states with third countries. Article 112 is concerned with export aids to third countries and art. 113 regulates the position after the expiry of the period of transition. Article 114 connects art. 111 (2) and art. 113, providing that customs agreements and commercial treaties with third countries shall be concluded by the Council on behalf of the Community, acting unanimously during the first two stages and thereafter by qualified majority. Article 115 deals with the difficulties individual states may experience as a result of the common commercial policy and authorises such states to take protective

---

[6] On 20 July 1968, [1968] J.O. L189.
[7] See *Second General Report*, 1968, p. 110.
[8] (1974) O.J. L152.

measures under the guidance of the Commission. During the period of transition, in emergency situations, states may take unilateral measures but have to notify these to the other member states and the Commission. In chosing these measures, they must cause least disturbance to the operation of the Common Market. Finally, art. 116, with reference to the end of the transitional period, brings the principle of co-ordination and common commercial policy into operation with regard to the participation of the states in international organisations of an economic character.

As a result of the above provisions, the member states surrender a certain amount of their treaty making power and the Community, at the same time, assumes a corresponding responsibility in the field of commercial relations regulated by the E.E.C. Treaty. Whilst the details of the common commercial policy remain yet to be elaborated, certain developments[9] have taken place and proposals for certain import regulations are currently under consideration. The Communities, as we have noted earlier,[10] have already entered into a number of external trade agreements and associations.

(H) SOCIAL POLICY (ARTICLES 117–128)

1. *Social Provisions*

In the blueprint of the Community one can see a close connection between economics and social problems expressed in the general principles of the Treaty (arts. 2 and 3 (i)) and the specific "social provisions". In this way, the Community law of the economy has been linked with social policy.

It seems, at this stage, premature to speak of a "Social Law" of the Community, as art. 117 merely expresses an agreement between the member states "upon the need to promote improved working conditions and an improved standard of living for workers" and their belief that "such a development will ensue not only from the functioning of the Common Market, which will favour the harmonisation of social systems, but also from the procedures provided for in this Treaty and from the approximation of provisions laid down by law, regulation or administrative action". A great deal of effort, both domestically and at the Community level will be required to implement this programme.

Whilst social services and welfare state benefits are essentially a matter for the domestic concern of the member states, the Community

---

[9] E.g. in the field of dumping practices, quantitative quotas, import of steel and agricultural and other products.
[10] See pp. 37 *et seq.*, above.

is also interested not only because of its professed aim of a "better Europe", but more practically because of the social problems consequent upon the movement of labour.[11] Hence the special concern with "workers". As the scope and standards of the social security systems differ as from country to country, it is essential to improve some and harmonise all into a system where the migrant worker and his family would find an adequate level of protection whether at home or in another member state. The long term policy of the Community seems to have this object in mind.

It follows that, in accordance with the general pattern of the Treaty, the Commission, assisted by the Economic and Social Committee must address itself to certain specific tasks enumerated in art. 118, viz. employment, labour law and working conditions, basic and vocational training, social security, prevention of occupational accidents and diseases, occupational hygiene, the right of association and collective bargaining between employers and workers. This may be the broad outline of the European Social Law.[12]

Whilst it may be taken for granted that the member states are, within the general terms of the Treaty, committed to work towards an improvement of their social security system art. 119 specifically enjoins the member states to "ensure and maintain the application of the principle that men and women shall receive equal pay for equal work".[13] This reflects the trend towards the equality of the sexes and the specific recommendations of the Convention of 24 June 1951 sponsored by the International Labour Organisation.

Article 120 is concerned with the maintenance of the existing equivalence between paid holiday schemes. Articles 121 and 122 are concerned with the function of the Council and Commission, and with studies and reports on social developments within the Community.

2. *The European Social Fund*

The Treaty sets up a European Social Fund to be administered by a Committee under the supervision of the Commission and governed by its own statute.[14] The title is rather misleading because the scope of the Fund is limited to "the task of rendering the employment of workers easier and of increasing the geographical and occupational mobility

---

[11] See pp. 304 *et seq.*

[12] See Lyon-Caen, G., *Droit Social European* (1969).

[13] Council directive 75/117 of 10 February 1975 Cf. Case 80/70: *Gabrielle Defrenne* v. *Belgian State*, [1974] C.M.L.R. 494 at p. 509; but see also Case 43/75, *Times*, 9 April 1976.

[14] For the Statute, see J.O. 1201/60, 31 August 1960.

within the Community" (art. 123). The real purpose is to provide
financial assistance, that is, to provide fifty per cent of the expenditure
incurred by a state or a body governed by public law for the purpose of
re-employment of workers or relief of temporary unemployment resulting from the conversion of an undertaking to another type of production (art. 125 (1)).

The Fund has been reformed recently[15] in accordance with art. 126
to undertake two different functions, i.e. to implement the Community
policies and to deal with difficulties which impede the smooth working
of the Common Market.

Article 128 gives the Council authority to lay down general principles
for implementing a common vocational training policy capable of contributing to the harmonious development both of the national economies
and the Common Market.[16]

Clearly, the rudiments of social policy and its implementation are
too fragmentary to provide more than a modest beginning of what may
become in the future a body of rules complementary to the economic
and commercial policies of the Community.

(K) THE E.E.C. LAW OF THE ECONOMY

The brief analysis of the relevant provisions of the Treaty projects
a concept of the Law of Economy of the Community. In accordance
with the legislative techniques developed in the Civil Law countries,
the Treaty codifies the basic principles (i.e. the economic freedoms)
of the Common Market, outlines the essential policies, sets up institutions and provides machinery for the implementation of the design.
The law is used as an instrument of definition and enforcement.

As blueprints go, the design is clear but not as comprehensive as it
could be, whilst the social aspects of this *Economic Community* are
traced in rather pale colours. This is understandable in view of the
responsibilities of the member states for their social services and it
seems sufficient, at this stage, to emphasise the link between the
economy and social and human problems.

Being only a reflection of a federal concept, the Community Law of
the Economy has to be accommodated to the role of the sovereign
state in the Community. Therefore, within the *dirigist* concept of the
economy, the Treaty grants the bureaucratic organs of the Community

---

[15] [1971] J.O. L28.
[16] Cf. "General Guidelines for a Community-level Programme on Vocational
Training", J.O. C81, 12 August 1971.

only as much authority as is necessary to organise and harmonise the national economic systems by advice and persuasion rather than by the exercise of power. Where a decision is thought necessary, the Community organs are equipped with the requisite power backed by the corresponding treaty obligation undertaken by the member states.

The strengthening of the Community institutions would, it seems bring a greater cohesion of the national economic systems and a more intensive degree of uniformity at the expense of the member states. Such a development is undoubtedly linked with the future evolution of the Community.

Appendix

LISTS OF FURTHER READING

CHAPTER 1

ANDERSON, S. V., *The Nordic Council. A Study of Scandinavian Regionalism* (1967)

AUBREY, H. G., *Atlantic Economic Cooperation. The Case of the OECD* (1967)

CAMPS, M., *Britain and the European Communities, 1955-63* (1964)

ESMAN, J., & CHEEVER, D. S., *The Common Aid Effort. The development assistance activities of the Organisation for Economic Co-operation and Development* (1967)

GALTUNG, J., *The European Community: A Superpower in the Making* (1973)

GLADWYN, Lord, *The European Idea* (1966)

GRZYBOWSKI, K., *The Socialist Commonwealth of Nations* (1964)

JACOBS, F. G., *The European Convention on Human Rights* (1975)

JOHN, I. G. (editor), *E.E.C. Policy towards Eastern Europe* (1975)

KARELLE, J., & DE KEMMETER, F., *Le Benelux: Textes Officiels* (1961)

KITZINGER, U., *Diplomacy and Persuasion* (1973)

KITZINGER, U., *The European Common Market and Community* (1967)

KITZINGER, U., *The Second Try* (1968)

LAMBRINIDIS, J. S., *The Structure, Function and Law of a Free Trade Area: The European Free Trade Association* (1965)

LORETTE, L. DE S., *Le Marché Commun* (1961)

Manual of the Council of Europe, Structures, Functions and Achievements (1970)

PALMER, M., & LAMBERT, J., et al., *European Unity, A Survey of the European Organisations* (1968)

PRYCE, R., *The Politics of the European Community* (1973)

RANSOM, C., *The European Community and Eastern Europe* (1973)

ROBERTSON, A. H., *European Institutions, Co-operation, Integration, Unification* (Third Edn. 1973)

SPINELLI, A., *The European Adventure* (1972)
STEIN, E., & HAY, P. (editors), *Cases and Materials on the Law and Institutions of the Atlantic Area*, 2 vols. (1963)
The European Free Trade Association and the Crisis of European Integration. An aspect of the Atlantic crisis? (1965)
TORELLI, M., *Great Britain and the Europe of the Six: the Failure of Negotiations* (1969)
URWIN, D. W., *Western Europe Since 1945* (1968)

CHAPTER 2

ALTING VON GEUSAU, F. A. M., *European Organisations and Foreign Relations of States*, 2nd Edn. (1964)
ANANIADES, L, C., *L'association aux Communautés européennes* (1967)
AXLINE, A. W., *European Community Law and Organisational Development* (1968)
BATHURST, M., *et al.* (editors), *Legal Problems of an Enlarged European Community* (1972), Part IV
BRUGMANS, H., *et al.*, *The External Economic Policy of the Enlarged Community* (1973)
CARDIS, F., *Fédéralisme et intégration européene* (1963)
HALLSTEIN, W., *Europe in the Making* (1972)
HAY, P., *Federalism and Supranational Organisations* (1965)
HENIG, S., *External Relations of the European Community* (1971)
L'association à la Communauté économique européene. Aspects juridiques, Bruxelles, Institut d'études européennes (1970)
Les aspects juridiques du Marché commun, Collection scientifique de la Faculté de Droit de l'Université de Liège (1958)
Les Communautés européennes et les relations Est-Ouest, Colloque des 31 mars-1er avril, 1966 (1967)
NERI, S., *De la nature juridique des Communautés européennes* (1965)
PUISSOCHET, J.-P., *The Enlargement of the European Communities: A Commentary on the Accession of Denmark, Ireland and the United Kingdom* (1975)
RAUX, J., *Les relations extérieures de la CEE* (1966)
SCHONFIELD, A., *Europe: Journey to an Unknown Destination* (1973)
WALL, E., *Europe: Unification and Law* (1969)
WEIL, G. L., *A Foreign Policy for Europe?* (1970)

ALTING VON GEUSAU, F. A. M., "The External Representation of Plural Interests" (1967), *Journal of Common Market Studies* 426

COSTONIS, J. J., "Treaty making power of the E.E.C.", [1967] *European Yearbook*, 31

RAUX, J. and FLAESCH-MOUGIN, C., "Les accords externes de la C.E.E." (1975), *Rev. Trim. de Droit Européen*, 227.

CHAPTER 3

AKEHURST, M., "Preparing the authentic text of the E.E.C. Treaty", in Wortley, B. (editor), *An Introduction to the Law of the E.E.C.* (1972), at p. 20

L'Avocat à l'heure du Marché Commun, Rouen, Colloque International (1972)

BRINKHORST, L. J., & MITCHELL, J. D. B., *European Law and Institutions* (1969)

DAGTOGLOU, P. D. (editor), *Basic Problems of the European Community* (1975)

DONNER, A. M., *The Role of the Lawyer in the European Community* (1968)

LECOURT, R., *Le juge devant le Marché Commun* (1970)

MITCHELL, J. D. B., "Lawyers and the European Communities" (1971), 22 N.I.L.Q. 149

PESCATORE, P., *The Law of Integration* (1974)

POLACH, J. G., "Harmonization of Laws in Western Europe", [1959] *American Journal of Comparative Law* 148

SEIDL-HOHENVELDERN, I., "Harmonization of Legislation in the Common Market", [1962] *Journal of Business Law*, 247 and 363

SCHNEIDER, H. H., "Towards a European Lawyer" (1971), 8 C.M.L. Rev. 44

STEIN, E., "Assimilation of National Laws as a Function of European Integration" (1964), 58 *American Journal of International Law* 1

THOMPSON, D., "Harmonization of Laws" (1965), 3 *Journal of Common Market Studies* 302

CHAPTER 4

DETTER, L., *Law Making by International Organisations* (1965)

ECONOMIDES, C. E., *Le pouvoir de décision des organisations internationales européenes* (1964)

Institut d'études européennes, La Décision dans les Communautés européenes (1969)

LAUWAARS, R. H., *Lawfulness and Legal Force of Community Decisions* (1973)

Les Novelles : Droit des Communautés européenes (1969), Nos. 483–806, 1134–1172

MATHIJSEN, P., *Le Droit de la C.E.C.A.* (1957)

MITCHELL, J. D. B., "Community Legislation" in Bathurst, M.E., *et al, Legal Problems of an Enlarged Community* (1972), 100

MORAND, C.-A., *La législation dans les Communautés européenes* (1968)

PESCATORE, P., *L'Ordre juridique des Communautés européennes* (1971)

RIDEAU, J., *et al. Droit Institutionnel des Communautés européennes* (1974)

CHAPTER 5

BRAUN, N.C., *Commissaires et juges dans les Communantés européennes* (1972)

La Commission des Communantés Européennes et l'Elargissement de l'Europe, Bruxelles, Institut d'études européennes (1974)

COOMBES, D., *Politics and Bureaucracy in the European Community* (1970)

LINDBERG, L., *Political Dynamics of European Economic Integration* (1963)

MAYNE, R., *The Institutions of the European Community* (1968)

SPINELLI, A., *The Eurocrats* (1966)

HALLSTEIN, W., "The EEC Commission: a new factor in international life" (1965), 14 *International & Comparative Law Quarterly* 727

NOEL, N., "The Commission's Power of Initiative", (1973) 10 C.M.L. Rev. 123

CHAPTER 6

CAMPS, M., *European Unification in the Sixties* (1967)

CONSTANTINESCO, V., *Compétences et pouvoirs dans les Communautés européennes* (1974)

ECONOMIDES, C. P., *Le pouvoir de décision des organisations internationales européenes* (1964)

HOUBEN, P. H. J. M., *Les Conseils de Ministres des Communautés européenes* (1964)

Institut d'études juridiques européenes, *La Fusion des Communautés Européennes au lendemain des Accords de Luxembourg* (1967)

JAUMIN-PONSAR, A., *Essai d'interprétation d'une crise* (1970)

Institut d'études européennes, La décision dans les Communautés européenenes (1969)

LOUIS, J.-V., *Les règlements de la Communauté économique européene* (1969)

NEWHOUSE, J., *Collision in Brussels* (1968)

ROSENSTIEL, F., *Le Principe de Supranationalité* (1962)

TORELLI, M., *L'Individu et le Droit de la C.E.E.* (1970)

VON LINDEINER-WILDAU, K., *La Supranationalité en tant que Principe de Droit* (1970)

WALLACE, H., *National Governments and the European Communities* (1973)

ESCH, B. VAN DER, "Legal policy in an enlarged European Community" (1973), 10 C.M.L. Rev. 56

MORTELMANS, K. J., "The Extramural Meetings of the Ministers of the Member States of the Community" (1974), 11 C.M.L. Rev. 62

CHAPTER 7

ALLOTT, P., "The Democratic Basis of the European Communities" (1974), 11 C.M.L. Rev. 298

BIRKE, W., *European Elections by direct suffrage. A comparative study of the electoral systems used in Western Europe and their utility for the direct election of a European Parliament* (1961)

COCKS, SIR B., *The European Parliament* (1973)

COOMBES, D., *The Power of the Purse in the European Communities* (1972)

EUROPEAN PARLIAMENT, *The Case for elections to the European Parliament by direct Universal Suffrage* (1969)

FITZMAURICE, J., *The Party Groups in the European Parliament* (1975)

FORSYTH, M., *The Parliament of the European Communities* (1964)

HENIG, S. (editor), *European Political Parties* (1969)

HOUBDINE, A. M., & VERGES, R., *Le Parlement Européen dans la Construction de l'Europe des Six* (1966)

HOVEY, J. A., *The Super-parliaments* (1967)

LASALLE, C., *Les rapports institutionnels entre le Parlement européen et les Conseils de Ministres des Communautés* (1964)

LINDSAY, K., *European Assemblies* (1960)

MANZANARES, H., *Le Parlement Européen* (1964)

NIBLOCK, M., *National Parliaments in Community Decision Making* (1971)

STEIN, E., In NADELMAN, K. (editor), *XXth Century Comparative & Conflicts Law* (1961), 509–530

DRUNKER, I. E., "Strengthening democracy in the E.E.C." (1964), 2 *Common Market Law Review* 168.

DUVIEUSART, J., "Le rôle des parlements nationaux et du Parlement européen dans le developpement des Communautés", [1968] *Institutions Communautaires et Institutions Nationales* 49

CHAPTER 8

BECKER, M., *La Banque européenne d'investissement* (1973)

BERNARD, N., *et al.*, *Le Comité Economique et Social* (1972)

Institut d'études européennes, *La Décision dans les Communautés européennes* (1969), 127–132

MENAIS, G. P., *La Banque européenne d'investissement* (1968)

BERTRAM, C., Decision making in the E.E.C.: The Management Committee Procedure (1967–68), 5 C.M.L. Rev. 246

GENTON, J., "La représentation et l'influence des opérateurs économiques dans la Communauté européenne", [1968] *Institutions Communautaires et Institutions Nationales* 75

SCHINDLER, P., "Problems of decision making by way of the Management Committee Procedure in the E.E.C." (1971), 8 C.M.L. Rev. 184

ZELLENTIN, G., "The Economic and Social Committee" (1962), 1 *Journal of Common Market Studies* 22

CHAPTER 9

BRAUN, N. C., *Commissaires et juges dans les Communautés européennes* (1972)

BEBR, G., *Judicial Control of the European Communities* (1962)

BEBR, G., *Rule of Law within the European Communities* (1965)

BRINKHORST, L. J., & SCHERMERS, H. G., *Judicial Remedies in the European Communities* (1969) and Supplement

COLIN, J. P., *Le Gouvernement des Juges dans les Communautés européennes* (1966)

DELORME, J.-P., *L'Article 169 du Traité de Rome* (1971)

DONNER, A. M., *The Role of the Lawyer in the European Communities* (1968)

FELD, W., *The Court of the European Communities: new dimension in international adjudication* (1964)

FERRIERE, G., *Le controle des actes étatiques par la Cour de Justice des Communautés européennes* (1968)

GREEN, A. W., *Political Integration by Jurisprudence* (1969)

LAUWAARS, R. H., *Lawfulness and Legal Force of Community Decisions* (1973)

MANN, C. J., *Function of Judicial Decision in European Economic Integration* (1972)

REEPINGHEN, C. VAN & ORIANNE, P., *La Procédure devant la Cour de Justice des Communautés Européennes* (1961)

SCHEINGOLD, A., *The Rule of Law in European Integration* (1965)

VALENTINE, D. G., *The Court of Justice of the European Communities*, Vol. I "Jurisdiction and Procedure", Vol. II "Judgments and Documents" (1965)

WALL, E., *The Court of Justice of the European Communities, Jurisdiction and Procedure* (1966)

HARDING, C. S. P., "Decisions addressed to Member States and Article 173 of the Treaty of Rome" (1976), 25 I.C.L.Q. 15.

TOTH, A. G., "The Individual and European Law" (1975), 24 I.C.L.Q. 659

CHAPTER 10

BATHURST, M. (editor), *Legal Problems of an Enlarged European Community* (1972), Parts II and IV

CONSTANTINESCO, L. J., *L'Applicabilité directe dans le droit de la C.E.E.* (1970)

CONSTANTINIDES-MEGRET, C., *Le droit de la Communauté économique européenne et l'ordre juridique des Etats membres* (1967), 244

DONNER, A. M., *Le juge national et le droit communautaire* (1966)

Droit communautaire et droit national, Semaine de Bruges, Colloque 8–10 avril 1965, Bruges (1965)

JACOBS, F. G., & DURAND, A., *References to the European Court* (1975)

PESCATORE, P., *L'ordre juridique des Communautés européennes* (1971)

RIDEAU, J., *et al. La France et les Communautés Européennes* (1975)

SAINT-ESTEBEN, R., *Droit communautaire et droits nationaux* (1967)

BEBR, G., "How Supreme is Community Law in the National Courts?" (1974), 11 C.M.L. Rev. 3

IPSEN, H. P., "Relationship between the law of the European Communities and National Law" (1965), 2 C.M.L. Rev. 379

CHAPTER 11

ADAMS, J. C., & BARILE, P., *The Government of Republican Italy* (1972)

BERGSTEN, E. E., *Community Law in French Courts* (1973)

CONSTANTINIDES-MEGRET, C., *Le droit de la Communauté économique européenne et l'ordre juridique des Etats-membres* (1967)

DONNER, A. M., *et al., Le juge national et le droit communautaire* (1966)

DONNER, A. M., *Le rôle de la Cour de Justice dans l'élaboration du droit européen* (1964)

FORRESTER, I. S., & ILGEN, H. M., *The German Legal System* (1972)

GAUDET, M., *Conflits du droit communautaire avec les droit nationaux* (1967)

HAURIOU, A., *Droit Constitutionnel* (1970) (France)

HERLITZ, N., *Elements of Nordic Public Law* (1969)

HOLBORN, L. W., *et al., German Constitutional Documents since 1871* (1970)

HOLT, S., *Six European States. The Countries of the European Community* (1970)

Institutions communautaires et institutions nationales dans le développement des Communautés (1968)

LESGUILLONS, H., *L'application d'un traité-fondation : le traité instituant la C.E.E.* (1968)

MAJERUS, P., *L'Etat Luxembourgeois* (1970)

PEASELEE, A., *Constitutions of Nations,* 3rd Edn., Vol. III Europe (1963)

SENELLE, R., *Revision of the Constitution 1967–1971* (1972) (Belgium)

WAELBROECK, M., *Traités internationaux et juridictions internes dans les pays du Marché commun* (1969)

DAGTOGLOU, P. D., "European Communities and Constitutional Law", [1973] C.L.J. 256

DONNER, A. M., "Les rapports entre la compétence de la Cour de Justice des Communautés européennes et les tribunaux internes" (1965), 115 *Recueil des Cours de l'Académie de la Haye* 5

HAY, P., "Supremacy of Community Law in National Courts" (1968). 16 A.J. Comp. L. 524

CHAPTER 12

BATHURST, M., *et al.*, *Europe and the Law* (1968)

COLLINS, L., *European Community Law in the United Kingdom* (1975)

KEETON, G. W., & SCHWARZENBERGER, G., *English Law and the Common Market* (1963 Current Legal Problems)

LANG, J. T., *The Common Market and Common Law : Legal Aspects of Foreign Investment and Economic Integration in the European Community, with Ireland as a Prototype* (1966)

Legal and Constitutional Implications of United Kingdom Membership of the European Communities, Cmnd. 3301 (1967)

PISANI, E., *et al.*, *Problems of British Entry into the E.E.C.* (1969)

The United Kingdom and the European Communities, Cmnd. 4715 (1971)

WALL, E. A., *European Communities Act 1972* (1973)

WATSON, G., *The British Constitution and Europe* (1959)

BRIDGE, J. W., "Community Law and English Courts and Tribunals: General Principles and Preliminary Rulings" (1975–1976), 1 *European Law Review* 13

DE SMITH, S. A., "The Constitution and the Common Market: a tentative appraisal" (1971), 34 M.L.R. 597

FORMAN, J., "The European Communities Act 1972" (1973), 10 C.M.L. Rev. 39

GREMENTIERI, V., & GOLDEN, C. J., "The United Kingdom and the European Court of Justice: an Encounter between Common and Civil Law Traditions" (1973), 21 A.J.C.L. 464

HUNNINGS, N. M., "Constitutional Implications of Joining the Common Market" (1968–69), 6 C.M.L. Rev. 50

MARTIN, A., "The Accession of the United Kingdom to the European Communities: Jurisdictional Problems" (1968–69), 6 C.M.L. Rev. 7

MITCHELL, J. D. B., "What do you want to be inscrutable *for* Marcia?" (1967–68), 5 C.M.L. Rev. 112

MITCHELL, J. D. B., *et al.*, "Constitutional aspects of the Treaty and Legislation relating to British membership" (1972), 9 C.M.L. Rev. 134

SIMMONDS, K. R., "*Van Duyn* v. *Home Office*: the Direct Effectiveness of Directives" (1975), 24 I.C.L.Q. 419

THOMPSON, D., & MARSH, N. S., "The United Kingdom and the Treaty of Rome: some preliminary observations" (1962), 2 I. & C.L.Q. 73

TRINIDADE, F. A., "Parliamentary Sovereignty and the Primacy of the Community Law" (1972), 35 M.L.R. 375

WADE, H. W. R., "Sovereignty and the European Communities" (1972), 88 L.Q.R., 1

CHAPTER 13

DAINTITH, T., *Report on the Economic Law of the United Kingdom* (1974)

FIKENTSCHER, W., *Rechts Fragen der Planifikation* (1967)

FROMONT, M., *Rapport sur le droit économique français* (1973)

HUBER, H., *Wirtschaftsverwaltungsrecht* (1953)

JAQUEMIN, A., & SCHRANS, G., *Le droit économique* (1970)

JEANNENCY, J. M., & PERROT, M., *Textes de droit économique et social français* (1957)

MORSIANI, G. S., *Rapport sur le droit économique italien* (1973)

PIEPENBROCK, R., *Der Gedanke eines Wirtschaftsrechs in der neuzeitlichen Literatur bis zum ersten Weltkrieg* (1964)

PROUDHON, P. J., *De la capacité politique des classes ouvières* (1865)

RINCK, G., *Wirtschaftsrecht*, 3rd Edn. (1972)

SVOBODA, K., *La Notion de Droit Economique* (1966)

VERLOREN VAN THEMAAT, P., *Le droit économique des Etats membres des Communautés européennes dans le cadre d'une Union économique et monétaire* (1973)

VERLOREN VAN THEMAAT, P., *Rapport sur le droit économique néerlandais* (1973)

ZACHER, H. F., *Rapport sur le droit économique en république fédérale d'Allemagne* (1973)

ZAPHIRIOU, G. A., *European Business Law* (1970)

CHAMPEAUD, C., "Contribution à la définition du droit économique", [1967] *Dalloz Chron.* 215

DAINTITH, T., "Public Law and Economic Policy", [1974] J.B.L. 9.

FRIEDMANN, W. (editor), *Public and Private Enterprise in Mixed Economies* (1974) Chapters 1, 2, 5 and 7

KIRALY, F. DE, "Le droit économique, branche indépendente de la science juridique", *Recueil d'études sur les sources du droit en honneur de F. Geny* (1935), Vol. 3

LIMPENS, J., "Contribution à l'étude de la notion de droit économique", (1966) *Il Diritto dell' Economia*, No. 6

MACKINNON, V. S., "Experience in Common Law Countries of the Constitutional Problems encountered in regulating Economic Activity" (1963–64), 1 C.M.L. Rev. 183

SCHMITTHOFF, C. M., "The Concept of Economic Law in England", [1966] *Journal of Business Law* 309

WILBERFORCE, Lord, "Law and Economics", [1966] *Journal of Business Law*, 301

CHAPTER 14

ANDREWS, S., *Agriculture and the Common Market* (1973)

BALEKJIAN, W. H., *Legal Aspects of foreign investment in the European Economic Community* (1967)

BAROUNOS, D., et al., *E.E.C. Anti Trust Law* (1975)

BATHURST, M., et al. (editors), *Legal Problems of our Enlarged European Community* (1972), Parts V, VI and VII

BAYLISS, B. T., *European Transport* (1965)

BELLAMY, C., & CHILD, D. G., *Common Market Law of Competition* (1973)

BLAKE, H. M., *Business Regulations in the Common Market Nations*, Vols. 1, 2 and 3 (1969), Vol. 4 (with J. A. RAHL), *Common Market and American Antitrust: Overlap and Conflict* (1970)

BONTEMPS, J., *Liberté d'etablissement et libre prestation des services dans le Marché Commun* (1968)

CAWTHRA, B. T., *Industrial Property Rights in the E.E.C.* (1973)

DERINGER, A., *The Competition Law of the European Economic Community* (1968)

DESPICHT, N., *The Transport Policy of the European Communities* (1969)

European Competition Policy. European Aspects Law Series No. 12 (1973)

FISCHER, A., *L'organisation des transports dans le cadre de l'Europe des Six* (1968)

GOLDMAN, B., European Commercial Law (1973)

Institut d'Etudes européennes, *L'harmonisation dans les Communautés* (1968)

JACQUEMART, C., *La Novelle Douane Européenne* (1971)

JOLIET, R., *Monopolization and Abuse of Dominant Position* (1970)

JOLIET, R., *The Rule of Reason in Antitrust Law* (1967)

KORAH, V., *Competition Law of Britain and the Common Market* (1975)

LIPSTEIN, K., *The Law of the European Economic Community* (1974)

LYON-CAEN, G., *Droit social européen* (1969)

MAZZIOTTI, M., et al., *La Libre Circulation des travailleurs dans les Pays de la C.E.E.* (1974)

McLACHLAN, D. L., & SWANN, D., *Competition policy in the European Community* (1967)

PENNINGTON, R. R., *Companies in the Common Market*, 2nd Edn. (1970)

PERRET, F., *Coordination du droit des sociétés en Europe* (1970)

RENAULD, J., *Le droit européen des sociétes* (1969)

RIBAS, J. J., *La politique sociale des Communautés Européennes* (1969)

SCHMITTHOFF, C. M., *The Harmonisation of European Company Law* (1973)

SEMINI, A., *La C.E.E. Harmonisation des législations* (1971)

SHOUP, C. (editor), *Fiscal Harmonization in the Common Market*, 2 Vols. (1967)

STEIN, E., *Harmonization of European Company Laws* (1971)

THOMPSON, D., *The Proposal for a European Company* (1969)

VENTURA, S., *Principes de droit agraire communautaire* (1967)

Index

357

Printed in Great Britain by Chapel River Press, Andover